# Fund
# Managers

Founded in 1807, John Wiley & Sons is the oldest independent publishing company in the United States. With offices in North America, Europe, Australia and Asia, Wiley is globally committed to developing and marketing print and electronic products and services for our customers' professional and personal knowledge and understanding.

The Wiley Finance series contains books written specifically for finance and investment professionals as well as sophisticated individual investors and their financial advisors. Book topics range from portfolio management to e-commerce, risk management, financial engineering, valuation and financial instrument analysis, as well as much more.

For a list of available titles, visit our website at www.WileyFinance.com.

# Fund Managers

## The Complete Guide

MATTHEW HUDSON

WILEY

This edition first published 2019

© 2020 John Wiley & Sons Ltd

*Registered office*

John Wiley & Sons Ltd, The Atrium, Southern Gate, Chichester, West Sussex, PO19 8SQ, United Kingdom

For details of our global editorial offices, for customer services and for information about how to apply for permission to reuse the copyright material in this book please see our website at www.wiley.com.

Wiley publishes in a variety of print and electronic formats and by print-on-demand. Some material included with standard print versions of this book may not be included in e-books or in print-on-demand. If this book refers to media such as a CD or DVD that is not included in the version you purchased, you may download this material at http://booksupport.wiley.com. For more information about Wiley products, visit www.wiley.com.

Designations used by companies to distinguish their products are often claimed as trademarks. All brand names and product names used in this book are trade names, service marks, trademarks or registered trademarks of their respective owners. The publisher is not associated with any product or vendor mentioned in this book.

Limit of Liability/Disclaimer of Warranty: While the publisher and author have used their best efforts in preparing this book, they make no representations or warranties with respect to the accuracy or completeness of the contents of this book and specifically disclaim any implied warranties of merchantability or fitness for a particular purpose. It is sold on the understanding that the publisher is not engaged in rendering professional services and neither the publisher nor the author shall be liable for damages arising herefrom. If professional advice or other expert assistance is required, the services of a competent professional should be sought.

Library of Congress Cataloging-in-Publication Data

Names: Hudson, Matthew, 1962- author.
Title: Fund managers : the complete guide / Matthew Donald Jeremy Hudson.
Description: First Edition. | Hoboken : Wiley, 2019. | Series: The Wiley
    finance | Includes index.
Identifiers: LCCN 2019026640 (print) | LCCN 2019026641 (ebook) | ISBN
    9781119515586 (hardback) | ISBN 9781119515593 (adobe pdf) | ISBN
    9781119515340 (epub)
Subjects: LCSH: Asset management accounts. | Strategic planning. | Capital
    market—Government policy.
Classification: LCC HG1660 .H83 2019 (print) | LCC HG1660 (ebook) | DDC
    332.1068—dc23
LC record available at https://lccn.loc.gov/2019026640
LC ebook record available at https://lccn.loc.gov/2019026641

Cover Design: Wiley
Cover Image: © Кристина Пахомова/Adobe Stock Photo

Set in 10/12pt TimesLTStd by SPi Global, Chennai

Printed in Great Britain by TJ International Ltd, Padstow, Cornwall, UK

10 9 8 7 6 5 4 3 2 1

# Contents

# Preface

*Is your world a fund, Daddy?*

– Rafe Hudson, aged 10

I am writing this book as a natural sister to my earlier book, *Funds: Private Equity, Hedge and All Core Structures* (which I will refer to as the 'funds book'). This book concerns the managers of the funds. The funds book proved popular with asset managers that use it as a structuring reference guide to their own funds or to check structures of funds different from their own, MBA and finance students, and more widely as part of training for managers, finance professionals, lawyers, and accountants.

This book sits alongside the funds book and examines the managers and their structures, as well as their day-to-day issues, hopes, and aspirations. As such, it is a little more anecdotal than the funds book and contains quotes and ideas from many managers and investors that I work with. The company that I work at – MJ Hudson – advises over 600 asset management groups and 200 institutional fund investors.

I also reference a number of lessons that I have learned (often the hard way) over more than 30 years (so far) in asset management. During this time, I have been a lawyer, asset manager, business builder, chief executive officer (CEO), chief investment officer (CIO), and chief compliance officer (CCO) – a wealth of experience to draw upon.

The funds book focused on alternative asset management. This book is broader and considers managers across all asset classes – although alternatives is more my zone. There is an emphasis in this book on creating and building management companies, as well as the current trend for mergers and acquisitions (M&A) to build scale in an effort to counter complexity, regulation, and multi-investor demand.

In the past, I worked within a fund managers' incubator at a bulge-bracket investment bank (Credit Suisse First Boston), and I also created a tech-incubator (Far Blue Ventures) which backed new IP-focused companies. I currently help others create new managers, such as Alpha Hawk (an emerging hedge manager incubator, where I am a co-CEO and MJ Hudson runs the infrastructure). Personally, I love new creations, and most of my career moves have involved starting something new. In this book I endeavour, therefore, to focus on the refreshing, the creative, and the new.

Starting an asset management company from scratch is always possible, although regulation has made it harder. I started one from scratch myself in 2000 and have helped many others start theirs. Creation is often the best fun. However, be aware that it might take several years of loss making. No doubt, your first plan will be too complex in its initial excitement and, for all your own joy, investors will want to wait and see. Do not be put off by increased regulatory requirements, but double your annual budget. Also, like any building project, double your first timescale estimates.

Spinning out a manager from a larger group is quicker. My top tip is to have your previous parent invest in the fund as a precursor, but not to invest in the manager, save with a call option in your favour, as this can put off new investors.

Ask yourself whether you genuinely have partners with whom you can establish a management company. If you think that you do, then be super clear, from the start, on what your strengths and weaknesses are. Also, each partner should commit hard cash to the venture in similar proportions and you should map out how the partnership will survive the first bad years. A fund manager 'seeder' is a group that invests in the management company. Seeders typically want 20% to 25% of the management company. Ensure there is a call option in your favour at an agreeable valuation. A cornerstone is an investor that cornerstones your fund. Such an investor will want a share of the performance of the fund and possibly a management fee break. Seeders and cornerstones can accelerate your business. The first investors are the hardest to close; everyone wants in once you are successful.

This book considers the ups and downs of the last ten years, as well as future-gazing to threats and opportunities of the next ten. The funds book came out during the immediate aftermath of the credit crisis (that I define as the period from mid-2007 to 2009, that saw the bankruptcy of Lehman Brothers and the collapse of Bear Stearns – to mention just two) and in the midst of the longer financial crisis (that I define herein as the period of negative to low growth from 2008 to 2013).

This book is also most timely, because it is set at the start of what I call 'the new era of asset management'. This new era is marked by a shift in the focus and energy of regulatory authorities onto the asset management industry, which have been distracted until now with their endeavours to remove the major systemic risk of modern-day capitalism – mass bank failure. In addition (as a Brit), we also find ourselves in interesting times with the United Kingdom (UK) winding up for its departure from the European Union (EU) in 2019 (perhaps!) and dealing with the inevitable fallout. The new era we find ourselves entering is also one of AuM scale or very deep niche skills. The middle is the valley of death. M&A in asset management is becoming prevalent. Regulation, increased substance, increased disclosure, and technology-led threats and opportunities are very much with us, and scale is helpful in managing these challenges.

This book spends some time on the regulators' new focus on industry practices, as well as the effects changing legislation will have on the UK, EU, and US – the three largest asset management blocs. Chapter 12, however, examines regional differences in asset management, with a particular focus on jurisdictions outside of these three blocs. Clearly, Asia is on a dramatic ascent in asset management.

I postponed writing this book to await 29 March 2019 – the planned date for the official departure of the UK from the EU (Brexit). At the time of writing, the date for Brexit is uncertain (but a second extension on the deadline has been agreed for 31 October 2019), and some words have now entered my swear-word vocabulary; such as 'longstop', 'extension', and 'red lines'. Still, the world spins on and the asset management community must continue to thrive and get on with the day job. Similarly, authors must finish books. Thus, in this book, I have assumed that the UK will 'Brexit' and leave the EU. That, in my own business, I have assumed from the date of the referendum result in 2016. Hence, I set up a regulated Luxembourg platform in 2017 in preparation for loss of EU financial passports. Also in this book, I have assumed that some sort of withdrawal agreement is signed and trade talks commence soon (or the UK stays in the EU customs union). Either way, I have written this book on the basis that at some point the UK loses the EU passports. More on the B-word later in the book.

The ongoing tussle between man and machine is another important backdrop to this book. Each side to the 'man versus machine' debate professes to have humanity's best interests at heart. Those supporting the use of robots argue that everyone's quality of life will vastly improve, whereas those that are sceptical of technology's rise claim that mass unemployment in an already wage-stagnant economy is a dangerous combination. This debate does not escape the boardrooms of asset managers as they look to cut costs, increase efficiencies, and stay relevant to the young.

So-called 'ESG' and 'impact' fund managers receive a heavy emphasis in this book, as rapidly growing key issues, as explained in Chapter 4.

This book does not examine the prior performance of different types of asset classes. Neither does it predict their future performance or make any detailed assessment of risk and return. Rather, it is a guide to all things fund manager – a mini-encyclopaedia to their structures, governance, regulation, taxation, technology, and, most especially, their challenges and opportunities.

Included in this book are some quotes from interviews that I have conducted with CEOs of asset managers to help me formulate a more immediate and relevant context for the technical aspects of the book. I have deliberately chosen CEOs from a range of asset classes, and all being founders of their company or strategy. This makes them all 'lively' and interesting. Their summary biographies are at the back of the book, and they are:

- Private Equity – Wol Kolade, CEO of Livingbridge, a UK-based private equity firm investing in growth and small to mid-cap, also with offices in the US and Australia.
- Hedge – Richard Novack, co-CEO of Alpha Hawk, a new multi-boutique hedge manager investing platform.
- Venture Capital – Alice Bentinck, MBE, general partner and co-founder of Entrepreneur First, a modern and widely acclaimed VC that is a business builder and start-up accelerator based in London.
- Listed manager – Tony Dalwood, CEO of London-listed Gresham House, focused on listed equity and alternatives.
- Social impact –Nigel Kershaw, OBE, Chairman of The Big Issue Group, the world's most widely circulated street newspaper.

To help with the navigation of this book, a short summary of each chapter is set out below.

| Chapter | Contents |
| --- | --- |
| 1 | **Seismic Shifts** – a look at the macroeconomic, technical, and political changes in the last ten years, with a focus on the most influential trends within the asset management industry. |
| 2 | **What Is it Like Being an Asset Manager?** – a fly-by tour of some hot topics discussed by managers, and the public's perception of them. In addition, what is it like being an asset manager, and do various strategies lead to different behaviour? |
| 3 | **Structures and Economics** – an introduction to the inner workings of an asset manager. It offers a snapshot of the structuring, fund manager economics, popular manager jurisdictions, fees, and differences between listed and private managers. |

| Chapter | Contents |
|---|---|
| 4 | **Governance** – a look at how the business of an asset manager is run, with a particular focus on the relevance of boards, committees, and non-executive directors. The growing influence of both external regulation and ESG are also considered. |
| 5 | **Investment Strategies** – a review of the major investment strategies employed in asset management and how they influence asset managers themselves. |
| 6 | **Investors' View of the Industry** – an analysis of different fund investor entities and how they view their asset managers. This chapter therefore considers pensions plans, SWFs, family offices, charities and other investors in your funds. |
| 7 | **Asset Allocation and Portfolio Construction** – a look at how your investors and, by extension, you as the manager, construct a portfolio and some of the theories behind asset allocation. This chapter also reviews historical methodology and considers how some of these theories are holding up in 2019 and what the future holds for them. |
| 8 | **Technology** – an exploration of how technology is being harnessed for investment research and algorithm-driven investment, as well as the threat technology giants pose as potential asset managers in the near future. |
| 9 | **Regulation in the Asset Management Industry** – an overview of the regulatory environment in which asset management operates globally, with a particular focus on the UK, EU, and US. |
| 10 | **Risk, Compliance, and Regulatory Trends** – an exploration of the future of regulation, covering emerging rules, as well as the hot topic of risk and risk strategies in asset management. |
| 11 | **Taxation** – a brief guide to taxation within the asset management industry. |
| 12 | **Regional Trends** – a comparison and analysis of regional trends affecting asset managers, as well as the asset management industry outside of the core blocs of the UK, EU, and US. The future of offshore is also debated. |
| 13 | **Future Trends** – so where does this all lead us? This chapter considers makes some predictions for the next ten years. |

Finally, I hope you enjoy this book, as well as learn from it. I have tried not to hold back from voicing my opinions or the opinions of others. Occasionally, I have been deliberately provocative. The funds book is technical and a little dry, whereas this book does contain an element of my own philosophy and personality, and with that (as people that know me would attest) comes both a long historical perspective and a healthy dose of humour.

Taking yourself too seriously, or not casting a questioning eye on either yourself or others makes for dullness and mild flattery.

Enjoy! – London, March 2019

# CHAPTER 1

# Seismic Shifts

*There is nothing impossible to him who will try.*
*Remember on the conduct of each depends the fate of all.*

— Alexander III of Macedon

I decided to put down my two favourite Alexander the Great quotes, as someone that distinctly lived for both the moment and the long-term future (which, dying aged 32, he sadly never saw, but I suspect he glimpsed and deliberately defined).

This chapter takes a brief look back at the very long history of asset management, before examining the most influential trends within the asset management industry over the course of the past ten years, including volatility (Vol), growth in passives, rise of the internet and technology, extremism, migration, unemployment, Brexit, generational shifts, the Arab Spring, quantitative easing and then tightening, and the expansion of China. Although an investor's office may seem like a bubble, the asset management industry does not operate within a vacuum. This chapter draws connections between the key social, political, and technological developments over the past decade and relates them to the asset management space.

## THE CODE OF HAMMURABI

The origins of asset management can be traced back to at least 1754 BCE and the Code of Hammurabi in ancient Mesopotamia, which set out a primitive system of property law, including basic rules about credit and security. The principal asset class at this time was land and the only people involved in 'asset management' were a limited demographic of powerful individuals. Later, in ancient Greece, international trade fuelled the development of basic banking activities, such as loans to seafaring merchants. At this time, the asset managers were slaves of the wealthy (think The Parable of the Talents). By the end of the Roman Empire, the first basic pension scheme had been invented – with some Roman military officers being given country estates (both for the modern-day financial reasons and to keep military leaders away from the politics of the city).

The Renaissance really ushered in the beginnings of modern-day asset management: mercantilism thrived, the Venetians invented double-entry book-keeping, the merchant banks grew, and commercial fairs (protostock markets) developed. The sixteenth century saw the rise of extraordinarily large businesses like the British East India Company and the Dutch East India Company, which were so-called 'joint-stock companies' – companies in which shares of its stock could be traded by shareholders. This led to substantial wealth creation and the emergence of public markets, culminating in the establishment of the first proper stock exchange in 1787 – the Amsterdam Stock Exchange. Meanwhile, the First Presbyterian Church established the first modern-style pension scheme for its ministers in 1759.

Industrial revolution and technological development throughout the eighteenth and nineteenth centuries led to a dramatic increase in productivity, which gave rise to surpluses, and surpluses meant more investable assets. The asset management industry became much more established and in 1884 Charles Dow created the first stock index. The beginning of the twentieth century (the 'Roaring Twenties') was a wild time for asset management with the development of investment theory and rapid economic growth ending in the Wall Street Crash in 1929 and the ensuing Great Depression (which sparked significant US regulatory reform).

In the second half of the twentieth century, asset management experienced a golden age that set the scene for today's financial sector: the first hedge fund was established by Alfred Winslow Jones in 1949; private equity was 'invented' in 1946 by the American Research and Development Corporation and pioneered in the late 1970s (and onward) by KKR; and the first index fund emerged, created by Jack Bogle of Vanguard in 1976.

## CREDIT CRISIS TO FINANCIAL CRISIS

*The financial crisis is a stark reminder that transparency and disclosure are essential in today's market place.*

– Jack Reed

On Monday, 15 September 2008, Lehman Brothers filed for bankruptcy. Images of former employees packing their personal items into cardboard boxes flew round the world. The anger, despair, but mostly shock of the 25,000 individuals who lost their jobs signalled a fact that many did not want to believe – Lehman Brothers was *not* too big to fail. Rewind to March of that year when Bear Stearns (subsequently sold to JPMorgan Chase) failed and it is difficult to imagine why systemic risk in other banks was not addressed sooner. This was just a snapshot of what was to come. What happened in the following years would be known as the 'credit crisis'.

The collapse of Lehman Brothers resulted in large government bailouts in order to stabilise the rocking financial system. With Bank of America purchasing Merrill Lynch and AIG receiving a bailout from the United States (US) Federal Reserve, the financial ecosystem looked shaky at best. The cause of this is not singular and has been well documented in other literature – for example, collateralised debt obligations (CDOs), excessive leverage, mortgage mis-selling, securitisation of bad debt, poor judgment by agencies, and disproportionate risk-taking by financiers. This period, chronicled by the media and in film, is seen as a defining episode of the last two decades. A key consequence of this financial meltdown was the increase in financial regulation.

In the US, the Dodd–Frank Wall Street Reform and Consumer Protection Act (Dodd–Frank Act) was signed into US federal law by President Barack Obama on 21 July 2010. This legislation was implemented in direct response to the financial crisis and was the single largest overhaul of financial regulation since the 1930s. Underlying the many rules, which were enacted to prevent similar events occurring again, is a theme of transparency. This has become the watchword for financial reform over the past ten years; used as a stick to beat, but also a badge of pride for those who follow through on their promises. The championing of transparency has been a key trend since the credit crisis.

The 2008 market crash was attributed partly to the housing bubble that burst in the US. The Dodd–Frank Act, in attempting to prevent this happening again, includes provisions to protect borrowers against predatory lending and to prevent abusive mortgage practices. The legislation aims to achieve this by establishing US government agencies to monitor banking practices and oversee financial institutions. Of course this reaction is seen by some as too little too late. The Federal Reserve did little to prevent the housing bubble and central banks in general should have done more to address the financial instability leading up to the crisis. The Bank of England (BoE) took a limited approach in maintaining a financially stable system (post-independence) and the European Central Bank (ECB) did not act in response to the credit surge.[1] Capital reserves pre-crisis were wafer-thin and not sufficient to cover more than a few percent of loan defaults. Some argue that high interest rates made it difficult for these institutions to influence the housing and credit boom. But the regulatory changes that have been enforced across Europe and the US are tools that could have been utilised before. For example, ensuring that banks kept aside more capital (and were not too leveraged, like Bank of America, Merrill Lynch, and Lehman Brothers, which almost entirely financed their purchasing of CDOs and mortgage-backed securities (MBSs) through loans – leverage on leverage) or requiring lenders to lower the maximum loan-to-value ratios for mortgages.

In Europe, these sentiments regarding minimum capital requirements resulted in the Basel III framework. The basic premise is that banks will be liquid enough next time to prevent the domino-like defaulting that occurred in 2008. Banks have also been required to improve the standard and quantity of their capital. This means having a higher proportion of equity to assets or debt. Furthermore, the importance placed on stress tests was felt by several major institutions that publicly failed. This led to banks limiting their diversification and retreating from certain asset classes as they feared the illiquidity and capital adequacy that came with them.

The credit crisis saw many banks fail or bail. Citibank went from being essentially a hedge fund to a retail bank in a sickening squeal of brakes. The credit crisis was a period of bank failure and subsequent regulation and ring-fencing. The financial crisis then consumed the credit crisis. All asset classes suffered. A number of EU member states went bust in all but name (for example, Ireland, Greece, Cyprus, Spain, and Italy) often from excess real estate (RE) excitement pre-crisis. The term 'PIGS' (Portugal, Italy, Greece, and Spain) was first used. For a few years, it felt like all the money had gone to the moon.

## QUANTITATIVE EASING

A continuous programme of quantitative easing (QE) has kept interest rates artificially low following the financial crisis. QE is a form of monetary policy, the ultimate aim of which is to boost spending in order to increase inflation levels. QE is a process whereby central banks (like the Federal Reserve and the BoE) buy back existing government bonds (gilts) as a way to shovel money into the financial system.[2] As the demand for the assets increases, so do the prices of those assets which helps to raise inflation. As commercial banks receive more funds from the repurchase of the gilts, they will be encouraged to fund more loans to companies and private individuals.

During the period from 2008 to 2016, the BoE bought GBP 435 billion[3] of government bonds. Although critics of the policy have argued that it helped to inflate asset bubbles, the BoE's own research has pointed to the benefit seen by individuals on the lower end of the housing market.[4] For those people, the increase in housing prices meant a bigger proportional rise in the value of their assets than those towards the top of the market. However, the gains made on cash were far more substantial for the wealthiest in society. What is clear from the BoE's research is that every age group and every income group was better off as a result of the QE policies that were introduced.

The US and UK have both ceased QE (for now) and, in December 2018, the ECB also ended its policy of QE, although it might change its mind in 2019, as the EU lurches towards a wild recession. The ECB's policy entailed spending EUR 30 billion a month on buying bonds, which, similarly to the policy in the UK, was introduced in the years after the financial crisis. Since this was introduced, more than EUR 2 trillion has flowed into the European economy,[5] which the ECB states arrested deflation and prevented any progression of the economic crisis. Similar to the criticisms of the BoE, this policy was derided by some because of the disproportionate gain for the wealthiest in society. However, it seems stating the obvious that those with a greater share of assets will benefit more when those assets increase in value. What the evidence suggests is that the individuals at all levels benefited from the policy and it helped prevent a further decline in the world's major economies.

## SPOOKY MARKETS

As the financial crisis settled, spooky markets developed.

I would describe the last 20 years as the 'Long Sideways', which first started after the biggest of post-war economic implosions – the dot-com bust of 2000 (see later on dot-com bust II). Despite an even odder period from 2004 (launched by the 'success' of the Iraq War) to the credit pop of 2007 (a period characterised by extreme credit pumping and wild times), the markets have moved sideways since 1999. The FTSE 100 was below its 1999 peak in 2018.

With QE lifting the markets from their drop, and with generationally low (effectively nil) interest rates, we have spent the last four years in warm treacle – little growth, little activity, little Vol – all in all, somewhat false and spooky. This also gave rise to significant growth in passive or index funds that drifted gently upwards on these warm winds.

The years since the credit crisis also saw also saw the banks pumped up, sometimes unwillingly, with too much capital. Barclays tried to escape state financing with a Qatari investment, which one might have thought a courageous thing to do – to not take money from the nanny state. However, its senior management are now, in 2019, being pursued by a previously wounded and maligned Serious Fraud Office (SFO). Banks had to spend the excess capital and QE somewhere, and have (in the UK and US) pushed much of it towards the residential mortgage market (as first-house mortgages are highly balance-sheet 'good'), as well as investing a lot in private equity (PE) leveraged buy-outs (LBOs) and bonds on large leverage multiples.

However, since February 2018, we have finally seen some changes – action – Vol. If President Donald Trump is to be believed, this is partly caused by the Federal Reserve increasing interest rates quickly. But the cessation of QE and beginning of quantitative tightening (QT) has also been a major factor – with some encouragement of Vol around trade wars and a slowdown of growth in some parts of the world (China, especially). In 2018 there were 110 market swings of at least 1% in the S&P 500, compared to only 10 in 2017 – yes, 2017 was really spooky.

Perhaps 2018 marked the end of the 20-year Long Sideways. We should also now see the strike back by actively managed funds from 2019. That said, Japan has been in the Long Sideways since the end of the 1980s, so I do not believe the Long Sideways in the UK, EU, or US has ended yet.

Ageing populations, anti-youth immigration, the distraction of politics, the rise of passive funds, and lack of investment panache in both the UK and US will keep us longer moving sideways.

## RISE IN ALTERNATIVES

During the financial crisis and beyond, alternative asset classes – private equity (PE), real estate (RE), hedge funds, illiquid credit, and other such asset types – have been growing more popular. The total assets under management (AuM) of alternative assets sits at over USD 7 trillion globally,[6] which is principally spread across 562 managers as at 2018.[7] PE managers alone have experienced an 18.5%, or USD 325 billion, increase in funding from investors between 2015 and 2018. Even more impressive are the levels of 'dry powder' that PE managers are holding. Dry powder is a market term referring to money raised by PE managers that has not yet been allocated towards the purchase of whatever assets the manager specialises in. The 2018 levels sit at USD 1.5 trillion,[8] which suggests that PE managers are having a tough time sourcing deals they believe are reasonably priced.

Alternative assets have been seen as a form of diversification since the early 1990s when Yale Endowment created annual returns of nearly 20% through allocating roughly a third of its portfolio to alternatives. The increasing difficulty in generating alpha and hitting investor targets post-financial crisis has led many investors to start to pursue similar strategies to those of Yale Endowment. This is a step-change from a management model to an outcomes-based approach. Added to which, the return of Vol to the public markets in 2018 and the possible end of the 30-year bull market in bonds might make the long-term nature of closed-ended PE, RE, and infrastructure funds more attractive to pension plans. That being said, the increasing prevalence of alternative assets in sovereign wealth funds, pension funds, and both active and passive portfolios begs the question – are alternatives now mainstream?

The increasing popularity of alternatives and what that means for the wider industry is discussed further in the book. In addition, with interest rates at effectively nil, and banks handicapped by regulators, the thirst for yield has seen a ballooning of both private credit[9] and infrastructure funds.[10]

## THE ARAB SPRING

The term 'Arab Spring' was used by the American political scientist Marc Lynch to define the period from 18 December 2010 to the current date of violent and non-violent protests and civil wars in the Arab world.[11] The advent of the Arab Spring was not foreseen by experts in Middle Eastern politics. This misreading of the situation begs the question – what caused the Arab Spring? It has been suggested that there are four possible causes: demographic change, social media, *karama* (human dignity), and economic liberalisation without political reform.[12]

First, the uprising against authoritarian regimes may have been caused by the population of the Arab world almost tripling from 1970–2010.[13] This resulted in a generational shift, with around 30% of the population in the 20–35 age bracket. In tandem with this change came high unemployment, increases in the cost of living, and limited opportunities. This was a key reason why the Arab Spring occurred.[14] Second, the increasing prevalence of social media was a main driver. This enabled the flow of resentment felt by the increasing youth population to disseminate quickly amongst the Arab world. Third, the underlying theme amongst the range of uprisings across the Arab world was the focus on 'human dignity (*karama*), freedom, and social justice'. This pursuit of an intrinsic respect for the human experience by members of the Arab world is a unifying theme and indicates that commonality can be felt in the pursuit of social and economic improvement.

## MIGRATION

In August 2015, the image of a young boy lying lifeless on a beach near Bodrum in Turkey shocked the world. Yet what was the cause of the largest migration Europe had seen since the Second World War? Why were so many people dying? What could be done about it? When examining the biggest trends in the past ten years it is impossible not to ask these questions about an issue that permeated every news outlet across Europe and the world.

As a brief introduction, it is important to outline the key moments that resulted in over 1 million migrants crossing the Mediterranean Sea in 2015 and many hundreds of thousands since. War and terrorism in Syria and Iraq, along with the Arab Spring, are perceived as the principal causes of the migration crisis. This has facilitated the flow of migration through the Central Mediterranean Route. The EU was able to stop migrants travelling along other routes through negotiation and compromise with more stable governments (for example, the EU–Turkey Deal prevented migrants from entering Europe through Turkey). In 2015, the migration crisis hit critical mass with high death tolls and a constant news cycle of despair. In response, the EU began Operation Sophia to prevent people-smuggling. In 2016, assaults on German citizens during New Year's Eve created a huge backlash against Chancellor Merkel and her government's migration policies that had allowed over 1 million migrants into the country. Originally, her position was widely praised, especially considering other countries with strong economies were reluctant to take migrants. However, news reports that German citizens had been assaulted quickly resulted in negative press and a suggestion that opening the borders had been unwise. Chancellor Merkel has since decided not to run for re-election in 2021.

Migration has been a constant theme for millennia, however. People and tribes move for security, out of fear, hope for the future, or need for food or water. Migration built the global superpower that is the US and equally caused the collapse of the Western Roman Empire.

## RISE IN POPULISM

*What is there to be nervous about?*

– Toomas Hendrik Ilves

Populism can be broadly described as a political approach that attempts to appeal to anti-establishment sentiment amongst the general public, and, in particular, to those who believe their values and interests have been ignored by the ruling elite.

Within the last ten years, there have been clear examples of this strategy characterising the political discourse as a binary division between legitimate and illegitimate. The level of debate is reduced so that nuance and context is often erased. This results in the framing of political arguments in the simplistic terms of 'us' versus 'them'. By 'othering' their political opponents, populists race to the edge and base their ideological strategy on a siege mentality. Often perceived as a criticism of the 'Right', this approach is felt on both sides of the political divide. If anything, the allegiance to one particular movement or another is counterintuitive to the populist movement. Although this may appear to be a reflection of the democratic will of the people, populism reaches for the base fears of the public. This perception that populists speak truthfully is a combination of our own prejudices against establishment politics and the conventional political class's inability to connect with the people. Populists are no more transparent than establishment politicians are, but they often have the media savvy to present themselves in this way. It is the politics of appeasement, and in the pursuit of the top job, populists encourage a race to the bottom.

Yet, in a world where soundbites rule the airwaves and image is more important than substance, populism is on the rise. According to the Institute for Global Change, since 2000, the number of populist parties in Europe has nearly doubled.[15] The rise of populism in Europe over the past two decades marks the most significant transition in political thought since the Cold War. From Central and Eastern Europe to the Baltic, and now Italy and the US, populism has entered the political discourse and integrated itself into government. However, although populism appears to just be the positioning of oneself against the establishment, it is no easy feat. It is a deliberate strategy designed to influence and change mainstream politics. Although it may seem scattergun, the policies of populists are not random. They share common themes (for example, protectionist economic policies) and embrace similar political processes (for example, referendums).

In Eastern Europe, populist parties have acted against fundamental components of a pluralist society (for example, free press, constitutional courts, and civil rights). President Vladimir Putin's influence as a strongman and populist-in-chief is also felt strongly throughout East and Central Europe.

In Western Europe, the spread of populism has not been as extensive but the impact it has made is arguably greater. Marie Le Pen doubled the voting share of her father and made the second round of the election in France. Although she did not win, undoubtedly she shaped the political landscape for that period. The German parliament has had a shake-up with around a quarter comprising members from the Alternative für Deutschland (AfD) and Die Linke.[16] In the UK, Nigel Farage (and others) pushed a patently populist message ('freedom' and 'independence') to swing the Brexit debate in favour of the 'Leave' campaign. It was partly the threat of the United Kingdom Independence Party (UKIP) that pushed Prime Minister David Cameron to call the Brexit referendum in the first place. Farage's anti-establishment, anti-immigration, and anti-institution approach carried all the hallmarks of a traditional populist message. His 'take back control' message and persona as a man of the people holds commonality with other politicians (for example, Vladimir Putin, Donald Trump, Marie Le Pen, and Boris Johnson) who have positioned themselves as 'outsiders'. Of course, the irony of populist outsiders is that they are often themselves from super-privileged backgrounds. President Obama tried to make this point about then presidential candidate Donald Trump, but the blow obviously did not land.

The resurgence of populism in France, Germany, and the UK (amongst others) has caused the mainstream political parties in these countries to move closer to their respective leanings.

In Southern Europe, the Left-leaning populist parties have enjoyed the most traction. They project themselves as standing up to the establishment and aim to find and eliminate corruption. Synonymous with other general themes of populism these parties tend to endorse self-determination and a reclaiming of sovereignty. In contrast with more Right-leaning groups, this iteration of populism espouses anti-austerity rhetoric in the form of economic sovereignty through financial self-determination. Similarly to Western Europe, the rise in populism has resulted in some politicians running to the Right or Left. In Italy, we have a curious government from both the edge of the Left and the edge of the Right. Brazil has just appointed a heavily Right-leaning president who admires President Trump openly.

Although it can be shown that there has been a growth in populism throughout Europe over the past decade, it is less clear what its impact has been or will be. Specifically, whether the rise in populism has caused centrist parties to become more populist as well. Not a day goes by when something sensationalist is said in the press or on social media by a politician wishing to make a statement. Whether this translates into actual policy is another question. Suffice to say, politicians are becoming simpler in their messaging, less statesmanlike, and, frankly, ruder.

So where does this leave asset management? With nowhere to hide perhaps. Embrace the populist move or stay very quiet? Either way, I suspect politics will reach further into asset management. With social media, populist rhetoric is in constant circulation. There is little chance for asset managers to avoid being labelled as part of the 'elite' or 'establishment' against which populist politics rallies.

I wish I had the answers. My best advice is to stay dynamic and flexible. New laws might usher in higher taxes, the flattening of the offshore world, and the restructuring of the elimination of double taxation on returns (such as limited partnerships, Open-Ended Investment Companies (OEICS), investment trusts or offshore funds). Whacking rich bankers (and related finance managers) has always been popular since the credit crisis, and we can expect more regulation to this effect. So far, asset management has had a comparatively easy time of new regulation. Expect this to change.

## BREXIT

*Brexit means Brexit*

– Prime Minister Theresa May

On 23 January 2013, Prime Minister David Cameron gave a speech at Bloomberg discussing the future of the EU. In this speech, he put forward his opinion that he was in favour of an in-out referendum to decide on a new settlement for the UK in relation to the EU. This was followed by a pledge in the Conservative Party Manifesto for the 2015 general election to hold an in-out referendum. On 23 June 2016, the UK voted to leave the EU. This result was not widely anticipated by the national media or the markets. What ensued was a collapse in sterling and disbelief amongst large portions of the political elite. There were arguments on both side of the spectrum – some strong, some weak. Broadly, these were structured around democracy, the economy, politics, 'foreigners', togetherness, and credibility.[17,18]

'350 million pounds a week for the NHS' . . . 'immigrants are taking your jobs' . . . 'the economy will collapse' . . . 'house prices will crash' – this was the start of the 'project fear' that arguably both sides ran. Both campaigns fell into blunt, simplistic, 'who cares if it is fake', rude, political soundbites.

So what does Brexit mean for fund managers? To me, Brexit means that at some point, the UK will leave the EU. I know this sounds obvious, but this simple fact is sometimes lost in the angry noise. Thus, asset managers have to assume that the UK will lose its passport for raising money in the EU. Similarly, EU member states will lose their passport to market to the UK. This is the safest bet, even in light of the FCA's agreement with ESMA and EU regulators in February 2019 regarding cooperation in the event of a no-deal Brexit.

Therefore, prepare early and create an EU hub for distraction and management. This, combined with the increased need for 'substance' (more on this in Chapter 10), means money flowing out of the UK to establish a real presence in the EU, if we want to access it (we do not have to).

Beyond that, the effect of Brexit is minimal on the day job. However, its mid-term effect on the UK economy and trade and its long-term effect on the world's view of the UK, appearing small and in need of 'independence' (I thought people declared independence from the Brits, not the other way around?), cannot be properly measured yet. Nor can what will be a hit on the City of London. I have a lot of faith in London to continue trading as it has so successfully for the last 2000 years. Londoners are, on the whole, pragmatic and reasonable. However, the City was a bit of a damp backwater until the Big Bang (the period of drastic financial services deregulation in the UK during the 1980s under Prime Minister Margaret Thatcher), and the helpful US 'invasion'.

As a Brit, I hope that the US stays with us. We need the US to maintain some idea that we are a strong nation in the post-Brexit world. The only other option for greatness without the US supporting us as a 51st state, is to dramatically cut tax and regulation and out-Singapore Singapore. The problem is that Singapore is located in the young and fast-growing powerhouse of South-East Asia.

The notion that the Commonwealth nations will come back and help their former master, especially after their major assistance in two world wars, is clutching at very short straws. I wish some of the people that now produce Brexit-related soundbites had studied history more carefully at school.

## SOCIO-ECONOMIC DIVIDE IN EUROPE

The interrelation of migration, health, populism, education, intergenerational conflict and wealth all lead into the discussion concerning inequality throughout Europe. It is not just a discussion about people who have money and those who do not. It is a more nuanced discourse, which requires an understanding of the transmission of wealth through generations and the perception of what it means to be advantaged or disadvantaged. This section will examine some of the key reasons why the socio-economic divide in Europe is growing and what that means for generations to come.

Broadly, since 2007, the economic recovery has not led to issues of inequality being redressed. First, income inequality is at its highest level since records began. According to the Organisation for Economic Co-operation and Development (OECD),[19] during the 1980s, the wealthiest 10% had average incomes 7.5 times higher than the poorest 10%. Today, the difference is around 9.5 times. This is combined with high levels of household debt, which in times of Vol is particularly dangerous. In the UK, the levels of household debt are a serious concern amongst analysts examining the risks associated with the property market. Underlying this is the perennial problem of wealth distribution. Today the unequal distribution of wealth means that 10% of the richest households possess 50% of the total wealth.[20] Perhaps a more revealing statistic is that the poorest 40% in society hold barely over 3% of wealth.[21] How you examine the data will always bear a significant impact on the conclusions you draw. For instance, were you to examine the salary increases within the technology or finance sectors over the past ten years you would notice that they have seen an upsurge. In contrast, unskilled workers have seen far greater pressure on their pay packets and face a relative change in their wages which helps drive the inequality seen in those industries. This perhaps explains, in part, the recent voting patterns of certain demographics in various elections and referendums within the eurozone. It is not just the salary that is contributing to the rising inequality throughout the EU, but also the changing working patterns.

The flexibility afforded by part-time work and zero-hour contracts was championed as a solution to changing family structures, youth unemployment, and new approaches to work. Yet, with the growth of the gig economy and the lack of safeguards for employees, this particular solution for unemployment is not necessarily a perfect solution for everyone. For example, despite unemployment levels in the UK at a four-decade low[22] the rest of Europe has in the past ten years faced significant levels of unemployment. Indeed, in 2015, Greece had an unemployment rate of 24% compared to Iceland's 4%.[23] This is partly caused by less structured working patterns in the form of part-time and temporary work, but also wider issues concerning working conditions and labour market structures.[24] This is particularly prescient in the UK where zero-hour contracts have become a political talking point in the past couple of years.

When comparing nation to nation, there have been major inequalities in employment. Indeed, during 2015, there were still 1.4 million fewer jobs then there were during 2007.[25] Older people have postponed retiring or have applied for lower-skilled jobs – a major issue in Italy, Greece, and Spain.

## ACTIVE VS. PASSIVE

The growth in passive investing is a key trend of the past decade. Post-financial crisis, passive investing has risen inexorably. A manager's goal is generally to beat its benchmarks (the market). In contrast, passive investing does not require an assessment of an individual investment. Passive investors follow a particular index by trying to own all the stocks in that index in the proportion they are held in that index.

The debate over whether it is better to invest in passive or active funds has been going on for years and is one that is constantly referenced in all sections of the financial press. One of the most scathing reports of recent years has been the FCA's on actively managed funds. Perhaps unfairly, active asset managers (mainly of retail funds) have been staring down the barrel of the FCA's Beretta. They are the subject of current proposals for greater pricing transparency, as a result of some startling statistics showing that actively managed funds underperform passively managed funds due to the high and often quasi-hidden pricing. Whilst the logic is sound, and index-hugging should be a passive activity, you cannot help but feel sympathy for active fund managers trying to compete with funds that have been tracking a rather healthy economy, a false market driven by QE, and interest rates engineered to zero.

Passive funds and their proponents articulate their perceived advantages regularly. Some of the typical arguments that are made in favour of passive funds are that they are cheaper and have performed better than their active counterparts since the financial crisis. Research has shown that 75–85% of active managers in the US underperform their benchmark.[26] Passive funds are unemotional and their construction merely follows the rise and fall of the companies share prices in their portfolios: follow your winners and reduce your losers. Investing in a passive fund also, they claim, prevents the risk of an investor inadvertently choosing an active fund that is actually an index-tracker in disguise[27] (although the FCA is cracking down on this in the UK).

Whether one form of investing or the other is better is up for debate. The truth, and sometimes the facts, often depend on who you ask. Dan Hunt, a senior investment strategist at Morgan Stanley makes this point. He states that it is important to take a nuanced view, but that ultimately it comes down to the priorities, goals, and timeline that an investor has. For example, someone who is anti-risk and does not want to incur any fees that are not strictly necessary would undoubtedly plump for a passive fund. In contrast, someone who is not so averse to risk and wants a higher return than tracking the index could provide would invest in an active fund. Interestingly, an actively managed portfolio can also offer the risk-averse investor steadier returns, even though they may be lower, as compared with an index-tracker, as hedging strategies are often implemented to counter market fluctuations rather than follow them.[28] The truth is that most investors probably sit somewhere in the middle. Investing in a combination of the two would provide a better answer for most investors.

I have to confess to a prejudice in this debate, as an active PE investor myself. I predicted, at the start of 2018, that passives were due a correction, as the soft momentum of the gentle upwards for the previous four years – with little Vol – was due to end. Passives were also in danger of creating an existential issue, where they could not get bigger than actives. If passives represent too much of a market, they end up eating it. Like yin and yang, or the Jedi light and the Sith dark side, both need each other. Passives need a larger active market created by actives to be able to have a 'market' to passively follow.[29] If more money flows away from actives and into passives, companies with significant index weightings will see their stock over-purchased and companies that do not, or rarely, appear in indices will be under-purchased, resulting in serious market distortion, as the underlying financials and other fundamental indicators of portfolio company value are increasingly ignored in favour of simple market capitalisation.

## GENERATIONAL SHIFTS

The evolving combination of Baby Boomers, Generation X, and Millennials in the workforce is a topic of perennial discussion within the commercial world. Every generation faces new and old challenges. Some are not inherent to the world of work, but part of a much wider discussion about the role of society and where we fit within it. Housing, job prospects, politics, and even avocados have been part of the discourse centred on what it means to be a Millennial. However, the influx of Millennials into the workforce has also created a discussion about the different approaches to work. Often derided as lazy, weak, self-absorbed, profligate, and erratic, a dominant trend in the media is how fickle the Millennial workforce is. This section will attempt to debunk some of these suggestions but also understand why they are made in the first place.

'Millennials do not like work. They do not want to hold down a job and work for long-term rewards. Instead, they want to go find themselves on some far-flung island or at a full moon party in Thailand, where they can drink niche spirits and dance whilst covered in luminous body paint.' The *Harvard Business Review* (*HBR*) suggests[30] this characterisation is unfair. Indeed, the reputation that Millennials put in less than what they expect to get out is quantitatively and qualitatively not true. *HBR* points out that Millennials want to be seen to be working hard and are more likely to forfeit unused holidays. Yet they are perceived as entitled and lacking in motivation. One study[31] points out that there is probably little validity in any claim pointing to differences between generations in the work place as a new trope. Indeed, young people have always been perceived as different. The qualities that older generations associate with Millennials are the very same qualities that they were once accused of. Rather than assuming young people are different now, perhaps the answer is that older people have changed. The differences that are oft-cited are in fact minimal. A point convincingly illustrated by a study[32] from IBM's Institute for Business Value, which measured ten variables. One particular variable, the desire to make a positive impact on their organisation, demonstrates that Millennials actually care more about where they work.

Another criticism of Millennials is that they do not stay in one role for long and that young people today will have three, four, or five different careers. However, in the US, the average length of time a person in their twenties stays in a job is broadly similar to what it was in the 1980s.[33]

So, the real conclusion here is likely that young people want and need more money, they take time finding out what it is they are good at, and what it is they want, and their motivations have always been thus and always will be. Job turnover will be particularly high in the early stages of a person's career and relatively low in the latter stages.

There is equally some truth that the Baby Boomers have ridden strong economic waves and have significant RE value and large pensions, 'taken' by us (I am a Baby Boomer) as a gift from our parents' darn-your-own-socks postwar spirit. The credit crisis we caused for the young today has also kept the younger generations' pay low for over ten years. So, perhaps we owe the younger generations something here.

Each generation seems to perceive the ones that follow it as soft and luckier than they are. Certainly, my grandparents' generation thought the postwar children had it better than they did. Each younger generation perceives the one before it to be out of touch. A classic line from West Side Story – a child to his parent in response to the parent's "when I was your age" – sums it up best – 'you were never my age'.

Asset management has also grown tremendously with the Baby Boomer generation in charge of the rise of global growth. We are now seeing increased succession questions, and managers like Blackstone, KKR, and Carlyle are all appointing the next generation. Expect subtle changes, such as technology growth and a closer focus on environmental, social and governance (ESG) issues, under the new and youthful leadership.

We all need to be sensitive to generational differences – even though I suspect they are actually small differences – if we are to build businesses with strong cultures. Listen, adapt, give a little, and build loyalty. Provide roles with clear direction and be sure to understand younger people's philosophy on work in order to attract the best talent in the marketplace.

## GLOBAL INFLATION

The first method of understanding inflation that is commonly used is the Phillips curve. It demonstrates that as levels of unemployment change there is a direct and foreseeable impact on the rate of price inflation. This theory was modified during and after the 1970s, where it looked like the correlation did not actually exist. The Phillips curve is now characterised as a series of smaller curves operating within a long-run Phillips curve. This theory is important as it gives central banks the potential to manipulate inflation levels through fiscal stimulus. By spending money, the government generates growth, which in turn reduces the number of unemployed. As this talent pool restricts, companies have to offer more competitive wages to attract employees. This puts workers in a stronger negotiating position to facilitate better wages, which will have to be met by their employers. The companies who now have a higher wage bill will pass this on to the customer by increasing the price of their products, resulting in price inflation.

Apart from the Phillips curve, the Fisher equation is also widely used as a tool in comprehending how inflation works. The Fisher equation, also known as the Fisher effect, is a theory proposed by Irving Fisher that scopes out the dynamic between inflation and both the real and nominal interest rates. The Fisher effect posits that the real interest rate is equal to the nominal interest rate subtracted by the expected inflation rate. Thus, unless nominal interest rates rise at a rate equal to inflation, real interest rates will fall as inflation increases.

Post-2007, the party line was economic recovery. Yet, for a large part of the past ten years, there has been a general global trend of low inflation rates, with the targets set by central banks often being missed. Along with the decline in oil prices, 2014 saw inflation rates wane to low and sometimes negative levels. This raises two obvious problems for any economy that has been stuck with this problem. First, when inflation is below the target set by a central bank it suggests that the monetary policy in place is ineffective or that the central bank is not serious about meeting its inflation targets. Second, low inflation is linked to periods of deflation, which in turn is symptomatic of a poor economy.

There are several non-financial theories as to why there has been low inflation across the world over the past ten years. In the US, prior to 2018, inflation rates had not reached the 2% target set by their central bank since 2012. One of the core arguments for this trend is the higher productivity attributed to improvements in technology. The argument is that this technology not only helps productivity growth, but also results in suppressed unit labour costs, which has in turn restricted inflationary pressures. Japan has suffered low inflation for a prolonged period, with one theory suggesting that ageing is a primary cause. The argument states that where old workers with firm-specific skills lose their jobs, they tend to go into entry-level jobs instead. This has a negative impact on younger workers' wages, which results in deflationary pressure. We have seen this in Italy and Spain. On a larger geographical scale, one of the contributing factors to this trend of low inflation is globalisation.

Another problem with inflation is an increasing trend for banks to set inflation targets. Since 1989, when New Zealand introduced the first form of inflation target, the number of such targets has grown to 28, with 21 emerging market economies and nine advanced economies doing the same thing. By making inflation the focus of their monetary policy, a globally low rate is to be expected. As the number of central banks that set inflation targets increase, it is likely that inflation levels will stay low.

As discussed above, there have been signs that this Long Sideways era of low growth, low inflation, and low interest rates may be coming to an end with US government bond yields, and yields of those issued elsewhere, tending to rise.[34] Whether this really does signal increased growth, inflation and interest rates remains to be seen.

So, how do asset managers deal with inflation? I have found over the last ten years that they do not reduce their anticipated returns low enough to handle a low inflationary environment. They stick for too long setting out their previous returns. Frankly, with no inflation, why set returns more than a few per cent in equities, and 2% or so for fixed-income? Growth is hard to come by in a low-inflationary economy.

## IMPACT OF THE INTERNET

Tim Berners-Lee, Robert Cailliau, and a team of incredibly talented individuals (along with some abstract thinking) changed the world. Very few people leave an indelible mark on history, but the members of *Project ENQUIRE* and its later incarnations at the European Organization for Nuclear Research (CERN) did. The 'World Wide Web', which we now more commonly refer to as the 'internet', and all that has been made possible because of it, has helped shape the way people interact, do business and experience their lives. First created during 1990, the utility of the internet has grown dramatically over the past three decades. Specifically, over the past ten years there has been a notable shift in how it has impacted business and the asset management industry as a whole and with the rise of broadband, mobile dependency and efficiency, and social media – the 'always on' culture – has ensnared us.

Comparisons are often made between the latest iPhone and the computers used for the Apollo space mission or the technology available to President John F. Kennedy during the Cuban Missile Crisis. The processing power of the latest smart phones would be unimaginable to employees 10, 20 or 30 years ago. The transmission of information and the sharing of ideas is now infinitely easier. This has altered the way people engage with their work and how they interact with others. The ability to communicate seamlessly through video, conference calls, and encrypted chat from any location provides an unprecedented degree of flexibility. This provides a variety of advantages for asset management that engender a more dynamic and collaborative work force.

First, modern technology's association with the internet has improved the access which clients and colleagues have to employees. This means that decision-making can occur at a faster rate, and that the right people can be involved from the word 'go'. This simplifies the process by putting all the right parts in place, requiring less organisation and effort.

Second, for the majority of businesses, client contact is vital. Therefore, from the perspective of the client, the care they receive is directly related to how easily they can contact an employee. Consider that, in 2016, 89% of asset managers had a social media presence.[35] Mobile phones and other technology have enabled a higher rate of communication which gives clients more contact time. Although, this perhaps has raised the bar higher and perhaps in some situations creates an unrealistic expectation, which will inevitably not be met. The French have enshrined the 'right to disconnect' in the workplace by requiring employers to ensure employees do not have to check their emails outside office hours. The encroaching presence of mobile phones in people's home lives may be mostly beneficial to their employers but it is also being blamed for relationship issues, lack of sleep, and high levels of stress. The value of talking to someone face to face has not been erased. It may be that the increase in technology has actually raised the premium placed on business relationships being maintained in person. Moreover, as it becomes easier and easier to send an email, the value in arranging to meet with someone will be higher.

Mobile phones have not just made communicating easier, they have had a dramatic impact on the rest of our lives. This is driven by the vast majority of mobile phone owners using their devices to view content and information. Anybody with a product to sell or market needs to utilise this technology to be organised, drive connectivity, and network. Yet what is apparent is that these high usage levels are now forging change at a societal level. Try walking down a street in London and counting the number of fellow walkers that are not reading their mobile devices. Look across a restaurant and spot those diners actually talking face to face with others. Mobile devices and the internet have changed our lives. The ultimate punishment for a parent is to remove the device from the child or change the Wi-Fi code.

Third, the internet has facilitated not just how we talk with each other but how we interact financially. Money transfer services such as PayPal, Worldpay, Apple Pay, and Google Pay are now being integrated into our daily lives. From relatively humble beginnings, PayPal began as an idea for an online encrypted library. The original concept was imagined by Max Levchin, who upon seeing a lecture by American businessman Peter Thiel (who later invested USD 750 000 in Facebook) combined forces to develop PayPal. The speed at which this market has grown is marked by the arms race between the major players in today's technology sector. Google and Apple have both launched their own products in the last ten years. Apple Pay, which is combined with finger print technology, has changed the day-to-day shopping dynamic. Carrying cash or lending someone change becomes obsolete with the facility to pay the exact amount by using your phone. This method of payment is both incredibly intuitive and prevalent. Individuals with mobile banking and money transfer services are now completely autonomous from high street banks.

The speed and depth of the internet and mobile devices has not only changed the way asset managers operate over the last ten years, but also given them significant opportunities to grow. Access to clients – and retail – has never been easier, and tech-savvy younger people expect to be able to flip in and out of finance units and ideas. The US Jumpstart Our Business Startups Act (JOBS Act) allowed USD 50 000 unit ticket sizes, and pension reform enables individuals to have more control over their money. Increasingly, PE, private debt, and RE managers are now accessing what we would have all called retail money.

The internet really has changed everything. Clever asset managers embrace its possibilities, facilitating immediate and transparent access, information, and investment. However, clever managers appreciate clients still value old-school, face-to-face relationships.

## ENVIRONMENTAL, SOCIAL AND GOVERNANCE ISSUES

Environmental, social and governance (ESG) considerations (see more in Chapter 4) are no longer niche or part of a specific investment strategy. It pervades everything and every strategy. This has been an incredible change over the last ten years. ESG is also the Achilles heel of passives, which is why they talk about it so much. Essentially buying an index and all of its constituent parts means it is hard for passives to have an effective ESG policy or take ESG steps.

ESG is, however, in my view, much spoken of, but still minor in its actual effect. Expect this to change over the next ten years. Expect increased focus, especially if managers increasingly are labelled the evil global elite that protect or, even worse, create inequality. ESG is one defence.

## COMPLEXITY, TRANSPARENCY AND SCALE

With increased internet speed and access, being 'always on', and the demand for greater transparency, managers have to up their game. Then factor in the three to five lettered 'words' (CRS, GDPR, AIFMD, FATCA, MiFID – need I go on?), and the demand for greater regulatory and tax substance and reporting, you can see how asset management has become harder over the last ten years.

In addition, compliance and regulation are only heading in one direction, and the world regulators have only barely got going on asset and wealth management since the financial crisis. The joke in banks these days is that for every ten people in the lift up to work each day, only one is a client-facing banker.

All this leads to the need for scale – see the recent asset management mergers, such as Henderson Janus and Standard Life Aberdeen. This trend is sure to continue, so: (1) be very niche, (2) get into the trillion-dollar AuM club fast, or (3) go home.

## SOME CONCLUSIONS

The economic strategy during the financial crisis (and beyond) of austerity in the UK, US, and EU has also no doubt fed into an increase in phenomena such as populism and the growth of socio-economic division. The US has only just announced – ten years later – that austerity has 'ended'.

Similarly, the Brexit referendum result, President Trump's 'America first', and the rise of populism, are the first major challenges to globalisation. The world views of Prime Ministers Tony Blair and David Cameron and President Obama are in retreat.

Private credit is on the rise. Italy only recently allowed non-banks to lend. Many PE managers see private debt as the way to scale AuM. The last ten years saw the regulators whack Wonga-esque high-rate lending, but regulated private lending, and debt has seen a dramatic rise in the last five years.

Asia is on the rise, but this is not just about China. India is a force to be reckoned with.

Data is big! And this trend has become unstoppable. A third of all digital data out there has been created during the last three years.

I write more on these and other trends in Chapter 13.

## ENDNOTES

1. www.economist.com/news/schoolsbrief/21584534-effects-financial-crisis-are-still-being-felt-five-years-article
2. www.bankofengland.co.uk/monetary-policy/quantitative-easing
3. www.ft.com/content/a2f0c024-32ac-11e8-ac48-10c6fdc22f03
4. www.ft.com/content/a2f0c024-32ac-11e8-ac48-10c6fdc22f03
5. www.bbc.co.uk/news/business-46552147
6. www.blackrock.com/latamiberia/resources/education/alternative-investments-education-center/what-are-alternative-investments

7. FT: Global shift into alternative assets gathers pace: www.ft.com/content/1167a4b8-6653-11e7-8526-7b38dcaef614

8. Ibid.

9. www.ft.com/content/e405a256-1fbf-11e7-b7d3-163f5a7f229c

10. www.ft.com/content/5fb18f06-a1d9-380f-b237-6b4c24d88dcf

11. Mushtaq and Afzal, 'Arab Spring: Its Causes And Consequences' [2017] 30(1) Journal of the Punjab University Historical Society. http://pu.edu.pk/images/journal/HistoryPStudies/PDF_Files/01_V-30-No1-Jun17.pdf

12. Martin Beck and Simone Huser (2013). 'Explanations for the Arab Spring', Center for Mellemoststudier, Syddansk Universitetf.

13. Ibid.

14. Volker Perthes (2011) Europe and the Arab Spring, Survival, 53:6, 73-84, DOI: 10.1080/00396338.2011.636273. www.swp-berlin.org/fileadmin/contents/products/fachpublikationen/111123_Survival_EU_ArabRev_Prt_KS.pdf

15. Institute of Global Change. https://institute.global/insight/renewing-centre/european-populism-trends-threats-and-future-prospects

16. Ibid.

17. http://lup.lub.lu.se/luur/download?func=downloadFile&recordOId=8931444&fileOId=8934759

18. Trebbin Harvard, Nadja LU(2018) MRSK61 20172 Human Rights Studies. https://lup.lub.lu.se/student-papers/search/publication/8931444

19. www.oecd.org/els/soc/cope-divide-europe-2017-background-report.pdf

20. Ibid.

21. Ibid.

22. www.bbc.co.uk/news/business-42802526

23. www.oecd.org/els/soc/cope-divide-europe-2017-background-report.pdf

24. Ibid.

25. Ibid.

26. www.fin24.com/Opinion/the-age-old-debate-active-vs-passive-investing-20171103

27. www.investmentnews.com/article/20180406/FREE/180409949/13-active-fund-managers-agree-to-reveal-closet-indexing

28. www.ft.com/content/2cefb44c-2c32-11e7-bc4b-5528796fe35c

29. https://internationalbanker.com/brokerage/beware-rise-passive-investing/

30. https://hbr.org/2016/08/millennials-are-actually-workaholics-according-to-research

31. www.jstor.org/stable/41682990?seq=1#page_scan_tab_contents

32. http://www-935.ibm.com/services/us/gbs/thoughtleadership/millennialworkplace/

33. https://fivethirtyeight.com/features/enough-already-about-the-job-hopping-millennials/

34. www.nytimes.com/2018/04/26/upshot/the-era-of-very-low-inflation-and-interest-rates-may-be-near-an-end.html

35. www.pwc.lu/en/asset-management/docs/pwc-asset-management-in-the-social-era-june16.pdf

# CHAPTER 2

# What Is it like Being an Asset Manager?

*People may say I can't sing, but no one can ever say I didn't sing.*

– Florence Foster Jenkins, amateur operatic soprano, 1868–1944

**A**sset managers have a certain view of themselves that they sometimes find hard to express, or convince the broader world about. Fund managers have been labelled 'locusts', 'squid', 'pigs', and 'dogs'. They have been described as 'boring', 'academic', 'aggressive', 'self-important', and 'unaware'. Yet the majority of people in the world never interact with fund managers and have no idea what they do. They are, nevertheless, suspicious of them. They suspect that they are far too rich, do not pay their fair share of taxes, and along with the bankers, likely caused the credit crisis. How many managers, when they meet someone they suspect of having no engagement with finance, will say that they are a hedge fund or PE fund manager? More likely, they might say that they 'manage money' or are 'involved in finance'. It is easy to ignore or disengage from outsiders to the sector, but this is done at the manager's peril. Governments regulate and tax the industry; meanwhile, social media opens up managers to direct criticism and even bullying. This chapter therefore attempts to give an overview of what it is really like to be an asset manager.

Since asset managers are driven either by delivering alpha or beta – or variants between like smart beta (return-orientated, risk-orientated, and something in-between) – I am going to approach this chapter with the assistance of the ancient Greek alphabet. This is partly in homage to the first and most important two letters within the asset management industry and partly as a two-thousand-year-old apology by Western civilisation to the destruction of the Alexandrian library of ancient Greek knowledge.

*A α, Alpha*, is clearly the holy grail of active management. Alpha is outperformance of the market. Delivering alpha is expected as an active manager, and there is much serious discussion (and light-hearted banter) in the industry surrounding top decile, top quartile, beating benchmarks, and not being beta in disguise or hugging an index.

PE, venture capital (VC), hedge, and most other alternative strategies, aim to deliver alpha. Alternative managers like to say that they deliver 'uncorrelated' returns to assets that follow markets. This is true to a point, but when things feel gloomy, people do not buy technology companies, antiques, or fine art either.

***B β, Beta***, is the aim of passive managers and index-trackers. The pursuit of beta entails minimising risk as much as possible. Beta is a historical measure of Vol. Beta measures how an asset (for example, a stock, exchange-traded fund (ETF), or portfolio) moves versus a benchmark (an index), whereas alpha is a historical measure of an asset's return on investment compared to the risk-adjusted expected return.

To aim for beta is to aim to achieve exactly the same results as the chosen market. 'Mr Market' is not really a person and does not speak; however, it (which is the accumulation of millions of trades) can be replicated by essentially buying the entire index (and its weightings).

Active managers can also seek some beta. However, in recent years, following the financial crisis, with major QE, freakishly low interest rates, and little Vol, passives have grown to such a size that they are arguably 'eating' the market that they are supposed to be following. In other words, can you track a market if you (and not your alter ego – the activists) also make the market? This has led to a strange years-long horizontal lack of activity, and an almost existential problem hitting trading. However, with the return of Vol, rising rates, and the reduction of QE, actives should make a comeback.

***Γ γ, Gamma***, is for 'good'. Managers aim to do social good. They might not believe, like some of the large technology companies in the US, that they are making the world a better place, or 'doing God's work' as one CEO once jokingly said (and I am sure has regretted ever since); however, managers do intend to make the world richer and people's savings last longer, and many have other specific social (or 'ESG' – more on this in Chapter 4) aims. Entrepreneur First, for example, makes the point that 'what the most ambitious people choose to do with their lives has a profound impact on society, the economy and culture'.[1] Nigel Kershaw OBE, best known for *The Big Issue*, is a prime example of this, spending his career helping to promote a better society through creating, developing, and managing social enterprises.

*Δ δ, Delta,* or 'day job'. What is it like? Is it about making a nice salary, enjoying the markets, working in a team, negotiating a complex obstacle course of regulations, or just winning? Many managers simply love their asset class. PE managers think they have the best job ever and VCs wax lyrical about new types of technology and disruptive models. Fixed-income managers spend time worrying about their particular bond market and what state governors are up to. Meanwhile, RE managers often read 'property porn' late at night and infrastructure people spend all day walking around ports or staring at bridges. Hedge fund managers in my experience actually just like winning and listed portfolio managers are similarly fixated on beating their benchmark. Overall, for whatever reason they may give, asset managers tend to love their jobs.

On the flip side, fund structures can drag down their mood. With very long life funds comes very long commitments. Worst of all, failing to beat their benchmark or being accused of index-hugging can send a manager into a tailspin.

The world is proving a challenging place for asset managers at the moment. We are finding politics increasingly frustrating, owing to the uncertainties that it is creating. Some managers can exploit politics – for example, when George Soros famously 'beat' the BoE on Black Wednesday in September 1992. When John Major's government was forced to withdraw sterling from the European Exchange Rate Mechanism (ERM), it was reported that Soros made over USD 1 billion in just a few days.

*E ε, Epsilon,* is for 'engagement' with portfolio companies, both by passive and active managers. There has been considerable press coverage for active managers who have taken a stronger approach to their engagement with portfolio company management, whilst passive managers continue to struggle with a lack of meaningful engagement. Engagement is important in the promotion of both growth and ESG compliance. Chapter 4 on governance goes into detail about the impact a manager can have when it practises engagement.

*Z ζ, zeta,* is a much disputed letter and sound in ancient Greek, so I am taking the liberty of using it as I wish, to represent 'sea'. The migration of managers to islands with better taxation is a popular trend. However, it brings with it not just transportation issues, but often greater regulation (the opposite of what is frequently assumed). With major countries fighting a race to the bottom on corporation tax (just look at President Trump's recent moves, as well as developments in the UK and Ireland), the tax benefits of a manager relocating 'offshore' make less sense. Indeed, some high-profile hedge funds have recently actually moved back to the UK from Switzerland.

*H η, eta,* is for 'hurdle' or 'high-water mark' (both discussed in Chapter 3), a word or expression that keeps managers awake at night. The hurdle to clear or high-water mark to stay ahead of can break a management group. Slip below it and the whole operation can disintegrate as investors fall away and team members follow the money. That said, whilst meeting the benchmark will keep investors happy (just about), achieving the hurdle is not exciting and managers will always aim to exceed expectations.

*Θ θ, theta,* is for 'theatre' – acting, pretending, and convincing. All entrepreneurs are actors. Richard Branson said he spent two years pretending to run an airline, until one day he woke up and believed he was running an airline. Managers have to convince their team of their strategy, convince investors to invest, and convince portfolio companies to sell to them. Generally, if you start your own operation you have to fake it until you make it. We are all actors on the world stage, and sometimes the main difficulty is not knowing your part, as Rosencrantz and Guildenstern found in Shakespeare's *Hamlet*.

*I ι, iota,* well I do care one 'iota', and so do most managers. The financial crisis illustrated the interrelation between economics and society, and recognising the industry's mistakes in the build-up to the crisis, managers have signalled their intent to become stewards of change. Indeed, this is a core part of MJ Hudson's philosophy and is commented on in detail in Chapter 4.

*K κ, kappa,* is clearly for 'cappuccino' and the original coffee houses that spawned many of the original finance houses, which have since developed into the complex financial ecosystem we know today. (Interestingly, certainly in the UK, coffee houses came before tea houses and later gin dens.) The hubbub of the coffee houses developed into the drama of the trading floors, but with the rise of the all-pervasive and always-on internet, trading floors are also on their way to becoming a relic of history, and much of the human interaction of investment has disappeared – see 'loneliness' below.

*Λ λ, lambda,* I am taking for 'loneliness'. When I was a VC fund manager, it was easy to spend time with companies, but rarely other VC fund managers. This is not just a problem in VC. Hedge fund managers are notoriously protective of their trading model and ideas, as they eke out returns by being somewhat contrarian, finding minute cross-market discrepancies, or betting against other people's behaviour.

Asset class specific industry conferences help managers to get out more and the internet facilitates connectivity between managers, but as an adviser to asset managers now, I am frequently surprised by their thirst for current market issues and themes. Unfortunately, conferences isolate managers by asset class, when understanding the broader spectrum is more empowering. Hence, we have seen the growth of the 'asset library' managers that manage assets of all classes for broader knowledge, such as Apollo, Blackstone, and Carlyle. Similarly, being both a limited partner (LP) (i.e. investor) and general partner (GP) (i.e. manager) does not have to be a conflict, and can add considerable value and expertise.

*M μ, mu,* is for 'machines'. With the advent of artificial intelligence, predictive analytics, machine learning, and natural language processing, the orthodox approach to investment analysis is being constantly reimagined. As Tony Dalwood notes, 'a lot of money can be made by machines exploiting inefficiencies'. Alice Bentinck MBE mentions the future of synthetic biology. Wol Kolade talks of the way we currently access software so inefficiently – typing in words. The number of words spoken is so much more than the number of words written; thus current data is actually small. Take a step further, and just imagine if we could simply think and it could be recorded in software and code.

Machines and technology are explored in more detail in Chapter 8.

*N ν, nu,* is for 'nuts', or commodities, as a significant asset class. Some huge public companies (Glencore, for example) produce, manage, and trade commodities. Trading commodities was historically about getting an edge on a crop or well (who can forget new trader Eddie Murphy trading frozen orange juice futures in the film *Trading Places*). Now, it is about both knowledge and attention to operational detail.

*Ξ ξ, xi,* or XL, which is for 'extra large' and takes us to equities and bonds – the largest asset classes. These two asset classes dominate asset management. They have also been hit the hardest on fees. Each asset class has multiple individual strategies. In equities, strategies fall into categories such as venture, growth, momentum, and turn-around. In bonds, we talk about high yield, junk, senior, junior, mezzanine, listed, and private debt. As such, the investors that manage these asset classes are very different from each other. These asset classes are the 'mainstream' classes but how 'alternative' are the rest, I wonder.

There is considerable overlap between private and public equity, and private debt and mainstream credit for managers. The joke is that private equity is not always 'private' or 'equity' (PE managers love investing debt, as well as equity, in portfolio companies).

**O o, *omicron*,** is for 'outsized' returns. Outsized is a word that generates excitement amongst PE managers, but is a dream for most credit managers. How do equity investors garner outsized returns? Well, largely, it is down to risk, or luck, or both. Excessive leverage can also help. Timing is vital (finding willing buyers and sellers at the right moment at the right price), as can be seen when measuring PE fund returns – and the emergence of 'vintage funds' in the fund units secondaries space.

Personally, I prefer growth. Growth is not a popular strategy, but in the current low interest rate environment, growth is making a comeback. The reality is that asset managers cannot really create growth, nor do closed-ended funds timescale really allow time for growth to create outsized returns. Growth is made by portfolio company management, not fund managers. The push for growth from funds can lead to frustration for both asset managers and portfolio company executives. I can vouch for that from my experience on both sides.

**Π *π, pi*,** (given its importance in mathematics) is for 'algorithmic trading'. Humans are often too slow and too fallible. In the hedge fund world, computers are increasingly used to make investment decisions using complex algorithms. Algorithmic trading enables trades to be executed at optimal times and prices, with minimal risk of error, and with reduced transaction costs. Instead of spending time on the many detailed and stressful aspects of trading, managers can focus their attention on big-picture strategy and maximise productivity. However, never trust a machine called HAL.

**P *ρ, rho*,** is for 'remuneration'. Most managers expect a base salary to cover their mortgage, grocery shopping, and other family expenses. Beyond that, there is typically a bonus. One of the reasons why so many managers left the clearing banks during the financial crisis was the legislative restrictions on the bonus or performance payments payable by banks.

Bonuses are usually based on individual and/or company/fund performance. Many managers also own shares or options in the management company (which may go public, like KKR, Apollo, and Aberdeen, or get sold, like Fortress – more on public managers in Chapter 3) and can therefore also receive dividends and capital gains.

Managers (especially senior managers) aim for big returns to maximise performance fees and carried interest, which flows into bonus pools, dividends, and capital gains. Regular performance fees are typical in mainstream open-ended strategies and hedge funds, which are paid when the manager clears its high-water mark. PE, VC, and RE funds are often closed-ended, however, and thus performance is rewarded in the form of carried interest (a share of capital gains). Mostly, it is only measured at the end of a fund. Thus, some PE management companies have to consider shorter-term rewards for younger managers.

**Σ *σ/ς, sigma*,** is for 'skin in the game'. Many managers invest in their own funds. This is not a conflict, but alignment. What is better than to have your manager with skin in the game? Many listed equity and bond managers invest much of their own wealth in the funds they manage. In addition, alternative managers invest or 'co-invest' significant stakes in their own funds. Sometimes this is, in effect, a reinvestment of the management fee, but it can be much more.

In addition, sigma is for specialisation and its rise. Tony Dalwood of Gresham House emphasises the popularity (and really necessity these days) of specialisation in the assets that he manages – 'It used to be that I was given management of a general portfolio, but nowadays these portfolios are specialised between the class of the asset, its size, or geography'.

*T τ, Tau*, is for 'teamwork'. The cult of the star manager pervades in asset management. An individual manager or small team leaving an asset management company can significantly impact a group's share price if listed, and can cause AuM to be sucked out or slowly leak away. An example of this was seen in 2010 with Gartmore when star managers, Roger Guy and Guillaume Rambourg, left. Gartmore was subsequently sold to Henderson. Similarly, the recent drop in share price and capital AuM shrinkage experienced by GAM Investments following the suspension of star manager Tim Hayward further illustrates the point.

Despite this, many of the asset managers we work with highlight teamwork and the camaraderie of working in an asset management firm as one of key reasons for enjoying the job or choosing the career. Tony Dalwood joined Phillips & Drew after having spent most of his youth playing rugby at a high level and being impressed by a similar team culture when he first started working in asset management. Tony also mentioned to me that the wide range of characters and the dynamism of people working in asset management makes the nine-to-five much more interesting.

*Y υ, upsilon*, is for 'unicorn' – a term coined by Aileen Lee for a privately held start-up company valued at over USD 1 billion. This is the ultimate goal for VCs who invest large amounts of capital into companies that go stale, bust, or never even make it to the starting line. It's the diamond in the rough that VCs seek, as a few diamonds (or a single unicorn) makes it all worthwhile.

*Φ φ, phi*, is for 'philosophy' and education. I cannot overemphasise the need for constant learning. This can really give a manager the edge in a competitive market. There is also nothing more impressive than the Renaissance manager. A deep knowledge of history can give you sight into the future. History does not exactly repeat, but it keeps performing the same plays. Furthermore, whilst specialism has become market standard (see 'Sigma'), a broad knowledge base (e.g. of different asset classes, foreign geographies, domestic and international politics, economics, and technological developments) can help a manager stay ahead of the game. You are never smarter thank when you know you don't know something.

*X χ, chi*, is for the 'children'. Wol Kolade of Livingbridge told me that he was so impressed with a PE speaker at his school, that he knew he wanted to be a PE manager from an early age. Similarly, Alice Bentinck MBE of Entrepreneur First wants to back young inspired people.

The importance of education, mentoring and apprenticeship cannot be underestimated. Fostering future talent should be a top priority. In addition, what fun it is, running and training a young and hungry team!

In addition, chi is for change. One of the largest areas of change (detailed in Chapters 9 and 10) is the growth of regulation, rules, and red tape. Managers joke that for every manager, there are five people behind him or her in compliance, finance, and HR, whereas historically it would be five portfolio managers for every back-office person – that has been a massive change in the last few years!

Chi is also about the huge changes in technology that we have seen over the past 10–20 years. The curve has been particularly steep recently, with the impact of mobile phones, the internet, and big data hugely influencing the asset manager at both a micro and macro level. This trend is set to continue and is a core constituent of Chapters 8 and 13.

The change in asset allocation itself has also been one of the larger shifts in the industry. Allocation towards alternative assets such as PE, VC, RE, private debt, and hedge has shot up from practically zero 20 years ago to now being a significant component of pension fund portfolios, perhaps more so in the US, but in the UK as well.

*Ψ ψ, psi*, is for 'p.s.' one must not forget that the asset management industry is a blessed industry and we are all very privileged. Especially as the world increasingly divides between 'haves' and 'have nots', it is important to remember our good fortune. It is also incumbent on us to help to give the returns people need to enjoy an equally blessed life. Before we all moan in the future about increased regulation, administration and transparency, just remember the words of the prophet known as Spiderman's Uncle Ben – 'with great power, comes great responsibility'.

*Ω ω, omega*, is for 'Omega' watches, and the ability to build a specialism or niche from a small place – Switzerland in this case. Managers build boutiques. They also increasingly build multi-boutiques. They also build multi-managers, as the demand for one-stop-shops increases.

Increasingly there is no excuse for not knowing large detail in small things. Even if your AuM is huge, each aspect of every investment should be specialised.

## From the CEOs

I thought it would be helpful for the younger readers of this book to ask the five founding CEOs that I interviewed why they joined the asset management industry and what advice they would give to young entrants to the market.

**Tony Dalwood** of Gresham House talked of the team spirit he encountered when he first entered the world of asset management, which he held in high esteem, having played rugby at a high level. Tony's top tips for youngsters are:

1. You do not know everything.
2. Always listen.
3. But do not believe everything you hear – question it.
4. Read as much as possible.
5. Invest your own money across as many asset classes as possible – experience the highs and lows.
6. Get as much experience as possible in internships.

**Wol Kolade** of Livingbridge was so impressed with a speaker from 3i in his A-level economics class that he decided at that moment that he wanted to get into PE (as it later transpired, via a graduate programme at Barclays). Wol was only a schoolboy, but he was interested in businesses, and he loved the idea of backing people. 'People change the world', Wol told me.

Wol recommends studying a degree subject with a heavy focus on quantitative analysis, such as engineering. He also advises learning how to code, because 'IT is everything'. He says we should look at every process and try to automate it. Keep innovating – do not just stop and admire the latest thing – look for the '*new* new thing'.

Wol also regularly reminds himself that in PE, that there are three choices:

1. Buy.
2. Sell.
3. Do nothing.

Sounds obvious, but really a PE manager should stick this fine advice on their computer screen. He also emphasises that whatever choices you make, anyone can get lucky if they diversify enough. Therefore, the big secret in PE investing is to diversify, and then not lose too much in bad companies. Back your winners and drop your losers.

**Richard Novack** of Alpha Hawk got into hedge fund management following many years of trading. Richard explains that a hedge fund manager is not only about a trading/investment strategy intended to produce returns – it is a multifaceted business. Richard's decision to establish his own hedge fund was, of course, predicated first on exploiting his skill set derived from nearly 30 years of trading, but equally enticing to him was the opportunity to be involved in the many other facets – business development, operations, and marketing, for example. Richard told me that, 'At this point in my career the opportunity to build a complex business and learn in the process was exciting. Moreover, after spending the better time of the last 20 years surrounded by trading screens and with a focus, primarily on the capital markets, I embraced the idea of being out and about with real people contact.'

Richard emphasises the importance of passion ('the manager needs to be hungry and still have a twinkle in their eye when they explain what they do, even after years in the industry') and commitment ('skin in the game in the form of investment capital or sweat equity').

**Alice Bentinck MBE** of Entrepreneur First, is one of the most focused (co-)founders (along with Matthew Clifford) in asset management that I know. She knew from university that she would get a first and then join McKinsey (and she did!). Whilst a consultant, she recognised that business is all about people. At Entrepreneur First, they back the person first and foremost, and the ideas or business plan can follow (known as 'talent investing'). Alice's number one tip is that, to be a good asset manager, you have to be good with the people as well as the numbers.

Alice also sees a lack of innovation in the asset management industry and suggests there is a world of opportunity in the sector for inventive young individuals – 'Do not try to recreate what exists, as it may already be dead anyway'.

**Nigel Kershaw OBE** of The Big Issue came into asset management late, and via a career in printing. As such, he never saw himself as a fund manager. Instead, he wanted to make a significant social impact through product.

Nigel – a reincarnation of Plato to my mind – sees a need for democratisation of capital and socialisation of product. Nigel thinks big (pun intended). He knows that 'ordinary people want involvement in investment'. Nigel reminds us all that, for the retail investor, it is really hard to look at the underlying portfolios. As such, common investors instead look at the managers themselves, their investment framework, and governance.

Personally, I have a concern for the cult of the star manager, or the loud, ego-driven managers that like to tell us all how awful everyone else is (people in glass houses . . . ). Some cults do well for a long period, but most start believing their own rhetoric and convince themselves (with no one employed to remind them when they are not wearing any clothes) that they are unbeatable. Star managers that set up their own houses or strategies can fail without their previous institutional infrastructure, team and balancing governance. Like any team sport, the team that supports the star player(s) is vital to success. Also, like athletes, it is impossible to be at your very best all of the time and all ideas become old.

A clear unifying theme running through the thoughts of the five CEOs that I interviewed is the importance of teamwork and innovative thinking.

## Some Conclusions

What is it like to be an asset manager?

Those that move mid-career to asset management typically believe that the 'buy side' is more fulfilling. They believe (especially if managers were once their clients or they moved from the 'sell side') that the buy side is the glory side. However, the grass is not always greener. Different stresses emerge, such as loneliness, and the nightmare of not reaching your goal can (Matrix film-like) become reality as you chase the elusive nirvana of the industry benchmark, only to find when you get there, that the benchmark (Wizard of Oz-like) actually just exists in different subjective forms of interpretation. Do not let me put you off, though!

Chasing alpha and beta, and staying on top of hurdles and high water marks sets asset managers' pulses racing; client wealth generation and impact investing gives asset managers meaning beyond the numbers; working with teams of diverse individuals in a fast-paced business environment keeps the day job interesting; and becoming a master of one's asset class is something most asset managers are truly passionate about.

A career in asset management is challenging – investors can be demanding and the markets can be uncooperative. In addition, if you find yourself in a fund that will never make carry, owing to one poor investment (why are the worst investments always the biggest?), then the rewards are not there.

Life as an asset manager is like the markets themselves: the lows can be tough and the highs can be almost dream-like.

## ENDNOTE

1. https://medium.com/entrepreneur-first/tech-entrepreneurship-and-the-disruption-of-ambition-4e6854121992

# CHAPTER 3

# Structures and Economics

*I like terra firma; the more firma, the less terra.*

– George S. Kaufman

This chapter will introduce different types of asset managers currently operating in the market. Each type will include sections on its structuring, popular jurisdictions, their fund economics, fees that are charged by the manager to the investor and portfolio companies, and the differences between managing a listed or unlisted fund. A number of asset managers are listed and I can see this trend continuing – so what is the listed effect on how they operate? This chapter will also explore the squeeze on players in the middle of the market from the larger funds growing on the one side, and the increase in smaller, more niche funds.

## JURISDICTION OF ASSET MANAGERS

When initially establishing themselves, asset managers will choose their geographic base and will take into account a range of factors. These factors include their place of birth, the country they currently work in, availability of future team members, access to investors, schooling options, or, indeed, the weather.

It is also often the case that they will jurisdiction 'shop' based on the tax regime that is most favourable, or for regulatory reasons, or even because their target investors prefer a certain jurisdiction. Sometimes asset managers choose their jurisdiction based on the fact that there are better investment deals to be found there.

A combination of these factors also come into play during a manager's growth phase, when they intend to open multiple offices across separate jurisdictions. Readers may assume that I would come out swinging for the UK as the jurisdiction to establish an asset management practice; however, I believe in being jurisdictionally agnostic and recognise that each jurisdiction has its benefits and limitations. Unfortunately, the UK is certainly not the jurisdiction *du jour*, with Brexit putting managers off opening in the UK or even making them leave.

It is, however, the case that a manager can be located easily in a different jurisdiction than the fund that it manages, although increasing rules on 'substance' for tax or regulatory purposes is making this choice harder. That said, sub-managers or investment advisers using the delegation rules allows operations to be based in a number of jurisdictions.

**UK** The UK as a jurisdiction for asset managers is (currently) the number one spot in Europe. London and New York are often vying with each other for the title of financial capital of the world. Other than having a favourable tax and regulatory regime set in place for asset managers (discussed further in Chapters 10–12), there are also many non-legislative reasons as to why the UK is popular amongst asset managers. For example, being (almost) geographically situated between the Asian and American time zones. The UK also benefits from high quality universities that indirectly translate into a strong service-sector economy. The most obvious benefit, however, is English being the main language spoken by the business community.

The UK also has hundreds of years of open trading, is mostly welcoming to foreigners, is liberal, reasonable, and accessible. It is often forgotten, but the UK also has the best legal system in the world, built up over hundreds of years. Its constitution benefits from not being written down (and therefore being flexible as required) and there are clear demarcations and balances between the executive, parliament, church, monarchy and judiciary. The judges are not appointed by politicians (thank goodness), and are smart and (this is important) incorruptible. Thus, managers can get on with business in the UK.

Another principal reason for the UK attracting non-resident investors (including hedge funds) is the ability to appoint UK-based investment managers without creating a risk of UK taxation for themselves. Her Majesty's Revenue and Customs (HMRC) is committed to maintaining this environment by offering the 'investment manager exemption' (IME). The IME provides a tax exemption where the manager meets certain conditions, which are discussed in Chapter 11.

**US** The asset management industry in the US is the most developed around the world and is the country with the largest AuM. In 2017, North American assets hit USD 54 trillion, leaving Europe in the dust at USD 29 trillion.[1] The size of a market is only one indicator as to the overall offerings and health of the asset management industry in the US – but it is a strong one. One would assume that if the managers did not approve of the market in the US or the way in which it was heading, they would just leave. There is very little in the way of physical infrastructure that an asset manager requires.

The recent tax reforms (discussed in more detail in Chapter 11) passed by President Trump have already benefitted US-based asset managers, with many enjoying a tax-cut windfall due to the decrease in the top rate of corporate tax falling to 21% from 35%. With the extra cash, asset managers have the option to increase their dividend payments or even offer share buybacks. Managers themselves, however, will be hit substantially (as will many other high earners) by the changes in the way state and local tax regimes interact with the federal tax system. It used to be the case that the federal tax rate would be reduced by the amount of taxes paid at state and local level. The deductible amount, however, has now been capped at USD 10 000, which is a far cry from the average deducted from those earning over USD 1 million, which was USD 275 000 in 2015.[2] The introduction of the cap may bring about the uprooting of asset managers from the coasts to states with lower tax rates.

The US also has the deepest pool of capital to raise money. US investors continue to represent the largest capital pool for managers across the globe. In 2017, nearly 60% of the total AuM was raised from US investors, slightly over USD 30 trillion.[3] US investors continue to dominate the top rankings by AuM as well. Of the top 20 global asset managers, 12 were based in the US and raised nearly 70% of the total assets (which, surprisingly was down from 13 managers raising over 70% the year before).[4] US pension plans are the largest in the world by AuM, and allocate far more to alternative or private strategies than most other pension funds by jurisdiction. Of the USD 54 trillion of US AuM, nearly half (USD 25 trillion) is held by pension funds.[5] Within that USD 25 trillion, 28% is allocated towards alternative or private strategies (assets that are not cash, equities, or bonds), which is 3% higher than average across the P7 countries, and 12% higher than the UK's allocation towards the same asset class.[6]

There are many different types of players within the US asset management industry, which keeps it highly competitive. Industry firms ranging from pure-play independent asset managers to diversified commercial banks, insurance companies, and brokerages that offer asset management services in addition to their core business activities all jostle over the purchase of assets. The vast size of the US asset management market is hardly done justice by the facts and figures above. It is so vast that the second largest region by AuM, Europe, which has a population twice the size of that of the US, only has slightly over half the level of AuM. In other words, it will take a few generations before the US asset management market plays second fiddle to any other jurisdiction, with regards to both fundraising and investing. Until that happens, asset managers across the globe will nearly always have to consider courting US investors, another shining example of the US as *the* global superpower. With such a high concentration of global assets based in the US, asset managers domiciled in the region have enjoyed the power of being able to move the market by sheer size alone. Terms that govern the existence of fund managers will often have originated from the US, meaning managers based in the US are often exposed at an earlier stage to changes in the market.

**Switzerland** Following watches and chocolate, financial services is usually what people associate with Switzerland. In the past, this has often been private banking; however, the asset management industry is fast-growing within this small land-locked country. There are many reasons why an asset manager may wish to set up shop in Switzerland – aside from its panache for financial services. Switzerland's public infrastructure is second to none, with a rail system allowing workers to travel seamlessly across the country (I read the advert . . . ). Switzerland also has a high quality of life, especially for those who can afford it. Other than the beneficial social aspects, Switzerland also boasts the highest per capita wealth in the world, with an average just below USD 550 000 per adult, providing asset managers with a rich domestic market of investors.[7] Another attractive factor for the asset management industry is its leadership in innovation, with a number one spot it has maintained since 2011 according to the Global Impact Investing Network report (although Switzerland's ease of starting a business rating is worryingly low, at 58[8]).

Switzerland also offers a consistent crop of assets for asset managers. Swiss workers have a high level of disposable income and a high savings rate that feeds into an established pension system, both of which provide ample opportunities for asset managers. Asset managers within Switzerland manage over CHF 2 trillion for both domestic and international investors, more than twice the size of the total Swiss pension pot.[9]

Switzerland is governed on both a federal and cantonal level, with 26 different cantons setting their own economic agendas. This often means that each canton is competing not only on a local level within Switzerland, but also on an international level against other attractive business hubs such as London, New York, and Hong Kong. The BAK Taxation Index is a form of measurement used to review a location's attractiveness for both businesses and skilled individuals, taking into account the location's base tax rate as well as various other tax rules, presenting a more complete picture of a city or canton's and individual's tax burden. When reviewing the corporation tax burden, the 'effective average tax rate' is used, for which the international average is 29%.[10] The closest canton to the international average is Geneva, with an average of 21.4%, whilst the lowest rate of any canton is found in Nidwalden at 10.1%, just losing the top spot to Hong Kong at 9.9%.[11] These figures are often reviewed by businesses (including asset managers) when deciding where in Switzerland to set up shop. The rate for highly qualified individuals is also calculated in the BAK Taxation Index and has found that Zug, with an average rate of 23%, is the lowest within Switzerland, which is again considerably lower than the international average of 38.5%.[12] Depending on the structure of the asset management firm, the personal tax rate may be of more importance to managers.

Zurich and Geneva often rank closely in global rankings for asset management popularity. Both cities are beautiful and provide easy access to other jurisdictions (Germany and Austria for the former and France for the latter). Geneva has historically been known for its popularity amongst wealth managers (who feed into the asset management industry) and the international crowd living in Switzerland (see Red Cross, the UN, and hundreds of other NGOs). Zurich, on the other hand, is the central hub for business in Switzerland and has always been competing for financial services business with Geneva and was not as much caught up in the money laundering scandals as its French cousin was. In rankings compiling various political, economic, social, and technological indices in order to determine a leader board of asset management hubs, both cantons performed exceptionally well when compared with other cities. With regards to each of the categories, both cantons rank close to equal, and lead the board with regards to political/legal rankings, highlighting it as a key strength.[13] The category that hamstrings both cantons is – unsurprisingly – technology, which, according to the compiled study stems from a lack of online governmental resources and a lack of will for Swiss residents to take part in the e-revolution.

**EU**   The EU has successfully harmonised asset management markets across its 28 (maybe now 27) member states through the introduction of various regulatory regimes. The high level of harmonisation has made it easy for asset managers to offer access to their funds to would-be investors, who, a generation before, they would never have had access to. PE managers based in the Nordic region can apply for passporting rights of their alternative investment fund (AIF) (discussed more in Chapter 9) with their competent authority, and receive investment from Dutch pension funds. Of course, the system is not perfect. The concept of pre-marketing, for example, which is the idea that asset managers can hold discussions with potential investors before their fund has been fully established, has no EU-wide definition (and in some countries simply does not exist). To the EU's credit, however, this oversight is currently being addressed, with a proposed definition of pre-marketing set to be passed at some point this year (as at the time of writing this is predicted to be mid-2019) and therefore be implemented by member states by 2021. In a draft report published in September 2018, the definition proposed by the European Commission (EC) states pre-marketing as being:

> '*a direct or indirect provision of information or communication on investment strategies or investment ideas by an EU AIFM or on its behalf to potential professional investors domiciled or registered in the Union in order to test their interest in an AIF or a compartment of an AIF, which is not yet established in the Member State where the potential investors are domiciled or have their registered office.*'[14]

Straightforward, no? For jurisdictions within the EU that do not already have a pre-marketing regime in place, the above definition will be a welcome relief and will lead to further convergence across the EU. Other jurisdictions that have implemented a definition of pre-marketing which may read wider than the above will not be as happy, however, which includes jurisdictions such as the UK who generally permit the circulation of draft documentation to potential investors before the fund vehicles are established.

In addition, not all of the EU member states have implemented national private placement regimes (NPPRs) under the Alternative Investment Fund Managers Directive 2011 (AIFMD). Essentially, the goal that the AIFMD set out to achieve has not yet been reached. Similarly, the Markets in Financial Instruments Directive (MiFID) (the first) was only implemented properly once MiFID II came out.

As well as the harmonisation of regulations making it easier to offer investment services to neighbouring jurisdictions, the EU has also created freedom of movement. With the EU able to act as one trading bloc, the concept of the freedom of movement of workers means that investment professionals can move from country to country and apply for work without the need to apply for a visa. Aside from the obvious benefits created by this system that were originally envisioned by the founders of the European Coal and Steel Community, freedom of movement makes it easier to gain inside knowledge (contacts or a cultural understanding) on investors that only a local originally from that country would have.

Although I firmly believe that London will continue to prosper as a financial city outside of the EU, there has been some leakage of professionals to various EU cities that has slightly shifted the balance of power. Luxembourg, Paris, and Frankfurt have all managed to lure businesses out of London and onto the continent. Dublin has attracted a few too. Luxembourg and Dublin especially, have been particularly successful at creating desirable fund jurisdictions. The asset managers, other than the 12 based in the US, that make up the top 20 in 2017 were all European, except for one, which was based in the UK.[15] The investor capital on offer in this bloc is deeper than that found in the UK, with managers receiving over 15% of their AuM from the bloc, just under twice as much as available in the UK.[16]

**France**  France boasts one of the largest asset management centres on continental Europe, with nearly EUR 4 trillion AuM. France is host to some of Europe's largest bank-owned asset managers, including Amundi (created by the merger of Crédit Agricole and Société Générale's asset management businesses) and Natixis, who hold the top two spots.[17] These financial institutions groups (FIGs) are leading the charge for the European goliath managers, leveraging existing distribution networks and relationships created by the banks to distribute their product.

**Germany**  Unsurprisingly, Germany has done well to effectively promote its asset management industry on a European-wide scale, with BVI Bundesverband (the Germany Investment Funds Association), being one of the founding members of the European Fund and Asset Management Association. Over the last 10 years, the Germany asset management industry has seen impressive growth, having recently exceeded the EUR 3 trillion mark (a 77% increase from 2008), which has largely been attributed to a consistently low-interest rate environment by BVI.[18]

**The Netherlands**  The Netherlands as an international trading hub goes back hundreds of years. It is in their blood to be outward-looking. This characteristic is one of the reasons why so many international businesses base themselves in the Netherlands, and large institutional investors based in the Netherlands act to attract asset managers. ABP, the pension fund for Dutch civil servants and PFZW, the pension fund for the Netherlands' healthcare sector, are listed as the second and third (respectively) largest pension funds in Europe (with a third pension fund not far behind in seventh place).[19] The combination of large pots of money, an established asset management industry, and Brexit, means that Amsterdam is well-positioned to become a likely asset management centre for Europe. (I confess to a small prejudice, as I am a quarter Dutch).

**Luxembourg**   As far as I have seen, Luxembourg has situated itself as the most likely successor to London for closed-ended private fund domiciliation following Brexit. The size of its asset management market has recently topped EUR 4 trillion, which from the previous year was slightly over 10% growth, and which is unlikely to slow down as Brexit looms and uncertainty engulfs London.[20] The largest contingent of that EUR 4 trillion is equity funds, sitting at EUR 1.5 trillion.[21] Importantly, Luxembourg offers a wide field of service providers, ranging from fund administrators to depositaries, all of whom are itching for more business. The fund structures are well thought through too (having copied ideas from the UK), as well as Luxembourg being one of the two main centres for UCITS (with Ireland – see the section on Dublin).

This is why MJ Hudson opened a Luxembourg funds platform in 2017, shortly after the UK's EU referendum result.

**Dublin**   Dublin is the sibling of Luxembourg, also set to inherit a large portion of those asset managers or funds that leave London. With its first language being English and a strong asset management industry in place before the likes of Brexit came along, Dublin will be a serious contender to Luxembourg. Many asset managers have already, or are in the process of, opening up new offices in Dublin that will act as either their main office in Europe following Brexit, or the main recipient of investment. Dublin is proving especially popular as a destination for UCITS (funds created pursuant to the Undertakings for Collective Investment in Transferable Securities Directive, in order to benefit from EU passporting rights) domiciliations, with nearly 80% of the Irish domiciled funds held being held in UCITS.

Hedge funds also find Dublin and the Irish Collective Asset-management Vehicle (ICAV) particularly attractive. With over 40% of hedge fund assets globally serviced in Ireland,[22] Dublin is a hedge fund service global centre.

I see Dublin as more for hedge and credit and Luxembourg more for PE, VC, RE, and infrastructure. Ireland also needs to address the limitations around its limited partnership structure to challenge Luxembourg for closed-ended funds.

**Liechtenstein**   Liechtenstein is home to the largest family-owned private banking and asset management group in Europe, the Liechtenstein Global Trust (LGT). LGT have an AuM of over CHF 200 billion and offers one of the largest fund-of-funds or managed services to institutional investors. Liechtenstein enjoys incredibly close regulatory alignment with Switzerland, facilitating investment in asset managers across their border.

**Malta**   Previously known for attracting large amounts of hedge fund business, Malta has now switched its interest in catering for smaller funds and start-up asset managers, aiming to provide a regulatory flexibility that might not be on offer in other jurisdictions in Europe. With the recognised incorporated cell company, Malta is following Jersey and Guernsey down the route of offering an incorporated cell platform to investors, which offers segregated liability whilst retaining control at the core. The current total net asset value (NAV) of Malta-domiciled funds is EUR 10.8 billion, but once more asset managers take the time to familiarise themselves with the new direction the island is taking, Malta argues that it will grow its AuM.[23] Malta is also geographically close to the Middle East and North Africa (MENA) region and the rest of the African continent and, therefore, attracts funds from these regions.

**Offshore**  Other than the obvious benefits of living life as a fund manager on an offshore Caribbean island (think *Death in Paradise* meets *Billions*), there are a few other reasons why a fund manager may choose to be based offshore rather than onshore. Offshore jurisdictions tend to have smaller populations that makes it easier for fund managers to get in contact with the members of their local executive branch. Lawmakers and regulators in the offshore world generally have a better understanding of funds and the way that they operate, as finance is better promoted in offshore locations. Offshore regulators are often more responsive than their onshore counterparts and will be able to provide greater assistance to a fund manager when they are going through the initial establishment stage of their business.

The variety of fund vehicles on offer, although used by onshore managers so long as they provide offshore substance, is often greater in the offshore world than those offered in jurisdictions such as the UK and US. Jurisdictions such as Guernsey and Jersey offer entities such as the protected cell company and the incorporated cell company for fund managers. The protected companies are popular amongst fund managers, especially within the infrastructure world, as they provide ring-fencing opportunities that are not available to other types of vehicles. Even the Guernsey limited partnership has been slightly tweaked to allow fund managers to choose whether it has a separate legal personality or not, an option not available to UK fund managers.

## REGULATION OF ASSET MANAGERS

Chapters 9 and 10 contain more detail on the regulation of managers. However, we discuss regulation in some depth in this chapter as it directly affects managers on choice of jurisdiction.

It is impossible to consider the jurisdiction of a manager without considering its regulation. Asset management is a regulated industry. Some very successful managers cease to manage external capital, partly to avoid the perceived 'hassle' or restrictions of regulation (example of Soros).

We look below at the mainframe of regulation for UK, EU, and US. EU managers are also regulated by their home regulator, but at all times with the overlay of EU regulation surrounding AIFMD, MiFID II, and the overarching European Securities and Markets Authority (ESMA).

It is probably time to mention again the B-word. Brexit has bust open the EU, and poses a threat to the continued existence of the EU (whatever the politicians say in Brussels). Combine Brexit with the threats to the EU of immigration, extremist political parties, and an anti-establishment or collective herding by Trump's America, it is hardly surprising that EU politicians have fought the UK hard on Brexit.

I delayed finishing this book until 29 March 2019, in the hope that Brexit and its implications on asset management would be clearer. At the time of writing, the UK parliament is 'considering' (let's be nice ... Zero-Three down as of 5 April 2019) the agreement to agree, known as the 'Withdrawal Agreement', as approved on 25 November 2018 by leaders at a meeting of the European Council. This agreement really is an agreement to agree and contains scant real detail, other than that there is a transitional period for financial services until December 2020. During this transitional period the UK will still be treated as an EU member state and have to follow the applicable EU law (as it already does) for which it will benefit from freedom of establishment and services. Whilst the UK is in the transitional period, it shall therefore have access to the current EU passporting rights it presently enjoys.

Perhaps more significant than the Withdrawal Agreement is the Political Declaration between the EU and the UK that was published 25 November 2018. The Political Declaration effectively sets out (in incredibly high-level terms) the parameters of an intention to agree an agreement constituting the relationship between the EU and the UK following the transition period. The agreement put into place following the transition period is intended to be an ambitious free trade agreement resembling recent free trade agreements (FTAs) between the EU and Canada and South Korea, including deeper security and economic partnerships. Importantly for the asset management world, the EU and UK shall each 'conclude ambitious, comprehensive and balanced arrangements on trade in services and investment in services and non-services sectors',[24] ensuring that investors and service providers are not treated in any discriminatory manner. The provision of financial services also had its own heading within the Political Declaration with wording surrounding an equivalence framework to be in place by June 2020.[25] Unfortunately, however, as the old adage goes, nothing is agreed until everything is agreed, meaning that we will have to wait until the end of the transitional period (if there is one and no hard Brexit) to know exactly on what terms the UK will be beginning its new relationship with the EU. At the time of writing, it is still possible that there is no Brexit at all.

**The UK Financial Conduct Authority**   Within the UK, promoters, fund managers, and investment advisers must be authorised by the Financial Conduct Authority (FCA) where they perform 'regulated activities'. Separately, any employees or officers of those firms who carry out key functions (known as 'controlled functions') in that firm must be authorised separately as individuals by the FCA as well. Not everyone within the authorised firm needs to be an authorised individual.

The FCA has split the types of authorisation into two separate categories, significant influence functions (SIFs) and customer functions (CFs). SIFs are functions that enable the individual to have a significant level of control and influence over the authorised firm insofar as that function is a regulated activity.[26] Individuals who hold SIFs are typically executives/management at a firm. The SIF function is then broken down into the following further categories:

- **FCA-governing functions:** The individual falling under this category will be those that are in charge of a firm's affairs, such as a director or chief executive (the full list of functions being CF1-CF5).
- **FCA-required functions:** These are functions that each firm needs to have in place, which includes oversight, money laundering reporting, and benchmark functions.
- **Systems and controlled function:** This function encompasses the reporting by an employee to the governing body of a firm about the firm's financial health, setting risk exposure limits, and ensuring adherence to internal controls.
- **Significant management function:** This is the function undertaken by an individual who is a senior manager with significant responsibility for a significant business unit.

The Customer Function is self-evident in that it covers functions that relate only to those activities that are customer-facing, i.e. not related to a firm's internal functions. The main Customer Functions include:

- **Advising on investments:** Other than a non-investment insurance contract.
- **Giving advice:** Either in connection with corporate finance business, pension transfers, or on becoming a member of a Lloyd's syndicate.
- **Dealing and arranging:** In investments, with, for, or in connection with customers where the acts are governed by COBS 11.
- **Acting as an investment manager:** And carrying out functions related to the role.[27]

The above functions will often be a part of an asset manager's day-to-day life, such as arranging deals to invest in, providing investment advice to clients and inducing prospective investors to participate in a fund. All authorised individuals and the authorised firms that they belong to are listed on the FCA's online registry.

As defined under Schedule 2 of the Financial Services and Markets Act 2000 (FSMA 2000), arranging deals in investments is another regulated activity. This potentially has a broad scope, and often covers a wide range of marketing activities as well as more mechanistic forms of deal-making. It also will likely cover an investment adviser. The 'overseas person exemption' reduces the need for authorisation in respect of certain (but not all) 'arranging' activities where a person carries on regulated activities in the UK but not from an established place of business in the UK. As it is only a partial exemption it is not a particularly worthwhile exercise to seek to base the manager offshore to avoid authorisation, as the activities not covered by the exemption will require an authorised person to conduct them in any event. For a manager who is not based in the UK, it is common to engage an authorised person in the UK to act on its behalf in these respects. Unauthorised persons must not communicate invitations or inducements to participate in the fund. Such communications must be issued by an authorised person or approved by an authorised person. There is a wide range of exemptions applicable to this restriction. If the fund is not a CIS, the restriction on financial promotions is narrower and so communications approved by an authorised person can often be circulated to a wider range of persons.

**Regulatory Umbrellas**  In the UK, there is the concept of the 'tied agent'. In turn, this has accelerated the use of FCA-regulated umbrellas or regulatory incubators in the UK. This enables a manager to utilise a larger platform.

Indeed, MJ Hudson has both an AIFM platform and a MiFID platform to house either younger managers, managers from other locations, or for passporting. Increasingly, these platforms are growing, as both regulators and fund investors want to see a large team in the back office with qualified compliance and risk individuals, or see the oversight outsourced. There is no shame in regulatory or compliance outsourcing. There is only downside in doing it yourselves and not doing it properly or extensively. Whole or partial outsourcing is a significant and growing trend.

## The US Securities Exchange Commission

In the US, the primary regulator of the financial sector is the Securities Exchange Commission (SEC). Some regulatory authority is also exercised at the state level, generally by the state attorney general. For more details about its background, structure and remit, see Chapter 9. PE funds in the US are subject to a wide range of legislation but in many instances may be able to rely on exceptions from the provisions of those pieces of legislation.

The Investment Company Act of 1940 (ICA) regulates funds and other entities that engage primarily in investing and trading in securities and whose own securities are offered in public offerings. The manager of a fund will have to ensure the fund complies with this legislation. Unless an exception applies, under the ICA a fund will have to register with the SEC as an investment company. Typically, a fund will seek to qualify under two specified exemptions: ICA section 3(c)(1), which requires that the fund securities are beneficially owned by not more than 100 persons; and ICA section 3(c)(7), which requires that the fund's investors are exclusively institutional investors (known as 'qualified purchasers' who, generally speaking, are those who own as an individual at least USD 5 million worth of investments or as an entity at least USD 25 million worth of investments) and knowledgeable executives. If the fund solicits investments through general advertisements or general solicitations, then certain additional rules are applicable. These rules have fairly complex anti-avoidance provisions which look through those investors that are corporates or other legal entities to their ultimate beneficial owners.

The Investment Advisers Act of 1940 (IAA) regulates the manager or adviser of a fund (if separate entities) by requiring them to register as an investment adviser with the SEC unless an exception applies, or the applicable state. The historical exception, known as the 'private adviser exemption', was for an investment adviser which had fewer than 15 clients (and each fund advised was a separate client). Therefore, it was a fairly simple matter for most advisers and sponsors – advise fewer than 15 funds. However, the provisions of the Dodd–Frank Act (see more below) have eliminated this particular exception.

Under the IAA an investment adviser is subject to a number of provisions determining whether or not it is required to register with the SEC. It owes a fiduciary duty to the fund and is prohibited from any action that is fraudulent, deceptive or manipulative with respect to the fund.

Offerings and sales of securities in the US (including interests in PE funds) must be made in compliance with the Securities Act of 1933, which requires a registration statement filed with and approved by the SEC unless an exemption is applicable. A registered offering (i.e. a public offering) is both time-consuming and expensive and many will subject the fund and its operations to the obligations under the Securities Exchange Act of 1934. Consequently, PE funds are structured and marketed to avoid these requirements. The exception used most frequently is provided under Section 4(2) of the Securities Act 1933. This is a fact-sensitive exemption. Factors that are often present in an offering that does not involve a public offering under Section 4(2) include a limited number of offerees and purchasers, and no general marketing and solicitation of the fund.

The Securities Act of 1933 regulations provide a 'safe harbour' known as Regulation D. This regulation generally permits sales to accredited investors and requires the filing of a form with limited information with the SEC. An additional benefit of using Regulation D to solicit and sell securities is that part of the regulation – Rule 506, which is the most commonly used part of Regulation D – generally exempts the offeror (fund) from state securities law filings, other than notice filings, the payment of a fee, anti-fraud provisions, and certain other provisions of state law. Recent changes in Regulation D that were adopted by the SEC on 10 July 2013 permit an offering under this safe harbour to include general solicitations and advertisements (factors that were not permitted prior to this change) as long as each of the purchasers is an 'accredited investor' as defined under the SEC regulations. This is a significant change and allows placement agents and issuers to widely solicit investment. Advertisements can be in any form, ranging from electronic means such as websites and Twitter accounts to outdoor advertising (billboards). An SEC report regarding Netflix clarified the SEC position on social media. Effectively, the content provided through social media messaging such as Twitter will be evaluated in a manner similar to content distributed through traditional media (for example, a private placement memorandum) – Elon Musk recently discovered this the hard way.

**Dodd–Frank Act** The Dodd–Frank Act expands provisions of previous legislation such as the IAA to broaden the range of sponsors and advisers who must register with the SEC. Foreign investment managers/advisers are required (as of 31 March 2012) to register with the SEC. The previously relied upon 'private adviser exemption' under the IAA has been removed by the Dodd–Frank Act. The new exemptions to the requirement to register with the SEC are extremely narrow and are summarised below:

- 'Private Fund Adviser Exemption' – applies to those that solely advise private funds with less than USD 150 million in private fund assets under management in the US. Only assets managed from within the US can count towards the threshold and the exemption is not available to any adviser that manages any separate accounts for a US client.
- 'Foreign Private Adviser Exemption' – to obtain this exemption the adviser must (i) not have a 'place of business' in the US (an office or location in or at which it regularly provides advisory services, solicits, meets with or communicates with clients); (ii) have fewer than 15 US advisory clients and investors in private funds; (iii) have fewer than USD 25 million under management with US clients and investors in private funds; and (iv) not offer advisory services to the US public or advise a US registered fund.

The requirement to register with the SEC brings a significantly increased regulatory oversight. In addition to requiring the adviser be registered, the IAA requires compliance with Rule 206 – referred to commonly as the custody rule. This requires the adviser to comply with detailed procedures that are designed to keep the investor informed about the location and person that maintains the custody of their assets. This includes performing surprise inspections or (in lieu of certain procedures) ensuring that their external auditors are also registered with and subject to monitoring by the Public Company Accounting Oversight Board and that the assets are subject to the audit. External auditors must also comply with the SEC's independence rules. Additionally, financial statements must be produced in accordance with US Generally Accepted Accounting Principles (GAAP) and enhanced anti-affiliate rules that strengthen the reporting and custodial procedures. These rules are generally in response to the Madoff scandal where an affiliate of the investment adviser purported to hold the assets of the investment adviser whilst in fact facilitating a massive fraud.

Under the Dodd–Frank Act, the IAA is amended to require an investment adviser with AuM between USD 25 million and USD 100 million (or if the SEC requires, a higher amount) to register with the US state of its principal office and place of business only if it is subject to a requirement to register within that state in question. This is subject to any applicable exceptions within those states as well.

**The EU Alternative Investment Fund Managers Directive** The Alternative Investment Fund Managers Directive (AIFMD) was implemented by member states of the EU on 22 July 2013.

The provisions of the AIFMD are extensive and require careful consideration in planning a fund and consultation with compliance experts. The AIFMD seeks to create a harmonised legislative framework for alternative asset managers that operate within the EU, whether they are established within the EU or not and regardless of where the fund under management is established. Managers who are within the scope of the AIFMD are alternative investment fund managers (AIFMs) – those individuals or legal persons whose regular business is the management of (one or more) AIFs, which, broadly speaking, includes all non-UCITS funds together with some joint venture arrangements and managed accounts. More information in relation to AIFs can be found in Chapter 9.

All EU-based AIFMs are required to be authorised and subject to supervision in their home state, although the definition of who is the AIFM may lead, in certain fund structures, to only certain 'onshore' managers being the AIFM. The home regulator may qualify any authorisation granted by limiting its scope, such as by placing restrictions on the investment strategy.

An AIF can have only one AIFM and it must have one. In applying for authorisation, the AIFM must provide both information relating to the AIFM and information relating to each AIF it intends to manage. The information required includes the credentials of the people conducting the AIFM's business, shareholders with 10% of the voting rights or with an ability to exert 'significant influence' over the management of the AIFM, the organisational structure of the AIFM, a plan on how it intends to comply with the AIFMD, the remuneration regime of the AIFM and arrangements regarding delegation.

Where the AIF is internally managed, it will need to be authorised as the AIFM and in other circumstances (including the typical limited partnership structure of a PE fund) the AIFM can be an external party. Managing the AIF includes providing portfolio management and risk management services. The provision of risk management services is not frequently referred to in PE fund agreements and this may result in a fund being deemed to be self-managing in the absence of express reference to risk management. Some managers will also need to consider the wording of the agreements vesting managerial responsibility on them by the GP. If the manager is a delegate of the person in whom managerial responsibility is vested, then it will not be the AIFM. Only the person directly appointed by or on behalf of the AIF will be the AIFM.

There is a partial exemption for the manager from the requirements of the AIFMD if it manages (across all AIFs for which it is the manager) small AIFs with either:

- assets under management of less than EUR 500 million, provided that there is no leverage and investors do not have redemption rights for the first five years; or
- assets under management of less than EUR 100 million, including assets acquired by leverage.

The partial nature of the exemption means that if an AIFM managing small AIFs wishes to take advantage of the management or marketing passporting provisions it will require full compliance with the AIFMD. In any event, a small AIFM must register as such with its local regulator (e.g. the FCA).

**Markets in Financial Instruments Directive II** The Markets in Financial Instruments Directive II (MiFID II) was fully implemented in January 2018, after a year's delay to allow market participants to prepare for the changes in reporting requirements in a bid to increase market transparency, which, amongst other things, was the goal of MiFID II.

Arguably, the most talked about piece of the new directive is the separation of research and transaction charges, meaning financial institutions will no longer be able to bundle these costs (and effectively provide a discount on pricing), also known as unbundling. Funnily enough, it was the UK that pushed for this unbundling, with continental Europeans pushing to keep the research costs bundled with transaction costs. If the investment firm does not swallow the costs themselves, they will need to provide detailed reports to investors. Under Article 24, when providing detailed costs, firms will need to provide:

- **Ex-ante costs:** also known as before the event costs, which detail expected costs of a certain investment and need to show expected costs on an annualised basis over periods of time.
- **Ex-post costs:** which are costs actually incurred during the previous year.[28]

Ex-ante costs need to be submitted to investors before each investment is made and by this time investors should already have been receiving reports of these from managers. The first set of ex-post costs will be available on an annualised basis, but only once the first anniversary of the investment has been reached (which should be happening shortly). Both types of costs listed above will detail the impact of the costs on the performance of the investment.

The various costs that must be disclosed include:

- **One-off charges:** Costs that are usually charged either at the beginning or end of the provision of the investment service, which can be termination costs, switching costs, signing costs or deposit costs.
- **Ongoing charges:** Costs paid for the continual provision of services such as monitoring costs, custodian costs, or advisory costs.
- **Transaction charges:** Costs incurred by every investment that are charged by the investment firm, such as broker commission costs, forex costs, and fund entry costs.
- **Ancillary charges:** Costs often grouped as miscellaneous, which include research and custody costs.
- **Incidental charges:** Costs charged that vary depending on the result of the investment returns, such as performance fees.

Within the transaction charges umbrella there are two main types or components of costs: explicit costs and implicit costs. Explicit costs include costs such as the broker's commission and are easily identifiable by investment firms when undertaking investments.[29] Implicit costs are embedded within the costs of the execution price when undertaking an investment, or the cost of bringing an asset into the fund. As they are harder to quantify, implicit costs have a set way in which they must be calculated, which is the difference between an asset's mid-market costs immediately before it is ordered on the market and the cost when the deal is executed (also known as the 'arrival price').[30] For some financial instruments, calculating the arrival price may be straightforward for the asset manager as they can use a single historical data point; however, for products that are not traded at a high frequency (or with regards to those stated explicitly by MiFID II) Packaged Retail and Insurance-based Investment Products (PRIIPs) (see further below) may provide further calculation methods such as the use of spreads or indices.

Under MiFID II, transaction reporting requirements have also greatly increased from the requirements for harmonised reporting that were originally introduced in MiFID I. Virtually every aspect of reporting has been increased in scope, from the types of transactions to the types of entities that now need to provide reports. Entities that are required to provide these reports include investment firms, trading venues, and approved reporting mechanisms, which must be delivered to the national competent authority (NCA) within which the business is conducted.[31] Originally there were only 24 fields in each trade that required completion; however, MiFID II now has 65, with the final report due by no later than the close of business of the following day that the trade was made (T+1).[32] Fields include the legal entities involved, the trader or specific algorithm, the trading venue and delivery types and optionality (the last two are included when dealing with over-the-counter (OTC) derivatives only).

However, it is not only asset managers and trading venues that have had to prepare for the new reporting standards. The FCA states that it captures roughly 500–700 million transaction reports monthly, which is roughly equivalent to an over 50% increase from before MiFID II was introduced.[33,34] The FCA has stressed that mistakes about the content of the information and report duplication cannot be permitted to deteriorate the quality of the reports, stating that they expect reporting firms to adapt internally to the changing regulatory landscape.[35] The FCA is not looking to punish firms that are making genuine attempts to provide concise and consistent data reports; rather, it will be making examples of firms that make no real attempt to provide the information required under MiFID II.

What does all of the above mean for asset managers? The initial impact showed that the market for European equities research took a USD 300-million dive, possibly due to European and UK firms cutting their research budgets by 32% and 17% respectively.[36] This means that the regulator's attempts to provide a more transparent system have been met with a mass cutting of firms' research budgets that in turn has made it harder for some smaller companies to attract investors, as research into them is proving too costly. This is not a good thing for listed small and medium-sized enterprises (SMEs). This criticism has been picked up by the Autorité des marchés financiers (AMF), the French financial regulator that, in November 2018, called for a review of the unbundling rules citing poor performance and drop in profits at various SME research providers.[37]

Some of the largest asset managers are choosing to absorb the costs instead of passing them onto their clients, flip-flopping their decision over the course of 2017 between the two options.[38] A few asset managers have instead opted to build up their internal research teams, which perhaps results in a higher upfront cost with lower future costs and a possible new profit line should they decide to sell their research externally.

Managers based outside of the EU that undertake transactions (and purchase research) of a European nature have had difficulties with the 'Brussels Effect' (the unilateral ability of EU politicians to regulate markets outside of the European Union, leading to a global regulatory standard[39]). The SEC has had to issue three 'no action' letters due to the confusion faced by some US firms when purchasing research from the EU due to conflicts with the existing US regulatory framework. During the time these letters are in force the SEC will monitor the effects of MiFID II and determine what changes (if any) need to be made to the regulations governing the US's markets.[40]

There is also the question as to how these new rules have affected research providers. Those with a focus on European research only have had to adapt their business model, as this research is now no longer a free 'extra' to be included with other services, it therefore needs to meet standards set by asset managers and consumers of the research. If the standards are not met, purchasers of the research are going to have a hard time justifying the cost to their investors. Research providers that have a global focus have started to unbundle costs on a global scale to harmonise their approach across the US, Europe, and Asia. One final frustration faced by providers comes from the split in execution services and research services. Whereas before the two services may have been provided by the same service provider, it may be now that multiple parties specialising in certain areas of research are feeding into one transaction, raising questions about information sharing.

**Packaged Retail and Insurance-Based Investment Products Regulation** From January 2018, Packaged Retail and Insurance-Based Investment Products Regulation (PRIIPs) came into force that requires managers to provide investors with a pre-contractual key information document (KID). The main goal of PRIIPs is to enhance investor protection standards for retail clients. Any manager that advises a retail investor on a PRIIP or sells a PRIIP to a retail investor must provide the retail investor with a KID in good time before any transaction is concluded.

## STRUCTURES OF MANAGEMENT VEHICLES

### Public or Private

It used to be the case that asset managers were private companies (or partnerships), controlled by the few founding members that started them. However, many of the larger asset managers (in the mainstream and the alternatives) have sought out larger pools of capital than their traditional investors and have since undergone initial public offerings (IPOs) and are being traded on public stock exchanges like the London Stock Exchange (LSE) or the New York Stock Exchange (NYSE). The two main examples of 'going public' are a PE firm's management company listing on the public markets providing shareholders with access to management fees and carried interest, or when the managers list a particular fund on a public market, allowing access to investors who may previously have been locked out or barred from PE investments.

**Public Managers** In the US, prominent PE groups such as KKR, Blackstone, Carlyle, and Apollo took portions of their management vehicle public through listings on the NYSE. The PE groups in the US have recently reached an age where publicly listing management vehicles allows founders to free up or monetise their capital that has been tied up from when they set up their first fund. Other reasons for listing management vehicles include:

- **Capital Access:** By listing on exchanges, firms gain access to a permanent pool of capital that they can use to invest in their underlying funds as part of the GP commitment (discussed in more detail in the internal team economics section of this chapter), instead of having to pony up their own money or provide more capital to an existing investment rather than issue a new drawdown notice to investors.
- **More investors:** PE funds are often restricted in the type of investor they can accept into their funds, but by listing on exchanges, anyone can become an investor in them, greatly increasing the number of potential investors/shareholders.
- **Lack of buyers:** There are not many potential buyers of a multibillion-dollar asset manager, especially for those firms that make only highly specialised investments. Going public eliminates the need for a single strategic buyer.
- **Build reputation:** As stated on the tin, PE firms tend to be private and therefore fly under most people's radar, but those wanting to fast-track their brand recognition and build a

solid reputation may choose to do so by listing on a stock exchange, where the information on constituents is more readily available.

- **Portfolio purchases:** When it comes time for a fund to sell its interests in an underlying portfolio company, the manager may wish to hold onto the portfolio company for a few more years before selling it. To do so, it could use publicly available funds to purchase the portion of the company currently held by investors.
- **Employee incentivisation:** Oftentimes only more senior employees receive a portion of carried interest, but by listing shares in a management vehicle, every employee would have a chance to either buy shares in the vehicle or receive options that vest over time. Access to quicker employee incentivisation is therefore possible.

An offer of listed PE provides investors exposure to PE; but also liquidity, which they may not get with unlisted PE (disregarding the secondaries market). The liquidity is also complemented by the diversification an investor receives when the underlying assets are PE funds. Whilst not a pure investment into a PE fund, this will still grant exposure to a market that may have previously been unavailable entirely to retail investors. There is an obvious demand for this form of investment and one can point to the multiple listed PE indices that are tracked by banks and made available to retail investors as evidence of this. An example of such is the LPX Indices, which, following its launch in 2004 now has multiple PE series focussing on certain characteristics, such as size, region, and underlying investment strategy.[41]

With the new pool of capital, asset managers are often cornerstoning their own funds, which on the one hand provides more skin in the game from the management vehicle, but also brings into question whose interests the managers are looking after. It comes as no shock that what investors believe is best for their capital may not be the same as what the manager believes is best for their capital, which may create serious conflicting interests between the fund manager as an investor and as a manager of the investment. Further conflicts could arise when interests of those new shareholders in the management vehicle differ from those in the underlying funds, forcing the fund manager to compromise between the two. Is the manager working for their fund carried interest or their quoted manager share price? Of course, granting up to 50% of all fund carried interest to the public shareholders to an extent alleviates this conflict. That said, unless an investor is both in the public company stock as well as the funds as an LP, the issue still can have consequences.

With the increase of listed alternative asset managers, many financial analysts question how to value their shares. Alternative asset managers' income (carried interest and management fees) is a lot more volatile and cannot always be predicted in advance, with analysts unwilling to place a price/earnings ratio on the carried interest income stream received by these types of managers.[42]

Listed managers, such as Apollo, like to report in terms of 'economic net income', which also reflects the change in unrealised investments. With a dip in public company valuations in late 2018, this has a double whack on listed managers that report in economic net income, both in terms of their own public stakes, as well as their mark to market private stakes. In addition, there is the public managers' report in 'distributable earnings' that is a measure of cash earnings that can go to their shareholders. This is perhaps easier to grasp.

The more long-term views of alternative asset managers along with their cyclical style for investing has meant that it is necessary to move away from more traditional methods of valuing shares in asset managers. Groups such as Blackstone, Carlyle, and KKR have already made these changes in how they value their shares.[43]

A further recent dilemma for US public managers is that many are listed as partnerships for taxation purposes (lower tax on carried interest in closed-ended funds). However, from 2018, if they convert to companies then they would both benefit from President Trump's corporate tax-cuts, as well as gain entry into larger indices. With the rise in passives, these indices have a stronger value – arguably up to 15% in increased value, so brokers tell me. Being a company could therefore boost valuations, whereas staying as a partnership keeps taxation lower, especially for the management shareholders. If listed PE firms convert to a corporation from listed partnerships, their carried interest (or performance fees) are suddenly subject to a 21% tax charge. This issue coincides with succession issues for the original founders. Listed PE management complain that their stocks are undervalued, in part, because of the lack of inclusion in big indices that would be solved through the shift in structure.

Ares Management has recently made the conversion. Mike McFerran, Ares's chief financial officer (CFO), said at the time that the conversion 'will simplify our structure, broaden our potential investor base, improve our liquidity and trading volume and provide a more attractive currency for strategic acquisitions'. The corporation change also opens share ownership to foreign investors, as under the partnership structure an investor from outside the US that owns units in a listed PE group needs to file a US tax return. That is not the case in a corporation.

I very much admire these US listed alternatives giants. To an extent, I am trying to build a service provider version of them at MJ Hudson. They have diversified way from their roots in PE (Apollo, Blackstone, Carlyle), or credit (Ares and to an extent Apollo), or fund of funds (Hamilton Lane, or Partners in Switzerland) and now are major players in other alternative classes such as RE, energy, infrastructure, and to a smaller extent, hedge. Carlyle also became an LP by purchasing Alpinvest, and so, to an extent, did KKR by (masterfully) acquiring its heavily discounted USD 5 billion listed feeder from Euronext a few years back. These groups are effectively public pioneers in Alts, leading the way for alternatives to become more mainstream, and giving the public the ability to invest in their management groups, and access to uncorrelated carried interest. So, hurrah for them.

**Public Funds**   In the UK and US, there are a number of listed fund types. Real estate investment trusts (REITs), investment trusts, and venture capital trusts (VCTs) are all good examples of funds with tax breaks to allow just single taxation on profit. So for example, VCTs focus purely on riskier, unlisted VC investments.[44] As at the time of writing, these vehicles provide a 30% income tax relief to the investor if the shares are held for a minimum of five years, and any dividends received on them do not incur any income tax charge.[45] There is also no capital gains tax charge on profits made when shares in a VCT are sold.[46]

Mutual funds and ETFs provide investors with a broad range of diversity across asset classes, regions and risk levels. Since their introduction over 20 years ago, there is now nearly USD 3.5 trillion worth of ETFs, which is dwarfed, however, by the USD 18 trillion worth of mutual funds.[47] Be that as it may, currently the more popular product is ETFs, which received USD 464 billion of inflows in 2017.[48] Both are classic examples of financial products that are available to retail investors and are incredibly popular in the US.

ETFs trade similarly to stocks, attempting to replicate the performance of a selected index. This means that ETFs can be traded multiple times throughout the day with pricing constantly updated; however, over time this accrues trading commissions, reducing pay-outs. There is no lower investment minimum when trading ETFs, however, because the risks are usually lower for an ETF, the dividend yields tend to be as well.

Mutual funds are usually purchased directly from the asset manager, rather than via an index, and can be either actively or passively managed (discussed in further detail in Chapters 1, 5, and 13). The pricing of mutual funds is only updated at the close of business each day, rather than constantly throughout the day.

Access for retail to investors to public funds is important to spread ownership. However, one of the larger problems with listed closed-ended funds is that they typically trade a discount to NAV. This is a real problem for UK listed investment trusts, where the spread can be horrible. Again, it is the illiquidity of their holdings that causes most of the problem with their share value to NAV discount. Brokers try various ways to narrow this discount, such as providing liquidity in the shares. Groups such as 3i aim to raise funds to become more a listed manager than a listed fund (it tried this for years), as has Intermediate Capital. Electra successfully balanced the public fund and public manager concept for many years, but then was attacked by an activist for favouring the manager, and subsequently the manager span out and the investment trust is being wound up.

## Entities

**UK Limited Liability Partnership** In the UK, incorporating a limited liability partnership (LLP) as the management vehicle of a fund was the norm until the last ten years. LLPs are flexible in that they incorporate both corporate-like elements as well as elements from traditional partnership entities. The ability to use LLPs in the UK is relatively recent, as the vehicle had only been created under the Limited Liability Partnerships Act 2000. Unlike limited partnerships, LLPs have a legal personality, bearing traits of both companies and partnerships. The advantages of using an LLP as a management vehicle are that:

- **It has limited liability:** This means that the members of the LLP are only liable to the amounts agreed between them.
- **It has separate legal personality:** This allows the LLP to enter into a contract in its own name.
- **It is tax transparent:** This means that the income of the members of the LLP are taxed rather than the entity – pay-as-you-earn (PAYE) and national insurance contributions (NICs) – on the members' income.
- **It is unrestricted by articles of association:** LLPs are governed by an LLP deed which is the constitution of the entity, and can be drafted to the members' requirements, and amended without ever needing to file it at Companies House.
- **They typically attract low costs:** The costs related to establishment are low, as are secretarial and administrative costs.

The flexibility of the LLP deed is possibly the most attractive trait of the LLP to fund managers. An LPP deed can be drafted to any specification so long as they do not break any laws. Managers can therefore more easily apportion carried interest between members of the management vehicle and also make it easy for the LLP to accept new members (as well as kick some out).

As always, however, there are some disadvantages to using an LLP, which include:

- **Lack of LLP deed:** Where no LLP deed is signed between the members, the LLP will be governed by the default rules under the Limited Liability Partnerships Act 2000.

- **Auditing:** Most LLPs will have to file audited accounts with Companies House, meaning financial information is not kept private.
- **Profit retention:** Profits have to be distributed to members on an annual basis and cannot be retained.

Whilst not a disadvantage, when operating an LLP as the management vehicle, members need to ensure that they are not recategorised as 'salaried members' and lose their favourable tax treatment. The introduction of the salaried member rules attempted to curb individuals' abuse of the favourable tax treatment.[49] The government felt that when members of an LLP do not act as a partner should, and instead behave more like employees, then they do not deserve the corresponding tax benefits. Members of an LLP were deemed to be employees (and taxed thusly) where their engagement with the LLP meets all three of the following conditions:

- **Disguised salary rule:** This condition will be met when 'disguised salary', which is an amount payable to a member, is either fixed, variable (but without reference to profits and losses of the LLP) or doesn't vary in practice, and makes up at least 80% of the total amount payable to a member.
- **Significant influence:** If a member does not have significant influence over the business of the LLP then they are effectively an employee.
- **Capital contribution levels:** If capital contribution levels of a member are below 25% of what that member is expected to receive under their disguised salary then they will be deemed to meet this condition.[50]

**UK Limited Company**  The fund manager may also be established as a limited company. The management team of the manager will be shareholders (and possibly directors) in the company. This will have tax implications, as a company is not tax transparent, and the management team will therefore receive a salary and potentially bonuses or dividends.

However, personally, I prefer companies to LLPs, as it feels like a more grown-up entity. In addition a company:

- is more able to attract capital;
- can be listed; and
- can create stock option schemes for employees.

Thus, companies can scale and diversify easier.

**US Limited Liability Company**  Similar to LLPs in the UK, the US offers the use of a limited liability company (LLC), a hybrid vehicle with traits of both partnerships and companies. Like a company, the members of the LLC benefit from limited liability, whilst at the same time it is treated as tax transparent. Members of LLCs can be individuals, companies, or other LLCs. There is no maximum number of members and states permit single member LLCs. An LLC also provides significant flexibility to the members or members of the executive team in establishing their relationships, including finance, governance, and equity-based incentives.

**General Partner in Limited Partnership Structures**  In a typical closed-ended fund, the limited partnership structure is most common. In such a fund, there is typically only one GP, which is often an entity controlled by the manager. The GP has unlimited liability in such a partnership. Hence, it is often itself a limited company.

The GP has responsibility for the decisions of the fund, can make legally binding obligations and has unlimited liability for the debts and obligations of the fund. The limited partners will seek to avoid intervening in the operation of the fund in order to avoid accidentally attaining GP status and, therefore, assuming unlimited liability for the debts of the fund.

The GP will usually be a subsidiary organisation of the fund adviser or manager. It will have a legal structure (such as an LLC) which limits the liability of its owner(s) – including the authorised adviser/manager entity (regulated in the UK by the FCA), and any seed or other investors who have taken a share in the ownership of the general partner – shielding them from liability in the event that the fund incurs losses or liabilities. The PE executives are usually directors or employees of either the GP or the manager (or both) and will also have ownership of either or both of these entities alongside any seed or other investors.

While a GP could, in theory, be regulated, owing to the GP having by law unlimited liability status, using an authorised entity as a GP is unattractive. Thus, the GP typically appoints a separate entity to be the regulated manager. The manager is appointed by the partnership to act as its manager and operator. Therefore, the manager takes all the day-to-day decisions related to the operation and management of the partnership including the acquisition, management, and disposal of investments. The role of the GP is limited to monitoring and supervising the manager and a small number of more formal matters.

In a corporate structure, where the fund will often be an LLC or a company limited by shares, there is no requirement for a GP, and the fund entity itself will enjoy limited liability status. The liability of the manager of the fund, which itself will often be a corporate entity, is limited to the amount which is unpaid on its shares in the fund and itself.

**GP as an LP Structure**   In a 'GP as an LP' structure, the general partner will be a limited partnership and therefore will not be a separate legal entity. The GP will itself have a separate general partner, often a company. These structures are more common in US closed-ended funds, and the GP in such a structure will usually receive the carried interest. The management fees can flow through the GP, but more typically in the US direct to a separate LLC manager. The formation of limited partnerships is governed under state and federal law. The majority of US limited partnerships are formed as 'Delaware LPs', under the Delaware Revised Uniform Limited Partnership Act. An advantage is that a Delaware LP is not required to reveal the identity of its partners. In addition, there is an established body of case law regarding the governance of Delaware LPs.

## MANAGEMENT COMPANY ECONOMICS

### How They Make Money

Fund managers will charge a fee, mostly based on a percentage but sometimes a flat fee, on each investor's capital invested with the manager. This fee may be charged as soon as the investor contractually commits (typical in a PE-style fund), wires their manager their capital (typical in a hedge fund), or it may be paid when the asset manager makes the underlying investment (this is a growing trend even in PE).

According to an FCA report on UK asset managers, 13 of the 16 asset managers they sampled recorded that 80% of their revenue came from managing assets that are either pooled or segregated.[51]

Many investors find it hard to compare fees, however, as even when asset managers use the same word for a fee, the underlying definition of the fee could be completely different.

Some managers may use the same term 'management fee' as one another, but manager A's management fee includes administration costs, whereas manager B's administration costs are separate and, therefore, manager B may appear more expensive at first glance. Thanks in part to PRIIPS (as discussed earlier), all funds marketed towards retail investors must disclose their costs in a manner more easily understood. This includes listing direct and indirect costs, costs that are recurring and one-off and any additional costs charged.

## Fund Management Fees: How Different Funds Produce Different Fees

### Closed-Ended Funds – Typical in PE or VC

**During the Investment Period** The management fee is generally calculated during the investment period as a percentage of the fund's total commitments. It is typically between 1% and 2% depending on a number of factors including the fund's size and investment strategy. The management fee will be lower for a secondaries fund or a fund of funds, reflecting the fact that making investments into other funds is less costly than making investments into underlying assets such as portfolio companies, and also in recognition of the fact that the underlying funds will also charge management fees.

Investors will often take the view that the purpose of the management fee is simply to provide the manager with sufficient funds to allow it to manage the fund, not to allow the manager to generate a profit. Therefore, investors may wish to compare the management fee against a specimen budget for the manager in order to ensure that the management fee is not significantly in excess of what is required to meet the day-to-day expenses of the manager. This approach has hardened from investors during the financial crisis, but has loosened a little since.

**After the Investment Period** The management fee is typically calculated as a percentage of the acquisition costs of the investments that the fund continues to hold after the investment period, so not fees on fees. For this purpose an investment that has been written off is treated as having been disposed of, so no management fee is payable in respect of it. Alternatively, the management fee 'steps down' to a reduced percentage of total commitments to the fund.

Investors may want the management fee to take into account any write-downs in investments (that is, if an investment has been written down below its acquisition cost, the amount of the write-down is taken into account in calculating the management fee). If this approach is taken, the manager will typically request that the test be applied only on a portfolio basis so that any write-ups can be offset against any write-downs to determine whether there has been any overall write-down of the investment portfolio. This approach should only result in the management fee being reduced and not result in it being increased as a result of an overall increase in the value of the fund's investments.

Instead of being a fee payable directly by the fund to the manager, in the UK and US, the management fee is typically structured as a priority profit share (known as the GP's share or GPS), which is paid by the fund to the GP and then by the GP to the manager. Further information is set out in Chapter 11.

### Open-Ended Funds – Typical in Hedge or Mainstream Equities

**Management Fee** The management fee is designed to cover the manager's operating costs and is typically set at 2% per annum in hedge (although I have seen it as high as 5% pa in hedge), but a fraction of that in mainstream equities, and in each case is charged on the NAV of the fund's assets. Whilst represented as an annual charge, the management fees are often paid monthly or quarterly.

**Redemption Fees**   An additional layer of fees also deals with where an investor seeks to withdraw its funds. In such circumstances, the investor may be charged a fee to withdraw, which generally operates to charge investors a redemption fee if they withdraw money within, say, a 12- or 18-month period. Redemption fees may also be applicable where an investor seeks to withdraw a large amount from the fund, as they may be limited to withdrawing a fixed amount or percentage at any given time.

**Transactional or Monitoring Fees**   Managers may receive certain additional fees, including:

- transactional fees from investors, such as entry and exit fees;
- monitoring fees from portfolio companies;
- directors' fees from portfolio companies; and
- consulting or other fees from portfolio companies.

However, these fees are not very popular with fund investors, and are, therefore, either fully or partly refundable to the fund (or often set against managements fees).

## Performance Fees and Carried Interest

### Closed-Ended Funds

**Distributions/Carried Interest**   As a limited partnership fund typically operates on a draw-down/distribution model, the fund will typically distribute any income or capital gains that it receives to investors periodically in the case of income (often quarterly) and as soon as possible in the case of capital gains.

The profits which are available for distribution are split between the investors and the carry vehicle held by the executives of the manager and others, on pre-agreed terms. The amount paid to the carry vehicle is called carried interest and is the performance-based remuneration which the management team is eligible to receive. The provisions in the partnership agreement which deals with the calculation of these distributions are commonly referred to as 'the waterfall'.

There are a number of different ways in which the waterfall can work. The principal concept is to motivate the investment team to make profits. Once investors have received their money back, plus a 'hurdle', then the investment team of the manager receives a carried interest (often 20%) of the fund's profits.

The hurdle in a closed-ended fund can be structured in a number of ways, but a PE hurdle is often just that – a hurdle – and once cleared (referred to, therefore, as a 'soft' hurdle), the profits taken by the carry vehicle constitute all the profits of the fund; whereas, in RE or infrastructure, the hurdle is more like a fixed coupon (a 'hard' hurdle).

**Carried Interest, Escrow and Clawback**   With most waterfalls, it is possible that too much carried interest could be distributed or, more precisely, that the amount of carried interest distributed may exceed the amount that would have been distributed had all the distributions been at the same time on a consolidated basis. Upon termination of the fund, the carry limited partner will be required to repay any distributions it received in respect of its carried interest (the 'clawback') to the extent that such distributions exceed 20% of the fund's cumulative net portfolio gain. A further protection for limited partners on carried interest overpayment is holding part of the carried interest in escrow until the fund's investment returns are known. In investment bank-sponsored funds, the escrow is often held by the bank. The escrow also has the effect of protecting the partners of the carry vehicle (known as carry holders) from overspending by other carry holders of the carry returns (jokingly referred to as 'Porsche protection').

**Carried Interest Vehicle**  The partners of the carry vehicle are the principals of the fund manager, together with any cornerstone or seed investors that have negotiated a share of the carried interest. The carry vehicle is often structured as a partnership and in line with the memorandum of understanding between HMRC and the British Private Equity and Venture Capital Association (BVCA), which allows for carried interest to be treated as capital by the executives for tax purposes rather than income. The carry deed governs the terms of the principals' returns with the manager, such as share of income, joiners and leavers, consents, etc.

**Underlying Control of the Carry Vehicle**  Invariably the main principals of the manager or investment adviser 'control' the carry vehicle and operate a form of carry 'board' or adjudication committee that regulates the carry vehicle. The carry vehicle, if it is a partnership, is bound by general laws of partnerships, such as fair dealing, and confidentiality. If a carry partner leaves the manager or investment adviser, then he will be treated as a 'leaver' and his carry might be cancelled in whole or in part. The carry documentation will contain rules about leavers, often defining them 'good' or 'bad', and further penalises the leaver if he competes post-leaving (hence why many individual managers 'retire' for a year or two between investment houses).

## Open-Ended Funds

**Performance Fee**  The second principal level of fees for open-ended funds is the performance fee, which is designed to be an incentive for the manager and reward stellar performance. A typical 'performance fee' will often be set at 20%. However, this can range from as little as 10% to as much as 50%. Performance fees are usually taxed as income.

**Hurdle Rate**  Often built into the performance fee mechanism is what is known as 'hurdle rate' (historically often set at 8%), which is a rate of return that must be paid to investors before the manager can claim its entitlement to the performance fee. The hurdle rate can also either be soft or hard, 'soft hurdle' being that after the hurdle is cleared a catch-up mechanism applies so that the performance return is calculated on all returns once cleared, whilst alternatively the 'hard hurdle' only allows the performance fee to be calculated on the returns above the hurdle.

**High Water Mark**  Most performance fees also include a 'high water mark', which essentially works to carry forward any losses from the manager to ensure that the manager only receives a performance fee over its highest performance level. Effectively, this means that any previous losses must first be recovered. The high water mark 'issue' is often a reason why open-ended funds are later liquidated by the manager if the fund's returns start to decline.

## COSTS OF RUNNING A MANAGEMENT COMPANY

There is a plethora of different costs associated with running a management company of a fund – some of which are unique to the asset management world, others are not. Unless you have been hiding under a rock, there has also been some serious recent debate over fees charged by asset managers to their clients, and pressure is mounting from investors for managers to find ways to cut costs. This has bled into the topic of passive versus active investment strategy. Arguably, the work that an asset manager does has changed very little, the same basics of researching investment opportunities and corralling capital from investors still exist, it's just that there's now much more information and more competition.

Increased regulatory regimes bring with them higher costs, especially following the introduction of MifID II, whereby research and other transaction costs and investment services can no longer be bundled together and fees charged must be disclosed to clients (discussed further in Chapter 10). This unbundling has forced many managers to simply absorb the costs precipitated by the new regulation, taking away from their bottom line. As investors win more rights in the ongoing investor versus manager match-up, more detailed information across an increasing number of reports must also be disclosed, further pushing up reporting costs.

Some of the costs of running an asset management company are listed below:

- **Board:** Board costs can include anything from paying non-executive directors to provide oversight to the management company, pay packages for directors, and even costs of the investment committee, costs for which are often charged to the fund.
- **Strategy:** Different asset managers running different strategies will have costs associated with their deal strategies; for example, the costs of margin calls on options for a hedge fund, or costs of an acquisition in the case of a classic PE buy-out strategy.
- **Deal team:** The deal team for the strategy will require heavy amounts of investment, as these are the people that undertake the research and eventually present investment ideas to investment committees.
- **Compliance team:** As discussed above, more regulation equals more costs, which could not be better evidenced than the increasing numbers of compliance employees within the asset management sector. Gone are the days of having one compliance officer for the whole bank. These days compliance teams are tasked with reviewing mountains of regulation and guidance and ensuring that the asset managers adhere to them.
- **Back office:** There has always been a market for the supply of back-office services and asset managers are faced with the choice of keeping this in-house, or outsourcing it. Amongst others, back-office services can include administration, fund accountancy, custody, and transaction processing.
- **Office:** It may have already been apparent, but the popular jurisdictions for asset managers tend to be in cities (capital or otherwise) that are seeing increasingly high costs of rent for office space, which won't change until we are all sat in our garden sheds holding a virtual conference call with colleagues across the globe.
- **Insurance:** Perhaps a sub-threshold to deal with team costs is key person insurance, which, as the teams grow in size, only gets more expensive.
- **IT:** I have dedicated an entire chapter to the rise of technology in the asset management sector, and investments by asset managers to build their own IT ecosystem will only increase as we find more ways to become more efficient with technology; however, large up-front investment into more efficient IT systems may improve costs savings later on.

- **Other costs:** Other incidental costs of running an asset management company include paying licences for the relevant regulatory authority.

Of course, there is a deep irony that regulators are making the costs of running an asset management firm higher, but at the same time, the regulators are attacking the higher fees.

## INTERNAL TEAM ECONOMICS

The internal economics of the manager predominantly concern how the senior investment executives are remunerated. The management team as a whole will want to ensure that everyone is equally motivated by the success of the manager and the pay and reward structure will aim to reflect this. That said, investment houses established by dominant founders can have structures skewed against the majority of the team, with founders also expecting to pick up more carry (in a closed-ended fund) as the fund matures, and team members leave (or are forced out).

I have always been surprised why investors do not really look into who gets the performance fees in a team. Then again, I have also been alarmed at how little due diligence (DD) investors do on the management company, its governance, and culture. Seemingly, the larger an investor or fund ticket is, the less DD they do. Pension plans or endowments can invest hundreds of millions in just one PE fund, and yet these plans employ a handful of staff and pay them little to boot. Pension plans, state plans, endowments, and SWFs really should do a lot more work – have bigger teams – and pay them better – to play their social role of protecting the savings of the masses.

**Salary and Fixed Draws**  The remuneration of the investment team depends in part on the legal vehicle chosen for the structuring of the manager. Whether it is a corporate or a partnership vehicle, the team and other staff will be paid a base of some description. The senior members of the team will also participate in a profit share. In a partnership structure this is achieved by permitting fixed and variable drawings by the partners of the firm. For a corporate structure, the senior members can also hold either ordinary shares or a secondary class of shares that pay out dividends. In both cases, the payments of fixed amounts of remuneration can be linked to milestones. Since 22 July 2013, the policies underlying remuneration in the form of both salaries and fixed drawings are required to be in line with the provisions of the AIFMD, which may require a change in policy depending on the manager in question.

**Bonuses**  Bonuses are typically awarded on a discretionary basis and in order to incentivise the team these are fixed to certain milestones. Again, since 22 July 2013 the award of bonuses has been subject to the provisions of the AIFMD.

**Share and Option Ownership of the Management Company**  Share option plans may exist in relation to a listed company or a private company. The success of the manager is aligned with the investment team that participates in the rewards through the increase in share price (more significant with a listed company) and by any payment of dividends. If the manager is structured as a partnership, then such a scheme would still be possible where a corporate entity is established as a partner of the manager, through which the payments of dividends are made and options granted.

**Performance Fee Share and Carried Interest**  This is discussed above and is designed to both motivate and retain key staff. Investors expect managers to be aligned to them by principally being interested in the performance elements of fees, and not be mere management fee gatherers.

**Co-Investment**  Individual members of the investment team may also be permitted to co-invest alongside the fund on a deal-by-deal basis, an arrangement which is not entirely favourable to the investors of the fund as a whole, unless it is fixed to every investment. Alternatively, if it is a deal-by-deal co-investment arrangement then it can be fairer to investors if it invests where the fund does not have the firepower to invest the full amount of an investment.

Banks have in the past also allowed their in-house team access to bank leverage to allow individual members to invest into deals. Certain private management companies allow effective lending to staff to acquire LP interests in the funds.

**Fund Investment or the GP Commitment**  The investment team may be incentivised by investing fully alongside the investors in the fund. The investors of the fund will indeed commonly expect a commitment to be made by the investment team in the whole fund (known as the 'GP commitment' in a closed-ended fund) in order to ensure its commitment is aligned with the success of its investments. These commitments are often expressed as a percentage of the investors' commitments or as a hard cap. Historically, this requirement was set at 1% of a fund for certain US tax purposes. However, especially during the financial crisis, investors have been expecting up to 10% GP commitment, or 10% of all fund commitments.

There are banks that will lend to executives of the GP or the GP itself to make this investment.

## DOES SIZE MATTER?

### Manager Size

There is a squeeze on players in the middle of the market from the larger funds growing on the one side, and the increase in smaller, more niche funds. Notwithstanding my earlier point regarding a lack of buyers within the asset management market, there have been an increasing spate of mergers and acquisitions of asset managers within the last few years. As costs have increased due to regulations that are more stringent and investors are becoming more cost-aware when reviewing product ranges, there has been an increased squeeze on profits within asset management firms.

Reports are suggesting that revenue per AuM will decrease, whilst costs per AuM will slowly increase.[52] Whilst an increase in the onboarding of technology will cut costs, many will turn to the open market, or look to amalgamate other firms to increase their offering.

Similar to what has happened in the legal sector, many mid-sized asset managers that have no competitive advantage will find themselves squeezed between the members of the trillion-dollar club and the smaller, specialised managers. There will be a few mid-market firms that survive due to an established investor network or a distribution network belonging to their parent bank or insurance company – however, these will likely be a minority.[53]

It appears that many asset managers are taking the merger and acquisition (M&A) route. In the last 20 years, 2018 was the only year where total deal value of M&A activity involving asset managers as the target was higher than USD 20 billion, other than 2009.[54] The question remains, however, as to whether multiple mid-sized asset managers clubbing together means that they become better quality managers, or simply add an extra '0' to their AuM. Houses that grow larger but do not manage to improve their offerings will only be prolonging their decline.

It is believed by Yves Perrier, the current CEO of Amundi, that in the near future there will be two types of asset managers – asset gatherers (managers offering all services globally) and asset specialists (boutiques specialising in certain products).[55] The former requires low fees and low costs spread across each strategy, quick adoption of technology and a large offering of passive investments. The latter, meanwhile, requires a specialised offering of a niche strategy in order to justify charging higher fees than their Goliath counterparts.[56]

### Multi-Multi

**Multi-Manager** Some management groups are becoming multi-manager as well as sometime multi-brand. The centre or holding company will offer marketing, legal, and administration, leaving the underlying managers to manage.

Large groups such as Legg Mason, Affiliated Managers Group (AMG), and Principal Global Investors are good examples.

**Multi-Boutique** A multi-boutique is a series of specialised boutiques, but with the advantage of more scale. Such firms are taking over the role that banks and insurance companies played prior to the credit crisis. Under pressure from post-crisis regulations – such as the US Volcker Rule that limits banks' ownership of hedge funds – large banks also sold their stakes in niche managers.

**Multi-Stakes** This is also leading to new funds being created to acquire stakes in managers.

Especially if such funds are managed by the banks themselves, then this helps avoid the limitations of the Volcker Rule.

From the managers' perspective, investment from these multi-boutiques or funds brings two obvious pluses. First, it helps them manage the process of succession. Thanks to the valuation and equity injection that come with an outside investment, it becomes easier for a founding team of managers to pass the reins to the next generation. Second, it can help with distribution and back-office functions.

The holding entity can win many new outlets and help to market, and someone else can take on some of the bureaucracy that might otherwise distract its investment team.

Also a strategic or large LP or asset-owning backer to your management company can lead to cornerstoning of future funds by such investors that is effectively getting a fee discount on these funds.

**Multi-Strategy** Strategy diversification is becoming more common, whereas a few years back it was called – negatively – strategy drift. That said, as long as each fund sticks to its knitting and strategy, then multi-strategy offers investors a shop window to many products all managed with the integrity and skills of their favoured brand.

Managers such as Blackstone and Apollo offer a 'library' approach, which they say offers investors a complete offering from the manager – one that can spot trends across and industry or industries and invest up and down the internal rate of return (IRR) stack.

The one-stop shop.

**Multi-Fund**   Similarly, the multi-fund offering can offer different year vintages, different fund economics (such as lock ups – and income versus capital) and different products.

Holding groups such as AMG and Legg Mason get some of the diversification benefits of a fund of funds (which invest in other funds), but with a steady stream of income and less of the overall investment risk.

## SOME CONCLUSIONS

I write more much about regulation and compliance throughout this book, for good reason. Broadly, regulation is only going one way – up. Similarly, compliance is on the same journey. These days I feel like you cannot onboard a new client without knowing where their mum gets her hair done.

Costs are also on the increase owing to not just increased regulation and compliance, but also tax and regulatory rules on substance. As (formerly) offshore jurisdictions seek to change the way the world views them, they move away from the post box-style offering and require more substantive decisions be made within their jurisdictions, which means more decision-makers be based offshore, raising costs.

The good/bad old days of taking it in turns to be the compliance officer, a lack of interest in spelling the word, risk, and having a retired favourite accountant or lawyer as your entire back office, are long gone – thankfully.

Similarly, the days of a brass plaque in somewhere like the Cayman Islands and two local directors – one a 'jumbo director' with 200 directorships and the other a local Sark farmer – have similarly gone.

The results of the FCA's study on asset managers also calls for better protection for the investors and other compliance-heavy remedies.

There will be more pressure on compliance and fees coming our way before deregulation sweeps in to restart the party. For now, this all means increased costs – and the only way is up from here – so all of us need to adapt.

## ENDNOTES

1. https://willistowerswatson.pl/aktualnosci/pdf/2018.10.29-TAI-PI-500_2018.pdf
2. www.ft.com/content/8ff0974c-fd3c-11e7-a492-2c9be7f3120a
3. https://willistowerswatson.pl/aktualnosci/pdf/2018.10.29-TAI-PI-500_2018.pdf
4. Ibid.
5. Ibid.
6. Ibid.
7. www.amp-switzerland.ch/en-gb/why-switzerland/success-factors
8. https://passthrough.fw-notify.net/download/272550/https://prismic-io.s3.amazonaws.com/sfama-cms/0a638a04-79ff-4b94-a638-963d585a325b_gii-full-report-2017.pdf p. 323.
9. IFZ/AMP Asset Management Study 2018: An Overview of Swiss Asset Management, p. 23.

10. Swiss cantons are still leading in global tax competition; BAK Press release: BAK Taxation Index 2017, p. 3.
11. Ibid.
12. Swiss cantons are still leading in global tax competition; BAK Press release: BAK Taxation Index 2017, p. 4.
13. IFZ/AMP Asset Management Study 2018: An Overview of Swiss Asset Management, p. 25.
14. European Parliament Draft Report 2.10.2018; Committee on Economic and Monetary Affairs.
15. https://willistowerswatson.pl/aktualnosci/pdf/2018.10.29-TAI-PI-500_2018.pdf
16. Ibid.
17. www.euromoney.com/article/b180dn1wr0c4rv/why-the-french-are-leading-europes-asset-management-shake-up
18. www.investmenteurope.net/investmenteurope/news/3713152/german-fund-industry-hits-eur3trn
19. www.ipe.com/analysis/analysis/ipe-top-1000-european-pension-assets-grow-by-9/10014864.article
20. www.pwc.lu/en/asset-management/docs/monterey-insight-luxembourg-press-release-2018-incl-leaders-ranking.pdf, p. 1.
21. Ibid p. 2.
22. www.irishfunds.ie/getting-started-in-ireland/why-ireland
23. www.financemalta.org/sections/funds/
24. Political Declaration, p. 7.
25. Ibid., para 38.
26. SUP 10A.5.3R (FCA Handbook).
27. SUP 10A.10.7R (FCA Handbook).
28. http://iscltd.com/library/MiFID_II_Costs_and_Charges.html
29. Ibid.
30. https://fundcentres.lgim.com/srp/lit/mKK4pm/MiFID-II-costs-and-charges-QA_Unit-Trusts_31-01-2018_UK-ADV.pdf, p. 1.
31. Guidelines Transaction reporting, order record keeping and clock synchronisation under MiFID II p. 10.
32. PWC; MiFID II Transaction reporting: Detecting and investigating potential market abuse; p. 5.
33. www.cordium.com/insights/mifir-transaction-reporting-key-issues-highlighted-by-the-fca/
34. FCA Transaction Reporting Forum: July 2018, p. 7.
35. Ibid., p. 28.
36. www.thetradenews.com/mifid-ii-story-far/
37. www.ft.com/content/74138918-f236-11e8-9623-d7f9881e729f
38. www.ft.com/content/6edc5960-9a27-11e7-a652-cde3f882dd7b
39. https://papers.ssrn.com/sol3/papers.cfm?abstract_id=2770634; p. 3.
40. The research revolution: investment research rules in the era of MiFID II, p. 39.
41. www.lpx-group.com/lpx_indexing/lpx-indices/
42. www.valuewalk.com/2014/01/alternative-asset-managers-value/
43. https://seekingalpha.com/news/3430304-private-equity-firms-adopt-distributable-earnings
44. www.ftadviser.com/investments/2018/08/29/half-of-hnw-investors-unaware-of-venture-capital-trusts/
45. www.gov.uk/guidance/venture-capital-schemes-tax-relief-for-investors
46. Ibid.
47. www.schwab.com/resource-center/insights/content/etf-vs-mutual-fund-it-depends-on-your-strategy
48. www.bankrate.com/investing/mutual-fund-vs-etf-which-is-better/
49. Salaried Member Rules: Revised Technical Note and Guidance (HMRC).
50. www.michelmores.com/news-views/news/llp-salaried-member-rules

51. FCA Asset Management Market Study, Nov 2016, p. 5.
52. After the Easy Money Boom, Stark Choices for Asset Managers; www.bain.com/insights/after-the-easy-money-boom-stark-choices-for-asset-managers/
53. Ibid.
54. www.ft.com/content/35797ffa-df3d-3df5-87a7-75f7f6ba6b5e
55. Ibid.
56. After the Easy Money Boom, Stark Choices for Asset Managers; www.bain.com/insights/after-the-easy-money-boom-stark-choices-for-asset-managers/

# CHAPTER 4

# Governance

*Aristocracy, Timocracy, Oligarchy, Democracy, and Tyranny.*

– Plato

This chapter will discuss the growing body of rules and opinion surrounding 'governance' – an undefined term in any usage that literally means all rules. Its origin can be found in the Greek verb 'Kybernein' that meant guiding, steering, or manoeuvring a ship. Many words and expressions can be found from travelling, although most expressions created in the twenty-first century seem to derive from instant social media (LOL, bantz, OMG, etc.). First used metaphorically by Plato to describe the governing of people, its use has been applied widely to include political structures (governments), high office (governors), or teachers (governesses). Within asset management, its scope has been enlarged to cover the measures that organisations employ to promote what, in the eye of the beholder, represents best ethical practice.

This chapter will touch on measures that asset managers are implementing internally, but will also review measures that asset managers are pushing on the companies that they hold ownership. This chapter will also discuss ESG policies as well and the impact asset managers are having when putting these measures to companies' boards. Lastly, this chapter will discuss the rise of the impact fund and what can be inferred from its recent popularity.

There are numerous definitions of what 'good' governance is. The orthodox version of fund manager governance as their principal role of managing other people's money is usefully articulated by Paul Roye (former director of the SEC's Investment Management division). In the speech he gave to the Investment Company Institute in Washington D.C. in 1999, Roye outlined what he understood as the four pillars of governance. First, to ensure that the fund's objectives guide how the fund is managed. Second, to make sure that the assets of the fund are kept secure. Third, when investors redeem their investment they are given their pro rata share of the assets. Fourth, to ensure that the fund will be run for the benefit of its investors or owners and not its service providers. In short, fund manager governance refers to a system of checks and balances which ensures that an investment fund is operated by the fund manager in the best interests of the fund and its investors.

Importantly, from the perspective of the investor, 'governance involves understanding if the individuals controlling your money are organised around a reliable framework that is of high standing'.[1] Pre-financial crisis, there were many examples of conflicts of interest, fraud, lack of independent directors, and a weakness in knowledge and experience of both fund directors and fund managers. For example, the Weavering Capital fraud in which investors lost GBP 350 million through a series of catastrophic trades. As I write this book, a series of investigations are starting around the large Abraaj fund management group.

Yet today there is a notable step-change in the importance placed on governance. This is conspicuous at both investors' levels of operational due diligence and with high-profile managers discussing its value. For example, Larry Fink of BlackRock recently sang the praises of ESG in the pursuit of sustainable growth – 'A company's ability to manage environmental, social, and governance matters demonstrates the leadership and good governance that is so essential to sustainable growth, which is why we are increasingly integrating these issues into our investment process.'[2]

The importance of due diligence (DD) for investors in funds has never been more critical. Some providers of this (plug – MJ Hudson, as providers of DD services for fund investors) are noticing an upswell in demand.

In order to establish how the asset management industry got to this point of increased governance, it is necessary to examine the regulatory background that underlies this conversation. Much more on regulation is covered in Chapters 9 and 10.

## REGULATORY BACKGROUND

### UK Regulatory Environment

At the height of the financial crisis, the government felt obligated to promote stronger regulation and oversight of the financial services industry. To achieve this, it gave the BoE the authority to instil stability within the industry. Many of the banks had created systemic risk and this highlighted the need for an overhaul of the supervisory system. On 1 April 2013, the new 'twin peaks' system was introduced, comprised of the Financial Conduct Authority (FCA) and the Prudential Regulatory Authority (PRA). These two bodies are now responsible for preventing future market failures.

### FCA

- Primary role is to protect consumers, enhance the integrity of the UK financial system, to help maintain competitive markets, and promote healthy competition. Underlying this is a focus on the prevention of harm to customers and markets.
- Under FSMA, any person who carried on a 'regulated activity' must either be authorised by the FCA or come within one of the statutory exemptions.
- For each regulated activity, an applicant for FCA authorisation must identify which investment types their activities concern.
- Alternatively, the content of the 'promotion' being made to would-be investors must be approved by an 'authorised person'.
- In order to monitor and regulate firms according to the risks they present, the FCA places them into four different categories determined by size.

### PRA

- Primary role is to promote safety and soundness of those firms it regulates.
- (In relation to insurers) to ensure there is an appropriate degree of protection for policyholders.

- Firms need to apply to the PRA to receive authorisation for certain regulated activities.
- Although the PRA does not give a definition of a bank, it lists the types of banks it already regulates.
- Similarly to the FCA the PRA delineates firms into categories dependent on how frequently and intensely they wish to supervise them.
- Section 59 FSMA – individuals who carry out 'controlled functions' on behalf of a firm must be approved by the PRA.

## US Regulatory Environment

The 1929 stock market crash was a wakeup call for the US financial services industry. Although described as a 'death sentence', the introduction of the Public Utility Holding Company Act of 1935 along with the Securities Act of 1933 and the Securities Exchange Act of 1934 provided much needed oversight. With the objective of promoting market confidence and protecting the public interest, the SEC was the first step towards a more transparent system.

**SEC**  The SEC's primary role is to protect investors. It fulfils its role by requiring companies that publicly offer securities or have more than 2000 shareholders (or at a minimum, 500 that are not accredited investors) and have total assets in excess of USD 10 million to register the applicable class of stock under the Securities Exchange Act of 1934. It also requires these companies to be open and honest about their business, any securities being offered, and the risks involved. Furthermore, the SEC instructs those that trade in securities to treat investors fairly and honestly.

### Dodd–Frank Act

- Restricts the types of trading activities that certain financial institutions (such as banks) are allowed to practise.
- Increases the oversight and supervision responsibilities of the SEC and Commodity Futures Trading Commission (CFTC, a division of the SEC), particularly in swaps and derivatives.
- Contains provisions to protect borrowers from predatory lending and to prevent abusive mortgage practices.
- Created Financial Stability Oversight Council (FSOC) to oversee financial organisations and fill in the regulatory gaps created by the numerous agencies responsible for regulating the various corners of the financial markets.

### The 'Volcker Rule'

- Sets out explicitly permitted activities, services, capital requirements, and restrictions on transactions with affiliates for banking entities and non-bank financial companies.
- Prohibits a banking entity from engaging in 'proprietary trading', acquiring or retaining any equity, partnership, or other ownership interest in a hedge or PE fund, or sponsoring a hedge or PE fund.

## EU Regulatory Environment

The key piece of legislation is AIFMD. The directive was transposed fully by all 28 member states on 22 July 2013. This directive is designed to cover managers of investment schemes which have been created for professional investors. Examples of types of fund include hedge funds, PE funds, RE funds, and a variety of institutional funds.

AIFMD has had a widespread effect on asset managers that are based in or wish to market in Europe. In order to market across borders, managers will have to comply with new capital requirements, information standards, standards of disclosure to regulators, requirements to use certain functionaries such as depositaries, and a plethora of other obligations. There is a Euro threshold limit for the 'full scope' of the AIFMD rules, but the implementation of this threshold varies across member states of the EU. In the UK, for example, asset managers operating under the threshold are still required to seek authorisation from the FCA, which entails compliance with a significant proportion (but not a majority) of the new AIFMD rules.

**AIFMD** The AIFMD provides a framework for the regulation of AIFMs. Its key provisions cover:

- General conditions relating to investors including conflicts of interest, fair treatment, and risk and liquidity management.
- Requirements pertaining to the organisation of the AIFMD, including internal governance.
- Reporting requirements such as annual reports, disclosure to investors, and regulatory reporting.

**Code of Conduct** In addition to specific rules, the AIFMD contains a wide-ranging set of general principles. These principles include acting in the best interests of the fund and investors as well as obtaining the client's approval before investing all or part of the client's portfolio in units or shares of the AIFs it manages. The FCA made proposals following a market study (MS15/2.3) to strengthen the requirements for asset managers to act in the best interests of investors. This is through a combination of clarity of our expectations, introducing independence on governance boards, and introducing prescribed responsibility under the Senior Managers and Certification Regime (SM&CR).

As well as following a set of principles regarding conflicts of interest and treating investors fairly, AIFMD requires (subject to issues of proportion and scale) AIFMs to have a permanent risk management function and that risk management is 'functionally and hierarchically' separated from other operating units, including the portfolio management function.

**Transparency** Certain information must be provided to investors and the regulator during the marketing process and on an ongoing basis. Before investors make an investment, the manager must disclose to the investors information including the investment strategy, the legal implications of the investment contract and the identities of the manager, depositary and other third-party service providers. An audited annual report must be disclosed in respect of each EU AIF within six months of the end of the financial year. AIFMs must also regularly report trading information and information regarding the portfolio to regulators.

**MiFID** MiFID was applicable in the UK from November 2007 but was incorporated by MiFID II, which became effective in January 2018. MiFID II is seen as necessary in the wake of the financial crisis in order to increase investor protection. To achieve this goal MiFID II introduced new measures to increase transparency and standardise the regulatory disclosures necessary in certain markets. In essence, the objective is to create a cohesive and unified regulatory framework that will prioritise the protection of investors.

See Chapters 9 and 10 for more information and the effect of MiFID.

**BASEL III**  Basel III is a collection of measures designed by the Basel Committee that have been internationally agreed as a response to the financial crisis. The objective of the measures is to add weight to the regulation, supervision and risk management of banks.[3] These measures are an extension of the previously agreed Basel II framework.[4] Broadly, their aim is to reduce bank leverage and increase liquidity. Consequently, the amount of capital that banks have to hold on to is greater and of better quality than previously agreed.

See Chapters 9 and 10 for more information and the effect of Basel III.

**Anti-Bribery Legislation**  The UK Bribery Act 2010 was created to answer the requirements of the 1997 OECD Anti-Bribery Convention. In essence, this legislation improves the previous UK law and represents one of the most stringent global regulatory frameworks. This is, in part, because of the creation of a strict liability offence for partnerships and companies who fail to prevent bribery. Importantly, the UK Bribery Act 2010 represents an increased liability risk for companies that operate or are incorporated within the UK.

Anti-bribery legislation has now pervaded the industry globally – see Chapters 9 and 10 for more information.

**Anti-Money Laundering**  The Money Laundering, Terrorist Financing and Transfer of Funds (Information on the Payer) Regulations 2017 came into force on 26 June 2017 and transposed the Fourth EU Money Laundering Directive (MLD4) into UK law. The regulations aim to prevent terrorist financing and money laundering, and involve increased due diligence requirements.

**CRS**  The Common Reporting Standard (CRS) requires jurisdictions to acquire information from their financial institutions and automatically exchange that information with other jurisdictions in a reciprocal arrangement. The objective is to prevent tax evasion through reporting. It is often said that CRS is the FATCA for the rest of the world.

**Foreign Account Tax Compliance Act**  The Foreign Account Tax Compliance Act (FATCA), was enacted by the US congress in 2010 in an effort to address non-compliance by US taxpayers. This is achieved through a reporting mechanism that mandates foreign (external to the US) financial institutions to report to the IRS information about the accounts of US nationals. This process enhances cross border tax compliance through the creation of an international standard for the automatic sharing of information concerning US taxpayers. Underlying this process is a targeted movement towards greater transparency.

**Whistleblowing**  There are numerous examples of prominent whistleblowers (Edward Snowden, Mark Felt, Sherron Watkins, Linda Tripp, Coleen Rowley, etc.) who have hit headlines across the world. At its core, whistle-blowing is the action of reporting wrongful conduct in the work or other place.

In the event that an individual does 'blow the whistle' there are legal protections (if the individual in question is legally classed as a 'worker') that the Public Disclosure Act 1998 affords UK workers. Consequently, it is unlawful for that individual to lose their job or be treated unfairly. Breach of these rules is not taken lightly, as demonstrated recently by the Barclays whistleblowing scandal – the company was fined USD 15 million and its CEO, Jes Staley, was personally fined GBP 642 430.[5]

**Base Erosion and Profits Shifting project**  The Base Erosion and Profits Shifting (BEPS) project was designed by the OECD to prevent multinationals taking advantage of previous loopholes, gaps, and mismatches in tax rules. Its core aim is to introduce an effective taxation framework that stops multinationals from shifting profits to at best lower and at worst no-tax locations. Underlying this aim is a motivation to ensure that the economic benefit is retained by the country that facilitates the multinationals' presence.

The BEPS framework binds 100 countries together, facilitating a collaborative process that will increase the likelihood of the BEPS package being a success. This package sets out 15 'Actions' that countries have at their disposal to block multinationals from exploiting local tax laws.

**Beneficial Ownership and Registers**   Historically, there have been considerable differences in the transparency of registers across jurisdictions (Cayman Islands, Isle of Man, British Virgin Islands, Guernsey, EU, etc.). This has ranged from centralised registers, which the public can access, to opaque procedures where you physically have to go to a registered office to check. In general, this divergence between jurisdictions has narrowed as the asset management industry has embraced new technologies. The structural problems of enabling access to this information has been lessened considerably by the creation of, for example, the internet, as well as the introduction of new regulation. Moreover, with the rise of ESG and more rigorous governance and taxation practices, there has been a movement among investors for managers to be more forthcoming with who the shareholders really are. This has also been, it must be said, set against a backdrop of concern for criminal or terrorist financing (a major reason why MLD4 was introduced). This section will explore some of the changes which have been introduced across jurisdictions to close this gap in knowledge and increase transparency.

The European Parliament (EP)[6] has taken a proactive approach to transparency within the financial world with the updates to the EU's anti-money laundering legislation. MLD4 comes in response to the leaking of the Panama Papers and the terrorist attacks of 2015 and 2016 in Paris and Brussels, respectively. Various EU member states have followed suit with their own implementing measures. Not only states within the EU but also crown dependencies and British Overseas Territories have introduced their own frameworks. This is off the back of the UK government backing legislation that necessitates its 14 overseas territories to create public beneficial ownership registries by 2020, or face them being imposed. Although the UK government has insisted that its overseas territories make information public, this has not been followed by several territories. Similarly, some EU member states and offshore jurisdictions have decided to only enable law enforcement and appropriate regulators access. Although this is not entirely what was mandated it must be said that it is significantly more transparent than the previous regimes. The following is a brief outline of a selection of jurisdictions that have implemented a beneficial ownership registry.

The Isle of Man[7] introduced the Beneficial Ownership Act 2017 to replace the Companies (Beneficial Ownership) Act 2012. In part, this was because of international needs to be more transparent in light of greater scrutiny over the sourcing of certain funds but it was also a very business-centric approach. Importantly, this legislation introduced a central register, which helps the regulator and adds transparency to the system. This follows the EU's Anti-Money Laundering: Beneficial Ownership of Corporate Entities Regulations 2016, which apply to (for instance) any Irish[8] corporate entity and therefore will have a knock on effect for CISs, AIFMs and UCITS.

The British Virgin Islands (BVI) introduced the Beneficial Ownership Secure Search System Act in 2017.[9] The purpose behind the new legislation was to illustrate BVI's dedication to transparency and due diligence, which has been championed by other measures introduced by EU member states, Crown Dependencies, and British Overseas Territories. The Act introduced a search system that provides the secure, efficient and effective storage and retrieval of beneficial ownership details for every corporate legal entity.

In 2018, the Cayman Islands[10,11,12] government introduced into law the Beneficial Ownership (Companies) (Amendment) Regulations and the Beneficial Ownership (Limited Liability Companies) (Amendment) Regulations. Since the beginning of July of that year, companies and limited liability companies (unless an exemption is applicable) that have been registered or incorporated in the Cayman Islands must now create and maintain a beneficial ownership register at their Cayman Islands-registered office.

From March 2019, and off the back of MLD4 being implemented in Belgium,[13] companies, not-for-profit associations, foundations, trusts, and other similar legal entities are required to disclose their 'ultimate beneficial owners' (UBOs). The register that has been created is online and accessible to the regulators, entities under AML rules, and all citizens (even those without any legitimate interest, unlike the Isle of Man rules).

Malta[14] has introduced a beneficial ownership register, which is a new measure to promote transparency regarding the arrangements of legal entities. This process will require a rigorous analysis of the legal entities' ownership structure in order to ascertain whether sufficient disclosure of information has occurred. The obligation to release information concerning the ultimate beneficial owner must also be made to the respective registries. This information will then be accessible for national competent authorities, national tax authorities, the Financial Intelligence Analysis Units, and various qualifying persons.

The introduction of centralised registers for these and other jurisdictions is a promising step forward in transparency. Although there are differing levels of improvement, it looks like a progressive approach is being embraced. A key area of ongoing politicised debate is whether all registers should be seen by anybody, or just by regulators, tax and government bodies. The Channel Islands Registries for example can only be accessed by authorities and not the public.

**General Data Protection Regulation and Data Protection**  The General Data Protection Regulation (GDPR) came into effect on 25 May 2018, and impacted businesses both within and outside the EU. The regulation replaced the EU Data Protection Directive 95/46/EC and aims to update and harmonise the differences between EU member states' privacy laws. In the event of a data breach, the GDPR states that the controller should notify the supervisory authority (Information Commissioner's Office (ICO) in the UK) immediately and where possible within 72 hours of the controller becoming aware of the breach. The controller must also communicate the breach to the data subjects effected 'without undue delay' and this must be direct communication, i.e. the controller cannot simply post a notice on their website. The content of the GDPR impacts the operators within the asset management space in a number of ways (for example, compliance, business model, investors and information, selection of technology, and the integration of data protection throughout the business). In real terms, this will require asset managers to place a far greater emphasis on data protection. One solution is to encourage digitisation and promote new technologies, which will manage the data in a compliant way. This will fulfil the purpose of the GDPR, which is to reformat personal data protection as an inherent right, thus creating greater demonstrable transparency. The introduction of mandatory breach reporting requirements, fines of up to 4% of global turnover, and the removal of the Data Protection Act 2018's threshold for the 'right to erasure' means the GDPR will inevitably become a catalyst for further change in this space.

It is already having a major effect on data and user information, with social networking companies squirming especially. However, GDPR and similar protection rules do clash rather spectacularly with other recent developments on ownership transparency, CRS, know your customer (KYC), and AML (perhaps the clash of the four-lettered words against the three-lettered). I have already seen investors not investing in funds, as they fear that with all the information that they have to provide, and with no computer proving un-hackable, they are in danger of exploitation, bribery, and even kidnap.

See Chapters 9 and 10 for more information on data protection.

## BOARDS AND COMMITTEES

**Boards**   Fund managers are typically companies, and it is the board where most of the action lies. Boards can delegate to committees, such as the investment committee, to help efficiency. Directors on boards determine outcomes, only subject to shareholder rights and demands, and shareholders requiring changes to the directors.

**Shareholder Rights**   Typically, shareholders will have the same standard rights irrespective of whether the company is public or private. The specifics of shareholders rights are dependent on the rights attached to the shares under the company's articles of association or by-laws. Consequently, depending on what class of share you possess it is quite common for different shareholders to possess different rights. Shareholder rights are also extended by statute or case law, such as rules around investors or minority shareholders.

**Employees**   Employee rights, worker rights, trade unions, right to state-directed pensions, maternity and paternity allowances – the list is long. Employees are vital for managers' culture. Employees will also hold you to account on governance.

**Listed Managers**   For listed managers, assessing the management on an ongoing basis through corporate governance is vital to ensure the value for shareholders is generated appropriately. Enhancing corporate value and co-ordinating the various interests between stakeholders is a perennial challenge for the modern public company. Indeed, as globalisation impacts commercial decisions more often, different cultural and societal factors need to be considered. Listed companies are constantly having to re-evaluate their social responsibility, which, through transparent communication, can be illustrated to shareholders to reassure and drive value.

Shareholders will delegate authority to management to exercise their judgement to make decisions regarding the company practices. For their part, shareholders provide capital (and risk), which they hope will be used in line with corporate governance policies. Management in turn will be audited and held to account by shareholders who exercise their commercial and legal rights.

In the age of holding companies, it is important to shareholders that corporate governance is not just applied to the surface. Ensuring that the policies apply to the group as a whole is an ongoing concern for investors. Of course there are other stakeholders aside from shareholders who have an interest in the actions of a company. Creditors, for example, should be a concern for listed companies. Many of whom would be impacted by potentially off-colour actions by management.

The key watchword for listed companies when considering governance is 'transparency'. Ensuring that disclosures are made to the relevant parties in a timely and accurate way will go a long way in implementing effective corporate governance. The information provided should be reliable and comparable so that stakeholders can make an informed comparison. By releasing information this way it ensures that shareholders are treated equally, as the partial release of information to only certain parties is not good practice.

**LLPs and LLCs as Managers**   The LLP, in the UK, and LLC, in the US, are both company–partnership hybrids.

Both are used as management vehicles for funds and are transparent in nature. Governance is centralised within the partnership or members' agreement, as well as by statute.

**Limited Partner Advisory Committees**   The vehicle typically used to pool an alternative fund's cash and assets is a limited partnership, which is not controlled directly by a board of directors but is instead controlled by the GP. It is also common for the GP to delegate management of the fund to a separate manager. To give investors an opportunity to consult on certain matters with the fund manager, the GP will often approve the creation of a limited partner advisory committee (LPAC). Arguably, the most important responsibility is to decide whether or not to approve conflicts of interest flagged by the fund manager. An LPAC's function is to be consulted by the manager on a variety of matters. This includes the general policies and guidelines, prospective investment sectors, actual and potential conflicts of interest in respect of the partnership and the interests of the manager and its affiliates, and to perform other functions that will be outlined in an agreement between the committee and the manager.

When there is a decision to be made surrounding a conflict, the criteria of assessment would not be based on the commerciality of the situation. Instead, it will most likely be decided on whether a conflict exists, whether policy should be amended, and if the manager has the requisite skill and experience to handle the matter. LPACs do suffer from LPs not wanting to make actual decisions, partly in fear of their LP losing limited liability of being sued by other LPs or the GP. This is a shame.

**Fund Boards**   Funds can also have boards – principally open-ended or corporate funds. Certainly post-financial crisis, there is a desire for more independent directors and, especially, more independent directors with fewer directorships (fewer 'jumbo directors'), and clearly increasingly there is an investor need for directors to have more knowledge and experience, and certain investors want more full board meetings.

The FCA asset management market study published in 2017 outlined the FCA's criticism of certain governance standards within the asset management industry.

The FCA notes that many products and services are complicated and rely on complicated processes. In addition, there is a certain lack of transparency over the fees charged to the investor and a general lack of clarity in communication.

In summary, the FCA report found AIFM boards:

- Do not always convincingly consider value for money for their investors.
- Lack the autonomy, authority, and independence within the company structure to effectively hold the commercial strategy implemented by more senior boards and committee to task.
- Fail to take appropriate action to prevent and address underperformance.

As a solution to this appraisal, the FCA suggested several proposals that were received with moderate approval. First, fund managers could preserve the current governance structures, but clarify their duties and require the board to demonstrate their compliance. Second, extend the SM&CR to the senior managers of the AIFM. Third, create greater independence amongst current governance bodies through mandating an independent director majority on an AIFM board. Or fourth, establish an independent body modelled on the Independent Governance Committees (IGCs) in pension fund structures, which would carry out new duties. This would allow the current AIFMs to proceed as normal, with the new committee filling the gap in terms of responsibilities, which the FCA feels may be necessary.

**Managers of Listed Funds**    The FCA appraisal shone a bright light on listed funds. Here the fund can self-manage at listed company level or appoint a separate manager.

A recent example is Invesco, where a dispute in 2018 between Invesco Perpetual and one of its investment trusts managed by Invesco resulted in the shareholders calling for board members to be sacked and the FCA being brought in. The origins of this dispute started when the directors of Invesco Perpetual asked Invesco to cut the fees it was charging for managing the fund. Although the fund had been consistently beating the average returns of its competitors, the management fees were deemed too high as against the AuM. This request is within the remit of Invesco Perpetual to make, although you would expect it to be merely an opportunity for Invesco to put forward the case that, although expensive, their services were worth it. However, what transpired was very different. Invesco, through their other funds, held 16.8% in Invesco Perpetual at that time. Consequently, they demanded that the directors who challenged their fees resign and new ones be instated via a shareholder vote. Ouch.

Another recent example is Electra Private Equity, an investment trust that had outperformed the FTSE All-Share Index consistently. In 2016, it sacked its manager, Electra Partners (renamed Epiris post-spin-out, when they raised an even bigger fund as an independent manager from new institutions), and subsequently sold a large number of its positions. These decisions were sparked by an activist fund that ended up taking control of the board and is now winding up the Electra fund. Was this a good result  for shareholders?

**Investment Committees**    Most managers' boards appoint and operate an investment committee (IC), which broadly speaking is responsible for oversight, planning, and deals.[15] The core role of an IC is to approve the investment objectives of the fund, which is achieved by creating an appropriate investment plan. In short, the IC is incredibly important to the success and longevity of an asset manager.

There are some examples of best practice that help to illustrate the role of a competent IC. First, the IC should codify the roles, responsibilities, and specific duties of every member. This documentation process should not just be limited to the initial establishment. It should be an ongoing process that intersects with every part of the IC's role. This will provide continuity and aid in communication, which ultimately ensure the IC is held accountable for their actions. Second, the IC should have a complete understanding of the objective of the fund as well as what metrics they are using to determine success. Without this, it is much harder to fulfil their role of ensuring good investment choices are made. Understanding the goals of the asset manager as well as if they are realistic will help the IC immensely. Third, synonymous with this last point, the IC should only endorse an investment strategy that is realistic and derived from a reasonable set of assumptions about the investor's risk tolerance. Ensuring there is a meeting of minds between the IC, manager and investor is key. In order to avoid a mismatch of objectives, it is important that the IC consider the risk of an investment. Fourth, the hiring strategy and process for an IC should be clear and efficient. This should be articulated by the IC, as well as the process for terminating a relationship with a manager. This is a particularly important aspect of the IC's role as a mistake here could result in detrimental consequences. Lastly, the IC should at all times act in a disciplined manner, employing common sense and take a responsible approach.

It is clear that the IC is an integral part of any asset manager. As a fiduciary, it has a responsibility to carry out its role responsibly, with the aim of ensuring maximum success. Importantly, the IC should not just be at the whim of the management, owner or founders. I suspect that the days of the vetoing, strident CIO, and manager-owner might be over.

**Executive Committees**   These committees are often appointed by the board. The executive committee will normally have a range of duties but, broadly, their role is to provide organisational direction on behalf of the board as well as advising them on commercial matters such as policy, investment, risk, and strategy. This could be summarised as helping the board achieve its goals in the most efficient way. It could be a decision-making entity, act as a think-tank, a forum for conversation, and a filter for good or bad strategies. It should comprise the best members of the board and not be a reward. Ensuring the executive committee fulfils these characteristics will help an asset manager immeasurably. Indeed, these committees are typical in AIFMs.

**Role of the Non-Executive Director**   For many companies, the ideal non-executive director (NED) possesses competence and knowledge and can use their skills to help the company they are appointed by. Furthermore, independence is a vital quality and should not be considered as merely a natural progression in a corporate career. NEDs have specific responsibilities and can be governed by the SM&CR, the FCA's revised approved persons regime and the PRA's Senior Insurance Managers Regime (SIMR). This includes the roles of Chairman, Senior Independent Director and the Chairs of the Risk, Audit, Remuneration, and Nominations Committees. The FCA argues that NEDs with roles will create a more positive culture within these firms and provide better results for their clients and, more generally, the markets in which they operate.

Since 3 July 2017, 'Standard NEDs' (NEDs not holding senior management functions) have been subject to the FCA individual conduct rules set out in the Code of Conduct sourcebook (COCON 2.1) and the senior conduct rules. The purpose of this was to raise the standard of conduct and reduce the risk of potential misconduct.

## GOVERNANCE TRENDS

It is clear that the quality of the board at both an individual and group level has come under greater scrutiny in recent years. In particular the composition of the board in regard to age, gender, and number of additional chairs held is of concern to investors. Many investors would like to see more information to judge for themselves whether they are making a sensible financial decision trusting the board. Notably, investor stewardship, board quality, compensation, activist investing, ESG, cybersecurity, and human capital are prominent topics in the wider discussion.

**Investor Stewardship**   Globally, there is increased pressure from investors and governments to see better investor stewardship. This is, in part, a consequence of the financial crisis and the reaction to managers who, it is felt, should be more accountable.

**Board Quality and Composition**   Historically any change in the composition of the board would be driven by retirement or, less frequently, a need for a new perspective due to an emerging trend. One key factor behind the slow turnover of directors is the growing trend of increasing the mandatory age of retirement. According to the same index, 42% of S&P 500 companies with mandatory retirement ages have put the age limit at 75 years. This is combined with a small fraction of boards having mandatory term periods. These factors ensure that board turnover is low and make issues like gender representation much more unachievable. Despite this, it is clear that 2018 saw an increasing resistance to this anachronistic approach. For example, according to the Harvard Law School Forum on Corporate Governance and Financial Regulation,[16] boards in certain markets should expect increased votes against directors if there are less than two women on the board.

This traditional mindset will have to be confronted in an evolving commercial world. New challenges are emerging, especially in the technological, regulatory, and political spaces. Companies will want directors with direct industry experience and new perspectives to generate the necessary innovative and informed decisions required to succeed. The value of directors is their ability to inform a company's strategy. Without the relevant background this will become increasingly harder to do. Refreshment looks set to be a key trend going forward.

**Gender Balance** Gender balance on boards is a hot topic. Gender parity promotes better practice and better results.[17,18,19] There is a significant positive impact that gender balance can have on an organisation, yet it is still the case that the majority of firms do not recruit or promote women to the board. The Department for Business, Energy and Industrial Strategy released a report in May 2018 highlighting the 'pitiful'[20] excuses offered by FTSE 350 companies for their lack of gender representation at the top of their companies. For example, one representative suggested that 'most women don't want the hassle or pressure of sitting on a board', with another arguing that 'all the "good" women have already been snapped up'. Furthermore, it is also important to highlight the scope of this problem, with the following examples indicating the global nature of female underrepresentation:

- **United States.** Large institutional investors' patience is running very low regarding gender parity on boards. State Street Global Advisors is willing to vote against the chair or the entire nominating committee and previous attempts to address this issue have not been taken seriously.
- **Japan.** There is a particularly low level of representation of women on Japanese boards and it is submitted that investors will push for this to be changed in 2019. Some investors will share their guidelines with Japanese companies in a bid to aid them to promote gender equality.
- **India.** The 2013 requirement to have one female on the board has been subverted by the practice of appointing a female relative. The Kotak Committee is recommending that at a minimum, one of the independent directors should be female.

There is clearly some way to go before equality in the boardroom is felt.

**Compensation** Compensation for board members has increased significantly in the last decade. This looks set to continue but there is a growing concern surrounding both executive compensation and remuneration given to non-executives with a number of board positions. Value for money and the bottom line are obvious concerns to the investor and they will want greater clarity over the compensation schemes employed.

**Alignment of Interest** The relationship between an investor and manager is one based on trust. Historically, this was considered innate when the asset management industry was smaller.

However, the rapid growth of the market and the ensuing financial crisis undermined the orthodox opinion that alignment of interest was inherent rather than manufactured. Post financial
crisis, there have been significant concerns from investors, with some of the key points summarised as follows:

- **Fund size.** Funds used to be much smaller and there were fewer of them. They have bal-
  looned in size and managers have included other aspects to their role, such as consultancy
  and investment banking. Moreover, some managers have changed their business structure by going public. This has caused two major concerns. First, management fees will
  increase as they are typically in proportion to the size of the fund. Second, investors are
  concerned that there are not enough high quality investment opportunities to justify the
  size of some funds.[21,22]
- **Leverage.** Prior to the financial crisis, the leverage ratios for PE and RE investments
  especially had grown to what then became unsustainable. This raised the question as to
  whether investors were receiving any greater value then what they would get from a leveraged S&P 500 product. There were two key concerns for investors. The first was whether
  fund managers were incentivised to increase risk through over-leveraging in order to maximise their reward from performance fees. Second, were managers actually adding value
  beyond what could be found in a leveraging firm?
- **Fee income.** Especially the process where fund managers change acquisition companies'
  fees which they render to themselves. Examples include deal fees, consulting fees, and
  monitoring fees. This raises two concerns for investors, first, that managers may charge
  rates that would be considered above industry standard and, second, that managers are
  encouraged to acquire companies that would engender large services fees. There has been
  significant debate (and SEC fines) surrounding the lack of transparency of these fees.
  Charge what is agreed and tell the investors in advance!

**Performance Fees or Carried Interest**   Superficially, it is argued that performance fees create
alignment of interest between manager and investor. However, anxieties include the manager
taking a more risky approach to hit the target and therefore be able to pay the investor their
capital and clear the 'hurdle' for its own fee. Given that the manager faces little downside risk
but the investor does, it is argued that this differing risk appetite can cause misalignment.

When performance fees work, they work well to generate returns for investors. Management companies should work hard to show investors that performance fees help align
interests – not skew incentives. They have not yet comprehensibly won this debate.

**Managers Investing in the Funds**   One clear way of better aligning the interests of investors and
managers is for the manager to invest their own capital in the fund. In this way the manager has
'skin in the game', thus creating the same interests that an investor would when they invest.
As such, there is a clear synergy between the goals of both parties and an investor can be more
assured that the manager will make decisions that will benefit them both. It should be noted,
however, that the source of the funds matters.[23] Some fund managers will not have accumulated
enough wealth to invest their own capital into a fund they manage. As such, market practice
is for the manager to waive the management fee they would receive for their work. There is a
clear distinction, however, between investing your own money that you have worked for and
offsetting a future fee that would be part of your role. In this instance, it may be advisable for
the manager to be lent money by the investor or take out a loan. This would help crystallise

the significance of the investment and more closely intertwine the thought of the manager with the investor.

**Activist Investing**  There is a tension between the objectives of institutional and activist investors that will continue throughout 2019. The former endorse value for the long-term shareholder, in contrast to the latter angling for short-term value creation. As with all types of conflict, communication is key. For the companies that manage to open a form of dialogue between themselves and activist investors, this conflict will be more easily managed.

**Cybersecurity**  This will be an increasing concern for boards across all markets and regions as the prevalence of attacks increases. For more information, see Chapter 8.

**Human Capital**  There is a growing interest amongst institutional investors in human capital, evinced by the high-profile public debates surrounding gender pay, company culture, and a greater focus on the composition at the C-Suite level.

## THE RISE OF ESG

> *There is no wealth but life. Life, including all its powers of love, of joy, and of admiration. That country is the richest which nourishes the greatest numbers of noble and happy human beings; that man is richest, who, having perfected the functions of his own life to the utmost, has also the widest helpful influence, both personal, and by means of his possessions, over the lives of others.*
>
> – John Ruskin, Unto This Last

**Historical Context**  Environmental, social, and governance (ESG) policies are, in one form or another, as old as investing. Historically, religious principles governed how certain demographics invested their money. For example, in the eighteenth century, Quakers and Methodists had to follow guidelines when deciding what companies to invest in.[24] Using a form of ethics to influence the type of investments made is often characterised as 'responsible' investing. This was evidenced during the 1960s, where the concept of responsible investment was closely aligned to the civil rights movement. This helped elucidate the principle that there is a formal, rather than casual, link between the companies individuals invest in and the wider society they belong to. This only became clearer as investing became accessible to a wider portion of society. Indeed, the growth of the fund management industry from the 1970s through to the 1990s was marked by activist opportunism through encouraging shareholders to impact corporate behaviour. This culminated in the famous example of managers being put under pressure not to invest in companies working within the South African market. Environmental factors grew in prominence in the 1980s and more recently with incidents such as the BP oil spill. More recently, the financial crisis illustrated the patent interrelation between society and economics. Consequently, the role of the investor to promote good stewardship through endorsing ESG policies became increasingly popular.

**Drivers of Change?**  This is part of a broader realisation that asset managers themselves are able to become the drivers of change when they shout loud enough. Some managers, both active and passive, are starting to call on CEOs of their underlying portfolio companies to think about long-term growth plans and possibly ditching the quarterly reports. Similarly, in a letter to CEOs Larry Fink released in 2017, he stated 'index investors are the ultimate long-term investors – providing patient capital for companies to grow and prosper'. Unfortunately, however, because passive funds are – err – passive, they cannot pick and choose companies to invest in when their governance policies or remuneration policies do not align with their managers' ESG policies.

Although active managers have the facility to divest from a company if they disagree with its governance, it is much harder for passive fund managers. Managers such as BlackRock, Vanguard, and State Street have to hold on to their stocks in line with the index. Their level of influence is limited to softer forms of engagement despite the protesting by passive managers that they are very much about ESG, but it is clear that passive managers realise this is their Achilles heel. A few more scandals and the passive industry might suffer long-term damage from their lack of ability to influence ESG. This was very apparent in the wake of the Marjory Stoneman Douglas High School shooting in Florida. The divisive nature of the gun control debate polarises individuals across the globe. The morality of investing in companies such as American Outdoor Brands and Ruger leaves many investors uncomfortable. This has led to State Street to say they will be looking to engage with weapons manufacturers and their distributors over issues surrounding safety and the responsible use of their products. In contrast, Vanguard has indicated it will most likely be more effective in influencing gun manufacturers behind closed doors. It is likely that there will be differing approaches, with some being more successful than others, but an increase in interest in stewardship by fund houses has to be a good thing.

A key example of a pension provider embracing ESG is Norway's Kommunal Landspensjonskasse (KLP), which has total assets of around NOK 280 billion. It was originally created in 1949 to help manage the pensions of municipal employees. It now counts 337 municipal and county authorities, 31 health trusts, and 2300 public sector companies as clients. ESG has become a core tenant of its approach to investing – with detailed explanations of why it excludes certain investments made public. KLP also lists the companies it engages with along with its voting record.[25] Underlying this approach is a belief that transparency creates influence. Through making its decisions public it has more impact as a minority shareholder in certain investments. Moreover, by being open, there is an emphasis on disciplined decision-making, which they feel helps generate results.[26] Over time KLP has developed its position and has become a member of United Nations Principles for Responsible Investment (UNPRI). Through this process they have become a leader within the ESG field and have managed to provide consistent returns for their customers.

It is important, though, to remember that not every investor thinks alike. ESG is not a singular philosophy and it leaves room for divergence in thought. For one individual it may be unconscionable to invest in fossil fuel exploration but for another it may be that tobacco companies present a bigger moral dilemma. Presenting different portfolios for investors may be a solution that works in the interim, but activist investors will surely see far greater potential to influence corporate behaviour.

**The Cost of ESG** 'ESG-ifying' a portfolio comes at a cost, however, as the investment arm of Norges Bank (manager of in excess of USD 1 trillion AuM) found out in 2017. They detailed in a report that removing investments on ethical grounds, which included tobacco and weapons manufacturers, has meant they have missed out on an increase of 1.1% in their equity portfolio since 2006.[27] Whilst this may not sound like a lot in the grand scheme of things, this still equates to a USD 10 billion opportunity loss. Norges Bank has pointed out, however, that this was to some extent negated by the exclusion of mining companies on an environmental basis. Yet it is arguably more costly not to take into consideration ESG when investing. The importance of these policies has steadily grown over the last couple of decades[28] and the risk of damage can impact a company at many levels. First, there is a direct risk to the operations of a company, such as wage concerns (for example, the McDonald's wage dispute[29]) or carbon emissions (for example, the Volkswagen AG scandal[30]). Second, the supply chain can pose risks, as seen with child labour in the textiles industry.[31] Third, a product can pose a risk (for example, the Merk's Vioxx recall in 2004). This issue is further complicated by the lack of consistency in the reporting of ESG standards by companies. For investors this complicates the issue, and makes analysing the risk harder.

**So What Is 'ESG' and Why Is it Popular?** So what do I include within the definition of 'ESG policies'? They are often defined as policies with an approach to investing that aims to incorporate environmental, social, and governance factors in all investment decisions in order to enhance risk management and generate sustainable long-term returns. ESG policies were introduced to the PE industry by UNPRI, pushed by the UN's then Secretary General, Kofi Annan. The principles were developed by investors for investors and offered a menu of options to incorporate ESG issues into investment practice. As of January 2018, UNPRI had nearly 2000 signatories (including 369 asset owners, 1303 investment managers and 241 service providers) from over 50 countries, representing approximately USD 60 trillion[32] AuM.

Today, the unmitigated success of the UNPRI has meant that in a pleasant turn of events, it is no longer deemed sufficient in itself. The authors of UNPRI have achieved their primary purpose, to put ESG on the map. It is now time to push and develop it further.

It has been said that PE and other alternative fund strategies have passed through to their third stage of evolution. In its infancy, PE focused on financials; in its teenage years the emphasis shifted to operations; today is its middle age, the 'age of reason', and the focus is increasingly shifting towards environmentally and socially sustainable growth.

There are two factors driving this third stage of evolution. The first is non-exclusive to the asset management industry. The development of anti-corruption, health and safety, employee rights, and climate change legislation are changing the face of businesses around the world, and for the better. The second is investors. Investors care not only for strong returns, but also for responsible investing. Investors are in the driver's seat wishing to earn good returns for their stakeholders but more recently want to be seen to focus on more sustainable and responsible investments and push for their managers to be investing responsibly.

Asset managers have recognised that investing long-term in highly illiquid assets suits ESG to a tee. Managers seek the capital to invest in a company, and work alongside management to implement ESG programmes over a long period of time that can lead to tangible corporate value at exit. Currently, there is untapped value in ESG.

Today, ESG management is geared towards risks rather than towards opportunity. Investors and fund managers see ESG as a means of protecting rather than enhancing value. I hope that this will evolve further to value also.

**A Fund Investor's View of a Manager's ESG Policies** A fund investor that is preoccupied by ESG factors has various points along the investment process to make enquiries. At both the pre-investment and post-investment stage there is an opportunity for the investor to investigate the manager's proposed adherence to ESG policies, but also clarify their own expectations. On a broader level, there is a movement by investors to take into consideration ESG policies.

**Pre-Investment**   The investor is a passive partner. Once they have invested their funds, it is up to the manager to manage the fund. As such, the pre-investment stage is important for the investor to ascertain whether they should commit or opt out. It is at this stage that the investor should investigate whether the manager has incorporated ESG policies into its investment practices and operational processes. Further points for the investor to raise are: (i) their own expectations vis-à-vis the level of ESG compliance the manager should be adhering too; and (ii) the ESG disclosures the manager will make to them. It is important that the investor does this at the pre-investment stage as it will be harder for them to do it post-investment.

**Post-Investment**   Once an investment is made by an investor, their role is primarily passive. There is an element of engagement an investor can make, but their involvement would mostly be focussed on monitoring the manager's implementation of the ESG policies. This can be achieved through either a formal or an informal request for information. This will be centred around the actions the manager or portfolio companies have taken and its impact on ESG performance. If the manager has made defined commitments to an investor, then an investor should be able to ask for an update on the progress of these ESG-related goals. Indeed, where there is a risk to these goals or, a broader risk to ESG performance, the investor should actively encourage the manager to disclose this to the appropriate parties. In order to facilitate a manager's commitment to ESG performance, the investor may engage with the manager to promote greater transparency surrounding non-confidential information on ESG issues. Underlying this, the investor must respect the fact that they are a passive partner and that information may be commercially sensitive and therefore not appropriate to be shared.

**Current Investor Thought on ESG Policies**   The concept of investing responsibly as a niche practice is quickly becoming obsolete. The investment industry has seen how quickly the UNPRI have been signed up to. PricewaterhouseCoopers (PwC)[33] suggests that this is just one of many factors that point to the industry as a whole becoming far more focussed on ESG issues. In fact, they submit that they are becoming part of mainstream thought. This is based on the principle that through meeting ESG standards companies will perform better and thus portfolio returns will be protected and enhanced. ESG performance and how fund managers drive this will become a useful metric for many investors, who in general believe that value is added by adhering to these policies. Indeed, it is perfectly plausible that investors will avoid certain industries where fund managers do not take into consideration ESG, or perform badly compared to their competitors.

**ESG Policies of Underlying Companies Under the Microscope**   A recent study by BlackRock, which analysed the disclosures of 4000 listed companies worldwide, found that companies that implement ESG policies are more likely to be sued or face regulatory action.[34] Undoubtedly, this is surprising as common thought dictates that paying close attention to ESG will lower overall portfolio risk. Moreover, it should (in principle) lower the chance of damaging incidents, which, if made public, could cause serious reputational damage to the portfolio company, the fund that owns it, and the fund's own investors. This should mean less volatile returns for the manager, portfolio company, and investor alike. In pursuit of this goal, investors have invested billions of dollars into actively managed mutual funds and passive funds that factor ESG into their strategy. Yet it would be alarming to these investors if the companies they have invested in were more likely to be investigated, sued, and prosecuted. With average annual returns for companies reporting controversies at 0.3%, the year the controversies happened, compared with 3.2% for companies unaffected, the concern for investors is obvious.[35] Despite this, the results of BlackRock's study does not mean that ESG policies lead to ESG risks. They submit that what is needed is a better measurement of the link between a company's actions and social outcomes. This information would place investors in a better position to avoid choosing companies susceptible to controversies than if they were to use just ESG metrics in making a decision. Perhaps what it is needed is greater scrutiny of ESG policies and the governance scores that underlie the investment process of managers.

**ESG Policies Increasing Returns on Exit**   The main question investors would typically have when looking to incorporate ESG criteria into their investing process is whether there is a premium to pay for doing so. There is a range of views when considering a response to this question:

1. Implementing an investment thesis based on non-financial criteria such as ESG policies limits the pool of options one can choose. This consequently reduces the diversification of any portfolio ultimately hindering efficiency and impacting the rate of return and heightening risk.
2. Responsible investing in the guise of using ESG policies as a metric of ethical investing was accepted by certain investors who knew full well they would not receive expected market rate financial returns.
3. Investors, academics, universities, and others are now producing empirical evidence that demonstrates financial return is not hindered by taking ESG issues into account. Moreover, research shows that companies who implement ESG policies and adhere to them have a better financial performance and benefit from a lower cost of capital.
4. Some suggest that as investors use ESG criteria to value the price of stock, the subsequent gains will be priced in.
5. One way to prevent this is through active ownership, by engaging with the companies you have invested in to outperform their ESG criteria, this could generate better returns through positive ESG developments.

The rising popularity in using ESG as a metric for making a good or bad investment decision indicates that more and more people are seeing the second, fourth, and fifth school of thought above as accurate. This raises an important second question – are companies performing better (thus rewarding investors more) because they are following their ESG criteria, or are they following their ESG criteria because they are performing better? One study, which examined 180 companies in the US, suggests that the former is correct.[36] They demonstrate that the returns are higher to the tune of 2.3–4.8% per annum for sustainable companies in comparison to their non-sustainable counterparts. Therefore, it is submitted that ESG criteria should not harm company performance and the financial returns for investors. Appraising a company on the basis of their ESG performance and benefiting from their long-term investment in these policies would therefore make this metric ideal for PE firms.

Looking closer it is also possible to demonstrate how ESG practices can have an impact on Vol at a company, industry, and market level. Importantly, ESG practices will impact each of these three things differently. It would be an error to assume that all car manufacturers react the same to ESG policies or that the oil industry as a whole will be affected similarly by different ESG policies. The paper *ESG factors and risk-adjusted performance: a new quantitative model* argues cogently that the orthodox school of thought concerning risk and return is undermined by a mathematical analysis of the impact of ESG factors. From their research, they conclude that companies that incorporate ESG policies demonstrate less Vol then their contemporaries in the same industry.

**Private Equity**   As illustrated above, ESG policies have the potential, when complied with, to increase the performance of a company, and therefore the financial return for the investor. To give context, these policies are typically implemented across a longer time frame. Thus, for a PE firm looking to exit in five to seven years, continual adherence to ESG policies would make a company an attractive target. A study has found that PE firms use ESG as a core strategy to manufacture value.[37] Moreover, this is occurring at each stage of the investment cycle and being enforced from the board level. This implies that PE firms are looking to create value through ESG and are not just using it to mitigate risk through compliance.[38]

**ESG Policies and Re-Upping**   As institutional investors (and their own stakeholders) become more sophisticated in their understanding of ESG, they have started to pressure managers to become more serious and systematic in their approach to ESG. Some investors say that ESG is now a significant enough factor that they will often decline to re-up with a manager if it cannot demonstrate real improvements in its portfolio's track record on ESG.

An early booster of ESG-focused investing, APG Asset Management (APG), which manages the giant Dutch pension fund ABP, has been one of the first major investors to adopt this approach to the funds it evaluates. APG now requires managers to evidence their green credentials before deciding whether to reinvest with them. Managers with a strong ESG track record may soon find themselves speaking to a larger, more receptive, and loyal audience of investors.

**Other Examples of ESG Stress**   Despite growing pressure from the student and academic body, Cambridge University has decided not to divest from oil and gas. Its GBP 6.2 billion endowment fund was being lobbied by shadow chancellor John McDonnell along with 15 other Members of Parliament and a large percentage of the academic community to divest from these sources over the next three years. Calls for university endowments and other large institutional investors to put pressure on their portfolio companies (or even divest) over environmental issues has increased since the Paris Agreement in 2015. Yet, often with a large pension deficit, restricted government funding, and uncertainty surrounding the levels of funding that will be made available post-Brexit, there are legitimate concerns for its investors. What this highlights is the genuinely difficult ethical decisions that are created through investing. It is perfectly valid to call out a university that publishes a sizeable amount of research on the harm oil and gas companies do to the environment and then decides to invest in them. However, by divesting, that same university may jeopardise its ability to publish that research in the first place, as they need to generate returns to fund their research.

The embarrassment factor is not unique to universities, however. The Church of England was embroiled in their own scandal when it was revealed their fund had invested (indirectly) in payday loans company Wonga. Without labouring the point, the ignominy that must have been felt by the church leadership would have been considerable. What was particularly embarrassing was that the Archbishop of Canterbury (the principle leader of the Church of England),

Justin Welby, had publicly denounced Wonga's practices (and in particular, the interest rates they charged) before it was revealed that the Church Commissioners had indirectly invested in Wonga via their VC portfolio. The Church of England was also later revealed to hold investments in Amazon, after the Archbishop had criticised the company's tax avoidance practices and condemned the use of zero-hour contracts as 'the reincarnation of an ancient evil'.[39]

Perhaps one of the saddest trends of recent years has been the increasing prevalence of school shootings in America. Although it is unlikely that we will see any major reform soon, it does look like there is a change in attitude across the US. This has caused a variety of prominent asset managers to come out and denounce gun manufacturers for not increasing their efforts to prevent the most destructive types of weapon falling into the wrong hands. As investors become increasingly aware of the types of company they have a stake in, so to have managers become aware of their potential reaction. This has led to investors putting pressure on managers to sell the underlying portfolio companies that they feel contradict their personal ethical code. After the shooting at Parkland Florida, investors such as Blackrock, Bank of America, State Street, and others decided to release statements saying they will do more to engage with the companies they have invested in. This is, however, not the first time this issue has been raised at either the manager or investor level. Prior to the shocking events at Parkland, Vista Outdoor faced a shareholder proposal requesting them to report on whether they had complied with the Sandy Hook Principles (20 measures designed to prevent gun violence). This proposal did not gain much momentum because investors that have an ethical problem with gun manufacturers are unlikely to invest in them in the first place. The other main source of intervention will be to the vendors of these weapons. Walmart has come under significant pressure to restrict the sale of these weapons and has subsequently decided to sell them only to persons over the age of 21. Moreover, numerous companies that have an affiliation with the National Rifle Association have decided to cut ties in order to prevent a social media and investor backlash (for example, Hertz, MetLife, Symantec, and Delta Airlines). This is part of the growing trend of companies and institutional investors reacting to the retail market feeling. This movement is what is influencing large asset managers to be more proactive with their portfolio company management.

Another instance where portfolio companies are coming under more pressure is the backlash from environmental damage. Also environmental damage in a portfolio company can lead to liability to the manager and its LPs as a statutory offence in certain jurisdictions.

**Some ESG Conclusions** The role of ESG as a siloed concept, will, it is submitted, not be the future. The reality is that in today's world investors are concerned with what their money is being used for. As these principles are incorporated more regularly into companies' practices, they will become further engrained in the investors' psyches. This is a cyclical process, as investors' preoccupation with ESG reinforces the motivations for companies to incorporate them into their practices. This will, it is argued, become the accepted norm for how business is done. Importantly, the arc of progress in modern business is steeper than ever before. It is expected that this acceptance of ESG criteria as standard practice will happen at a particularly fast rate. Undoubtedly, this is a good thing for companies, investors, and wider society. With this in mind, in 2019 MJ Hudson acquired an ESG and investment impact reporting and consultancy business based in Amsterdam, that we will extend across other investment markets and geographies.

## IMPACT FUNDS

Peter Unger begins his book *Living High and Letting Die* with Oxfam's address. It is estimated that for every three dollars sent to Oxfam, a life can be saved. Were an individual to give USD

100, they would save 33 lives. Compare this to the fact that the richest nine billionaires in Silicon Valley are wealthier than the poorest 2 billion people and you can perhaps start to understand the scale of global inequality. But it is impossible to convey the visceral disparity in wealth and opportunities by just using statistics. However, this was not what Unger was attempting to do. Nor was he trying to shame or guilt individuals into donating money. Or indeed, apportion responsibility or hold people accountable. The point was that there is a moral dilemma in the pursuit of money. It is a truism that there will always be an individual who is less fortunate than you. Thus, the pursuit of individual financial gain, without acknowledging that others may be in more need than you, contains an inherent philosophical quandary.

This raises a second question – to what extent should finance, or more generally the commercial world, be responsible for those that are impacted by it? Or in other words, should finance be used for good? If we accept that in every financial transaction made there is a moral choice then perhaps good ethics should trump reward. This underlies the original premise of the 'impact fund'. Investors were, and still are, willing to engage with the morality underlying the financial world and accept a lower than market return in the pursuit of a higher moral good. What Unger observed so correctly is this innate transactional element.

**What Is an Impact Fund?** Impact funds are raised with the intent to generate and measure both a social and a financial return. It should be distinguished from socially responsible investing, which typically aims to avoid harmful consequences, rather than to foster a positive outcome. A fund may invest in a wide range of activities, or may specialise, but typical investments are in housing, rural water supplies, maternal health, primary education, and financial services. The expected financial return will depend at first glance on the investor base. Some may want investments which outperform traditional investment classes, others may allow for a reduced return as the price to pay for the social impact. Most funds instead aim to compete with the returns typically offered by other classes by looking at whether the venture will have a positive social impact first, and then looking at the commercial viability second.

**The Rewards of Social Impact Funds** Underlying the core purpose of impact funds is an outcome versus purpose approach. This question has been part of western philosophy for centuries and drills down to what the objective of impact investing is. Whether the outcome matters more than the purpose depends on the impact fund, but it can be a useful metric to examine the motivation behind a fund's philanthropy. For example, it is submitted that where a fund aims for below market returns and is investing in healthcare it may be reasonable to suggest that their focus is on purpose rather than outcome. In contrast, a PE firm that wants market-level returns and wishes to exit quickly may be more concerned with outcomes. The dynamic between outcome and purpose is not binary and many impact funds operate between the lines. Indeed, it is perfectly possible for a fund to consider themselves to be entirely outcome-driven, but in reality have a strong purposeful theme to their work. Equally, people who aim to fulfil a social goal can end up making a considerable amount of money. This is not to say that impact investing is an empty term, rather, that its use is flexible and in parts ill-defined.

The rewards of social impact investing are often divided into those which are financial and those which are social. There need not be a trade-off between the two if the investment is right, but sometimes the reduction of the financial reward can be offset by the social reward. What this takes is the kind of reporting that quantifies the social returns and allows for the best comparison with financial returns by expressing those returns with reference to cash. Such a subjective valuation could of course lead to distortions in the values given, especially so where individual groups use their own standards. If there is an industry-wide standard or standards (such as that provided by Global Impact Investing Network, or GIIN), there is both a greater pool of contributors to those standards (reducing the tendency towards bias) and a clearer system for comparing returns.

Most investors still seek reasonable rates of return versus traditional investments such as bonds or equities, within the range of 5–10% per annum as opposed to the higher returns offered by hedge funds and PE. Some investors will have restrictions on the minimum amount of returns to be sought, which may price them out of the social impact market. This would be true of pension funds, where a duty of the trustees is to seek the best return for the beneficiaries. The GIIN stated in its latest report that in 2015 USD 15.2 billion had been committed by 157 respondents to 7551 impact investments, who planned to increase their capital commitment by 16% in 2016. In their study, a sample of 156 of their members managed approximately USD 77.4 billion of assets. Further, it was confirmed that the vast majority of respondents reported that their investments have performed either in line with or exceeded both impact and financial expectations. The current financial, environmental, and political climate underscores the necessity for impact investing. In this time of economic Vol it is the vulnerable that are likely to suffer the most. Investing to effect social change could be a useful tool in combating society's fundamental challenges.

The use of auditing methods such as the GIIN's metric will help drive up investor confidence in the social impact investment market. It is important to develop a stable and consistent way of comparing the social return with the financial one. This in part may justify a lower rate of return if it can be said that the social benefit created was equivalent to (for example) a return of 30% in cash. For some charitable foundations that are investing in the social impact market, this is the key return. Some may look for a minimal financial return if it increases the social return, depending in part on the wealth and background of its backers (such as the Rockefeller Foundation or the Bill & Melinda Gates Foundation that want to 'give it away').

At the heart of what an impact fund looks like is its concern with environmental and social improvement. These areas are often cited by organisations in their approach to corporate social responsibility (CSR), but the two should not be conflated. A common critique levelled at CSR is that it is often compartmentalised within a business. In this sense, it is there to offset the outcome-based motivations rather than guide the actions of a particular company. A cynic would argue that CSR attempts to make profit-maximising business plans more palatable for the shareholder. At a normative level, the difference between the two is that impact investing relies on the business making decisions based on purpose which can be measured. Capital is the biproduct, with the important metric being the impact made, not the other way around. From this perspective, a vanilla impact fund must consider the societal or environmental improvement at every stage of the investment process, rather than an organisation thinking post hoc that they should mitigate their commercial strategy with some social investment.

**The Risks of Social Impact Funds**   The risks involved in social impact investing are not too dissimilar from existing classes of investment. They are still influenced by factors such as sector, location, and the stage in which the investment is made, but there are elements that increase the risk. A lot of the activities backed by social investing take place in less economically developed countries, and as such should be treated as similar to high-yield emerging market investments (in terms of risk profile, but not necessarily return). The risks involved can be legal, as the regulatory infrastructure may not be in place to seek redress and ensure the appropriate channelling of investment. It may also impede any necessary construction or other works. Other typical risks are company risk, currency risk, and other financial risks. Not all social impact investing takes place in such places, though. There are projects that deal with urban infrastructure and a wide range of voluntary sector organisations in more developed nations, although the risks will be reduced in scope and will still merit consideration. It should also be noted that given the current economic climate, many more developed countries are at risk of becoming poor targets for investment. This is especially clear for sovereign debt, which is a factor to consider, as many impact investments are made in conjunction with state funding or agencies. There are also reputational risks involved in social impact investing. There are critics who suggest that PE investment in otherwise charitable ventures leads to the risk of exploitation and 'mission drift', especially as the target groups are often the impoverished and potentially less well-educated.

The terminology and the goals set are important, too. There is a difference between 'output' and 'outcomes'. The output of the investment is more easily quantified – the number of development loans provided to farmers, for example. The outcome is less easy to quantify, and requires precise definition.

**What Do Impact Funds Look Like?** There is a common misconception that impact funds are not-for-profit foundations whose performance is hard to measure. Not all impact funds are the same, and there are a range of participants in social impact investment. These include development finance institutions (DFIs), private foundations, large-scale financial institutions, private wealth managers, commercial bankers, pension fund managers, and companies. There is a nascent field of regulatory and oversight committees, such as GIIN, established by JP Morgan; the Rockefeller Foundation; and the US Agency for International Development. Another landmark body of principles is the UNPRI, which since its launch in 2006 has seen over 1000 asset owners and investment managers become signatories to it.

A clear example of the definitional scope of the impact investing space is how 'impact' means something completely different for one manager in comparison to another. Indeed, examples range from passive funds being put under pressure to divest from gun manufacturers, or PE groups attempting to partner with social change entrepreneurs. There are also differing financial goals within the impact investing space. Some funds operate as not-for-profit and target below market returns on their investments, whereas others place financial performance at the core of what they do. Indeed, according to GIIN, 66% of the respondents to their most recent survey target risk-adjusted, market rate returns. Moreover, although 34% target below-market returns, 18% of that figure aim to target closer to the market rate. This indicates that there is a growing realisation that financial performance does not have to be negated in the name of social good. Perhaps the unifying thread amongst all funds, however, is an intention to make a positive impact. Indeed, the growth in investment is marked by the variety of causes being addressed.

Bamboo Capital, a fund that is trying to solve low-income individuals' biggest problems, has invested in a company called BBOXX.[40] BBOXX's business model is to install solar panels in remote parts of Asia and Africa, which can be financed through pay-as-you-go systems. This enables members of rural communities to gain access to clean energy. This will lay the foundation for all the associated benefits that come with a reliable source of electricity (internet access, mobile connectivity, and learning opportunities).

The Tony Elumelu Foundation[41] has a clear objective focussed on helping the private sector in Africa develop and become more competitive. This will, it is submitted by the foundation, impact the lives of the poorest and most vulnerable on that continent through the economic prosperity generated. In a similar vein, Investors' Circle hopes to foster business growth in the US to provide socially responsible and impactful companies the investment and help they need to succeed. Likewise, General Electric has created an accelerator to promote environmental solutions with five businesses in Africa.

Bridges Fund Management was founded by Sir Ronald Cohen (also founder of what is now called Apax Partners) nearly 20 years ago. Bridges was established as a very early UK pioneer in impact. There was some initial discussions on making financial (to investors) or impact or ESG type value returns. However, I for one was surprised they managed to achieve both a financial return and achieve significant impact objectives.

These examples are indicative of the variety of organisation types engaging with impact investing. What is particularly exciting is the combination of experience, innovation, and social consciousness that is being harnessed to address some of the world's biggest problems.

**How Do You Measure an Impact Fund?**  Most investors will be familiar with the usual metrics of business performance, with most of the analysis driven by the financial performance of the company in question. The obvious question when considering impact investing is how you can analyse a business, which supposedly does not focus on the bottom line. This perspective has hopefully, in part, been debunked by the discussion in this chapter already. However, it must be acknowledged that impact investing is designed primarily to engage with fundamental problems, which is not the same as stating they discard the economic logic of their business plan. There are, according to the Stanford School of Social Innovation,[42] three metrics which should be incorporated to assess the success of an impact investing fund.

First, management information systems can be useful in assessing the data derived from their portfolios. This includes other data aggregators, which can be utilised by fund managers in drawing conclusions from their fund activities. Second, impact ratings to provide comparisons for owners and managers to assess performance. Third, in keeping with the second point there should be standardised definitions of impact performance measures to allow benchmarking. To provide these three metrics, the review recommends the use of IRIS, PULSE, and the Global Impact Investment Ratings System (GIIRS) to give managers and owners the information they need to assess impact. They argue that this will improve efficiency and provide integrity to the assessment process. This will, they submit, enable the impact investing space to mature and develop the reputation needed for continual investment.

The Investors' Circle suggests the use of company-specific metrics will enable a more real-istic measurement. For example, they suggest that in the case of an environmentally focussed company, the metric could be how many pounds of rubbish are removed from the target area. This would give an indication of the operational efficiency of that project and enable some form of comparison and benchmarking. Through quantifying the success of their compa-nies, the Investors' Circle can report on the impact their investments have made. This in turn allows them to invest in the most suitable companies and further promote environmental and social goals.

Prophecy Impact Investments concurs with the Investors' Circle by stating that each com-pany will most likely use different metrics when determining impact. They also raise an impor-tant issue, which is the value derived by the investor in the process. Sometimes social good cannot be measured, but the investor's feeling about the impact can be a useful indication of how successful the project was.

The variance in different metrics, how they are implemented and how they demonstrate value is a consequence of the multifaceted nature of impact investing. What is crucial is that the social impact can be illustrated in some manner – whatever that is. For investors this may need to be in hard data, but for others it could be just the way they feel about how the project has helped. As indicated above, the type of investor is as varied as the challenges being tackled. What is exciting is that so many different groups, people, and businesses want to address these issues.

**What Does the Impact Investing Market Look Like?** The Markets and Markers research report[43] presents a comprehensive outline of the global impact investing market and indicates, amongst others, three key insights. First, the low-cost and affordable housing sector will make up the largest segment of the impact investing market. This will be seen in parts of Asia Pacific, Latin America, and Africa. This is driven by a huge demand for affordable housing solutions and an understanding that there is a significant tangible impact when capital is invested in this space. Second, until at least 2020, India will continue to be invested in heavily. As an emerging economy with inadequate government spending, considerable growth and a significant wealth gap, India remains a clear opportunity for impact investment. Third, access to clean energy will grow rapidly as an investment space. There is a large support base from which these technological solutions will be supported.

**What Factors Are Affecting the Market?** Despite the growth in the impact market, there remains significant challenges. Namely, whether the appropriate level of capital will be invested across the range of possible opportunities. An oft-cited criticism is that it requires a significant inflow of money to make a business profitable. Although many actors within this space do wish to invest, many are not prepared to invest at the same rate as seen in the wider commercial world. Underlying this is perhaps a perception that there is a lack of high-quality investment opportunities with a track record of success. This is in part due to a preconceived notion about what the impact investing space offers but also the lack of hard evidence showing the impact these projects make. A greater effort to create demonstrable evidence to investors of the strengths of an opportunity is necessary for impact funds going forward.

Another key concern for some investors is the lack of sophistication within the market. This manifests in four main areas. First, the lack of a common understanding about the differentiation within the impact investing market. Second, general practice of impact funds varies wildly in terms of proficiency. Third, the lack of a large talent pool to draw professionals from (a sign of an unsophisticated market). Fourth, the lack of creative deal and fund structures which would satisfy the commercial needs of investors. This combination of issues goes to the heart of impact investors' concern: that the market is not yet mature enough for some of them.

These issues sit on top of more general problems investors see with the concept of impact investing and the market. The foremost being the economic logic behind impact investing. Monetising solutions which solve the needs of the disadvantaged is incredibly tricky and therefore few and far between.[44] In order to do this, a significant amount of subsidisation is required, which may never lead to commercial success. The risk associated with investing in these ventures, unless accepted as the price of solving fundamental problems, is too great for some investors. This aversion is found in all forms of investing and is a by-product of a preoccupation with the downside risk and negativity bias many people have.

**Some Impact Conclusions** Impact, like ESG, means different things to different people. Impact, though, is way behind ESG in terms of understanding, debate, and investment dollars. Part of the problem is variance in definition. Also, much of the impact is not, in the end, felt due to local corruption (like charity investing), inefficiency, or too much enthusiasm being thrown at the wrong places or concepts. Perhaps at some point, impact will not need explaining, as it will become integral. I hope so.

## SOME CONCLUSIONS

ESG policies do not necessarily result in lower returns. It is likely that they will be an accepted norm going forward – so all businesses will incorporate them and investors will expect managers to only choose companies which employ them. This could mean that the concept of ESG as a siloed concept will become obsolete. The role of passive managers in influencing the underlying companies to promote ESG issues will hopefully grow as corporate stewardship becomes more important.

NEDs will remain as an attractive role, but will come under greater scrutiny. This is only natural as they continue to take on more and more chairs.

Governance is a central theme for the commercial world in general and any business will be keeping it central to their plans going forward. Globally, it is becoming more commonplace to question archaic practices. This is good not only for companies, but also society at large. However, governance cannot just become a derogatory stick to beat your enemies with. Greater sophistication and understanding is required. The key to good governance in my mind is time, skills, and reasonableness – only do things or get involved if you have all three.

## ENDNOTES

1. Butler, J. (2012) FT Guide to Wealth Management. Harlow, England; New York: Pearson.
2. https://www.ft.com/content/dd72c4b4-faca-11e7-9b32-d7d59aace167
3. www.bis.org/bcbs/basel3.htm
4. www.ibm.com/support/knowledgecenter/en/SSN364_8.8.0/com.ibm.ima.tut/tut/bas_imp/bas3_sum.html
5. www.bbc.co.uk/news/business-46614109
6. www.europarl.europa.eu/news/en/press-room/20180129IPR96112/public-to-get-access-to-information-on-beneficial-owners-of-firms-in-eu
7. www.gov.im/categories/business-and-industries/companies-registry/beneficial-ownership/
8. www.mondaq.com/ireland/x/564524/Fund+Management+REITs/The+Beneficial+Ownership+Regulations+2016+Implications+for+Funds
9. http://www.harneysfid.com/news/bvi-beneficial-ownership-regime---frequently-asked-questions
10. www.harneys.com/insights/cayman-islands-proposes-introduction-of-beneficial-ownership-registers/
11. www.jdsupra.com/legalnews/cayman-islands-requires-companies-to-53286/
12. www.collascrill.com/news/updates/the-clock-is-ticking-on-caymans-beneficial-ownership-regime-are-you-compliant/
13. www.bna.com/insight-obligations-belgiums-n57982093508/
14. www.grantthornton.com.mt/service/tax-and-regulatory/company-formation/the-beneficial-ownership-register/
15. www.vanguard.co.uk/documents/adv/literature/investment-committees-best-practice.pdf
16. https://corpgov.law.harvard.edu/2017/12/29/global-and-regional-trends-in-corporate-governance-for-2018/

17. www.sodexousa.com/home/media/news-releases/newsListArea/news-releases/gender-balance.html
18. www.tandfonline.com/doi/abs/10.1080/0958519021000029108
19. www.sciencedirect.com/science/article/abs/pii/S014829631730053X
20. www.theguardian.com/business/2018/may/31/pitiful-views-on-women-in-boardrooms-permeate-ftse-firms
21. https://goizueta.emory.edu/faculty/cai/documents/ECAI_Alignment.pdf
22. MJH Report.
23. https://goizueta.emory.edu/faculty/cai/documents/ECAI_Alignment.pdf
24. http://schroders.com/en/insights/global-investor-study/a-short-history-of-responsible-investing-300-0001/
25. www.ipe.com/pensions/country-reports/nordic-region/norway-ahead-of-its-time/10019227.article
26. www.ipe.com/pensions/country-reports/nordic-region/norway-ahead-of-its-time/10019227.article
27. www.ipe.com/news/esg/ethical-exclusions-dented-nbim-equity-return-by-11-since-2006/10018121.article
28. www2.deloitte.com/insights/us/en/deloitte-review/issue-12/finding-the-value-in-environmental-social-and-governance-performance.html
29. www.irmagazine.com/esg/media-banned-mcdonalds-agm
30. https://yoursri.com/media/msci-company-sample-controversies
31. http://www.robecosam.com/images/esg-risks-and-opportunities-the-textile-sector-2016-10.pdf
32. www.unpri.org/directory/
33. www.pwc.com/gx/en/services/sustainability/publications/responsible-investment.html
34. www.ft.com/content/08a3420e-05bf-11e8-9650-9c0ad2d7c5b5
35. www.ft.com/content/08a3420e-05bf-11e8-9650-9c0ad2d7c5b5
36. Eccles et al. (2014). www.hbs.edu/faculty/Publication%20Files/SSRN-id1964011_6791edac-7daa-4603-a220-4a0c6c7a3f7a.pdf
37. Cornelli, F., Ioannou, I., and Zhang, T. (2015) 'ESG moving out of the Compliance Room and into the Heart of the Investment Process'. ADVEQ Applied Research Series. The Coller Institute of Private Equity, London Business School.
38. https://spilplatform.com/wp-content/uploads/sites/329/2017/02/SPIL-The-Financial-Return-of-Responsible-Investing.pdf
39. https://news.sky.com/story/justin-welby-criticised-over-church-of-england-amazon-investment-and-zero-hour-contracts-11497125
40. www.forbes.com/sites/jaycoengilbert/2017/10/09/putting-the-impact-in-impact-investing-28-funds-building-a-credible-transparent-marketplace/#47b5cb9b3e5f
41. https://bthechange.com/15-companies-making-a-difference-with-impact-investing-9f3752774cc7
42. https://ssir.org/articles/entry/impact_investings_three_measurement_tools
43. www.marketsandmarkets.com/Market-Reports/impact-investing-market-265004523.html
44. https://ssir.org/articles/entry/the_trouble_with_impact_investing_part_1

# CHAPTER 5

# Investment Strategies

*An investment in knowledge pays the best interest.*

– Benjamin Franklin

*Gambling has really brought our family together. We had to move to a smaller house.*

– Tommy Cooper, UK magician and comedian

This chapter will examine the different types of investment strategies utilised by fund managers.

Increasingly, asset managers are becoming either specialised boutique managers of a single asset class or jumbo multi-asset managers. The niche manager strategies can range from healthcare properties such as doctors' surgeries or care homes, to peer-to-peer (P2P) lending. On the other hand, the jumbo multi-asset manager will manage investments in just about anything – from shares and bonds to other funds (known as a fund of funds).

We have also seen the rise of the listed (mostly US) manager, using its public status as an opportunity to spread across asset classes, often citing the 'library' and knowledge view of multi-asset investing.

## PUBLIC EQUITIES

Equity investment is the classic form of investment, and very much a 'mainstream' asset class.

Shares which are traded on the various stock exchanges across the world are the headline figures for day-to-day economic news reporting and this is where many first thoughts about investing stray. The common view on equity investment is to 'pick a winner' – investing in the shares of a company in the expectation that they will increase in value over time. This is a fairly simplistic approach to investing and inevitably leads to as much success as failure as share prices rise and dip due to a myriad of economic factors (many of which do not concern the direct performance of the portfolio shares). Some commentators suggest diversification needs at least 30 stocks. However, diversification will not help you when the market craters. Apparently, shorting stock does help you during market corrections, save that I have never really understood why long/short funds also seem to suffer during downwards market corrections.

The big short can make you a winner once in a career – the problem is that lightening rarely strikes twice and many big shorters then think they are gods and can go on a big losing streak.

The following section will look at the different types of pure equity strategies that are prevalent in the markets today. First, however, is a brief description of the two main types of analysis that are employed in assessing the worth of public equities.

## Types of Analysis

Broadly, there are two types of analysis that are used to examine equities – fundamental and quantitative.

**Fundamental**   Fundamental analysis looks to find the intrinsic value of an equity. It achieves this by looking at the financial, operational, and cultural structure of the company in an attempt to assess what the equity is really worth. Fundamental analysis of equities will emphasise looking at a company's financials, including the balance sheet, cash flow statement, and income statement. Moreover, a thorough analysis of the corporate structure, business objective, and how it performs within its sector, market, and geographical area is conducted. Comparisons are drawn to its competitors and an in-depth look at its actions is imperative to assessing its intrinsic worth. Through looking at the material qualities of a company, a fundamental analyst is trying to see whether the company they are analysing has a competitive edge which is not represented in its market valuation. Ostensibly, the fundamental approach aims to look at the qualitative rather than the quantitative.

**Quantitative**   Quantitative analysis is less associated with the intangible fundamentals that are used to get a feel of a company's intrinsic worth. Rather, a quantitative approach aims to look at the numbers. Often using vast amounts of data (see Chapter 8 on technology) quantitative analysts aim to identify patterns which they can exploit using pre-set algorithms. These algorithms can be based around earnings forecast, unexpected changes in price, and market shifts. Although the goal is to make money, quantitative analysis can also be employed to reduce risk. By looking at patterns or indicators in the market, analysts using this method can attempt to avoid pitfalls that others may fall foul of. Perhaps seen as a less romantic approach to investing, quantitative analysis is premised on the hard numbers in front of you. It removes the emotion from investing and limits the danger of an anxious investor. However, as discussed in Chapter 7, the use of historical data can result in algorithms making decisions based on false presumptions.

## Core Strategies for Investing in Equities

**Value Investing**   Value investing is based on the simple premise that certain stocks are under-valued by the market. It does not accept the efficient market hypothesis. One of the reasons it can be successful is that investors over- or under-react to good or bad news. This in turn causes the price of equities to rise and fall, which value investors argue does not correspond with the underlying value of the company. Thus, there is an opportunity for an investor to buy a security at a reduced rate and then sell it later once the market has valued it properly. As such, value investors heavily rely on the aforementioned fundamental analysis of companies. Their mantra is to buy the company and not the stock. The market places an emphasis on trendy companies (for example, Facebook, Amazon, Apple, Netflix, Alphabet's Google – or

FAANGS) and undervalues less glamorous companies. The position that an investor should put themselves in is as a business investor. Having this mindset allows value investors to see whether their view of the company itself, rather than the market perspective, is correct.

Typically, value investors are not interested in a small reduction in price. Rather, they look for a massive disparity in their valuation and the market's. This allows room for error but also the possibility of greater returns. As this method has become more and more popular, value investors have had to look further and further afield to find companies that present excellent investment opportunities. Partly, this is because of the wealth of public data available on companies listed in the major markets. In less well covered regions, there is a greater chance that a company has gone under the radar, with the forensic-like fundamental analysis offering richer rewards.

**Growth Investing**  This strategy's aim is to invest in equities whose value will grow faster than the average rate found in its industry or market. This means that, unlike value investing, growth investing permits buying equities that are overvalued. As long as the intrinsic value ultimately exceeds the market value at which they were bought at – it would be seen as a good investment. Thus, companies which are part of growing industries or offering new technologies are particularly popular with growth investors. The aim is for capital appreciation, rather than dividends, so established companies that have existed for a long time are less likely to appeal to growth investors.

Often, comparisons are used as a key metric to decide whether a company will grow. Through comparing the company in relation to its own past performance, competitors, and the wider industry an investor can interpret how successful it will be in the future. Other key flags to look out for are forward earnings growth, profit margins, historical earnings growth, and the return on equity. Strong performance in any of these categories is a good signal that the market valuation will be surpassed by its intrinsic value in the future.

**Momentum Investing**  Momentum investing is the strategy of investing in equities or other securities which have recently shown strong increases in their price (or some other measures, such as their earnings). This strategy relies on closely monitoring recent movement in the markets and picking those investments which have outperformed.

The main risk inherent in this strategy is fairly plain to see: market risk. This form of analysis entails following the market very closely and consequently if the market takes a dip then momentum investments will follow it down. In fact it will often be those securities which have grown the most recently which stand to lose the most. For example, a pure momentum strategy would have led an investor to be heavily overweight in tech stocks when the dot-com bubble burst, as those stocks had the most momentum leading up to the crash. However, momentum analysis is often combined with other strategies and forms of analysis to mitigate this risk.

**GARP Investing**  Growth at a reasonable price, or 'GARP', is a hybrid model between value and growth investing. The aim is to find equities that have a combination of both the qualities value and growth investors look for. The aim is not to split a fund evenly between value and growth stocks. This means that they look at the present value of the company to see if it is undervalued and assess whether it has good growth potential too. This requires them to look at the price/earnings, price to book, and the price/earnings to growth ratios. On top of this, GARP investors look at the fundamentals of the company and try to incorporate other metrics that growth and value investors use. This mixed approach does have an impact on the results a GARP investor will see. For example, when the markets are doing particularly well this strategy won't reach the heights found in a purely growth strategy. But, conversely, when the market does badly a GARP approach will not see the same level of suffering that a growth investor would. Although this sounds appealing it is a highly complicated approach and requires significant skill and care to get right. There is a danger that without appropriate skill an investor could be caught between two stools.

**Income Investing** The premise behind income investing is to pick stocks that provide a good dividend yield. Often looking at established companies that are no longer growing but producing strong financial results, this form of investing requires strong analysis. It is more than just looking at what equities provide the best dividends; it is just as important to look at how long the company can keep doing this. Perhaps maligned as less interesting than other forms of investing, this strategy can provide steady returns that over time represent sound financial decisions. Indeed, although it may seem less volatile then choosing growth or value stocks the reality is that the same underlying factors that present financial risks still apply. The macro events that influence equities generally will still apply and it is important to bear this in mind when picking any equity.

The above strategies, based on fundamental and quantitative analysis are the predominant strategies focusing on pure equity investment. There are, however, other broader approaches that are discussed in the following section.

## Other Strategies

**Long/Short** Some more advanced strategies towards equity investment have been adopted more commonly in the world of hedge funds. A primary example is that of long/short equities. The core approach is to buy long equities which are expected by the investment manager to increase in value and to sell short equities which are expected to decrease in value. When buying long, the investor (or manager) will agree a derivative contract (see later in this chapter for more detail on derivatives) with a counterparty to buy a specified number of shares of a company at a specified price on a future date. If the prediction holds and the market value of the shares increases, the investor exercises the contract and buys the shares at the now lower than market price. Selling those shares immediately following acquisition generates profit. Where the investor is to sell the equities short in anticipation of a falling market, he enters into a contract to sell a specific number of shares on a specified date at a specified price higher than that which is predicted for the future. When the market falls, he acquires the shares at the new lower price and then exercises the option (compelling the counterparty to buy) and makes a profit on the higher price paid for the shares. Sometimes the hedge fund will buy the stock both long and short, to 'hedge' its position (the origin of the term hedge fund).

**Passives or Index Tracking** Other approaches to equity investment include tracking a particular index. This may be accomplished by investing in all of the equities within a particular index (such as the FTSE 100) or a representative sample of them. The aim with either approach is to obtain portfolio growth in line with the growth in the market overall, rather than relying on a handful of equities beating the market trend. This style of investing is called passive investment, which in recent years has grown exponentially. For further discussion on passive investing see Chapters 1 and 13, where I have pitted passive investing against active investing.

**Leverage**  Managers often use leverage in order to enhance portfolio returns and different managers will utilise different levels and types of leverage. For example, equity funds usually use leverage sparingly whilst fixed-income funds will use leverage to boost their lower returns.[1] Leverage has also become a popular new offering by investment firms as credit dried up from banks after the financial crisis.

**Market Neutral**  The market neutral strategy is used by investors or managers when attempting to avoid a certain type of risk, whilst benefiting from increasing and decreasing prices of equities in one or more markets. The basic premise is to match long and short positions in different equities which should, in principle, increase the return from good stock selections.

The main upside of a market neutral strategy is its ability to mitigate market risks. When there is a significant amount of Vol in the market, this form of strategy tends to outperform others. Apart from strategies that just focus on short selling, market-neutral strategies have the lowest positive correlations.

The two main types of market neutral strategies are fundamental arbitrage and statistical arbitrage. The former uses fundamental analysis and the latter uses a quantitative approach. These two methodologies are discussed in more detail at the beginning of this section.

**Equities – Looking Forward**  Europe has seen significant political, economic, and social change recently (see Chapters 1 and 13 for further discussion) that has had an obvious impact on the markets. Indeed, European equities have had a particularly tough time of it in 2018. However, looking beyond the immediate past there are some key factors investors will be looking out for that signal a better horizon is in sight.

First, the corporate culture in Europe has meant that, in comparison to the US companies, it is not as focused. European investors have been far more reticent to oppose poor management than their US counterparts, which in turn means far greater opportunity for value and activist investors in this region. This may explain why more and more European companies are divesting and Europe is seeing an increasing number of spin-offs.[2] As European companies become less complex it is likely their more focused nature will make them more profitable. This in turn will increase shareholder return and provide excellent opportunities for those looking to invest in European equities.

Second, the cultural reticence for European investors to criticise their underlying portfolio companies makes this market an attractive proposition for activist investors. It is likely that more of these types of investors will make inroads into the European markets.

Third, it is impossible to ignore the impact of sociopolitical factors on the industries that operate within the EU. Certain industries will be hit harder by changing social standards and others may face increasing regulation. This may cause price discrepancies between the intrinsic worth of the companies and their market valuations as investors over- or under-react to the broader macro events present in today's world. Although there may be risks there are always rewards, and for the keen-eyed investor or experienced manager there is plenty of opportunity.

**Managers of Equities in 2019**  Managers focus on geographies, size, growth, value, income and have become more specialised as earlier described. As these are the most common strategies for retail, and retail platforms (such as St. James' Place and Hargreaves Landsdown), they are often in the financial news. The recent UK Woodford episode shows how what was not actually that significant an event  - no fraud or great losses  - can become mainstream news very fast. The Woodford discussion does shine a light onto well-known elements such as 'what is liquidity' and the nature of open-ended (an investor can redeem) vs closed-ended (no redemption) funds. The third choice of trading a holding company's securities (such as a

UK investment trust), but often with a heavy discount to NAV, is not perfect either. With the growth of secondary funds, perhaps closed is the new open and open is the new closed.

## BONDS OR CREDIT

The other mainstream asset class.

**Bonds** Bonds are the most common forms of debt financing freely traded on the market. Many bonds are seen as 'safe' investments due to the creditworthiness of the borrower and can be utilised to shore up the diversity of a portfolio.

Bonds are again not usually 'alternative' but 'mainstream', unless hedged or leveraged, or used as derivatives or derivative benching. Bonds are debt securities issued by either a company or a public body, such as central government or municipal authorities. Bonds are typically medium-to long-term investments, with a maturity of anything from one year to 30 years. They are often negotiable instruments, which are easily sold between investors on a secondary market. Traditionally, interest and capital repayments were made to the bearer of the bond (hence the now outdated term 'bearer bond'), although nearly all bonds are held and traded electronically through clearing houses and depositaries such as Euroclear.

The interest rate or the 'coupon' on bonds is dependent on several factors: the creditworthiness of the issue, the maturity date of the bond, and the prevailing market conditions at the time of issue. Some bonds carry an interest rate which is not fixed – these are technically floating rate notes rather than bonds and the interest rate is typically expressed as, for example, LIBOR + 125 basis points. The note will stipulate how often the interest rate is to be recalculated.

Bonds can be rated by rating agencies such as Standard & Poor's (S&P) or Moody's. The lower the perceived risk, the lower the yield. Bonds that are rated below 'investment grade' ('BBB' by S&P or 'Baa3' by Moody's is the lowest investment grade) were historically referred to as junk bonds, or high-yield bonds. These carry a higher risk of default, but offer higher returns. Investment grade bonds range from AAA to BBB (S&P) or from Aaa to Baa3 (Moody's).

**Government Gilts** Gilt-edged securities, or government gilts, are another form of 'safe' investment similar to bonds that are issued by the UK government. They are the UK equivalent to US treasury bonds and their name originates from the shape of the original certificates issued to investors that had gilded edges. Gilts can be bought primarily on the primary market, which is operated by the UK Debt Management Office, or on secondary markets through brokers. Due to their safe nature, the returns on gilts are not tremendous but are a staple amongst pension funds and life insurers (their popularity amongst the investors declining slightly due to their currently repressed yield rates). The main types of UK gilts have been:

- **Index-Linked Gilts:** Linked to changes in inflation.
- **Gilt Strips:** Strips stands for 'separate trading or registered interest and principal securities' where the interest rate and redemption payments are separated and exchanged independently of one another.
- **Conventional Gilts:** Most common type of gilt being the conventional gilt that receive a fixed payment every six months.
- **Perpetual or Undated Gilts:** Perpetual gilts differ from conventional gilts in that they do not have a maturity date. These gilts are to be redeemed at the option of the government; however, due to their low coupons there is very little incentive for the government to do

so.[3] With the exception of the certain war loans, all undated gilts are termed as 'rumps'.[4] The final undated gilt was redeemed on 5 July 2015.[5]

- **Double-dated Gilts:** Interestingly, a form of gilts called double-dated gilts were gilts in issue that had two maturity dates that could be specified by the government subject to three months' notice in the London Gazette.[6] The final double-dated gilt was redeemed 12 December 2013.[7]

**Private Debt** Credit managers, as an alternative to traditional bank lenders, have grown exponentially in popularity in the previous decade. Credit has now become a mainstream asset class for PE (and RE) managers. The main reason for this growth in credit as an asset class is the stifling of banks following the credit crisis. As global policy has forced banks to increase their minimum levels of capital and dispose of their riskier assets, credit lending has taken a back seat in main banks.

More recently, banks have begun to increase their levels of lending, especially in the mortgage space. However, the continued low interest rates of the last ten years have forced investors to engineer higher yields to satisfy their own investors' returns. This has precipitated an increase in funds' investment into credit, as well as infrastructure (see below).

A credit manager invests in fixed-income loan instruments ranging from senior and mezzanine debt to bonds and other short-term borrowings, as well as securitised products such as CDOs. Generally speaking, the cost of running a debt fund is lower than other funds, and so the management fees are correspondingly lower. Debt funds focus on preserving capital returns and will return a lower income than other investments. Funds will generally aim for absolute returns rather than returns relative to a benchmark. Credit funds can be structured as open-ended, closed-ended, or listed.

Credit's investment strategy will inevitably involve a degree of diversification in order to spread risk and still find investments that will deliver absolute returns. Government bonds and senior debt are examples of the more prudent debt investments to be found, but for many, such as institutional investors, the returns offered are simply not high enough. In order to attract a broader base of investors, investments in the higher-yield securities, such as mezzanine debt and high-yield corporate bonds (or indeed some sovereign debt) would need to be made. Given the current low interest climate, these riskier investments may make up 50% or more of the investment portfolio.

The size of private loan investments are growing and credit managers have identified a lending gap for SMEs. Loans may be made to commercial or residential RE developers for large-scale infrastructure projects, or to companies wanting to finance asset purchases whilst borrowing remains cheap. Credit managers will often be more flexible on loan terms than standard banks, offering varying levels of interest charged over different lengths of time.

Investments into start-up companies that offer P2P loans are also becoming more popular. Also known as crowdfunding, applications and websites offer an opportunity for people (and credit managers, on a larger scale) to invest in a lending system that offers loans to individual borrowers. This type of lending, like equity crowd funders, has a slightly Wild West feel about it, with little research done on borrowers.

**Senior Debt** Senior debt is debt that has the highest priority relative to other commitments of the investee or target. This priority is often secured by way of a lien over the investee's assets, which gives the lender the right to possess and sell those assets in the event of default. The senior creditor is also paid first compared with other creditors when interest payments or capital repayments are made. Although senior debt was typically provided by commercial banks, in the past decade an increasing amount has been provided by non-bank sources, such as institutional investors and hedge funds. This has only increased following the financial crisis, as banks are subject to tighter regulation on their investments and exposure and are generally more reluctant to lend.

The yield from senior debt is typically lower than other forms of debt where it is secured by collateral. The risk profile is low for senior debt because along with potential security, the legal systems in well-developed economies for dealing with the priority of creditors are sophisticated and can provide a fair degree of certainty. The presence of security alone is not determinative of the interest rate, as factors such as credit history, projected income, and ability to pay are also considered.

**Mezzanine Debt**  Mezzanine debt is debt that is subordinated to other commitments, such as senior debt. Generally speaking, it is only senior to contributions to shareholders in the distribution of the assets of a company when it is wound up. Therefore it is between the two levels of senior debt and equity, or 'mezzanine'. As such, its returns should also be between the two.

The mezzanine debt market can be divided into two broad sectors:

- the traditional mezzanine debt which is accompanied by equity or warrants to increase blended returns; and
- larger scale 'institutional' mezzanine finance which is not secured by warrants and is often syndicated.

The institutional finance transactions are typically 10 or greater times larger than traditional mezzanine deals. Institutional investors prefer warrantless debt because it comes with a greater interest rate and such investors typically have yield targets that their investments must meet. Equity sponsors also prefer warrantless mezzanine debt because the uptake of warrants will often dilute the equity holdings of other investors.

Mezzanine debt is a riskier investment than senior debt as it is not always fully secured and distributions are made only after the higher priority debts have been satisfied. To compensate, the yield on mezzanine debt is usually higher. Some issues of mezzanine debt carry warrants which allow the debt holder to elect to convert part of the debt into equity after a period of time, although this is restricted to smaller transactions.

Payment in kind (PIK) investments do not pay a current yield, but rather roll yield up, and therefore the coupon is higher than current yielding debt.

**Managers of Credit in 2019**  There is enormous growth in private debt, as well as alternative finance in public companies. This is due to the continued banks' retreat, increased bank regulation and capital rules, as well as a thirst for yield in a low interest environment. Banks are increasingly not top choice for PE seeking LBO debt. However still mezzanine struggles to define itself. The great 30-year bond bull market might be turning negative (some commentators suggest it has already) but the mainstream bond and debt markets still power away.

## ASSET-BACKED SECURITIES, COLLATERALISED LOAN OBLIGATIONS AND COLLATERALISED DEBT OBLIGATIONS

Asset-backed securities (ABSs) are bond issues by special purpose vehicles (SPVs) into which a financial institution has transferred secured assets such as mortgages. The aim is in part to take low value debts off a bank's balance sheet and the bond's interest payments and capital repayments are financed by the income stream from the underlying assets. The underlying assets do not have to be mortgages. ABS issues have been funded by a range of income streams such as recording royalties, credit card receivables, and life insurance premiums. The financial institution maintains its client relationships and simply diverts the income into the SPV.

The issue of ABSs can also be structured into more complex instruments. Collateralised Debt Obligations (CDOs) are issues of bonds derived from pooling various debt obligations into an SPV financed by the stream of income from this pool. The assets are pooled are segregated according to their creditworthiness. The division of assets is described as the difference between senior CDOs and junior CDOs. Senior CDOs are the highest quality, whereas junior CDOs are the poorest. This segregation allows for the pools to be tranched, and for CDO securities to be issued that have varying yields and risk profiles.

Collateralised Loan Obligations (CLOs) are similar to CDOs in structure. They are structured as SPVs which acquire debt obligations and issue securities (debt or otherwise) to investors to fund the acquisition of said debts. As a form of CDO, CLOs are a distinct subclass as they are syndicated bank loans rather than any other form of debt obligation. The loans are often highly leveraged – that is, the borrowers are borrowing much more than their equity.

An underlying flaw in ABSs, CDOs, and CLOs was exposed by and partly precipitated the financial crisis, where a large number were backed by sub-prime mortgages, and when it became clear that a large number of the mortgage borrowers would default, the holders of these securities (primarily banks and institutions that the bank sold these on to) found themselves with near worthless assets and large losses. Overleveraging of such investments was also rife pre-credit crisis, which meant that only a small movement in the 'equity' of such investments took the investment underwater. The market for CLOs and CDOs also ground to a halt during the credit crisis.

Following their role in the financial crisis, CDOs never properly recovered in popularity. Banks now find it difficult, due to high levels of required capital, to make significant profit on CDOs, even after pushing leveraging costs on to clients. Banks are putting down USD 1 million as an upfront margin cost for a USD 100 million trade.

CLOs, on the other hand, have made a tremendous resurgence. In 2017, over EUR 12 billion of European CLOs were issued, the largest amount seen since 2013. In the US, USD 54 billion has already been raised (as at July 2018) as the demand (and yield paid) is pushed up. However, one of the worrying issues about the rising fervour for CLOs is that investors are more willing to look beyond the AAA-rated tranches to lower quality issues. Worse still, in certain costs, covenants that are attached to the instruments that protect the investors are being stripped away to allow supply to meet demand.[8] Part of the surge in popularity can be explained by the US District Court for the District of Columbia's decision in early February 2018. Risk-retention rules governing US CLOs means that lenders no longer need to hold 5% of the CLO's value in capital, also known as the 'skin-in-the-game' rule.[9] The repeal of the rule also applies to existing portfolios of CLOs, as well as any issued following the ruling.

## REAL ESTATE AND INFRASTRUCTURE

RE and infrastructure funds operate with certain similar objectives and risk management profiles. Both fields can offer the reward of a long-term return on investment, and depending on the willingness to undertake risk, they can deliver substantial rewards. The risks which underline both are also similar. They are sensitive to the property market, they are largely illiquid and it can be difficult to assess how the fund's investments are performing until they have been realised. The time it takes for each investment to mature is significant too – it could be a period of up to ten years. Most investors in RE funds are pension funds, insurance companies, hedge funds, sovereign wealth funds, and other shadow banking operators that can play a long game. Some investors have recently taken on the acquisition and development in-house rather than by an intermediary, which adds to the risk and the cost of getting a management and development team in place, but can return a greater proportion of the income and capital profit. A lot of infrastructure projects are public–private partnerships (PPP) with the government and local authorities, which can lead to conflicts of interest in seeking a return and the publication of results.

**RE Strategies**   RE funds invest in a wide range of property types – housing, retail, commercial, and industrial. The return depends in part on the investment strategy and on whether the market grows during the period of investment. The main strategies are known as 'core plus', 'value added' and 'opportunistic'. RE funds are typically structured as an SPV.

Popular publicly available structures are the Jersey property unit trust (JPUT) described in Chapter 3 of my first funds book and the real estate investment trust (REIT) which is common in the US and a more recent development in the UK. The use of these specialised structures is not necessary. Many private funds are still structured as limited partnerships or as any other suitable structure, depending on the usual range of factors such as taxation of the investors or regulations.

RE funds can be more of a business than other fund structures. What this means is that the assets are managed on a more concentrated level with issues such as planning, construction, maintenance, insurance, and wider regulatory concerns and specialised tax regimes for property.

The RE market took a hit during the financial crisis (it does in most financial crises), especially as one of the triggers was the collapse in house prices in 2008 and the subsequent widespread default on mortgage payments. It has since recovered to an extent in both the UK and US.

A 'core plus' strategy is conservative, investing in high value property that does not need a large investment, with modest but safer and more immediate returns. The properties acquired will require little in the way of development and often have tenancies soon up for negotiation. This may be an opportunity to increase rents, although it may appear to be a less stable investment on acquisition.

The 'value added' strategy will look to properties which require more development and can offer greater returns. It may not be limited to the physical state of repair. Some value added properties may be so because of low occupancy rates. Such properties may be available at a discount and offer an opportunity to increase rent profit income along with capital growth where development is necessary.

The 'opportunistic' approach will often invest in greenfield sites, niche sectors, or emerging market properties that require the greatest amount of development, planning, and investment. Undeveloped and underdeveloped sites will often be unoccupied or have very low occupancy rates, and so this will present an opportunity to greatly increase the rental income and the overall value of the property (occupancy often increases market value). They target the greatest return but the investment period is longer and there are greater risks involved.

**Infrastructure Strategies**   The term 'infrastructure' encompasses a broad and diverse range of physical structures and services required for the functioning of a modern economy. This may include projects such as transport, education, health care facilities, telecommunications, water supply, and waste disposal. Certain types of infrastructure are not obviously recognisable as such. For example, scientific research facilities, banking, finance, and regulatory systems may all fall into the infrastructure bracket. Infrastructure is closely connected with energy. Infrastructure investment can take place at different phases of the development cycle. Riskier investments can be made, such as in greenfield sites and projects that have yet to receive authorisation, which will suffer from a longer period of time before they generate returns. The profit margin for such projects can be greater. Alternatively, investment can be made in the later stages of development, or when the project itself is complete. These can be safer investments but are often expensive, and the investor will have had no control over the previous development process.

Infrastructure funds seek to invest in developments as diverse as the projects themselves. Infrastructure projects are frequently developed as PPPs with the government or local authorities investing alongside institutional investors and banks. PPPs are often created following private finance initiatives (PFIs) driven by the state. PFIs are somewhat controversial in that private sector debt and equity are used to finance public projects but are underwritten by the public purse. This concept of underwriting of projects with public finances, together with the generation of profits for private interests and high profile failures, has led to PFIs and PPPs being perceived as politically unpopular. Equally they can be unpopular with investors that do not believe public policy should interfere with investment strategy.

PFI contracts are usually awarded by public authorities to privately held SPVs in order to utilise private sector project and financial management expertise. Contracts usually have a lifespan of between 20 and 30 years. Prior to the 2007 financial crisis, PFI infrastructure projects were overwhelmingly bank-funded. However, more recently the infrastructure funding market has seen a retreat by banks, which are faced with regulatory capital concerns and the regulation of the liquidity of their assets. The advent of shadow banking operators coupled with the withdrawal of banks has seen an increase in pension and hedge fund investment into PFIs.

Infrastructure initiatives such as PPPs and PFIs can deliver a high rate of return for investors in terms of the capital investment and, where appropriate, the receipt of ongoing contractual fees for the management of the facilities. Because initiatives are often underwritten by public authorities, they are regarded by investors as a relatively low-risk asset class which delivers long-term yields through contractual cash flow (which is often inflation-linked).

Certain infrastructure investments, such as utilities and public transport projects, are seen as particularly stable because they often have a natural monopoly status and operate within highly regulated sectors. An additional factor which makes infrastructure projects attractive to investors is that returns have a low market correlation and are not connected to investments in other asset classes such as bonds or equities. All that sounds great, but there have been high profile mistakes and government-led or regulatory interference, leading to the building blocks of certain investment strategies being knocked, in turn leading to losses, which are exasperated by the 'thinness' of allowable risk or equity. A good example is a government changing agreed rebates or tax allowances after the event.

**UK REITs**   REITs were introduced in the UK in 2007 to allow investors to obtain broadly similar returns from investing in the trust as though the investor had acquired the underlying property itself. A REIT is a company that owns and often operates income-generating RE. REITs can own many types of commercial RE, ranging from office space to hotels. Some REITs also participate in financing RE. The REIT structure was designed to provide a RE investment vehicle similar to the structure of a US mutual fund for investing in shares. Much of the US regime has inspired the UK's own REIT regime, for example the minimum distributions and the balance of business conditions.

REITs can be publicly or privately held. A public REIT would be listed. Following the passage of the legislation laying out the rules for REITs in the UK, nine UK property companies converted to REIT status, including five FTSE 100 members at that time – Slough Estates, Land Securities, British Land, Hammerson, and Liberty International.

REIT tax incentives aim to make the vehicle as tax neutral as possible. They also allow individuals to invest who would not otherwise be able to afford the high initial cost of investing in property. In addition, the requirement for the vehicle to be listed provides liquidity to investors. REITs must be approved by HMRC and are subject to rigorous regulation on application and during their lifespan, along with regulation applicable to a publicly listed company.

Following the vote to leave the EU, UK REITs have taken a slight knock on valuation. As a decent number of REITs are composed of offices and other commercial RE, the threat to London's (and the rest of the UK's) position as financial capital of the world has dented the appetite for REITs.[10] RE in retail shopping has also taken a dive for a combination of factors (that's a book in itself).

**US REITs** The US is the birthplace of the REIT. The US enacted a law authorising REITs in 1960 and in 1965 the REIT was first traded on the NYSE.

The primary benefit of a REIT is its tax efficiency. A large number of investors are able to participate in RE-focused investments with only one level of federal income taxation. An oversimplification of the federal taxation of entities is that: (i) corporations pay federal income tax; (ii) partnerships effectively pass-through federal income tax obligations including the character and amount of income, gains, losses, deductions, and credits; and (iii) a REIT is in-between. A REIT is a structure embodied in the US Internal Revenue Code (IRC) that has specified characteristics and consequences for its investors.

Shares in a REIT may be offered in a public offering that is registered under the Securities Act of 1933, that is, a public offering. This provides the REIT with the opportunity to increase its capital sources because investment is not limited to institutional investors or a limited number of investors, as it is in the context of PE investment funds.

A REIT acquires capital from its investors and, directly or indirectly, owns and controls the RE assets. This structure is similar to an operating corporation. There are two general alternative structures of a REIT: an 'UpReit' and a 'DownReit'.

In an 'UpReit', the REIT investors own the entity that is a REIT and the REIT owns an investment in a limited partnership that owns the investments in the RE assets. In a 'DownReit', the investors own the entity that is a REIT and the REIT owns and controls several single purpose limited partnerships ('properties'). The other LPs in the limited partnerships are the contributors of the applicable property.

There are three general types of REITs:

- publicly traded REITs;
- public non-traded REITs; and
- private REITs.

Publicly traded REITs are subject to the greatest amount of regulation. They are subject to the Securities and Exchange Act of 1934 and, accordingly, must adhere to the regulatory oversight of public companies. The majority of publicly traded REITs are listed on the NYSE. The investor benefits from the greater requirements for transparency and corporate governance, as well as the increased liquidity of their investment. The management of the investments is typically overseen by the directors of the company and operated in-house, rather than by outside agencies. The NYSE's rules require a majority of the directors to be independent by having no material relationship with the REIT as an investor or former employee, or by having an interest in a body which has a relationship with the REIT. The investors have a degree of control over the directors because they have the power to re-elect the board. The SEC rules and stock exchange rules also regulate corporate governance and require that the company has its own policy on corporate governance. The costs associated with investing in a publicly traded REIT are mainly in brokerage fees when buying or selling the shares. The REIT must also make periodic public disclosures of financial performance and yearly audited financial results must be filed with the SEC. Additionally, prompt public disclosure of significant events affecting the REIT must be made.

REITs may also be public entities but not listed on a stock exchange, known as non-traded REITs or non-exchange-traded REITs. A non-traded REIT is a riskier investment because it is less liquid than its traded counterpart, and the value of the stocks is not calculated as frequently as it would be on the market. Non-traded REITs often have redemption procedures in place to allow an investor to dispose of their stocks, but the process is not as quick as on the markets and could cost an investor more in fees than brokerage costs would. A non-traded REIT is often managed by an external investment manager, in contrast with a public REIT, possibly reducing the amount of profit available for distribution by dividend, and could potentially lead to a conflict of interests. The composition of the board is still regulated for its independence, but it is by the regulations of the North American Securities Administrators Association. Although there is the requirement to file accounts with the SEC there is no requirement to disclose to the investment community.

There are some REITs that are private – they are not traded on a stock exchange nor are they registered with the SEC. They are primarily aimed at institutional investors and high-net-worth individuals and provide the least amount of liquidity. It is generally difficult to have the stocks redeemed and they are often redeemed at a high cost. They are typically run by outside investment managers and there are no requirements for independent directors or regulation of corporate governance and disclosure.

**Managers of RE and Infrastructure in 2019**   The old RE guard is retiring says the trade news. The financial crisis was crippling and destroyed portfolios. Many of the managers have recovered and made money. However RE is cyclical and are we at the end of a cycle (I doubt it). Infrastructure is supposedly popular, but full of Government support and equal interference. Managers still struggle to raise money. Some asset owners still believe they can do it themselves. Leverage can be a struggle.

## OTHER HARD ASSETS

**Old Energy**   The old energy sector is made up of crude oil (in its various forms, such as Brent Crude and West Texas Intermediate), heating oil, natural gas, ethanol, and coal. It is a vital sector for the global economy, as it is made up of the fuels that have historically fired industrial growth as well as transportation, heating, and electricity. The market in old energy has seen a large growth in both prices and supply, as the appetite of developing industrial economies such as China consumes vast resources. That being said, China's latest five-year plan has set targets to reduce fossil fuel dependency and increase the relative consumption of natural gas, two moves which are likely to have an effect on the old energy markets if they are implemented. The growth of new technologies such as fracking and more economic means of locating reserves both onshore and in deep water for the extraction of oil and natural gas has provided new impetus to the old energy market. The US in particular has seen an expansion in its position as a globally prominent supplier of these forms of energy. PE investment in these sectors often takes the form of investing in the pioneers of exploration and extraction technologies rather than the energy output instead, as exploration and technology can deliver the higher returns.

**New Energy**   New energy concerns the development of alternative sources of energy from the old energy stalwarts. It is not only the development of renewable electricity or thermal energy generation such as hydro-electric, wind, and solar, but also alternative sources of fuels and other hydrocarbons such as the sourcing of ethanol from crops, wood, and agricultural waste. The industry saw large growth at the beginning of the twenty-first century as both investors and existing energy giants responded to public demand for reduced dependency on hydrocarbons and predictions that the reserves of old energy resources were limited, with scarcity driving up future prices. However, recent developments in the old energy sector have resulted in more economic access to known deposits and have revealed greater deposits of these resources. This has had an impact on investing in new energy.

Despite this impact, there have been some exciting developments in new energy. First, on 4 November 2016, the Paris Agreement became legally binding. Ratified by 55 countries that account for over 55% of the global greenhouse emissions, this was a significant step in addressing the environmental concerns of 99% of the scientific community. From a new energy perspective, this progress will prompt further investment in clean energy and encourage the growth of new technology. Second, the cost of solar components has reduced and their quality increased. Two common criticisms of renewable energy are that it is not cost-efficient and that it is ineffective. Big improvements in first-cost parity between conventional and high-efficiency monocrystalline cells suggest that solar power will become cheaper and more efficient. Third, there has been a significant uptake in the production and consumption of electric vehicles. In 2016, global sales were up 42%[11] with more and more car manufacturers announcing the development and production of new models. Fourth, the progress made by emerging economies is remarkable. The Climatescope 2016 report revealed that emerging economies are now deploying more renewables than their counterparts in developed nations. This debunks a common concern that less developed economies will compromise any progress made towards a greener global community. What these developments infer is that there is a clear appetite for a more environmentally friendly approach to energy. Inevitably, this will promote the use of new energy as common opinion shifts towards its use. President Trump's shocking withdrawal from the Paris Agreement is very bad (to use one of his complex expressions) and his approach towards new energy has been dismissive, his actions have received widespread condemnation from across the global political elite. The focus on new energy has entered the mainstream political discourse and it is unlikely to go away any time soon.

Various government policies may help the economic growth in this sector by the provision of tax incentives and subsidies but the benefit of new energy sources (reduced air pollution) is not factored into the market value of the energy produced, and they are still arguably expensive sources of energy compared with the old energy sources. In addition, as with infrastructure projects, they can be dented by government or other interference after the event.

**Commodities** The commodities market is divided into three broad classes of asset – agriculture, metals, and energy. Agriculture encompasses basic foodstuffs such as corn, wheat, soybeans, and sugar. The metals market ranges from aluminium to zinc and includes precious metals such as gold and silver. Energy is dominated by crude oil, natural gas, and coal; refined products such as heating oil and petrol; and alternative energies. Investing in commodities is traditionally seen as a hedge against inflation, and it is not often considered sound to invest too heavily in commodities due to the fluctuations in price that can occur. An investment in the commodities market can be made by directly purchasing the physical goods themselves, investing in the equities of companies which are involved directly in the trade (such as mining or oil companies), investing in ETFs or exchange-traded commodities, or speculating in the futures market. Each strategy varies the risks and rewards of investing but all are fundamentally linked to the prices themselves, which have over the previous ten years continually increased in what became known as a 'supercycle'.

**Agriculture** Like all commodities, the agriculture sector can often see volatile swings in prices. Long-term trends which are affecting prices include the desire for biofuels, pushing up the price as more staple foodstuffs such as corn and sugar are fermented for use as energy. It can also spike when there is a crisis in the oil markets, as consumers look for cheaper alternatives. The agriculture sector can also be affected by more traditional factors such as poor harvests, population growth, and political and social upheaval.

**Metals** The market in metals commodities can be divided into precious metals and base metals. Precious metals include gold, silver, platinum, and palladium. Base metals include iron, copper, zinc, tin, and aluminium. Although all have industrial purposes which can fuel demand and supply constraints, precious metals are also used as investments – gold is the best example, which is often used as a hedge against inflation or the decline of other investment markets. The market in base metals has seen price rises as part of the previous supercycle, with growth in demand fuelled by industrial growth, which has recently shown signs of slowing down. Base metals will see a growth in demand as more developing economies grow their industrial sectors, despite short-term cycles in pricing. Precious metals have some industrial applications and will see their prices affected by industrial growth as well, although they still will be valuable investments as hedges.

**Exchange-Traded Funds** Investment can be made through an exchange-traded fund (ETF) that is linked to the sector. Such an ETF may invest in one commodity or be spread across many. If it tracks just one, it may maximise its returns where there are good returns, but equally, where there is a poor return, the whole fund suffers due to the limited portfolio. A more diverse portfolio of commodities would spread the risk of losses more widely but reduce the maximum return where one has a standout performance.

**Indirect Investment in Operating Companies** Investments can be made in the commodities sector indirectly by investing in the equity of companies that operate in it. There is exposure to the movement of prices and where prices increase, in general, the revenues and profits of the producers rise, too. There are some factors with regard to equity investments in commodity producers that should be considered. The movement of the spot price of a commodity can affect a company's profit and loss profile in proportion to the company's size. Much like an ETF portfolio, the range of commodities that a company extracts or produces can also affect its susceptibility to market movements. An energy company dealing in crude oil and natural gas would suffer less in a crash in the price of crude oil than a company operating purely in crude.

**Futures** Rather than dealing in the commodities themselves or an ETF linked to them, some investors operate by investing in the futures markets. A futures contract is an agreement for the supply of a fixed amount of a commodity at a fixed price on a fixed date. Not all futures contracts are settled by physical delivery but by cash instead. They are useful for suppliers, for example farmers, as they allow them to guarantee a price for their crops when they expect prices to be low (provided that the crop is good and sufficiently bountiful), but could result in having to sell at less than the market rate if their judgement is wrong. The other side of a futures contract is often entered into by speculators who believe the price will rise, and that therefore they will make a profit selling at the market price (or spot price) once they have acquired the commodities or equivalent. A speculator of course has no intention of taking physical delivery of the crop. When the expiry date of the contract arrives, the investor will close the position by entering into a contract to sell the same amount of the crop. The movement of the price from the original position to the second closing position is the measure of the speculator's gain or loss. Most futures contracts are made exclusively between speculators, and are settled by cash rather than delivery.

## PRIVATE EQUITY

Private equity (PE) is a general term that encompasses investments made into private companies, public companies that are taken private (also known as a de-listing, a recent example of which was the de-listing of H. J. Heinz of tomato ketchup fame) or those that behave more like a PE-backed business (for example a buy-and-build strategy by a corporate). The horizon of a PE investment is usually three to five years, during which the aim is to increase the value of the business by either restructuring the company's group, adding companies through acquisition, encouraging growth, or changing the nature of the business. Once the timeline has been exhausted, the manager will realise its gains by selling off the company, or its shares in the company, through an IPO or sale (both known as forms of 'exit').

### Strategies

There are various strategies in use by fund managers to maximise their gains.

**Buy-Out** The most common is the leveraged buy-out (LBO) by which investment is made combining private capital with debt financing. The rationale is the classic justification for leveraging or gearing, that once the fixed cost of debt borrowing is paid for by the returns, the remaining capital gains from an investment are pure profit for the investors. The greater the ratio of debt to equity, the greater the return for the equity investors (in theory). LBO deals are more common when acquiring larger and more mature companies, as the proven track record of income and perceived lower risk will reduce the borrowing costs, and will increase the likelihood that debt financiers will commit to lending. The most common criticism of the LBO strategy is that it can encourage more financial engineering, with little operational or strategic value.

These types of deals were seen to be vulnerable to the commercial uncertainty generated by Brexit. Yet, in the run up to 2019, PE buy-out deals were almost 60% higher than they were during the last quarter of 2017.[12] Underlying this was a desire to get the deals over the line before Christmas and prior to any eventual departure from the EU. Key areas where there was a lot of movement were industrial products, telecoms, and business services. Despite concerns over the future of the UK's high street limited investment in the license and leisure sectors, Wagamama was still sold to The Restaurant Group for GBP 357 million[13] (and MJ Hudson advised on the deal!). Clearly, there is value to be found despite what some commentators feel could be a tricky time for PE. Indeed, although there is uncertainty in the short- to mid-term, PE houses have more money than they ever have had previously. Undoubtedly, they will want to put it in the ground and so it is quite likely that we will see bigger and bigger buy-outs.[14]

**Growth Capital**   Here, an established business is seeking to expand and requires investment. The aim is not necessarily to relinquish control of the company to the incoming investors, who may instead acquire only a minority stake (with appropriate safeguards). The existing business may or may not be listed. Where it is listed the transaction commonly takes the form of private investment in public equity (PIPE) whereby the incoming PE investors acquire convertible or preferred security that is unregistered with the markets for a period of time.

Growth capital in essence sits between traditional PE buy-outs and VC. PE houses that are involved in these deals will look for companies that sit in established markets and have a proven track record, even if that record is shorter than what would be considered in a buy-out. From the perspective of the founder, this kind of investment is suitable when they still want to be involved with the business and they are  not ready to sell all of it. Moreover, it is an excellent opportunity for them to get some outside experience which can help take their company to the next stage. Ironically, this often means that this kind of decision is not always necessary. Rather, they may prefer to grow their company at the current rate, or even decide that they do not want their business to innovate or expand. However, often this kind of capital is taken by owners because they want to grow their market share.

Despite growth capital ordinarily being accessed by businesses that are established, there are still risks. Predominately, these can be characterised as management and execution risks. For example, the growth of the business will inevitably require the development of the management team already in place. New members will have to be brought in to deal with the additional functions the business will be carrying out. This is a delicate and crucial process that has to be done well for the business to succeed.

**Development Capital**   Development capital is like growth capital, but is not so limited to high growth of the portfolio company, but more to a new 'development' of the business or a new business line.

**Recent Examples**   Recent examples of multibillion dollar buy-outs include the Blackstone Group's acquisition of a 55% stake in Thomson Reuters, specifically their Financial and Risk unit. For the 55% stake, the seller will be paid USD 17 billion, USD 3 billion of which will consist of equity provided by Blackstone (and its co-investors GIC and Canada Pension Plan Investment Board) and the rest will be a mixture of debt and preferred equity. The acquisition values the Thomson Reuters unit at USD 20 billion and coincides with the signing of a 30-year deal whereby Blackstone will pay USD 325 million per year for news and other content.[15]

Another large deal includes the hostile takeover of GKN, a producer of automotive and aerospace components in the UK by Melrose, a turnaround specialist, exemplified by their motto 'Buy, Improve, Sell'. Melrose paid GBP 8 billion for GKN. The hostile takeover was the largest of its kind in the UK since the Kraft takeover of Cadbury in 2010.[16]

**2019 News**   With stock markets having a troubling 2018, private investing is hot. This is despite the increasing amounts of 'dry powder' (amounts committed but not invested) in PE today. In addition, this is against a backdrop of generally increasing profit multiples being paid for businesses.

Debt in PE deals got very high in 2018 – and very free of covenants ('cov-light'), but is slightly declining today.

LPs are increasingly going direct into PE deals, and co-invest is still popular for LPs.

The push back on fees experienced by mainstream managers, has not really impacted PE.

**Managers of Private Equity in 2019**   PE is hot, hot, hot. The mega fund managers are becoming more mega and the niche are growing. The middle, the geographically or sized focussed, or undifferentiated are being squeezed. Dry powder is a real source of anxiety for investors, as is the higher deal and debt multiples. However PE managers have rarely had it so good.

## VENTURE CAPITAL

Due to the definition of PE encompassing such a broad range of investment activities (and due to its continued growth in popularity), I have dedicated a separate section of PE to venture capital (VC). VC is the strategy of investing equity into start-up or early growth stage companies in order to help fund the initial high costs the business faces. These costs can include establishing a suitable IT infrastructure, building a sales team, or renting space for the business. During 2017, the UK VC scene secured GBP 6 billion, putting it in second place behind North America, and slightly ahead of China.

High-risk and capital-intensive industries such as technology, biotechnology, and healthcare are the areas within VC that attracted the majority of the UK's VC funding. The UK's tech sector alone received GBP 2.99 billion in 2017, 80% of which was focused in London.[17]

A start-up company will usually go through several different rounds of investing, each of which will differ in type of investor, amount raised and capital allocation. Most of the investment rounds below fund the early stage or capital intensive loss-making period of a young company.

1. First round is the pre-seed round: a small round, generally less than 500,000, this can be raised by friends and family or from start-up accelerators. This round is usually used to hire a key team member or develop a prototype of the product.
2. Second round is the seed round: usually raising between GBP 1–2 million, this can be raised from angels, early-stage VCs, and start-up accelerators. This round is used for product development and to grow a larger team.
3. Third round is the Series A round: this round can raise anywhere between GBP 2–10 million from VCs (and perhaps larger angels). The funds raised help to develop new sales opportunities and perfect the product.
4. Fourth round is the Series B round: this can raise between GBP 10–20 million from VCs and later stage VCs. This funding is used by the start-up to build and expand the team and perhaps to move into new markets to find further revenue streams.

5. Finally, the fifth round is the Series C round, this and the rounds beyond can raise GBP 50 million or more; this is used for global expansion and perhaps to acquire competitors or start-ups that offer complementary products. At this stage the funding mainly comes from PE firms, perhaps late-stage VCs, and even banks.

## Strategies

**Biotechnology/Life Sciences** The term 'biotechnology' encompasses four separate sectors of investment, namely agriculture, medicine, industry, and environmental. With regards to the medical section of biotechnology investing, the industry focuses primarily on developing new drugs and new forms of therapy to combat diseases and illnesses. The bioscience industry has become extremely popular in the last decade, with investment pouring across multiple sub-sectors of the strategy. Nowhere is this better evidenced than by comparing the cost of sequencing a human genome. In 2007, it cost scientists USD 10 million to sequence a genome, whereas the cost for the same sequencing is now below USD 1000.[18]

In the US from 2014 to 2017, USD 66 billion was invested by VC funds into the biotech market, which allowed biotech companies to spend a staggering USD 42 billion in 2016 on research and development (R&D) alone.[19] To put that into perspective, UK-based biotech firms raised slightly over GBP 1 billion in 2016, GBP 681 million of which came from VC funds whilst GBP 105 million came from biotech firms listing on stock markets.[20]

Yet things look on the up for the UK biotech sector as GBP 2.2 billion was pumped into the market in 2018 – up from GBP 1.2 billion the year before.[21] This indicates that investors are still confident of UK innovation and hopeful that this sector is maturing. Although there has been an increase in investment there were, however, very few biotech companies that went public last year. This is not to say that biotech companies in the UK are not successful. Autolus Therapeutics plc enjoyed a very successful IPO and currently provides innovative treatments for individuals suffering from cancer. Indeed, areas such as cell therapy and genomics are particularly strong within the UK market and have attracted strong interest from VCs in the US. Given the strong history of life science success in the US this is a ringing endorsement for the UK's biotech sector.

**Physical Technology** Physical technology, rather than information or biotechnology, is the use of materials to develop products following research in the fields of engineering, chemistry, and physics.[22] Some of the highest spending on physical technology R&D comes from companies such as Volkswagen, Samsung, and Intel.[23] Perhaps the most important factor investors consider when investing in research and development is the path to commercialisation. For physical technology, the European Commission's (EC) definition of that path is as follows:

LEVEL 1    Basic principles observed
LEVEL 2    Technology concept formulated
LEVEL 3    Experimental proof of concept
LEVEL 4    Technology validated in lab
LEVEL 5    Technology validated in relevant environment
LEVEL 6    Technology demonstrated in relevant environment
LEVEL 7    System prototype demonstration in operational environment
LEVEL 8    System complete and qualified
LEVEL 9    Actual system proven in operational environment

A good example is how VC is helping the automotive industry develop new cutting-edge ideas. Particularly, their relationship with start-ups that are providing add on technology that can be utilised by vehicle manufacturers. This is in part because the traditional approach to R&D cannot keep up with the speed in which technology is developing. Traditional operators in this market are being disrupted by newer companies such as Tesla. Moreover, other companies, such as Dyson and Google, are moving into the market in the race to produce electric vehicles. Older stakeholders have bureaucratic decision-making processes that cannot keep up with these more modern nimble companies. In order to compete it is more efficient to partner with VC firms who can connect start-ups with more established players.

**Internet** The internet led to the dot-com bust of 2000, but since then has risen from the dead to become all-pervasive (now you don't have to dial it up and wait for an hour to download one picture). This has led in turn to the decade of internet unicorns, and the huge effect on the public markets (especially US) of the US internet giants – or FAANGS.

The collective impact of Facebook, Apple, Amazon, Netflix, and Google has led to the acronym FAANG. These stocks have led to the bull run in recent years and represent a significant percentage of the Nasdaq 100 index market capitalisation. Their growth has been backed by eminent managers such as Soros, Berkshire, and Renaissance who have included FAANG stocks within their portfolios. Their consistent growth has made them the darlings of Wall Street and there is significant momentum behind their increased valuation. Although the US has always produced huge companies (for example, General Electric, Standard Oil, IBM, and General Motors) there is a feeling these companies could surpass all predecessors. Their combined valuation is greater than the value of all the gold mined in a year[24] or the size of Russia's economy.[25] These companies, and their impact on the public markets, are a direct consequence of the creation of the internet. Facebook and Google can advertise to anyone who has access to the internet, Netflix can offer its content across the world and Amazon has the facility to provide products globally. The fear, of course, is that their performance and valuation is mirroring the dot-com bust of 2000. However, there are significant differentiators from that event which should be noted to refute these comparisons. In relative terms, the valuations are actually lower now and the companies in question have significantly better cash balances than their predecessors.[26] Moreover, the substance of these companies is emerging technology, which is constantly evolving and providing new opportunities. For example, although Google and Facebook may occupy a large percentage of the advertising market they are not confined to just one source of revenue. They have expanded into artificial intelligence (AI), machine learning, big data, and other developing technological fields. Indeed, as more and more people gain access to the internet and this new technology, FAANG companies gain an ever-growing customer base.

It is not just US companies that are impacting the commercial world. The explosion of Chinese unicorns has surpassed the number produced in the US.[27] In part, this is because of the efficient way that Chinese unicorns utilise the internet to satisfy their customers and grow the demand for their products.[28] With the majority of Chinese unicorns within the e-commerce and internet services industry it is apparent the adoption of the 'internet+' model has been worthwhile. Indeed, some analysts argue that this is the key differentiator between the Chinese economy and its competitors.[29]

At the end of 2018, the FAANGs took a bit of a market beating, but have recovered slightly as of the start of 2019. The success of the FAANGs and the unicorns has led to significant capital being pumped into copycats and niche startups. FAANGs are themselves creating spin-out teams and ideas (small teeth). This has put considerable impetus behind VC for now.

**Artificial Intelligence**   I only touch on this as an example of growth in VC investing. AI has quickly grown to become a sufficient stand-alone investment strategy in the VC world. In 2017 alone, USD 10.8 billion was invested into AI and machine-learning start-ups, a dramatic increase from USD 5.7 billion in 2016.[30] The cost of producing AI products is only reducing as we gather further data on one another, the main component required to improving AI. The continuing reduction in costs of production (Moore's law – discussed further in-depth in Chapter 8), also means that the hardware required by AI is improving and processing speeds are increasing.

**Mega VC Funds – Leading to Mega Rounds of Capital**   In May 2017, SoftBank Group, a Japanese conglomerate run by Masayoshi Son announced the first closing of the 'SoftBank Vision Fund' a technology-focused fund with USD 93 billion of commitments.

   Although the fund's focus is not restricted to early-stage companies, its investment strategy has a focus on 'companies and foundational platform businesses that seek to enable the next age of innovation'.[31] As of February 2018 it had invested 40% of its fund through investments in, amongst other companies, Uber, NVIDIA, WeWork, and DoorDash. SoftBank have, however, offered investments into deals it has previously undertaken as an acquiring company, such as its purchase of ARM Holdings, the UK semiconductor company which it stated that it plans to relist in five to seven years.[32,33]

   Part of this is the growing willingness on the part of the investor to take more risk and invest bigger. Rather than invest solely in a mainstream fund, investors are looking for smaller niche managers who have better sector experience. Whilst maintaining their considerable investment in big funds, investors will also look to put money into sector specialists. A consequence of this bar-bell style investing[34] will inevitably be the inflation in the valuation of start-ups as more and more money becomes available.

   It is important to remember that although mega funds are becoming more prevalent not all investors will have access to them. There will be a minimum amount for an investor to put in and many will just not be able to afford it. This being said, the speed at which technology and other sectors are growing will create plenty of opportunities for investors within the VC sector – irrespective of whether they put their money into a mega fund.

## Types of VC Managers

Other than the classic '2 and 20' fund manager, there are also HNWIs, family offices, hedge funds (they often pile into trends), and LPs going direct (see Chapter 6 for further detail). Beyond this, there is another class of VC manager called the corporate venturer.

**Corporate Venturers**   The traditional approach to innovation by a company was through R&D, crowdsourcing, experimentation, and strategic alliances.[35] Yet, the growth of corporate VC over the past five to ten years signals a shift in the way companies are seeking to grow and develop their businesses.

   The principle driving corporate VC is to target strategically important ventures that could provide excellent value for the parent company. To achieve this, in-house investment funds are created to find ventures that could afford potential for high-growth or possess valuable new technology. The basic process revolves around providing ventures with industry knowledge, access to markets, and capital, as well as often its first large customer. In this respect corporate VC is perhaps different from traditional VC. The aim is not to acquire the company to fill a void in the parent company's capabilities, although it might subsequently. Rather, the objective is to foster innovation and develop products that could provide value in the future.

Corporations with an in-house investment funds predicate their actions on what can best help their parent company's strategic goals. In this sense, corporate VC differs again from an orthodox VC approach. On the whole, VC focuses on the financial return and prioritises this as the core goal of their approach. In contrast, corporate venturers get actively involved in a venture to grow their knowledge, market intelligence, and provide solutions to their strategic problems.

A useful consequence of the corporate VC approach is the ability to test market hypotheses. R&D was historically the main arena in which this could be done but now corporate VC provides an alternative setting. Moreover, it can often be done for less cost and risk then keeping the process purely in house.[36] This is particularly apposite when internal innovation is lacking and it is looking outside the company can be a fruitful approach. Given that start-ups are hubs for creativity it is easy to see why this marriage of resources and ideas works.

## Where Next for VC?

There are mixed opinions about the impact both the FAANGs enviable success and the Vision Fund is having on the VC world. Some see private VC as changing the landscape for investing in technology, perhaps even providing an alternative to the IPO whilst others see it as a way to allow innovation to flourish. At the moment it may to be too early to call whether the Vision Fund will be successful or not. Perhaps a more important question, however, concerns the entire VC industry – is the Vision Fund meeting a market demand or straining start-ups further?

It is certainly meaning that raising what is essentially VC on the public markets might take more of a back seat over 2019. Private companies are delaying IPOs to raise further private capital.

Is a VC bubble waiting to burst? Certainly, parallels can be made with the dot-com bust, especially when a listed US iced tea[37] company changed its name to include 'blockchain' and its stock subsequently rose 500%. Originally called the Long Island Iced Tea Corp, the publicly listed company rebranded itself as 'Long Blockchain'. The business was valued at USD 23.8 million but this rose to almost USD 138 million later in that day after the open market bought into the hype. This is not the only example of the market being manipulated by rebranding. The Crypto Co saw a 17 000% increase in their stock price over a period of three months. What started this surge? An announcement that they would be introducing a crypto trading floor. The SEC had their concerns and suspended trading on Crypto Co referencing the unreliable nature of the information surrounding Crypto Co's future venture.

Evidently the buzz around blockchain and crypto currencies is not slowing down and this opens up the possibility for fraud to be committed, as well as copycat, naive, momentum-play or bullshit models (to borrow a technical phrase). Admittedly, it is unknown if that is what 'Long Blockchain' or 'Crypto Co' had in mind but it would be unsurprising if this tactic is not used in the future by another company. It feels very Dutch tulip, and I worry for the ponzi-caught lay investors.

That said, some listed unicorns trade at not insane profit multiples, and internet or web companies are having their day out on the sales field (look at its impact on the High Street retail), as well as truly disrupting markets (Skype, WhatsApp, and many more). With the cost to start such a company continually dropping there are plenty other opportunities in tech to get involved in.

The huge VC play of throwing extremely large amounts of money at a few companies to essentially 'disrupt the disrupters' and kill all other competition (the idea that there is one Google, one Facebook, etc.) is fascinating. Can WeWork really be anything beyond a landlord with a charismatic founder (and serious property liabilities)?

Personally, I feel that investing billions in suspect business models (such as bikes) or suspect markets (the concept of there being one taxi system across the world) to take over a market, smacks of hubris and feels like it will lead to dot-com bust II. In addition, I do not think some markets (like taxis that are tightly 'controlled' locally) can be killed by an algorithm run out of trendy offices on the west coast. That said, companies that win the race, such as the FAANGS and their Chinese equivalents are really coining it in. As of today, their only real threat is public relations (PR), and their (extremely annoying) evangelism and messianic 'making the world a better place' that eventually winds everyone up (at least old goats like me). Equally, regulators or taxmen can halt the march of the titans (as they did with Wonga).

**Managers of Venture Capital in 2019**   The classic '2 and 20' GP/LP models are strong. Like PE, mega or niche is good. Expect a major hit if public technology companies take a beating in the future. However the classic GP/LP model works very well and is here to stay.

## HEDGE FUND STRATEGIES

**Market Neutral or Directional**   Hedge fund strategies are described as absolute return strategies, in that they seek to deliver positive returns regardless of market performance, and can be described as directional or market neutral.

**So Buying Long and also Buying Short Is a 'Hedge'.**   A market neutral fund will seek a lower correlation to the current markets and will be less exposed to Vol in the markets. Directional funds are often exposed to market movements, as they seek to follow the direction that a particular market is moving and exploit any inconsistencies in the market movements.

**Discretionary or Systematic**   The way a hedge fund implements its chosen strategy and makes investments into its chosen instruments can also be divided into how the hedge fund operates when analysing the markets and selecting investments. They are known as either discretionary/qualitative strategies, under which investments are selected by managers who tend to rely on a fundamental or qualitative approach to their decision-making, or systematic/quantitative strategies, under which investments are selected using a systematic model.

**Strategy Implementation and Instruments**   The strategies set out above can be further broken down into how they implement this strategy to achieve the required level of returns and will depend on:

- the chosen market;
- the approach to the market;
- the types of instrument used to generate returns;
- the method and analytics used to select investments; and
- the desired level of asset diversification.

In addition, the level of diversification within a fund can vary dramatically. For a broader discussion on asset allocation see Chapter 7.

## Typical Strategies

Hedge funds cover a range of strategies and are constantly evolving. This makes it difficult to categorise a typical hedge fund strategy. However, as a rough guide, typical strategies fall into the following categories.

**Global Macro** Hedge funds utilising a global macro investing strategy take a view on an industry sector as opposed to individual companies in order to generate a risk-adjusted return. Global macro fund managers use macroeconomic ('big picture') analysis based on global market events and trends to identify opportunities for investment that would profit from anticipated price movements. Global macro is often categorised as a directional investment strategy.

The focus on an industry sector has resulted in global macro hedge funds having an interesting time of it as late. With rising bond yields and President Trump's stance on trade with China presenting a significant level of risk that managers have to side-step. However, this also means that there has been plenty of opportunity for global macro hedge funds to profit from these events. Indeed, many investors are looking to cash in on the success of these funds with USD 12 billion going to US macro funds in the first quarter of 2018.

**Directional** Directional investment strategies utilise market movements, trends, or inconsistencies when picking stocks across a variety of markets. Systematic models can be used or fund managers will identify and select investments. These types of strategies have a greater exposure to the fluctuations of the overall market than do market neutral strategies. Directional hedge fund strategies include US and international long/short equity hedge funds, where long equity positions are hedged with short sales of equities or equity index options.

**Event-Driven** Event-driven strategies concern situations in which the underlying investment opportunity and risk are associated with an event. An event-driven investment strategy finds investment opportunities in corporate transactional events such as consolidations, acquisitions, recapitalisations, bankruptcies, and liquidations. Managers employing such a strategy capitalise on valuation inconsistencies in the market before or after such events, and take a position based on the predicted movement of the security or securities in question. Large institutional investors, such as hedge funds, are more likely to pursue event-driven investing strategies than traditional equity investors because they have the expertise and resources to analyse corporate transactional events for investment opportunities.

Corporate transactional events generally fit into three categories: distressed securities; risk arbitrage; and special situations.

Distressed securities include such events as restructurings, recapitalisations, and bankruptcies. A distressed securities investment strategy involves investing in companies facing bankruptcy or severe financial distress, when these bonds or loans are being traded at a discount to their value. Hedge fund managers pursuing the distressed debt investment strategy aim to capitalise on depressed bond prices. Hedge funds purchasing distressed debt may prevent those companies from going bankrupt, as such an acquisition deters foreclosure by banks.

Risk arbitrage or merger arbitrage includes such events as mergers, acquisitions, liquidations, and hostile takeovers. Risk arbitrage typically involves buying and selling the stocks of two or more merging companies to take advantage of market discrepancies between acquisition price and stock price. The risk element arises from the possibility that the merger or acquisition will not go ahead as planned. Hedge fund managers will use research and analysis to determine whether the event will take place.

Special situations are events that impact the value of a company's stock, including the restructuring of a company or corporate transactions including spin-offs, share buy-backs, security issuance/repurchase, asset sales, or other catalyst-oriented situations. To take advantage of special situations the hedge fund manager must identify an upcoming event that will increase or decrease the value of the company's equity and equity-related instruments.

Other event-driven strategies include:

- a 'credit arbitrage strategy', which focuses on corporate fixed-income securities;
- an 'activist strategy', where the fund takes large positions in companies and uses the ownership to participate in or influence the management; and
- a 'legal catalyst strategy', which specialises in companies involved in major lawsuits.

**Relative Value Arbitrage**　　Relative value arbitrage strategies take advantage of relative discrepancies in price between securities. The price discrepancy can occur due to mispricing of securities compared with related securities, the underlying security, or the market overall. Hedge fund managers can use various types of analysis to identify price discrepancies in securities, including mathematical, technical, or fundamental techniques. Relative value is often used as a synonym for market neutral, as strategies in this category typically have very little or no directional exposure to the market as a whole.

This strategy requires the investor to invest in a 'pair' of securities. These securities will often have a high correlation, thereby moving up or down in value at the same time. When the cost of one security goes up and the other down (or vice versa) the investor will buy one security and short the other. When the prices return the investor will close the trade. This strategy is useful in a market that is neither bull nor bear but rather sideways. This can make it a particularly difficult strategy to employ as it requires significant skill and expertise to monitor how the markets are doing.

This balancing act made relative value arbitrage hedge funds work particularly hard in 2018. The Vol in the S&P has been out of step with its overseas counterparts. This means the traditional purchasing of foreign Vol and selling Vol in the US tactic has stung users of this strategy. It is likely that, going forward, relative value arbitrage funds will go long on Vol in order to counter equity swings.[38]

**Convertible Arbitrage**　　Convertible arbitrage is an equity long-short investment strategy that involves taking a long position in convertible securities of a company, whilst at the same time taking a short position in the shares of the same company. Convertible securities often take the form of bonds that may be converted to shares at a set time and price, usually at a discount to the market value of the company's shares.

The idea behind the convertible arbitrage strategy is that if a company's share price falls, the hedge fund will benefit from taking a short position in the company, and in addition, the value of the convertible bonds should decrease less than the company's share price. However, if the company's share price rises, a loss will be made in relation to the fund's short position of selling the company shares, but the hedge fund will benefit from taking a long position, as it may convert the convertible bonds to shares and sell at market price, hopefully making a gain overall.

**Fixed-Income Arbitrage**　　Fixed-income arbitrage is an investment strategy that seeks to profit from arbitrage opportunities between fixed-income securities. Fixed-income securities, such as government bonds, are debt instruments which provide a fixed stream of periodic payments to investors. A common fixed-income arbitrage strategy entails 'swap-spread arbitrage'. Swap-spread arbitrage involves betting on the likely direction of credit default swap (CDS) rates and other similar rates. A CDS is a type of credit derivative, and is a contractual agreement whereby the risk of a reference entity defaulting is transferred from a seller to a buyer. Payments are made by the buyer to the seller, but in the event the reference entity defaults on the loan, the seller agrees to compensate the buyer for the loss.

There has been a significant change in the market since the financial crisis for fixed-income hedge funds. In the US, outstanding corporate bonds totalled USD 2.8 trillion and dealer bond inventories totalled USD 269 billion.[39] Since then, outstanding corporate bonds have grown to USD 5.3 trillion and inventories have dropped to USD 40 billion. This is a swing from around 10% to roughly 1% as a consequence of regulation following the crisis. This raises serious liquidity questions and presents a tail risk for fixed-income strategies. Any investor using this strategy needs to ensure that they have stress-tested their strategy for a situation when liquidity has dried up.

**Multi-Strategy Funds (and Funds of Funds)**  Fund of hedge funds (multi-manager) are hedge funds with a diversified portfolio of numerous underlying single-manager hedge funds. Essentially, the investment is spread across separate sub-managers that invest in their own strategy. Alternatively a multi-strategy hedge fund is a hedge fund that uses a combination of different strategies to reduce market risk.

The obvious benefits of a multi-strategy fund is flexibility. It allows a manager to utilise the full gamut of investment strategies to pick which will best serve their clients. In contrast to a single strategy fund, which may allocate into cash or have to pick weak opportunities, a multi-strategy fund can move its resources to a different strategy. This movement of risk from one strategy to another relies on the principle of diversification, which is not just limited to different asset classes. It can be used as a tool to reduce risk on a strategy level as well. This finessing requires managers to not be fluent in just one strategy but many, and therefore necessitates staunch investment skills. For an investor this may be worth it as the consistency of results offered by this approach can provide better long-term results than hedge funds with a singular strategy.

**Commodities Trading Advisers Strategy**  Commodities Trading Advisers (CTA) funds use futures (discussed earlier in this chapter) and options. In the early stages of the execution of the strategy, managers of CTA funds tended to focus upon commodity-based investments. CTA funds tend to do well when the prices of securities are falling, and tend to underperform when the prices of securities rise. The investment strategies of a CTA fund fall into two categories: systematic and discretionary.

Systematic CTAs rely on computer programs to provide analysis of market data and to identify and make trades. Systematic trading is the most common CTA strategy, although it has drawbacks in that it can take a long time to implement changes to the computer programs, where changes in market or economic conditions occur.

A discretionary CTA which employs discretionary trading relies on its investment decisions being made by management based upon 'real-time' market data. Whilst a discretionary CTA is able to react to changes in market or economic conditions, they are less likely to be able to make an unbiased decision in the manner in which a systematic CTA can.

**Managers of Hedge Funds in 2019**  Hedge fund managers have never fully recovered from the financial crisis. It is still tough. Machines, mega-speed, algorithms and passives are the increasingly powerful enemy of stock picking and macro trends. The hedge fund of funds is all but dead. To grow, managers need to increase AuM and decrease costs. They also need to innovate. Change in hedge fund managers is glacial. The old way is not always the best way. Hedge fund AuM can evaporate like water in a desert. However, hedge and alpha managers have much to offer, especially when vol increases and interest rates rise. I really want them to succeed.

## OTHER STRATEGIES

**Secondaries**  Secondary investments in PE (or RE or hedge, for that matter) are effectively buy-outs by a second PE fund of PE assets from a first PE fund. This can also include the buy-out of a position in a fund as an LP or a direct acquisition of equity stakes in portfolio companies. These methods of acquisition can be broken down further.

### The Sale of Fund Interests

- **Straight sale:** For cash of a limited partnership interest at or around the GP NAV.
- **Structured joint ventures:** An agreement that does not completely relinquish the seller's interest.
- **Securitisation:** The process by which an interest in the fund is transferred to an SPV which issues loan notes to generate liquidity. Equity in the new vehicle may also be offered to investors.
- **Stapled secondaries:** Where a new fund is being raised by the general partner of the existing fund, a secondary interest in the existing fund may be offered to investors in the new fund as an additional incentive.

### The Sale of Direct Investments

- **Secondary direct:** The sale of direct portfolio assets.
- **Synthetic secondary/spin-out:** The sale of portfolio assets to a new fund partnership into which the secondary investors invest, which is managed by the previous manager.
- **Tail-end:** The sale of assets during the winding up of a fund.
- **Structured secondary:** Where the incoming investor agrees to provide the seller's capital contributions in the future in exchange for a preferred return on the portfolio income.

Secondaries are becoming more important as an exit route for PE investors (and other long-term investment) for several reasons. They shorten deal lifetimes and help achieve early exits for what are otherwise very illiquid investments, and many managers seek a more active portfolio policy in order to achieve the greatest returns possible. The regulatory landscape for investors such as banks and insurance firms is changing too – the Basel III and Solvency II regulations, respectively, will limit the investments these firms can invest in due to capital adequacy restrictions and rules on the risk weighting of assets, which in turn leads to secondary sales of alternative assets.

**Aspects of Secondaries Investment**  The key feature of portfolio or fund secondaries is the offsetting of risks involved in investing in PE at the primary stage. Secondary investment can reduce the effect of the 'J-curve'. The J-curve is the cash flow of a fund over time represented graphically. The initial outlays of the construction of the fund mean that the cash flow is negative for the first years, before returning to a positive line of growth later in the life cycle. Secondary investments often take place during the latter part of the construction phase or after, so the secondary investor should experience a positive cash flow either immediately or within a short period.

A secondary investment also mitigates the risks associated with blind pools, where an investment fund has no specific investments lined up on creation. The secondary investor has an advantage in that it can analyse the historical performance of the current investments and decide whether or not to invest on that basis, and also potentially negotiate a better price. Secondary investments are less 'blind' than primary investment.

Another benefit is that it is easier to diversify a portfolio with acquisitions of secondary interests than with a primary investment. When investing at the initial stage, the high commitments required prevent a quick diversification of the portfolio and the similar vintage years will often mean that it is harder to spread the Vol of returns and the lack of initial positive cash flow. Mature primary investment funds do not have such problems, but for newcomers it is easier to establish this diversity with secondaries.

**Some Criticism of Secondaries Investment** Secondary funds in themselves can be blind pools, especially when large funds are raised that take, say, five years to invest. In addition, as the demand for secondary investment increases, if the market of sellers (or primary direct funds) does not grow at the same rate, a greater proportion of secondary capital will be available and it will become more of a seller's market and the cost of acquisition will increase.

There is also the possibility of paying higher fees for secondary investments than for primaries. The investment in the primary fund requires the payment of fees to the managers of that fund. As most secondary investments are made through funds, the management of those funds in turn also charges fees. Also the larger secondary funds are effectively becoming an index for the wider PE asset class where the secondary manager hardly influences returns (other than through sharper or structured entry pricing).

Finally, 'pass the parcel' secondary investing (especially of single assets) is seen by some LPs as lazy, non-proprietary investing, and a means of extending management fees for an asset.

## Derivatives Funds

Derivatives are investment products which are based on an underlying asset, index, or other product. To buy oil is to acquire the asset. Agreeing to buy oil at a future date is the derived product. Derivatives originally developed to allow suppliers or purchasers of products to purchase the products they need and to simultaneously hedge against price Vol, in the belief that the price will increase or decrease. The derivatives market has now grown to encompass nearly any financial product – for example, equities, bonds, interest rates, and currencies. The counterparty to the derivative believes that the price will move in the opposite direction. The counterparty is often a speculator, and they often trade not to acquire or sell goods but only to make a profit by second-guessing the price movements. That is not to say they are unpopular, as their presence often provides liquidity in the market and a greater range of derivative options for those who are dealing directly in the products traded. Some of the recent regulatory interest, however, is investigating and seeking to regulate the perceived Vol that an excess of speculation can bring into a market. Derivatives are either traded through exchanges following a standard form, or are traded OTC derivatives where the form is often designed to the requirements of the parties. Funds have in the past decade begun to take an interest in the use of derivatives as sources of income.

There are funds that invest solely in derivatives as their investment strategy, whereas others hold them as part of the portfolio or use them to hedge against portfolio risk. The attractiveness of derivatives funds is on the increase as interest rates remain stagnant and other opportunities for investment income remain low.

**Issues Around Derivatives**   Derivatives carry general risks. There is counterparty risk where the contracting party that has unlimited exposure defaults on its obligations, leaving the other without the expected return, which can often be a vital hedge. Exchange-traded derivatives are guaranteed by the clearing house, which mitigates the risk of default. OTC derivatives, however, are not normally traded through a clearing house and therefore carry no implicit protection. Large-scale default by counterparties can cause wider market problems, such as the bailout of US insurance company AIG in 2008. As OTC derivatives are not frequently traded through a clearing house they are potentially more difficult to value, transfer, or liquidate.

Investing in derivatives by a fund can potentially create risk. Their use frequently involves leverage – enabling a fund to participate in gains or losses far beyond the initial investment. Instruments such as purchased call options do not expressly involve leverage, but can create an economic equivalent of leverage. Although leverage can allow gains far in excess of capital commitment, a fund stands to lose a large amount of its portfolio when at a loss.

One of the risks of funds for a stock market fund is where the equity markets grow at a rate which causes the losses on the call options sold to outweigh the gains the portfolio naturally makes. Derivative enhanced funds may, however, be better investments in a stagnant or bearish equity market.

**Specific Regulation**   The derivatives market came under close scrutiny following the financial crisis. Derivatives are seen as risky investments that were misused to excess, leading to some of the highest losses during the crisis. Not only that, but derivatives are often misused by traders to conceal losses, such as the case of Jérôme Kerviel of Société Générale, which resulted in losses of EUR 4.9 billion for the bank. OTC derivatives are now regulated more extensively in the US and EU. The Dodd–Frank Act has brought in sweeping reform, meaning derivatives known as 'swaps' are regulated by either the CFTC or the SEC, or in some cases both. Private funds will be regulated as 'financial entities' such that funds will not be able to take advantage of an exception, known as the 'end-user' exception. The regulations under the Dodd–Frank Act require reporting of each swap entered into, that the board or other appropriate committee approves uncleared swaps, and that other documentary requirements are fulfilled. The EU has also issued rules regulating the use of any derivative contract, the European Market Infrastructure Regulation (EMIR). These rules require the reporting of any derivative contract entered into to a trade repository and require that users implement management risk standards. They also introduce a category of OTC derivatives which must be cleared via a central counterparty (CCP). Both the provisions of the Dodd–Frank Act and EMIR will have indirect extraterritorial effect, affecting counterparties which are based outside of the applicable jurisdictions.

The SEC also considered direct regulation of the use of derivatives by funds. This was initiated by an announcement in March 2010 of a moratorium on the registration of new ETFs which were actively managed or leveraged and utilised derivatives. A consultation was launched in August 2011 exploring the benefits and risks of using derivatives in funds and whether or not there was a need for further regulation than that already required under US law. In December 2012, the SEC announced that it would lift the moratorium but would attach conditions to future registrations. An issuer would have to represent that it would assess and disclose its use of derivatives in accordance with relevant SEC guidance. The moratorium was only partially lifted, and ETFs which are leveraged by derivatives will continue to be prohibited.

## Currency Funds

Some funds will use currency investments as a core strategy whereas others look to currencies to hedge portfolio risk. For example, an investor in foreign currency denominated bonds would hedge against an adverse currency shift by investing in a currency derivative. Investment strategies rely on a variety of methods to calculate or predict changes in the exchange rates – some analyse market trends and the base statistics such as power purchasing parity to predict changes in the rates, whereas others look to investor psychology and behaviour to determine how the rates will shift on the premise that the majority of trades are conducted between investors rather than those using the markets in the course of their business. Many of the more sophisticated investors will use a blend of both techniques.

Investors in currencies who are seeking a return rather than to hedge against currency risk often seek to exploit changes in the exchange rates or differences in interest rates in different currencies. Most investments make use of derivative instruments linked to the currency trade.

Another technique is the 'carry trade' – borrowing money in a currency with a low interest rate, and then purchasing another currency with a higher interest rate and then investing in bonds denominated in that currency. The transaction is at risk of exchange rate fluctuations, which could wipe out the gain on interest. To protect against this, the arrangement to buy back the initial currency borrowed is made in advance by a forward contract. As long as the premium paid for the contract is less than the gain expected from the interest rates, the investor has a guaranteed return.

**Issues Around Currency Funds** Currency trading is notoriously difficult to succeed in or predict. The wealth of macroeconomic factors which affects the exchange rates in the first instance is difficult to evaluate but understanding and anticipating the psychology of the markets is an even more exotic art form. The Vol inherent in the markets is a key driver for commercial success but is also where big losses can be made. One of the recent problems arising from the economic downturn is that the EUR, USD, and JPY have all been subject to low interest rates and low swings of Vol, pushing investors into emerging market currencies, which often carry greater currency risk. As currency trades are frequently executed by derivatives there are also the risks attached to those instruments, such as counterparty risk, as mentioned above.

For the individual investor the most significant risk with currency funds is that currencies lack long-term consistent trends.[40] They are, in short, relatively unpredictable in the long term. This makes it difficult for individual investors to consistently make a profit. For example, rising interest rates can make a currency higher in a specific region as global investors will target it for its higher yields. Conversely, lower interest rates could also boost the same currency as low interest rates are indicative of rising equities, which could also attract global investors. It is easy to see, then, how an individual investor could make a miscalculation in their investment decisions.

Personally, I have always felt very few managers make money solely in trading currencies and it can be a lonely place for a manager. The arbitrage is getting harder, and currencies can be impacted by politics, the weather, and human emotion. A tough place to apply logic and make money.

## HOT TOPICS

### ETFs

ETFs were devised and refined in the US in the late 1980s and early 1990s. As of 2019, it is a hot place. The purpose of an ETF is to have investments that can be bought and sold freely which are linked to underlying interests in markets or indices. They are similar to an open-ended investment company (OEIC) as the shares can be redeemed (giving the fund its open-ended character). Some ETFs are actively managed rather than simply passive, although an original attraction of the ETF was that it was a cheaper investment than other funds, and active management pushes the fees up.

An ETF holds assets such as stocks, currencies, commodities, or bonds, and trades close to its NAV over the course of the trading day. Most ETFs track an index such as a stock index or bond index. ETFs can be attractive to investors because of their low costs, tax efficiency and stock-like features. A share in an ETF represents an interest in a unit of securities. The unit of securities can be all the shares of the tracked market or index in proportion to their weighting, a sample of the shares that aims to imitate the index, or made up of swaps or other derivatives. An ETF is priced continuously throughout the day, which makes it more attractive to short-term investors, along with the low management fees. It is, however, more expensive with regard to dealing costs, as there is a cost when selling the share or the bundle of securities it represents (on redemption).

Only authorised participants, which are large broker-dealers that have entered into agreements with the ETF's distributor, actually buy or sell ETF shares directly from or to the ETF.

Authorised participants may wish to invest in the ETF shares for the long-term, but they usually act as market makers on the open market, using their ability to exchange creation units with their underlying securities to provide liquidity of the ETF shares and help ensure that their intraday market price approximates to the net asset value of the underlying assets. Other investors, such as individuals using a retail broker, trade ETF shares on this secondary market.

**Pricing**   The price can vary in accordance with investor demand. If the price is pushed up, a market maker can purchase new baskets of securities and exchange them with the fund manager for shares in the fund. This increase of supply will reduce the price accordingly. When demand falls and prices drop, market makers can redeem the shares, which will increase the share price. With this open-ended approach, the shares in the fund are often quoted at close to NAV, although there can be brief fluctuations.

The shares are not purchased or sold at the NAV. When sold on the secondary market there will be dealing costs as with any quoted share, and when the shares are redeemed with the fund manager there may be additional redemption costs.

**Risk**   Investors have the ability to trade shares in the fund more frequently than with units of an investment trust, resulting in more flexible investments. This implies that these short-term trades will lead to greater returns. However, with the brokerage fees and potential fluctuations in price there is a risk that short-term gains are reduced significantly by the cost of frequent trading in comparison with a longer term investment. There is also a risk with regards to the synthetic models of an ETF that, as with any derivative product, the counterparty's collateral is dubious and the underlying investment fails.

**Regulation** In the US, ETFs are typically structured as open-ended retail funds. The primary source of law in respect of such funds is the Investment Company Act of 1940 (ICA). Under the ICA, the SEC is empowered to regulate ETFs and the ICA also imposes substantive requirements on ETFs. In addition, as ETFs are by their nature exchange traded, the funds must be compliant with the applicable securities laws (the Securities Act 1933 and the Securities Exchange Act 1934) and the relevant exchange's rules.

Most European ETFs are structured to fall within the UCITS IV Directive to take advantage of the European Economic Area (EEA)-wide freedom to sell and market them without reference to each national authority. In the UK, they are regulated by the FCA. The ETF will also be regulated by the exchange on which it is listed, and by the relevant law for the corporate vehicle and domicile chosen. Most European ETFs are domiciled in Ireland or Luxembourg with a public company structure.

They will also need to gain approval from the ETF's home authority. ETFs are considered UCITS, where the sole object is the collective investment in transferable securities or other liquid financial assets, by capital which is raised from the public, that is operating on the principle of risk spreading, and the units can be redeemed or cancelled out of the fund's assets. Steps taken by the fund manager to issue or redeem units in order to keep the price of the shares as close to NAV are acceptable. A fund which is closed-ended and either does not offer shares to the public or does so outside of the EU only, or which is prescribed by the home member state for the impropriety of its investment objectives or borrowing policy, cannot be a UCITS.

The fund will be authorised and regulated by its home member state for its compliance with UCITS (Article 5, UCITS IV). Most European ETFs are domiciled in Ireland or Luxembourg for taxation purposes and so will be regulated by those countries, both as a UCITS and for their compliance with local laws with regards to their corporate structure. They will also be regulated by the markets on which their shares are traded.

The regulatory landscape for ETFs may change in the near future. Several bodies at UK, EU, and international level have expressed concern about ETFs and the consequences of their activities on the markets for the underlying assets. For example, ETFs which invest in the commodities markets are considered to be affecting prices and reducing liquidity by holding onto assets. The FCA has identified that ETFs are putting investors at risk as well as market stability.

Retail investors are considered at risk, as the market for ETFs has grown rapidly in the past ten years and there are concerns that regulations have not kept up with this rapidly evolving market. Investors are at risk due to the increasing complexity and the increasing reliance on derivatives in synthetic ETFs. There is concern that despite the low fees and the ability to place the shares in tax exempt accounts, knowledge of the underlying risks (especially with derivative products) remains low.

One potential concern for ETFs is the EU's consideration of how the asset management industry should operate.[41] The current 'delegation' rules allow a firm to register a fund in one EU country (typically Luxembourg or Ireland) and then manage it elsewhere. This situation is not welcomed with open arms by other financial centres across Europe, with Paris and Frankfurt keen to change the rules. One way this may happen is that the EU may insist that the managers of these funds work from the country the fund is registered in. This would be enforced by national regulators and would prevent the UK asset management industry carrying on post-Brexit in the same way they have before. It would also have a major knock-on effect in the US and elsewhere outside the EU. The current delegation model reduces costs but changing this system will likely increase them.

Regulators are also concerned about the effect of ETFs on other markets. The Financial Stability Board (FSB) in 2011 published concerns that illiquidity, counterparty risk, and transparency issues connected with ETFs were connected to increased financial instability. It recommended a further study into whether more regulation was necessary.

**Management Fees** ETFs are often promoted for their low management fees over some of the competitor funds. Expenses for passive funds are typically in the range of 0.5% to 1%. Recently, there has been a race to zero! If there is an element of active management in the fund the fees can increase. Most fees are simply to deal with the cost of trading in the underlying securities, and investors can expect to pay brokerage fees when purchasing shares on the secondary market from the market makers. Some funds employ an 'all in one' fee system, where the expenses of the fund are deducted as a single flat fee calculated as a percentage of the NAV and paid monthly out of the fund. Many funds do not charge entry and exit fees. In 2019 will someone pay investors to invest but win from providing stock to shorters?

## Smart Beta, Alternative Beta, and Similar

As with a nascent musical genre, there is much debate over what to call this strategy – it is variously known as factor investing, smart beta, alternative beta, and (alternative) risk premia. All of these labels are perhaps best thought of as variations of and alternatives to the market capitalisation-weighted approach which underpins the more 'traditional' passive strategies covered towards the beginning of this chapter and in Chapters 1 and 13. Market capitalisation-weighted passive strategies track the market according to one 'factor': the size of the market capitalisation of the constituent companies in an index. If FAANG stocks make up 10% of the S&P 500 by market capital then a pound invested in a Vanguard passive tracker fund will own 10p of FAANG stock.

Factor investing allows for passive strategies to invest in stocks on the basis of factors other than size. This began in 1992 with Eugene Fama and Kenneth French's development and formal proposal of the factors of size and value. Since then, factors such as Vol, momentum, and quality have been developed, accepted and incorporated into investment strategies. Each of these factors defines a different characteristic of a stock. The names of these factors are an accurate guide to their meaning. 'Vol' focuses on a stock's movement up and down, 'momentum' on its recent gains, 'value' is defined by similar metrics to those an active value manager may use (such as price to book), and 'quality' by metrics such as debt to equity. Once these factors have been defined by a manager the stocks which exhibit them can be identified within an index and bought and sold systematically according to a predefined strategy. This is factor investing. The advantage of factor investing is that it is passive and cheap to run, allowing for low fees, whilst exhibiting an 'active-like' strategy with more sophistication and different priorities to a simple market capitalisation-based passive fund.

These factor strategies have extended beyond the equity markets to other asset classes including credit, commodities, and beyond, but equity is still the main focus. These strategies can also be market neutral, taking long as well as short positions based on the factor in question. This allows for some factor investing strategies to play a similar role to certain types of hedge funds in a portfolio. These strategies are known as alternative risk premia or alternative beta.

With factor investing the devil is in the detail. Keeping up to date with the latest market trends and looking beyond the broad labels of each factor to how each manager defines them and what their investment processes are is the only way for an investor to fully understand the product.

### Impact of Low Interest Rates and Decreasing Returns

One of the tools that central banks employ to stabilise economies when they are overheating or in need of a kick is the manipulation of the country's interest rate. Following the financial crisis, interest rates across the globe fell to unprecedented lows having been set by central banks such as the BoE, the Federal Reserve, and the Bank of Japan amongst others, in a bid to keep individuals and companies spending. However, keeping interest rates at low levels for a prolonged period of time risks increasing hasty investing by managers that are pushed to find higher returns in low-return projects. The demand for riskier assets that provide higher returns means that across the spectrum the price of assets increases to the point where asset managers cannot find suitable deals. Internally, asset managers that would ordinarily be restricted to assets of a certain risk class are having to go to their investors requesting that they be able to change the percentage allocations they set for certain assets or begin investing in entirely new asset classes. During 2018, however, interest rates rose from effectively zero in the UK and US (which was combined with QT). This led to a mini collapse in equity stock markets. During 2019, QT is under some challenge. QE might return in the UK post Brexit to deal with the economic change. QT is still some way off in Europe.

### Growing Popularity of Alternative Asset Classes

As the global economy continues to stumble (frankly) past 'levels not seen since before the great financial crisis', alternative asset classes – PE, hedge funds, RE, illiquid credit, and other such asset types – are growing more and more popular. The total AuM of alternative assets sits around USD 6–7 trillion globally, which is spread across 562 managers.[42] PE managers alone have experienced an 18.5%, or USD 325 billion, increase in funding from investors since 2015. Even more impressive (and perhaps equally scary) are the levels of 'dry powder' that PE managers are holding. Dry powder is a market term referring to the money raised by PE managers that has not yet been allocated towards the purchase of whatever assets the PE manager specialises in. The levels in 2018 sat at USD 1.5 trillion,[43] which suggests that even PE managers are having a tough time sourcing deals they do not believe are reasonably priced.

## SOME CONCLUSIONS

The diversity of investment strategies is such that it stretches categorisation to breaking point in certain circumstances. Many generalised funds will diversify their investment strategies in order to provide a balanced portfolio. This is not the case with niche strategies.

There is no doubt that uncorrelated alternatives are on the rise, especially as listed equities and bonds suffer declines. Banks have made a comeback in providing credit, but private debt is an enormous opportunity, currently being gobbled up by more traditional PE and hedge players.

## ENDNOTES

1. www.sr-sv.com/leverage-in-asset-management/
2. https://seekingalpha.com/article/4227635-european-equities-3-big-themes-watch-2019?page=3
3. https://www.dmo.gov.uk/media/14971/mb13062012a.pdf p. 14.
4. Ibid.
5. https://www.dmo.gov.uk/media/14971/mb13062012a.pdf
6. Ibid.

7. Ibid.
8. www.ft.com/content/e1b09a32-5863-11e8-806a-808d194ffb75
9. https://asreport.americanbanker.com/news/bell-tolls-for-clo-risk-retention-following-dc-court-order
10. www.whatinvestment.co.uk/opportunities-uk-property-investors-2017-2553155/
11. www.greenbiz.com/article/13-top-energy-developments-2016
12. www.growthbusiness.co.uk/private-equity-buyout-deals-to-slow-down-in-face-of-brexit-uncertainty-2555833/
13. Ibid.
14. www.cityam.com/270741/take-private-deals-worth-more-than-1bn-set-increase-2019
15. www.bloomberg.com/news/articles/2018-01-30/blackstone-to-acquire-thomson-reuters-unit-in-20-billion-deal
16. www.theguardian.com/business/2018/mar/29/gkn-shareholders-accept-melrose-takeover
17. www.londonandpartners.com/media-centre/press-releases/2017/20180105-2017-record-year-for-london-and-uk-tech-investment
18. Data from the NHGRI Genome Sequencing Program (GSP).
19. www.biopharminternational.com/report-shows-bioscience-industry-has-2-trillion-economic-impact
20. www.telegraph.co.uk/business/2017/05/23/uk-set-become-third-global-hub-biosciences-investment-booms/
21. www.ft.com/content/836832c2-1efc-11e9-b126-46fc3ad87c65
22. www.impactcentre.ca/wp-content/uploads/2017/11/171128-Physical-Technologies.pdf
23. 13.2, 12.7 and 12.1 USD billion respectively.
24. www.theguardian.com/business/2017/apr/29/fangs-breakneck-rise-facebook-amazon-netflix-google
25. www.theguardian.com/business/2017/apr/29/fangs-breakneck-rise-facebook-amazon-netflix-google
26. https://eu.usatoday.com/story/tech/talkingtech/2017/06/09/tech-stocks-fang-dead-long-live-faamg/385200001/
27. www.scmp.com/business/companies/article/2139684/heart-chinas-techno-nationalism-hit-list-200-unicorns
28. https://pandaily.com/chinese-unicorns-internet-companies-take-a-dominant-position/
29. https://pandaily.com/chinese-unicorns-internet-companies-take-a-dominant-position/
30. https://pitchbook.com/news/articles/2017-year-in-review-the-top-vc-rounds-investors-in-ai
31. https://softbank-ia.com/vision-fund
32. www.recode.net/2018/2/7/16984170/softbank-vision-fund-40-billion-technology-earnings
33. www.ft.com/content/c2fe7814-536a-11e8-b3ee-41e0209208ec
34. https://benhamouglobalventures.com/2018/06/28/emergence-mega-vc-funds-size-matter/
35. https://www.linkedin.com/pulse/rise-corporate-venture-capital-lando-barbagli
36. Ibid.
37. https://techcrunch.com/2017/12/21/long-island-iced-tea-shares-went-gangbusters-after-changing-its-name-to-long-blockchain/?guccounter=1
38. www.bloomberg.com/news/articles/2019-01-17/volatility-hedge-funds-hit-by-market-horrors-in-all-directions
39. www.hedgeweek.com/2018/09/05/268000/where-are-opportunities-fixed-income-oriented-hedge-funds
40. www.wsj.com/articles/the-smart-ways-for-fund-investors-to-deal-with-currency-fluctuations-1520219101
41. www.bloomberg.com/news/articles/2017-07-25/luxembourg-irish-funds-caught-in-brexit-rules-crossfire
42. FT: Global shift into alternative assets gathers pace: www.ft.com/content/1167a4b8-6653-11e7-8526-7b38dcaef614
43. Ibid.

# CHAPTER 6

# Investors' View of the Industry

*If the doors of perception were cleansed everything would appear to man as it is: Infinite. For man has closed himself up, till he sees all things thro' narrow chinks of his cavern.*

— William Blake, *The Marriage of Heaven and Hell*

**T**his chapter describes different types of investors – including sovereign wealth funds (SWFs), state-sponsored funds, pension funds, charities, family offices, and individuals – and their perspective on asset management. It explores the motivations of these investors and the types of investment they are drawn towards. This chapter is strongly linked to Chapter 5 on investment strategies and Chapter 7 on portfolio construction. As a fund manager, knowing your investor audience is critical to your success.

## SOVEREIGN WEALTH FUNDS

A SWF is a special purpose investment fund or arrangement owned and managed (directly or indirectly) by a government, created for macroeconomic purposes. A SWF is commonly established out of balance of payments surpluses, official foreign currency operations, the proceeds of privatisations, fiscal surpluses, and/or receipts resulting from commodity exports. SWFs are created to hold, manage, or administer assets to achieve financial objectives.

SWFs have existed for decades but are emerging as a potential large source of capital. SWFs have substantial resources and assets of high liquidity, and have grown significantly. These attributes of SWFs have seen them become an important investor group during the economic downturn/slowdown.

The first sovereign wealth fund named as such was the Kuwait Investment Authority (KIA) established in 1953 to invest in excess oil revenues. Since this date, the number and size of SWFs have increased dramatically. There are now more than 50 SWFs established with a combined total AuM of around USD 8.8 trillion.

There is a variety of sources from which SWFs are formed but, in general, they are the result of current account surpluses from a country's exports of commodities (commonly oil) and manufactured goods, fiscal surpluses, public savings, or privatisation receipts. SWFs are usually sourced from two categories – commodity or non-commodity.

Commodity SWFs are predominantly funded from oil revenue, although other natural resources such as gas and minerals provide a significant source of revenue. The main objectives of commodity-focused SWFs are to insure against the risk of volatile commodity markets, maintain economic stability, and provide an income source for future generations.

Non-commodity SWFs are funded by the transfer of assets directly from official foreign exchange reserves, budget surpluses, and privatisation revenue.

Historically, SWFs focused their strategy on fixed income. This approach has been adapted following QE and falling interest rates,[1] which has diminished the enthusiasm SWFs have for these products. Against this economic backdrop, SWFs have looked to other means to increase returns. After 2009, and the following bull market, equities became increasingly attractive. More pertinently, there has been a growing movement towards alternatives, which have enabled SWFs to diversify and produce superior returns. This has been bookended by SWFs move away from bonds, with the share in AuM invested in these products decreasing from 40% in 2013 to 30% in 2016.[2]

Clearly, the growing investment in alternatives by SWFs is based on a strategic decision to diversify in order to produce better results. Yet the traditional problem that alternatives are illiquid still rings true. However, for SWFs this is not as pressing a concern as it is for say, insurance companies.[3] This is because SWFs have a long-term perspective with broad goals. This enables them to take on more risk within their portfolio and, consequently, they do not need to retain a high level of liquidity.

## Types of SWF Investment Vehicles

SWFs are generally set up to do five things – stabilise, save, pursue, develop, and prepare. Underlying these objectives, are four general objectives that underline most SWFs,[4] as headed below.

**Stabilisation Funds** Stabilisation funds are often set up in countries that have rich supplies of natural resources to safeguard the economy from the effects of volatile commodity markets. A stabilisation fund is therefore established to help mitigate Vol by stabilising fiscal revenues and sterilising capital inflows. This is often achieved by building up a fund during times of favourable commodity prices and drawing on a fund when commodity prices or reserves fall low.

The investment strategy of a stabilisation fund is conservative, focusing on fixed-income rather than equity investments. This helps the fund achieve its purpose of protecting the economy of its founders' origin. Retaining liquidity is therefore vital and prevents stabilisation funds from having a high exposure to alternatives and equities.

For example, the Russian Reserve Fund was created to keep the federal budget balanced and guarantee that financing expenses could be met to ensure Russia's economy would be stable. Its investment strategy focused on low-yield securities and was characterised as a rainy day fund.[5] This came into play when oil prices started declining in 2014 and hit their record low in 2016. The Russian Reserve Fund had USD 89 billion AuM at the beginning of this slump and USD 32 billion at the end.[6] By the end of 2017, the fund had only USD 17 billion and had, according to the Russian Finance Ministry, ceased to exist by January 2018. The remaining funds have been merged with the National Welfare Fund, which was established to cover pension payments in the medium term. Another prominent example of a stabilisation fund would be Chile's Economic and Social Stabilization Fund. This fund was created in 2007 and replaced the initial Copper Stabilization Fund. The fund by its nature holds macroeconomic concerns at its core. When copper prices are high the fund accumulates excess revenue and invests it. When copper prices are low, the fund can funnel revenue into the budget to limit government expenditure. Similarly to the Russian Reserve Fund, the risk profile of its investments is low because of the short-term perspective it takes. This is synonymous with the Russian fund and based on the need for high liquidity. Consequently, the fund invests predominately in financial institution bonds, foreign government agency bonds, and currencies.

**Saving Funds**  Saving funds are intended to share wealth across generations. For countries rich in natural resources (in particular those countries which have non-renewable natural resources), a savings fund allows the benefit of that resource to be shared with future generations. This is achieved by converting that source into a diversified portfolio of international financial assets that will be able to provide for future generations and other long-term objectives.

Given the long-term nature and investment horizon of a saving fund, the fund tends to invest in a broad range of assets and forms of alternative investments such as RE, PE, hedge funds, and commodities.

**Reserve Investment Corporations Funds**  Reserve investment corporations funds are established for one of two reasons, either to reduce the opportunity cost of holding excess foreign reserves or to pursue investment policies with higher returns. These types of fund seek high returns and use leverage in their investments.

**Development Funds**  A development fund utilises returns to further develop a country's economic and development goals. This is achieved by investing in social infrastructure (for example, healthcare and education), physical infrastructure (for example, telecommunications, roads, and railways), and diversification of the economy (for example, investing in specific industries). Development funds take a more high-risk approach in their portfolio. Consequently, they invest heavily in equities and alternatives – utilising diversification to encourage better returns.

A good example of an SWF focused on development is Temasek Holdings, which invests mainly in equities. Established by the government of Singapore in 1974, their portfolio is comprised of shares in telecoms, energy, and financial services. The firm has also invested in debt funds, mezzanine funds, technology VC funds, and life sciences VC funds. This is combined with PE investments and the backing of SMEs. Furthermore, they encourage development in Singapore through financing infrastructure projects.

**Pension Reserve Funds**  Sovereign pension reserve funds are investment vehicles funded by a portion of assets set aside to prepare for the future needs and obligations owed to an ageing society. The objective behind the fund is to accumulate assets in the now to offset predicted higher liability in the future in order to sustain future pensions and social welfare. A number of countries, such as New Zealand, France, and Ireland, have established this type of fund.

Broadly speaking, SWFs are increasing in size and number thus ensuring that they will remain a staple of any future financial landscape. Historically, their presence has significantly influenced the capital markets and undoubtedly they will continue to do so. Beyond financial influence, their ability to impact the lives of everyone in the world through their investment in new sources of energy and technology will become ever more apparent. This section will now turn to a regional discussion of SWFs and the nuances that emerge because of the location they are both based in and operate in.

## UK

The increasing importance of emerging markets and the value of SWFs during financial instability has contributed enormously to their growth over the past ten years. Nowhere else has this been felt more than the UK. London is the pre-eminent Western centre for SWFs to manage their assets. The biggest SWFs have offices in London, with the International Forum of Sovereign Wealth Funds (IFSWF) relocating its secretariat to London from Washington DC in 2014.[7] Without doubt, the UK is a crucial market for SWFs offering a destination for their investments and a clearing house for their transactions. This section will look beyond what a SWF is, to why the UK is so popular and what SWFs think.

**Taxation**   SWFs are generally taxed in the same fashion as other government-owned or controlled funds. The UK provides a unilateral exemption to SWFs on their investment income. The exemption is granted as an extension of the doctrine of sovereign immunity. Because of the widespread adoption of the restrictive theory of sovereign immunity (with immunity no longer applying to commercial activities of foreign government enterprises), the unilateral tax exemptions typically apply only to passive investment income and do not apply to income from commercial activities.

The UK exemption for foreign governments is done administratively. The UK government has said that where an SWF is an integral part of a foreign government it will benefit from the exemption from UK taxes. Because the UK recognises the principle of sovereign immunity under which one state does not attempt to tax the activities of another state, the current practice of the UK government is to treat all passive income and gains beneficially owned by a foreign government as immune from direct taxes.

**Key Regulation**   In the UK, governmental policy has been welcoming of SWF investment and few deals are obstructed. The Enterprise Act 2002 restricted the capacity for ministers to refer potential acquisitions to the Competition Commission, except on grounds of national security, financial stability, or media pluralism. The scope for restriction is further limited by the provisions of EU law.

Concerns about the influence of SWF investment overseas have prompted calls to regulate or restrict the access of SWFs to domestic investment opportunities. The causes for concern include investments in industries which are of political and economic strategic importance and investments in currency reserves that are then used to manipulate exchange rates in order to aid the exports of the SWF's nation. These calls have generally been resisted on several grounds: such restrictions would be protectionist and could lead to retaliatory enactments; SWFs are an increasing source of finance and as a result can provide necessary capital where it is harder to raise locally; and there is a lack of evidence that such investments are made for political or economic strategic gain.

Broadly, investment in the UK or acquiring UK companies is less political, more open, and less protectionist than in other major jurisdictions, as can be seen especially in the US and France.

**Missed Opportunity?**   SWFs can be used as a tool for economic stabilisation that can steady the ship in the face of financial market Vol. Yet the UK does not have an SWF. In contrast to

Norway, which has the largest SWF in the world, the UK never spent the money it generated from oil in creating a fund. Instead, it used the cash flow to cut national borrowing and keep taxes low.[8] Perhaps the UK had to, and its economic growth, inflation and interest rate control and high employment since the 1980s is a discernible positive. In light of current economic and political trends, the utility of a UK SWF appears to be growing. It could be used to boost investment in the UK economy and help with broader socio-economic issues, such as unemployment. Given that national governments can borrow very cheaply[9] it would be possible for the UK government to create significant revenues through issuing debt and subsequently investing in the stock market. With the importance of SWFs increasing, the calls for a UK SWF will only grow.

Despite the lack of a UK specific SWF, there are many SWFs that operate within its borders. Norway's SWF helped protect UK jobs after 2008[10] and, in contrast to the fears Brexit has raised, China Investment Corporation (CIC) (China's SWF) is aiming to create a manufacturing investment fund in the UK.[11] The significant amount of activity of foreign SWFs within the UK is in part due to plentiful opportunity but also a welcoming tax and regulatory system. Clearly, SWFs have historically viewed the UK as a fantastic place to do business. What is crucial is that with their growing importance this perspective does not change.

The recent UK County Council pension plan pooling (see below) seeks to address, in part, the lack of a UK SWF.

Furthermore, with a more recent clamp down on possible money laundering and concerns about political or oligarch émigrés, foreign SWFs, and links to such SWFs have been further restricted from using London as a base.

## Europe

In general, SWFs have been accumulating assets at a considerable rate since the early 2000s. The EU, home of the largest SWF in the world, Norway's Statens pensionsfond utland, has seen considerable investment from SWFs in the last ten years in particular. However, the uncertainty generated by political instability across Europe (see Chapter 1) has impacted the level of investment by SWFs in Europe over the past two years. The year 2016 marked the first year that Europe was not the most popular destination in the world for SWFs to invest their money.[12] The contributing factors were most likely security issues, Brexit, the rise of populism in various countries, and poor economic growth. Moreover, with population growth slowing in the EU, emerging markets offer more fertile ground for SWFs to do business.[13] Large SWFs in Norway and the Netherlands may have to rethink their geographical strategy and focus more on areas such as Shanghai, Mumbai, Sau Paulo, and Lagos.

Although once met with scepticism (the OECD issued guidance urging countries to treat SWFs with 'restraint'[14]) and caution (in 2008 EU leaders called for an international code of conduct for SWFs[15]) in Europe there has been significant innovation around the SWF model over the past decade. For example, the Russian Direct Investment Fund was used to attract foreign direct investment (specifically USD) and was so successful that France, Spain, and Italy copied the method. Although the past couple of years have seen hesitation from some SWFs, Chinese investment has been significant. China Investment Corp. and Silk Road Rund Co. have just been two of the state-backed funds to invest over USD 255 billion[16] in Europe over the past ten years. The majority of Chinese deals have occurred in the top five economies in Europe, which has led President Emmanuel Macron to call for a unified strategy in handling Chinese investment.[17] The division between public and private is much harder to ascertain with

Chinese funds, so it is difficult to delineate what is just commercial business and what is foreign policy. What is clear is that a huge amount of investment has occurred in Europe at precisely the time it needed it after the financial crisis. The importance of SWFs in general is huge, with a significant amount of their investment promoting ESG goals and helping to stabilise a rocky financial ecosystem.

**Taxation**   In general, European countries encourage foreign SWFs to invest in their country, and withholding and related taxes are a small issue.

Similarly, European countries that promote their own SWFs typically grant them tax advantages.

**Key Regulation**   Investments made by SWFs in assets within the EU are subject to the same rules and controls imposed on any other type of investment. SWFs are therefore subject to EU legislation governing the free movement of capital and the rules on both merger control and state aid. The EU has traditionally pledged itself to be open to foreign investments and favourable to the liberalisation of transnational movement of capital. To this end, the Treaty on the Functioning of the EU (TFEU) prohibits not only restrictions to free movement of capital and payments between member states, but also between member states and third countries (Article 63, TFEU). Although Articles 64–66 TFEU provide some limitations to the principle laid down in Article 63, especially with respect to capital from third countries, the EU has not produced any specific restriction on the activities of SWFs. The EC issued a communiqué titled *A Common European Approach to Sovereign Wealth Funds* that repeated these concepts, which declares that 'the commitment to openness to investments and free movement of capital has been a long standing principle of the EU and is key to success in an increasingly globalised international system'.

## US

The concept of an SWF in the US has not been traditionally popular. With connotations of social handouts, the idea that the government should be paying a dividend to citizens automatically has not caused much enthusiasm. It may be surprising, then, that Alaska has a distinctly SWF-looking fund that has been running for over 35 years. The fund was set up under the guise of preventing oil revenue wastage. Every year since then Alaskans have benefited from an annual dividend, which many use to help pay down debt or put away to save. In 2017, 600,000 Alaskans received a cheque for USD 1100,[18] which unsurprisingly has contributed to Alaska being the most economically equal state in the US.[19] Even Hillary Clinton thought it might be a workable option in her campaign, with her memoir 'Hard Choices' detailing how her team tried to get the numbers to work. Underlying this objective to create a national wealth fund is the perspective from some parts of the political class that redistribution of wealth is not sufficient to overcome the inequalities that are entrenched between generations. It is interesting to see this attitude permeate the political discourse in the US, with the European situation discussed in more detail in Chapter 1. Despite Hillary Clinton's efforts, it appears unlikely that a US-wide SWF will emerge any time soon, especially under the incumbent president.

However, many states have set up their own SWFs to finance specific public services. For example, the Permanent School Fund in Texas, which was funded by commodities (oil and gas), gives funding for primary and secondary education within that state. Its origins date back to 1854 as an act of Texan state legislature to fund the regional school system. Although not plentiful, other funds do exist. Most of them are education based but some are designed to raise revenue for the local government.

**Taxation** The US grants a unilateral exemption to foreign governments. So long as the SWFs are either an integral part of a foreign government or an entity controlled by the foreign government, SWFs enjoy the benefit of a tax exemption.

**Key Regulation** In the US, investments made by SWFs have been a major political issue over the last two decades. The protectionist arguments and concerns about national security (including economic) are given greater weight in the public debates about such investment. Foreign equity investment is overseen by the Committee on Foreign Investment in the United States, chaired by the US Department of the Treasury. Notifying the committee is voluntary and it is under no obligation to investigate a referral. Only where there is credible evidence of a security risk and there is no other avenue to mitigate the risk will the committee be permitted to prohibit the investment. The powers of the committee have been strengthened by the Foreign Investment and National Security Act, requiring investigation of foreign government investment activity and broadening the scope of national security to include economic security and infrastructure.

## STATE-SPONSORED FUNDS

State-sponsored funds are pools of capital provided by various governments to be invested in line with public policy. They are distinguished from SWFs typically by their commitment to smaller scale investments (which primarily focus on stimulating economic activity within the state in question at particular times in the economic cycle), rather than investing surplus government income or capital in assets either domestic or international (usually with the sole intent of providing a direct economic return on investment). Many state funds have been established following the recent economic crisis in an effort to fill the commercial void with respect to lending to higher risk small enterprises. This void has been created by new regulation and changing attitudes within banking.

My biggest fear about state initiatives is that they find it hard to blend their political objectives with straight external economic objectives.

### UK

**Project Merlin** The government and the UK's four biggest banks, HSBC, Barclays, Royal Bank of Scotland, and Lloyds Banking Group, came to an agreement in 2011 in which the banks committed to lending more money, in particular to small businesses. As part of the agreement, the four banks (and Santander) stated both their capacity and commitment to lending GBP 190 billion of new credit available to businesses. GBP 76 billion of the lending commitment was allocated to small and medium-sized enterprises.

**Business Growth Fund** In addition, an initial extra GBP 1 billion of equity capital over a three-year period was given to the Business Growth Fund (BGF) and GBP 200 million to David Cameron's Big Society Bank that helps small businesses in disadvantaged parts of the UK.

The BGF was established in 2011 following recommendations of the Business Finance Taskforce (BFT), set up by the British Bankers' Association to consider what could be done to help the UK return to sustainable growth. It has been dubbed by PE investors the 'new 3i', a reference to the founding of 3i, or Investors in Industry.

The BGF provides long-term capital for medium-sized British companies. In order to get the scheme off the ground and to help the BGF invest in businesses, the sponsoring BFT banks provided an initial GBP 2.5 billion. The initial criteria stated that the fund would invest between GBP 2 million and GBP 10 million into businesses in return for a minority stake, ranging from around 10% to 40%, with each portfolio business having an annual turnover of between GBP 5 million and GBP 100 million.

It has to be said that the effect of the above initiatives were actually very small in the UK, although the BGF had some impact on UK SMEs, and still does.

**Funding for Lending Scheme**   The BoE and Her Majesty's Treasury launched the Funding for Lending Scheme in July 2012 with the aim of increasing the incentive for banks and building societies to lend to households and businesses within the UK.

The scheme was established with the view to reducing funding costs for banks and building societies so that consequently banks are able to make cheaper and more easily available loans. This was achieved by allowing banks and building societies to borrow from the BoE in the form of UK treasury bills for up to four years, for a fee.

**The Innovation Investment Fund**   The Innovation Investment Fund (IIF) was established in 2009 as part of an initiative to encourage investment in private sector companies specializing in clean energy and hi-tech industry. It aimed to use public funds as seed capital and to raise a projected GBP 1 billion for investment. Of the two funds initially set up under the initiative, only GBP 5 million of third party capital was raised between them. The government was to commit GBP 50 million to one fund and GBP 100 million to another, and the respective managers were to commit GBP 75 million and GBP 100 million.

The failure of the first funds to achieve what the government later described as an 'aspirational target' appears to have been in part due to their structure and the requirements for investing were much more restrictive than those of equivalent privately run funds, plus (as is often the case with these schemes) a suspicion on the part of private investors that government money comes with non-economic strings.

**British Business Bank**   A state-owned development bank established in November 2014 by the UK government, the British Business Bank (BBB) aims to target corners of the market where they believe there to be a lack of funding. It is wholly owned by the UK government through the Department for Business, Innovation and Skills and often lends money to SMEs through funds. Prime Minister Theresa May announced that following Britain's departure from the EU, the money that the UK government earmarked for the European Investment Bank (EIB) would now be going to the BBB. As well as funds, the BBB will provide loans to start-up companies, match investments in smaller businesses from angel investors or provide guarantees to other banks in an effort to increase lending to smaller businesses that may be lacking in track record or collateral.

The BBB has had a larger impact on smaller UK funds and SME funding than some of the other recent initiatives, and it is scaling up as I write this to invest more. Managers have found BBB comes with restrictions, and it has been criticised for being a tad slow and unwieldy, and some GPs or non-political LPs have sought to avoid BBB investing in a fund, but the situation is improving.

## EU

**The European Central Bank**  The European Central Bank (ECB), established in 1998, is a key part of the infrastructure of the Economic and Monetary Union (EMU) and the eurozone, but it is also an institution of the EU more generally – the central banks of the 28 member states of the EU (including those 19 states that have adopted the Euro) together with the ECB form the European System of Central Banks (ESCB). The ESCB does not take part in discussions or decisions concerning the monetary policy of the euro. Instead, this is reserved to those 19 central banks of the eurozone and the ECB, together forming the Eurosystem. This abundance of bodies and acronyms makes policy discussions and reporting a potential source of great confusion.

The main objective of the ESCB and by extension the ECB is to support the general economic policies of the EU without prejudice to price stability, set out in the TFEU, Article 127(1). It is left to the ECB to define 'price stability'. It has been interpreted as low inflation. The ECB's monetary policy aims to restrict inflation to a maximum of an annual increase of 2% in the Harmonised Index of Consumer Prices, and to avoid deflation. The ECB is also the sole issuer of euro banknotes and regulates the minting of coins.

The ECB operates two investment funds – one consists of its foreign currency holdings (the 'foreign reserves portfolio') and the other is euro-denominated (the 'own funds portfolio'). The foreign reserves portfolio is managed to provide liquidity, security, and return on investment in order for the ECB to have sufficient reserves of the key foreign currencies (such as USD and JPY). The own funds portfolio consists of the ECB's reserve capital and paid-up capital with the aim of providing income to cover operating expenses. Neither fund is put to direct use in line with the ECB's objective of price stability.

**The European Financial Stability Facility and the European Stability Mechanism**  The European Financial Stability Facility (EFSF) was a temporary fund set up in 2010 in the wake of the financial crisis to safeguard financial stability within the eurozone. It is funded by issuing bonds and other debt securities on the capital markets and then in turn lends to member states of the eurozone. It also undertakes an interventionist role in the capital markets to promote its objectives. The maximum that the EFSF was allowed to borrow was EUR 440 billion. A request for support is a formal procedure – the eurozone state must request assistance and negotiate with the EC and the International Monetary Fund (IMF) a support package, which must be approved by the other eurozone states unanimously. The need for support is tied to the cost of borrowing reaching an unacceptably high rate.

The EFSF has been formally replaced by the permanent European Stability Mechanism (ESM). The EFSF will continue to run the rescue programmes of Greece, Ireland, and Portugal, whilst responsibility for the recapitalisation of the Spanish banking sector has been turned over to the ESM. The EFSF will remain in operation until the last obligations are fully repaid.

The ESM is the permanent 'firewall' for the eurozone. It is funded in part by paid-in capital (EUR 80 billion) and the remaining EUR 620 billion of its authorised capital will be raised by debt issuances as and when they are needed. The eurozone states will back the total of EUR 700 billion in proportion to their economic capacity to support the programme. Germany is the biggest contributor, Malta the smallest. The total amount of bailout loans cannot exceed EUR 500 billion and the remaining EUR 200 billion is a reserve amount to guarantee the highest credit rating for the debt instruments issued. This has not proved entirely successful as the credit rating for debt issues was downgraded by Moody's in November 2012.

A request for assistance is made to the ESM and assessed for its potential impact on the eurozone and the sustainability of the applicant's public debt by the so-called 'troika' – the EC, the ECB, and the IMF. A memorandum of understanding is drawn up, which sets out the conditions attached to lending along with a facility agreement. The troika is responsible for monitoring compliance with the conditions attached to the facility.

Investors acquire the debt securities issued by the ESM in much the same way as other state debt is invested in. Although the eurozone states are contributors to the pooled funds, the securities issued are not attributable to the individual states. That has made little difference to the market's perception of such securities – Moody's downgraded the debt securities issued by the ESM in November 2012, in part motivated by concerns about the ability of France to fulfil its capital commitments.

**The European Investment Bank**   The European Investment Bank (EIB) is a long-standing institution that pre-dates the EMU by several decades, being established in 1958. It is a bank owned by the member states of the EU (rather than the eurozone states) and invests to bring about 'European integration and social cohesion'. The member state shareholders set the broad policy goals of the EIB and also oversee the decision-making bodies – the Board of Governors and the Board of Directors. The bank is financed by the member states and by raising money on the capital markets. The EIB does not loan exclusively to or within EU member states – about 10% of its lending was to or within over 150 'partner countries'. Its debt is priced at a similar level to prime sovereign debt and carries an AAA rating.

The investment policy is currently directed towards four areas – innovation and skills, access to finance for smaller companies, resource efficiency and strategic infrastructure. One of the EIB's divisions is the European Investment Fund which is a VC provider investing in SMEs.

**The European Investment Fund**   The European Investment Fund (EIF) was established in 1994 and is an entity formed by the EU to provide finance to SMEs. Its shareholders are the EIB, the EU (through the EC), and several private European financial institutions. It does not lend directly to SMEs, but instead provides finance through a range of tailored products offered to financial intermediaries (such as private banks and funds). It has two principal statutory objectives: (1) to foster EU objectives, especially relating to entrepreneurship, growth, innovation, and R&D; and (2) generating suitable returns to EIF shareholders. It is one of the largest investors in European VC funds with over 1 million SMEs having been supported by EIF investment. The EIF's annual report in 2017 stated that it had also backed 50% of Europe's unicorns.[20]

The EIF's many products include its Pan-European Venture Capital Fund(s)-of-Funds programme and its European Angels Fund, through which it co-invests with business angels. It has also provided finance to SMEs through investment in crowd-funding platforms such as Lendix.[21] In addition to its impressive VC presence, the EIF is an impact investor, most notably through its Social Impact Accelerator (SIA) and its European Fund for Strategic Investments (EFSI).

The EFSI is an initiative established in 2015. It is often called the 'Juncker Plan' as it is the main component of Jean-Claude Juncker's 'Investment Plan for Europe'. It is managed by the EIB with an aim to fill the current gap in investments across the EU for projects that are generally higher risk than those taken on by the EIB as well as helping to mobilise private investment. The EFSI states that its key aims include addressing gaps where investment activity is seen as too low, to shoulder some of the risks linked with activities that are carried out by the EIF and EIB, and to help raise EUR 315 billion of additional investment in three years.[22] The internal mechanisms within the EFSI include a 'steering board' and an investment committee, the former deciding on the EFSI's risk profile, strategy, and operation procedures, whilst the latter scrutinises project proposals, deciding on their eligibility for the EU guarantee. The projects that the EFSI will invest in come from a wide range but include infrastructure, education, health, R&D, technology, and energy. There is currently a proposal to extend the EFSI's lifetime until 31 December 2020.[23]

## US

The US Small Business Jobs Act of 2010 (2010 Jobs Act) created a number of initiatives and funds to support small businesses and manufacturers. These initiatives are administered by the US Small Business Administration (SBA). This federal government agency is part of the US Department of the Treasury. The SBA has numerous programmes that are designed to assist small businesses including educational programmes and a variety of loan programmes. Two major creations from the 2010 Jobs Act were the State Small Business Credit Initiative and the Small Business Lending Fund.

The Jumpstart Our Business Startups Act (JOBS Act) was much heralded in the US and aims to provide further support to small business and start-up funding by reducing federal regulation. Although the fund-raising platform known as 'crowdfunding' pre-dates the passage of the JOBS Act by several years, the passing of the legislation has seen an increase in the number of small investors using crowdfunding platforms to provide capital to start-ups and small businesses. The JOBS Act allows a business to raise up to USD 1 million a year from small investors who otherwise could not be approached without stricter regulatory approval or a public offering registered under the Securities Act of 1933. A potential investor who earns less than USD 100,000 a year may invest up to USD 2000 or 5% of their annual income (whichever is greater), and for those with greater income, a maximum of 10% of their annual income. The company must sell equity to investors through an SEC-registered broker but can offer non-equity rewards to investors without further registration (rewards such as discounted products or services once the business is established).

Several PE managers in the US see the JOBS Act, as route to encouraging individuals to invest in their funds and investment activities.

## PENSION FUNDS

A simple definition of a pension is a regular payment paid to a person during their retirement so that they have a continued source of income in the absence of work. It is unsurprising then that the word 'pension' comes from the Latin *'pensio'* meaning 'payment'. A pension fund therefore invests capital provided by employees and employers (and/or governments) during the working life of employees in order that these payments can later be made. The Roman practice of granting certain military officers country estates for their retirement comes close to being the first example of a pension scheme, but the award for first 'proper' pension scheme goes to the First Presbyterian Church for their Presbyterian Ministers' Fund in 1759. Pension funds can also be referred to as 'superannuation funds', which in some countries carries a specific meaning or is a broader term encompassing company pension plans or certain public sector plans.

**Types of Benefit Provisions/Arrangements**   The type of arrangement to which a pension scheme belongs is an important factor as this determines how the pension fund is taxed and withdrawn. There can be a number of arrangements to any one scheme. There are four types of arrangements.

In a defined contribution scheme, the contributions payable by a member are of a specified level (defined) but the final benefit of the scheme remains unknown until retirement. This is because the benefit the individual receives on retirement will be based on the total contributions made into the scheme, the level of investment returns on those contributions (which are dependent on the stock market) and the available rates for buying into an annuity that will provide the pension.

Under a defined benefit arrangement, the amount of pension received on retirement is fixed and is not dependent upon the size of the pension fund at the date of retirement. These schemes have become less popular over the years given the risk posed to the pension provider in making up any shortfall between the investment return on the contributions and the amount promised, which in some cases creates a slow decline in the main operating business.

In a cash balance arrangement, all or part of the member's pot is promised or guaranteed without direct reference to payments made by the member. The amount that is paid by the member (either actually or notionally) is fixed, meaning that there can be a shortfall, the risk of which is placed on the employer (sponsor) or the fund rather than the member. This promise or guarantee breaks the connection between the amounts going into the scheme and the pot that will eventually be made available to provide benefits, making these cash balance arrangements.

Hybrid arrangements are private pension schemes which are neither pure defined benefit nor defined contribution arrangements. One example of how such a scheme may work is that an individual would be allowed to accrue benefits on a defined contribution basis until a certain age at which benefits would then accrue on a defined benefit basis.

**Structure of Pension Schemes**   A pension scheme may be set up in various ways as, for example, by a trust, a contract, a board's resolution, or a deed poll. The most common structure used is that of a trust. A pension scheme trust is usually created with one or more trustees, who become the legal owners of the pension scheme assets. The governing document of a pension trust will be the trust deed and rules that not only create the trust but contain specific provisions and rules in relation to key elements of the scheme, such as administration and management.

The trustees' power to invest is often wide ranging, with legislation conferring power upon the trustees as if they were the outright owners of the assets. The trust deed will give trustees a number of powers. Importantly, the power to accept contributions into the scheme, to decide the investment strategy of the scheme, to invest the scheme's assets, and often detailed powers as to particular investments which they may make.

## UK

The first UK pension began life in 1670 for Royal Navy officers. It was not until 1908 that the Old Age Pensions Act introduced the first general old age pension on a means-tested basis.

In 1925 the Contributory Pensions Act established a contributory state scheme for manual workers and others earning up to GBP 250 a year. It was in 1946, following Sir William Beveridge's published paper titled 'Social Insurance and Allied Services' containing proposals for state welfare reform, that the National Insurance Act 1946 introduced a contributory state pension for all.

In terms of investment and meeting liabilities the defined benefit pension has significantly more regulatory oversight, with The Pensions Regulator enforcing Code 03, which helps providers meet the legislative funding requirements they are subject to. In comparison, for defined contribution providers there is guidance but far less regulation. It is ironic that despite both forms of pension trying to achieve the same goal, one is far more supervised than the other. Both want to match liabilities, comply with the rules they are subject to, and reduce the Vol found on their balance sheets. But for providers offering defined benefit schemes there is significant pressure from the state and far more regulatory constraints, especially in the types of investment that is permitted. Both serve a hugely important role in protecting the future wealth of investors, so it seems illogical that they have to meet different standards.

**The State Pension**   There are two parts to a state pension – a basic state pension and a state second pension. Individuals who have made a sufficient amount of NICs or accrued National Insurance credits during their lifetime will be eligible for the basic state pension.

The state second pension, previously known as the State Earnings-Related Pension Scheme (SERPS), provides additional money on top of the basic state pension. An individual may contract out of a state second pension and choose to join a private pension scheme instead. However, contracting out of SERPS has been a minor scandal and some people have contracted back in.

The UK state pension is a crucial element to many people's lives. Retirees who have worked for a considerable amount of time want to know how they are going to be able to structure their lifestyle once they have stopped working. In this vein, the impact of Brexit is causing consternation amongst investors who are hoping to enjoy the annual uplift of either wage growth, inflation, or 2%. This is especially true for British citizens overseas who are worried that they will have access to their pensions removed. Even if they are still able to access their savings, many are also concerned that they will not see the annual increases that a citizen living within the UK will enjoy. Given the general anxiety around saving for later in life, this confusion is not particularly welcomed by investors in, or approaching, retirement.

**Public Sector Pensions**   Individuals working for the public sector are generally entitled to join a public sector pension scheme such as the National Health Service (NHS) scheme for England and Wales or the teachers' scheme for England and Wales. The incentive of such schemes is to provide a more generous pension provision than the private sector schemes. However, in recent years due to government changes the benefits of public sector pensions have been disputed. However, they still divide opinion – if you are in them, they are not enough, whilst private employees criticise them for being too generous.

Although the benefit of public sector pensions has been debated in recent years, the impact that they may have on the public purse is still significant. Public sector schemes are typically unfunded (meaning that there are no underlying assets to pay for the future liabilities[24]) unlike their private sector counterparts. The current liability was estimated to be GBP 1425 billion, which is around 75% of the UK's GDP.[25] Given that life expectancy is rising through medical innovation and better standards of living, this presents a considerable problem for the public-sector pension schemes. If individuals live for another 10 or 20 years on top of the expected 20 post-retirement, then the numbers start to become very uncomfortable. One view is that individuals will have to work for longer. If people are regularly living to 90 or 100 then they will most likely be able to continue working past 60. This raises further questions about the job market and the impact it will have on younger generations. The repercussions of increasing public sector pension liabilities and increasing longevity in retirement is discussed further in Chapter 13.

**The Private Pension**  Private pensions can be established on an individual basis or through an employer's scheme. There are two main types of private pensions – workplace pension schemes and individual arrangements.

Workplace pension schemes are set up by an employer for the benefit of employees. This can take the form of a defined benefit scheme or a defined contribution scheme. The distinction between the defined benefit and defined contribution pensions is felt keenly in the UK. Employers would previously provide defined benefit schemes for their employees, but now workplace pension schemes are mostly defined contribution schemes into which both the employee and the employer must contribute a percentage of the employee's salary. From April 2019 the minimum contribution will be 3% from the employer and 5% from the employee. The scheme is administered by a trustee together with the employer.

A personal pension scheme is created through a contract between a pension scheme provider and an individual, and an employer may if they wish pay into an employee's personal pension. One important point to make is that often when setting up a private pension (which will most likely now be defined contribution) the default fund is selected. Pension providers will have multiple options for an individual to choose how their money is invested. The fund will select a default fund that may or may not comply with the investment objectives of the investor. It is important to thoroughly read the options when signing up to any scheme. Even more so when it can have a material impact on your future.

At the time of writing, UK private pensions are suffering from the same Brexit-related malaise as state pensions. Deficits have increased as a knock-on effect from markets reacting to uncertainty.[26] UK financial markets have seen falls in equities and there has been considerable pressure on sterling. Pension schemes traditionally invest heavily in these two asset classes, especially in the early part of the investment life cycle (see Chapter 7). For some companies, who have paid in further contributions, the industry is looking rosy. They are able to take advantage of their surpluses by investing in pension liabilities in the insurance market.[27] However, for others the outlook is not quite as promising. Firms such as BHS, Debenhams and Marks and Spencer have had a difficult time on the UK high street recently with some closing stores and others finding themselves in severe financial difficulty.

**Local Government Pension Schemes**  In addition to the state pension, the UK's county councils each run an Local Government Pension Schemes (LGPS) for their employees and the employees of related employers which take part in the scheme. Each of these schemes has been run since their creation by a group of professionals within the county council. As of 2018, these funds have over GBP 300 billion AuM.[28]

Chancellor George Osborne's Summer Budget in 2015 outlined the government's intention to encourage administering authorities to advance suggestions for pooling LGPS investments. With 89 separate administering authorities managing and investing their assets separately there was a clear logic to the Chancellor's proposal. Underlying this decision was a series of reports, but most notably the *Opportunities for collaboration, cost savings and efficiencies*[29] paper published in May 2014. This paper, which the coalition government penned, is the backbone to the Chancellor's proposal.

The underlying motivation was to reduce the high costs of each administering authority to run its own pension scheme but still maintain (if not improve) overall investment performance. Moreover, through combining the separate schemes the authorities would have access to the benefits of scale associated with large pension schemes. It will reduce investment costs and fees but also give the added opportunity for authorities to diversify and become infrastructure investment leaders and promote growth.

To achieve these goals the government proposed that the 89 administering authorities collaborate and invest through asset pools. These pools should have at least GBP 25 billion of scheme assets and their size, type, operating methods, and timetable will be set out by the authorities. This will be underpinned by an emphasis on strong governance and decision-making which will be articulated at the local and pool level. This should result in the lower costs and better value for money which the government has clear ambitions for. The government in its *Reform Criteria and Guidance*[30] has made this exact point and the expectation is that risk-adjusted returns over a long time is the priority. Alongside fee saving, one of the key advantages the government outlined in its criteria and guidance is the increased ability for authorities to invest in infrastructure. As of 2015, there were few LGPS assets invested in infrastructure, which the government was keen to change to facilitate the growth of the economy.

By 2017, the LGPS pooling proposal was underway with six of the eight proposed pools already in talks with Marcus Jones, who was at the time Parliamentary Under-Secretary for the Department for Communities and Local Government. The eight proposed LGPS investment pools were: London CIV, Northern, Central, Brunel, ACCESS, Wales, Border to Coast, and LPP (Between them they would have GBP 213 billion in assets). Having eight separate pools would, in an ideal world, encourage healthy competition between them. Consequently, driving performance and increasing better value for money. However, there is the danger of each pool competing for the same assets which would not be in the pension funds' best interests. Antony Barker[31] (director of pensions at Santander UK) raised this issue and stated that there must be sensible pooling to protect performance.

The pooling of the UK LGPS is an effort by the government to reduce investment costs charged by asset managers as well as to push pension funds into allocating more capital into infrastructure assets. The increased allocation that the pension pools are required to make towards infrastructure is mandated by the government following publication of guidance on investment reform criteria in November 2015. The government highlighted that the allocation of pension funds' capital in Canada and Australia towards infrastructure ranged from 10–15%, whilst similar reports from the UK's Scheme Advisory Board showed that only 0.3% of the total GBP 180 billion pool was invested in infrastructure.[32] Following the release of the UK government's guidance, each of the eight new pools have begun to increase their infrastructure allocation towards infrastructure assets, and in some cases have established bodies to focus entirely on infrastructure investments. However, they are still free to invest in infrastructure anywhere in the world so there may not be the benefit to the UK which the Government envisaged.

**CDC Pensions**  CDC pensions, which are popular in the Netherlands and Denmark, are beginning to make an impact in the UK. Their objective is to offer a form of regular income for retirees with changes in the funding position altering the benefit rather than asking for more money from the employer. In this sense, it is a hybrid between the defined benefit and defined contribution approaches. They are particularly attractive to employers who want to give their employees a solid pension but might be worried about long-term liabilities. From the viewpoint of the employee this can also be a good thing as the risk can be pooled between members of the scheme rather than each member having a siloed scheme. This could provide better returns and give employees in their retirement greater access to funds. However, the risk is that the pension scheme is not as successful as imagined and employees end up having their benefits altered. This could impact when they retire and cause the lifestyle they lead to be altered considerably. The UK government argues[33] that having another choice for individuals is part of the freedom employees should have when choosing their pension scheme. Indeed, it is codified in the UK Pension Freedoms. People should save for their retirement and promoting additional schemes is an effective way of doing this.

## EU

There is no consistent pension scheme across Europe. Pension rules, such as taxation and regulatory requirements, vary significantly across all member states. In order to bring a more homogenised system across Europe, the Institutions for Occupational Retirement Provision (IORP) Directive (Directive 2003/41/EC on the activities and supervision of institutions for occupational retirement provisions) was enacted in June 2003. The directive has made a step towards harmonising the pension provisions across Europe. The provisions in the directive recognise the fact that an internal market for financial services was needed for economic growth and job creation. Thus, company pension plans play a key role in ensuring the integration, efficiency, and liquidity, of financial markets. The directive is trying to provide a harmonised legislative framework for occupational pension funds to fully benefit from the advantages of the internal market.

One important feature of the IORP Directive is the establishment of a regulatory mechanism supporting the operation of cross-border occupational pension schemes. These rules apply only to funded pension schemes, and do not apply to state or personal pension schemes. The directive enables the establishment of pan-European pension funds that manage the pension schemes of employees in different member states. The directive states that the pension funds should:

- have sufficient assets to cover pension commitments;
- possess professionally qualified bodies, sound administrative procedures and adequate internal control mechanisms; and
- be transparent towards plan members by clearly communicating the target level of benefits, risk exposure, and investment management costs.

Under the directive, cross-border assets, and liabilities of a pension fund can be combined within a single legal entity.

Problem areas appeared due to the different interpretation and implementation of the IORP Directive. Member states have 'definitional differences' and clarification is required in four areas: cross-border activity, subordinated loans, ring-fencing, and investment regulations.

There is also reluctance from member states to see pension capital drift away from domestic markets.

However, some of the biggest hurdles faced by the multinationals have been discriminatory tax treatments in EU member states, although these barriers have recently started to break down. Others include complying with the social and labour laws of each country. As long as these laws are not harmonised within the EU, occupational pension products will be subject to different requirements in the various EU countries, which makes it very complex to administer cross-border schemes.

Following a review of the IORP Directive, the EU has set about with the creation of IORP II, which must be implemented in the UK by mid-January 2019. It will mandate pension schemes to implement further changes, some of which are as follows:

- All schemes are obligated to have 'key functions' in place, which is inclusive of internal audit and risk management.
- Pension benefit statements are required to be sent out annually to every active and deferred member.
- A remuneration policy will now be required and must be disclosed to the public with relevant information.
- Greater oversight from national regulators regarding certain activities (outsourcing and notification to regulators, etc.).

The Department for Work and Pensions has said that, regardless of the outcome of Brexit, the UK will implement the IORP II Directive (although many of the new regulations are already part of UK law).

**France**   The pension system in France is formed by a three-pillar system. Beyond the three pillars, all employees can enrol into a private retirement saving scheme.

This is primarily funded by social tax imposed on income from estates and investments, surplus sums from the French National Old Age Fund and the proceeds from the sale of certain state-owned assets. The statutory pension insurance scheme is a compulsory basic social security system, which provides earnings-related benefits for employees in the private sector.

These can be either defined contribution or defined benefit plans. Private pension plans are not mandatory; however, all employees must be enrolled in the basic and supplementary pension schemes. Therefore, all employees are subscribed to the first and second pillar pension plans, and can choose to enrol in a third pillar scheme operated by an insurance company. The third pillar pension schemes are administered by an insurance company authorised to do so by the French authorities.

**Germany**   The German pension system was one of the earliest universal national pension systems. It has been the model for many other social security systems across the world. The current system is mainly influenced by the 1972 reform that made the German pension system one of the most generous in the world.

Participation in the statutory pension scheme is mandatory for all employees. The statutory pension scheme provides for old age pensions (normal retirement age being 67), reduced earnings capacity pensions and widow's and orphan's pension. The monthly contributions calculated based on the employee's individual salary are borne by the employer, who can claim half of the contributions from the employee by deducting them from the monthly salary.

Hence, the contribution rate is equally shared between the employee and the employer. As a pay-as-you-go-system the statutory pension scheme is barely protected against the demographic change. Because of the decreasing capability of the statutory pension scheme due to demographic change, the coexisting company and private pension schemes are of growing importance. There are five different ways to carry out a company pension promise, as follows.

- Direct pension promise ('Direktzusage'): The employer contractually promises to grant the employee or his/her survivor pension benefits financed out of its own equity.
- Direct insurance ('Direktversicherung'): The employer enters into a contract in favour of the employee with a life insurance provider carrying out the contractual pension promise between the employer and its employee. The employer has to bear the insurance contributions and the employee is entitled to the insurance benefits.
- Company pension fund ('Pensionskasse'): Company pension funds are a special type of life insurance provider in the field of company pension schemes. As in the case of a direct insurance, the employer generally enters into a contract with the company pension fund for the benefit of the employee in order to carry out the contractual pension promise between the employer and its employee. The employer has to bear the insurance contributions and the employee is entitled to the insurance benefits.
- Pension fund ('Pensionsfonds'): The contractual structure between the employer, the employee, and the pension fund equals the contractual structure in cases of a direct insurance. Pension funds – as life insurance providers and company pension funds – are subject to the German Insurance Supervisory Authority, but are able to act more freely in their investment policy. In case of a shortfall the employer has an obligation to make additional contributions.
- Pension relief fund ('Unterstützungskasse'): Pension relief funds serve one company or several companies at once and are financed by allowances of the employer(s).

Company pension plans can be financed by the employee, the employer or both. The employer always has to promise a certain or at least determinable amount of pension benefits. As a result, independent of the type of financing or the way of carrying out the pension promise, the employer is always liable for the promised pension benefits. This even applies if the employer involves an external pension provider (e.g. direct insurance or company pension fund) to carry out the pension promise and if the promise is solely financed by conversion of employees' earnings.

## US

Employee benefit plan investors are generally subject to the fiduciary responsibility provisions of Title I, Part 4 of the Employee Retirement Income Security Act of 1974 (ERISA). These provisions impose standards of conduct on each individual or entity which has discretionary authority or control over the investment of employee benefit plan assets, or which is otherwise treated as a fiduciary with respect to a plan under ERISA. These rules require, amongst other things, that each fiduciary discharge its duties prudently and for the exclusive purpose of providing benefits to plan participants and beneficiaries. Fiduciaries are required to diversify plan investments so as to minimise the risk of loss and to invest the assets of a plan as a whole, in a manner that is consistent with the purposes of the plan, the terms of the plan insofar as they comply with ERISA, and the cash flow requirements and funding objectives of the plan. ERISA and related provisions of the IRC also prohibit certain specified transactions (or 'prohibited transactions') between a plan and a 'party in interest' (or related party to the plan) unless a statutory or administrative exemption applies.

Before proceeding to invest a portion of an employee benefit plan's assets in a fund, the fiduciary, taking into account the particular facts and circumstances of such employee benefit plan, should consider all applicable fiduciary standards, any prohibited transaction concerns, and the permissibility of such investment under the documents and procedures governing the administration of the plan.

**Plan Asset Regulations**   The Plan Asset Regulations set forth guidelines to determine when an employee benefit plan's equity investment in an entity, such as a fund, that is neither publicly offered securities nor securities of an investment company registered under the ICA, will cause the underlying assets of that entity to be treated as assets of the plan for purposes of the fiduciary responsibility provisions of ERISA and the prohibited transaction provisions of ERISA and the IRC ('Plan Assets').

The Plan Asset Regulations impose a 'look-through rule' based on the premise that, with certain exceptions, when a plan indirectly retains investment management services by investing in non-publicly traded equity securities of a pooled investment vehicle, the assets of the vehicle should be viewed as plan assets and managed according to the fiduciary responsibility provisions of ERISA. The Plan Asset Regulations distinguish pooled investment vehicles, which are subject to the look-through rule, from operating companies, which are not. Because VC companies may have characteristics of both pooled investment vehicles and operating companies, specific venture capital operating company (VCOC) and real estate operating company (REOC) definitions are included in the regulations, to provide guidance in determining when the operating company exception is available for a VCOC or REOC. The Plan Asset Regulations generally provide that the assets of an entity will not be regarded as plan assets if, amongst other conditions, the entity is a VCOC or REOC or if equity participation in the entity by 'benefit plan investors' is not 'significant'.

For the purposes of the Plan Asset Regulations, equity participation in an entity by benefit plan investors will not be significant if they hold, in the aggregate, less than 25% of the value of any class of such entity's equity, excluding equity interests held by persons (other than a benefit plan investor) with discretionary authority or control over the assets of the entity or who provide investment advice for a fee (direct or indirect) with respect to such assets, and any affiliates thereof. In this event, the entity's underlying assets would not be considered to be plan assets under ERISA or the IRC. For the purposes of this 25% test, 'benefit plan investors' include all employee benefits plans that are subject to ERISA or the IRC, including 'Keogh' plans, individual retirement agreements (IRAs) and any entity whose underlying assets are deemed to include plan assets under the Plan Asset Regulations (e.g. an entity of which 25% or more of the value of any class of equity interests is held by employee benefit plans or other benefit plan investors and which does not satisfy another exception under the Plan Asset Regulations), but only to the extent of benefit plan investors invested in such entity. Foreign pension plans, government plans, and church plans are not considered to be benefit plan investors. PE and hedge funds will typically seek to limit investments in the fund so that equity participation in the fund by benefit plan investors is not significant.

If the assets of a fund were to be deemed to be plan assets under ERISA, this would result, amongst other things, in the application of the prudence and other fiduciary responsibility standards of ERISA to investments made by the fund, and the possibility that certain transactions in which the fund might seek to engage could constitute 'prohibited transactions' under ERISA and the IRC. If a prohibited transaction occurs for which no exemption is available, the GP, and any other fiduciary that has engaged in the prohibited transaction, could be required to restore to a plan any profit realised on the transactions and to reimburse the plan for any losses suffered by the plan as a result of the investment. In addition, each disqualified person (within the meaning of IRC section 4975) involved could be subject to an excise tax equal to 15% of the amount involved in the prohibited transaction for each year the transaction continues and, unless the transaction is corrected within statutorily required periods, to an additional tax of 100%. Plan fiduciaries who decide to invest in a fund could, under certain circumstances, be liable for prohibited transactions or other violations as a result of their investment in the fund or as co-fiduciaries for actions taken by or on behalf of the fund. With respect to an IRA that invests in a fund, the occurrence of a prohibited transaction involving the individual who established the IRA, or his or her beneficiaries, would cause the IRA to lose its tax exempt status.

Regardless of whether or not the assets of a fund are treated as plan assets, the purchase and retention of any interests in a fund by an employee benefit plan will be subject to fiduciary standards of conduct and the prohibited transaction rules that are otherwise applicable to employee benefit plans under ERISA and the IRC.

It should be noted that ERISA generally does not cover pension plans established and maintained by government entities. The laws and regulations of the jurisdiction governing the government pension plans should be consulted to determine the fiduciary rules and any other issues that may need to be considered when a government plan invests in a fund.

## Pension Funds as an Investor

Pension funds are the largest class of institutional investors worldwide. There are trillions of dollars under management across the main markets such as the US, UK, Netherlands, France, Germany, Japan, and Australia. It is important for any fund manager to appreciate the strategies and concerns of pension fund managers, as they become increasingly significant investors in alternative asset classes. Therefore, for example, when US ERISA pension funds invest in PE partnership funds, they sometimes require their own rules or structures in separate ERISA-governed parallel partnerships.

Traditionally pension funds were very conservative in their investment strategies, investing in government bonds, or life insurance annuities – seeking low-risk long-term investment with a fixed rate of return. Inflation and other socio-economic pressures have led to pension funds needing to invest with strategies which led to greater returns, both to counter inflation and because pensioners live longer. To overcome these pressures, funds increasingly turned to other traditional investment classes, such as equities or bonds, in order to obtain a higher return and lower the eventual cost of pension plans. Further to this, pension funds have turned to alternative assets in order to seek ever greater returns. These investments include VC, PE, hedge funds, and debt finance.

Historically, pension fund managers across the globe have invested over 50% of their assets into fixed-income and cash, nearly a third into listed equities with the remainder invested into RE, PE, hedge funds, and unlisted infrastructure.[34] When looking at infrastructure as an asset class more specifically, it usually receives only 1% of assets through a combination of unlisted equities and debt. More recently, however, pension funds such as Canada's Ontario Municipal Employees Retirement System, France's Établissement de retraite additionnelle de la fonction publique, and Australia's Future Fund are increasing their target allocation to infrastructure. This increase in allocation is a welcome sign. Previously, there were limited plausible investment opportunities in the infrastructure market; however, the current existing macroeconomic forces will help to rebalance the supply and demand in favour of those able to invest in infrastructure. Infrastructure is key to a growing, functioning economy and failure to invest can lead to a major drag on a country's growth.

Once you understand that pension funds require low-risk, long-term investments, and that infrastructure projects have incredibly long durations and can offer diversity, you may question why pension fund managers currently allocate such tiny percentages of their assets towards investment in infrastructure.

There are some jurisdictions, however, that understand that infrastructure developments can counter a pension fund's long-term liabilities and can supply these demands better than others can. Canadian pension funds, for example, have been investing into infrastructure projects for over ten years and now even consider it a separate asset class that some allocate roughly 10% of their assets towards. Over the ten years, Canadian pension funds such as the Ontario Teachers' Pension Plan have now garnered enough experience to invest directly into infrastructure, as well as co-invest alongside PE groups. These managers do not need to depend on third party advisers as they have large enough in-house teams to handle such long-term and complicated projects. This level of expertise can be contrasted with that of the European pension fund managers, who have only seriously considered infrastructure investments a class unto themselves in the last five years or so. Allocations to infrastructure amongst European pension funds will usually range between one and three percent and for that smaller amount they will rely on external advisers to allocate their assets towards the appropriate infrastructure fund managers.

Regulations surrounding the area of pension fund investments have historically varied between continental Europe on one hand, and the UK and US on the other hand. In continental Europe quantitative restrictions were generally applied to institutional investors' investments. By contrast, in the common law tradition of the Anglo-Saxon countries, fund managers as trustees were under an obligation to invest as a prudent person would, with focus on their conduct and status (such as potential or actual conflict of interest) and a free choice of investment strategy so long as it was prudent and contained diversification, subject to any terms of the pension fund trust documents.

The interpretation by the courts of the prudential manager has frequently been narrow with the result that only investments such as government issued securities would be upheld as prudent. In the UK, more flexibility was given to fund managers in the 1960s and investment policy and trustee restrictions were rewritten completely in 1995. Trustees are free to (unless otherwise restricted) invest the fund's assets as if they owned those assets themselves. The trustees are obligated to draw up and maintain a written statement of principles governing investment decisions and addressing matters such as the investment assets to be held, the balance between different types, and the risk profile of the portfolio.

The US has provided flexibility to pension funds since 1974. Whilst the UK and US were the first ones to lift these restrictions, continental Europe remained concerned about high risk investments and gave priority to financial stability over higher returns. Over time, however, regulations have been liberalised in all countries. The IORP Directive required all member states to adopt prudent person rules for pension funds. The assets shall be invested in the best interests of the beneficiaries and members of the fund and in a manner as to ensure the security, quality, liquidity, and profitability of the portfolio as a whole. Member states are still allowed to impose some quantitative restrictions on investment management although these are heavily qualified.

The liabilities of a pension scheme are long term, and it is important that the scheme is able to meet its liabilities when they fall due. To ensure that liabilities can be met as they fall, the funding level, existing investments, and new contributions all need to be monitored along with the age of the members. It is generally the trustee who decides and is responsible for the investment strategy of the fund. A trustee will often take decisions on the investment strategy of a scheme following the professional advice of the scheme's advisers such as an investment consultant.

A number of factors will be taken into consideration when deciding upon the investment strategy of the fund, in particular: any limitations on investments contained in the trust deed and rules; any legal requirements such as the fiduciary duty to choose investments which are in the members' best financial interests and not for ethical or political purposes; the suitability of an asset class to meet the scheme's needs; the possible risks and returns in different types of investment; and ensuring diversification of the scheme's asset so as not to rely upon one particular asset class.

Once an investment strategy is established, the trustee will draw up a written statement of investment principles which sets out principles as to how investments should and must be made. The statement will govern factors such as the choice and types of investments, risk management, and the rights to be attached to investments. The statement will be reviewed every three years (or sooner if there is a significant change in investment policy).

I do think that many pension plans need to reconsider their expertise and cost base. I have wondered for a long time as to why it is that a pension plan allocating billions of capital spends so little money on their own investment team, and their core investment advisers. Frankly, many government-related schemes are fixated on low costs. The UK Government's cheap attitude drove Carillion into the dust. Often low cost equals low returns. Huge AuM asset owners pay their people and advisers poorly, whilst the managers they invest with are charging a multiple in fees and drive the sports cars. This doesn't seem to make much sense.

## CHARITIES

As charities have grown and the organisations have acquired greater supplies of funds, so their reach has expanded, and greater organisational complexity is the result. Today, the largest charities must function as businesses in order to guarantee efficiency and secure their long-term future. As such, charities must use their resources wisely and guarantee the availability of stable streams of cash flow. Like many other large businesses with similar demands, investing assets into funds is a way for charities to manage their resources and engage in long-term financial planning. With charities now investing into funds, the products themselves must be tailored to the needs of the charity. Often, charities may not wish to have their assets invested (even indirectly) into industries that they do not support. This so-called 'moral' investment strategy can result in funds that do not invest in areas such as tobacco, pharmaceuticals, defence, or oil and gas.

Similar to the various approaches taken by different investment portfolios such as hedge funds and pension funds, the goals and strategies of different charities occupy the full spectrum of the investment market. A charity will seek to adopt a strategy that serves to meet its operational objectives. Concerning a charity's investment strategy, this will usually be driven by either the terms of the endowments themselves or by strategic management decisions taken by the trustees.

Although the definition may vary from country to country depending on regulation and legislation, what is clear is that endowed charitable institutions are a significant investor group that should not be overlooked. Given that many charities derive a significant proportion of their income from investment returns, it is true to say that charities share certain characteristics with pension funds and private trusts. Indeed, there is often a need to be perpetual (although some funds may be finite) and derive an income, which can then be used to provide a sustainable stream of finance to support the overall charitable objectives. This stream of finance is typically in the region of 3–4% in order for the fund to continue to exist. Although there are other models that are discussed below, such as the 'spending out' model employed by the Bill & Melinda Gates Foundation (Gates Foundation). Of course, with this pressure to ensure a consistent level of finance, charitable funds are often very fee-conscious. Again, this illustrates another similarity a charitable investor will share with any other type of investor. Investors will always want value for money in the asset management industry.

One explanation for investment success for charitable foundations is that, unlike some hedge funds and pension funds, the foundations are able to focus on long-term investment strategies and do not have such severe restrictions in terms of the needs for liquidity and short-term returns.

**Taxation**   There is a variety of different tax reliefs available to charities. For example, provided a donation is used for charitable purposes only, a charity may apply for an exemption to corporation or income tax which would otherwise be payable on receipt of such a donation. Business rates relief can be applied in order to assist charities with their overheads and is applied to property occupied by a charity.

There are various tax incentives to encourage businesses and individuals to make charitable donations, such as relief from corporation and income tax.

Although charities typically enjoy favourable tax treatment, this will not usually extend to income or capital generated by financial investments. The tax exemptions applied to charities are normally restricted to charitable donations, trading in the charity's primary purpose (such as a religious charity selling holy books) or else trading mainly carried out by the charity's beneficiaries. Any non-charitable trading undertaken in order to raise funds to be applied for charitable purposes, such as financial investments, is taxable subject to small trading exemptions.

## UK

The practice of charitable giving has been common for centuries, with wealthy benefactors providing funds for the less fortunate as well as for the benefit of religious and learning institutions. Charity is a cornerstone of the Christian faith and before the advent of the welfare state, charity developed alongside society. However, early charity tended to be direct and disorganised with little forward planning. The industrial revolution saw the rise of great industrialists and bankers of the Victorian era and this coincided with a period of great hardship for the working poor. This in turn spawned charities such as the Peabody Trust for social housing, and the establishment of religious charities such as the Salvation Army. Consequently, this period saw the development of charities into something more similar to the sector we see today.

Charities are commonly defined as not-for-profit organisations established and run with a philanthropic goal. In the UK, charities must be established for exclusively charitable purposes, be set up for the benefit of the public or community and must use any profits generated for the purpose of the charity. It is important to note that charity is a status and not a legal form or structure. Various different kinds of organisations can qualify as a charity, whether they are companies, trusts, or bodies set up by specific legislation. Regardless, all charities in England and Wales are regulated by the Charity Commission and are subject to the general principles of charity law.

Historically, charities were prohibited from making investments that carried any significant degree of risk. UK legislation such as the Trustee Investments Act 1961 and the Trustee Act 2000 have brought changes that allow charities to manage their investments in order to focus on greater returns despite the increased level of risk associated with a high-yield strategy. The focus for trustees is to balance the opportunity of securing good investment whilst avoiding any undue risk. As such, a foundation's investment strategy should be in line with its charitable objectives. Specifically, a charity will try to make investments that will produce levels of returns sufficient to provide it with income and capital appreciation that will cover all the foundation's costs (including investment management fees) and, of course, facilitate its charitable objectives.

Under the UK Trustee Act 2000, trustees of unincorporated charities are permitted to delegate various aspects including:

- carrying out a decision that the trustees have taken;
- the investment of assets; or
- raising funds for the trust other than by the profits of trade which is integral to carrying out the trust's charitable purposes.

This means that UK charities are permitted to delegate their investment duties to professional investment managers and therefore gives the charity better access to the wider fund and investment market.

In the UK, investments made by charities are dwarfed by those made by pension funds. However, certain organisations such as university colleges and religious orders are relatively major players in the British investment scene. Broadly speaking, charitable funds aim to give financial assistance to people that meet their set criteria. However, their support is often not just limited to awards or grants but may include other forms of support to people who may need their help.

## EU

The UK model, which is also prevalent in the US, is only one form of charitable giving. The EU, because of its huge diversity, provides a wide array of approaches that should be recognised and appreciated. Each member state has a rich and diverse history of charitable giving, which, when consolidated into the 28 member states creates a network of both innovative and historical investment styles. The charitable sector has played a huge role in the development of Europe and the EU as an institution and will undoubtedly continue to do so. Generally, nations within the EU can be divided into three groups in their approach to charitable giving.

**The Rhine Model**  This model, inclusive of the Netherlands, Germany, and Belgium, is typified by staunch civil society organisations that have an institutional structure. These organisations will often benefit from state contracts who use them as a form of 'societal corporatism'.[35] This is in opposition to the traditional Anglo-Saxon model employed in the UK, where charities are seen as a balancing act to the state. In this form, the Rhine model operates symbiotically with the state as opposed to filling in the gaps. In areas such as education and healthcare, they are in effect subcontracted to work on the government's behalf to fulfil charitable goals. This interlink between charities and government means that awards and donations are not as popular within the fiscal and legal environment. Broadly speaking, foundations within this model have only begun to be seen as major stakeholders in the last 15 years.[36]

**The Latin/Mediterranean Model**  Often under this model, charitable funds are linked to the church, with a strong division in turn with the state. Historically, the church carried out much of the charitable work within each nation, with the state responsible for the operational side of social services. Within this model the state plays a crucial economic role and its relationship with the market is far more intertwined than in other models. Civil society organisations that operate within this environment often have difficulty being acknowledged as autonomous and independent. They often face attempts to control their actions by the political sector through legal intervention or a requirement for representation on charities boards. Similarly, to the Rhine model awards and donations are not common, with voluntary work perceived as direct competition to the job market. Whereas the Anglo-Saxon model is based on complimentary charitable services, it is less welcome under the Latin/Mediterranean model. Where a charity moves in to fill a gap left by the state, it is often questioned by politicians who paradoxically view this as their territory despite creating the space in the first place.

**The Scandinavian Model**  The Scandinavian model has the benefit of a strong state presence but also a welcoming approach to volunteering. Moreover, the protestant legacy in these countries means that personal initiative is viewed favourably.[37] This provides a potent combination helping civil society organisations to flourish in an environment that both welcomes and supports them. Typically, society will highlight an issue, which the state will go about filling. This flagging approach taken by many foundations gives the Scandinavian model a very proactive feel and enables charities to take action in partnership with the state. Unsurprisingly, there is a staunch bond between charities and government in these countries.

## US

The US, too, has a great tradition of philanthropy epitomised by the Rockefeller Foundation and the thousands of libraries and other public buildings funded by Andrew Carnegie. In the US, charitable endowments operate on a larger scale and as such investments into funds are also more common. The largest US investment portfolio is that of the Gates Foundation. Other squillionaires have since followed this model, such as Warren Buffett. Indeed, with around USD 36.4 billion of assets under trust, the Gates Foundation is the largest charitable foundation in the world. The Gates Foundation is unusual in its relatively aggressive approach to its investment strategy. The Gates Foundation effectively operates the 'spending out' model and as such will aim to spend all its resources within a finite period following the death of its founders. The Gates Foundation has been credited with developing the strategy of 'philanthrocapitalism', which includes using leverage to maximise investments.

This hybrid of philanthropy and capitalism is rapidly developing and there is fluid evolution of the charity fund model. For example, the Google Foundation, which is part of software giant Google's commercial arm, mixes for-profit and non-profit investments in order to maximise its impact. Also, see the development of social impact funds in Chapter 4 on governance.

## FAMILY OFFICES

Family offices, in many ways, behave like a fund manager or investment adviser for that family's money. Many family offices have a significant percentage (say 30%) of their 'non-core' business invested in PE, RE, and other alternative strategies. A family office is a private company that manages investments and trusts either for a single wealthy family or for several families.

Many family offices start within family companies where a wealthy individual will delegate certain personal matters to an assistant. However, the direct correlation between wealth and the volume of affairs such an assistant is tasked with will almost inevitably lead to the point where technical expertise is required.

The intergenerational factor with family officers will undoubtedly influence their view of the industry they operate in. For a significant number of family offices, the objective is to preserve wealth for future generations. This will have an impact on the types of asset classes they invest in, as well as the culture of the fund. They may have a less intense atmosphere and often are less formal than other forms of investor.

The impact of the family's business will perhaps also influence the types of investment that the family office practises. For a family that has made a lot of money in RE, they may feel that their strengths lie in this sector. This predisposition to invest in areas they feel familiar with is an understandable quality. Many of them will double down on their strengths and it is easy to see how this can impregnate the decision-making processes in this instance.

Others deliberately invest outside their main industry, similar to energy-sourced SWFs.

Family offices may expand beyond the original family that they were founded to support. These multi-family offices will then charge fees to other families who are seeking similar solutions. These operations may then eventually begin to fund-raise to support their investment activities – in which case it will need to become a regulated entity, and it begins to take on a character much like wealth managers. One such example is Rockefeller & Co., which expanded from the family office dedicated to the Rockefeller family to a regulated wealth manager with a wide range of clients.

Some family offices may be established in a reverse of the pattern described above. An example would be a successful hedge fund manager, which moves away from fund-raising from outside investors and begins to actively manage the wealth of its management team. This in effect is a multi-family office that has developed in order to cope with its own success and fund management.

**The Future of Family Offices**   Over the next decade, it is predicated that there will be a dramatic increase in the number of ultra-wealthy individuals across the globe.[38] By 2026, it is expected that the UK will be home to some 12 310 ultra-high-net-worth individuals (UHNWI)[39] and, according to Knight Frank, the number globally will grow by 43%.[40] Despite the uncertainty created by the Brexit process, London is still appealing to UHNWI. It is incredibly well connected and stocked full of high-value pursuits. Across the globe, it is Asia especially that will see the largest increase in UHNWI. In particular, Vietnam, India, and China will see dramatic rises in the super-rich as new markets open up and uncertainty is created across Western economies[41] (for example, the election of Donald Trump, Brexit, the failed coup in Turkey, and growing tension in the Middle East[42]). This undoubtedly has consequences for the socio-economic divide found across Europe and the rest of the world (see Chapter 1) – increasing wealth disparity and the antagonism that is associated with it. The underlying factors driving this growth in wealth include the increase in the number of women in work, urbanisation, and rising incoming levels.[43]

As the number of UHNW individuals grow, so will the demand for the financial and administrative support needed to manage their wealth. According to the Royal Bank of Canada, the cost of running an office is typically 1% of the assets being administered.[44] Therefore, to run a comprehensive office there needs to be a base level of wealth to justify more than the key services. For example, whilst a small family office will be able to provide general administrative, legal, and financial advice it will not have the breadth and depth of knowledge available to external council or financial advisers. Consequently, the use of third parties and specialists in tandem with the in-house team is often advisable. However, as the wealth of these individuals grows the need for a wider team with more experience is inevitable. This expansion increases overheads and makes the movement from a 'single' to 'multi' office particularly attractive.

The main advantage of a multi office is the ability to share the overhead costs associated with managing wealth. By utilising economies of scale, the cost of a wider pool of talent to run the office is reduced. Multi offices tend, therefore, to provide greater specialist legal, financial, and administrative support. Moreover, there is greater independence exhibited by the employees of multi offices, as they are not responsible for, and thus dependent on, one client. This might, in theory, provide greater clarity and objectivity when financial decisions are being made.[45] Although there are clear advantages to spreading the costs with other families, a multi office does present difficulties for particularly private families. The use of a multi office presents the risk that details of your family business may be shared indirectly with other families. Conflicts are more likely to arise as one family's objectives may clash with another and the boutique-style feel of a family office may be diluted as more and more families join.

Despite these risks, the advantages of a multi office are particularly appealing. The diverse requirements of an UHNWI necessitate a broad range of specialisms. These include, but are not limited to, succession planning, philanthropic programmes, wealth management, and logistical support. As these needs become more complex, the benefits of a multi office become greater. If the ultimate goal is to facilitate easier management of family assets, then then the value in using a multi-office is self-evident.

## INDIVIDUALS

Individual investors are not a homogenous group (talk about a statement of the obvious!). Like any category of investor, they are split into sub-categories. For example, the four most common are, UHNWI, HNWI, mass affluent, and retail. These divisions are not conclusive, but they offer a useful way to conceptualise the different operators within this space. Moreover, their views of the industry will vary considerably, and it is hard to prescribe a singular philosophy to each category. However, it is possible to gain an insight into their perspective by examining their very often specific objectives.

**Ultra-High Net Worth** The first World Wealth Report coined the term 'high-net-worth individual', which in the 1990s was sufficient to describe the wealthiest in society. However, by the early 2000s this moniker was not accurate enough to delineate the wealthy from the super wealthy. This is when the term ultra-high net worth came into use. Typically defined as people with over USD 30 million in investable assets, these individuals comprise the wealthiest members of society.

There is perhaps an assumption that UHNWI's have a special insight into investment. That their wealth is derived from (or at least maintained by) a secret understanding that other people do not have access to. More accurately, it can be surmised that UHNWI's are just particularly good at doing the things that most investors know they should do. Alternatively, frankly they inherited the money, married it, stole it, or got lucky by winning the lottery or had incredible timing on an exit (that is my list of how to make money the easier way than hard work!). They are not afraid to look at emerging markets, they rely on sound advice and they stick to a strategy. It must be admitted that certain asset classes which offer the biggest rewards are not always accessible to retail clients. Indeed, often UHNWI's make a considerable amount of their money in the private sector first – by starting their own business, for example. They, therefore, are far more comfortable investing in alternatives such as PE, VC, and other more niche real assets.

**High Net Worth** A HNWI is often stated as someone who has around USD 1 million in liquid financial assets. The majority of them live in the US, Japan, China, and Germany. However, there has been a growing increase in HNWIs in India and other parts of Asia. HNWIs' liquid assets make them very popular with wealth managers, with a range of customised services being offered to them to attract their business. This will include general investment management services, tax advisory and estate planning. Indeed, HNWIs are often fairly demanding of their advisers and will want sophisticated advice. One of the key concerns is risk, with many HNWIs citing it as their main concern in responding to FactSet's financial data survey.[46] For younger investors, it is about having access to the latest technology and feeling that they have stronger engagement with their managers. Moreover, these younger investors are increasingly conscious of ESG (see Chapter 4) and want to see more socially responsible investments in their portfolios.[47] Although it is hard to generalise about such a diverse group, there are some constants. A HNWI is likely to want sophisticated advice, easy access to their manager, better technology and a strategy that is ethically conscious. Underlying this is a staunch belief that any manager they hire should be socially responsible.[48]

**Mass Affluent** Following UHNWI and HNWI, is the mass affluent group. Traditionally, this sector has been underserved by finessed financial advice,[49] with a growing group that needs access to estate planning, pension consolidation and general investment management advice. Within the UK, this group typically have more than GBP 150,000 in household income and GBP 100,000 in investable assets. Often, this group rely on their immediate social group for advice on the industry and their view is framed by this process. What they want from the industry is a consolidated approach that takes a holistic approach to their financial well-being.[50] They do not have a considerable amount of time to make financial decisions and therefore need a service that encourages engagement and educates them on the importance of sound financial planning. Underlying this is strong preference for simplicity. This doesn't mean that the mass affluent sector wants less competence, but they need more clarity. This should be based on trust and clear guidance on what is best for their financial situation.

## SOME CONCLUSIONS

The requirement to bridge a culture gap is frequently commented on when working between different investing entities. The gap is sometimes thought of as being widest during commercial negotiations between actors in the public and private sectors. It is certainly useful to bear the cultural issue in mind when considering the behaviour and objectives of the organisations reviewed in this chapter. SWFs, state-sponsored funding bodies, banks, pension funds, and charities represent different investment classes but they are habitual sources of investment funding as well as being significant market players. Arguably, they hold a unique position, sitting at the junction between private and public sectors. Each of these organisations will have their own cultures that may be compared to greater or lesser degrees with the objectives of the solely private investor. Anyone who has worked alongside institutions from this sector will know that understanding where they come from and what drives them is critical to facilitating an investment.

Pension funds are, of course, the single largest sector source of this funding. Although some pension funds have, historically, kept clear of what they view as the high management charges of PE and hedge managers, in recent years many funds have adopted more aggressive investment positions, in some cases using the higher returns of PE to offset the damage caused to pension fund investments by the financial crisis and the consequent low interest rates and stock market Vol.

Since the 1980s, pensions' investment in PE funds has grown and pension funds have been the largest contributor of capital in PE investments in the US during 2001–2011. Pension funds make up 43% of capital invested, of which public pension funds comprise almost 30%.[51] SWFs are also a substantial source of funds. Middle Eastern state-backed funds, for instance, are thought to invest up to one third of their new investment into PE. SWFs focused more on the long-term wealth preservation model (e.g. the Abu Dhabi Investment Authority or Kuwait Investment Authority) tend to favour co-investment models, whereby they invest alongside a PE fund manager that they already back through a fund. In contrast, SWF funds attached to the development model tend to build in-house teams to conduct their own deals.

There are regional as well as public/private variations as to what different types of investors allocate to. Many still take a 'traditional' approach and largely avoid alternatives. Norway's SWF has recently rebuffed calls for it to invest in PE[52] and the UK's pension funds allocate far less of their AuM to alternatives than those in the USA. Each of the potential investors reviewed in this chapter needs to be carefully assessed, understood and accommodated. They each represent different opportunities along a wide spectrum of investment models. The long term view of an institution such as a pension fund, an SWF or a charity (the latter often being the most prescribed in their investment objectives) makes these institutions ideally positioned to engage with the long-term investment horizon and the limited liquidity of PE and other alternative asset strategies.

## ENDNOTES

1. https://preview.thenewsmarket.com/Previews/PWC/DocumentAssets/498560.pdf
2. Ibid.
3. Ibid.

4. http://fessud.eu/wp-content/uploads/2015/03/The-potential-role-of-Sovereign-Wealth-Funds-in-the-context-of-the-EU-crisis-working-paper-123.pdf
5. https://themoscowtimes.com/articles/russias-reserve-fund-ceases-to-exist-60157
6. https://preview.thenewsmarket.com/Previews/PWC/DocumentAssets/498560.pdf
7. www.thecityuk.com/research/key-facts-about-soverign-wealth-funds-in-the-uk/
8. www.bbc.co.uk/news/business-19871411
9. www.niesr.ac.uk/blog/mondays-macro-memo-uk-sovereign-wealth-fund
10. http://blogs.lse.ac.uk/businessreview/2018/06/27/how-norways-sovereign-wealth-fund-protected-uk-jobs-after-the-2008-crisis/
11. https://uk.reuters.com/article/us-china-cic/chinas-cic-sovereign-wealth-fund-plans-uk-manufacturing-investment-fund-idUKKCN1NO19K
12. www.ft.com/content/aa313492-6717-11e7-8526-7b38dcaef614
13. www.pwc.com/ee/et/publications/pub/sovereign-investors-2020.pdf
14. www.ipe.com/sovereign-wealth-funds-under-scrutiny/27923.article
15. Ibid.
16. www.bloomberg.com/graphics/2018-china-business-in-europe/
17. Ibid.
18. https://theintercept.com/2018/08/28/social-wealth-fund-united-states/
19. Ibid.
20. www.eif.org/news_centre/publications/eif_annual_report_2017.pdf
21. Ibid.
22. www.consilium.europa.eu/en/policies/investment-plan/strategic-investments-fund/
23. Ibid.
24. www.spectator.co.uk/2018/01/the-slow-death-of-the-public-sector-pension/
25. Ibid.
26. www.ftadviser.com/pensions/2019/01/02/uk-private-pensions-deficit-more-than-doubles/
27. Ibid.
28. https://pensionsperformance.com
29. www.gov.uk/government/consultations/local-government-pension-scheme-opportunities-for-collaboration-cost-savings-and-efficiencies
30. https://assets.publishing.service.gov.uk/government/uploads/system/uploads/attachment_data/file/479925/criteria_and_guidance_for_investment_reform.pdf
31. https://realassets.ipe.com/investors/european-investors/uk-lgps-pooling-takes-shape/10017857.article
32. Local Government Pension Scheme: Investment Reform Criteria and Guidance, p. 24. https://assets.publishing.service.gov.uk/government/uploads/system/uploads/attachment_data/file/479925/criteria_and_guidance_for_investment_reform.pdf
33. https://assets.publishing.service.gov.uk/government/uploads/system/uploads/attachment_data/file/479925/criteria_and_guidance_for_investment_reform.pdf
34. www.un.org/en/africa/osaa/pdf/pubs/2017pensionfunds.pdf pg 11
35. www.nef-europe.org/wp-content/uploads/2013/03/Philanthropy-in-Europe-A-rich-past-a-promising-future.pdf
36. Ibid.
37. www.nef-europe.org/wp-content/uploads/2013/03/Philanthropy-in-Europe-A-rich-past-a-promising-future.pdf
38. www.independent.co.uk/news/uk/home-news/uk-super-rich-numbers-rise-illustrated-graphic-ultra-high-net-worth-individual-knight-frank-a7608261.html
39. Ibid.
40. Ibid.
41. Ibid.

42. http://uk.businessinsider.com/wealth-x-super-rich-report-increase-in-wealth-number-of-ultra-wealthy-2017-6

43. Ibid.

44. www.rbcwealthmanagement.com/gb/en/research-insights/considering-a-family-office-heres-what-you-need-to-know/detail/

45. Ibid.

46. Ibid.

47. Ibid.

48. Ibid.

49. www.ey.com/Publication/vwLUAssets/EY-The-future-financial-wellbeing-of-the-mass-affluent-market-updated/$FILE/EY-The-future-financial-wellbeing-of-the-mass-affluent-market-updated.pdf

50. Ibid.

51. www.investmentcouncil.org/the-interdependence-of-pension-security-and-private-equity/

52. www.regjeringen.no/contentassets/569f03a08ee74350b3778fdbb24dd406/en-gb/pdfs/stm20172018 0013000engpdfs.pdf

# CHAPTER 7

# Asset Allocation and Portfolio Construction

*Those are my principles, and if you don't like them... well, I have others.*

– Groucho Marks

This chapter will examine the various methods used by investors – and by extension asset managers – to implement their investment strategy, to build their investment portfolios, and to balance their risk and reward. The most important strategic decisions that need to be made are those governing which asset classes to invest in and what proportion of their investments will be made in each asset class, and these require a decision-making framework. This is known as asset allocation. Asset allocation frameworks can be long term, also called 'strategic', or shorter term to address temporary opportunities or risks in the market, also called 'tactical'.

There are, of course, many different asset classes that an investor can choose. In a large part, this is dictated by the investment horizon, risk appetite, size of portfolio, and goals of the investor. A common example used for a simple 'classic' balanced portfolio would be a 60:40 split between equities and bonds (or 50 equities/30 bonds/20 cash equivalents to be more defensive). The governing principle being that if one asset class is performing poorly then the others will compensate if they are sufficiently diversified and not too highly correlated. This chapter will examine the different methods of asset allocation and the underlying tenants that guide these decisions.

I have also written this chapter to give asset managers and students of asset management a window into the life of the fund investor or asset owner (be it an SWF, pension plan, or other large allocator). As such, this chapter links up with Chapters 5 and 6.

One key benefit of the financial markets is the sheer scope of opportunity for investors. It is possible to move money through time zones into different parts of the world at any point, and there is a huge range of investments available for investors to choose from. As investors learn more about these different opportunities and receive more and more information regarding them, it is often the case that they wish to change their investments. Consequently, it is important for investors to have an idea about which investments they wish to make over the long term.

This, in short, can be described as portfolio construction. In addition to exploring the different asset allocation strategies, this chapter will look at what happens when an investor changes their mind or the market dynamic changes.

## PORTFOLIO CONSTRUCTION

Asset allocation is something that we all do in our lives. Unless you have renounced all worldly possessions, the readers of this book will have assets. These may be physical day-to-day assets (phone, computer, car, or house) or financial assets (such as equities or bonds). This composition can be referred to as your portfolio and will be structured according to the decisions you have made during the course of your life – whether to save for a deposit and buy a house at the expense of purchasing the latest computer or use a new app like Money Box to incrementally save your pennies and invest in equities as opposed to keeping the hard change in your pocket. There is a colossal range of assets which we choose from in our day-to-day lives and we are all familiar with the rationale behind these decisions. This chapter will try to use that understanding to illuminate the methods investors use to balance their risk and reward. Before we dive into the current methodologies, it is important to get a general overview of what portfolio construction looked like historically.

Harry Markowitz published 'Portfolio Selection' in the *Journal of Finance* in 1952 – establishing the theory that generating returns is not just about picking a winner. In this paper, he put forward the theory that it is the combination of assets as well as the assets themselves that impacts the results of the portfolio. Before this, portfolio construction theory was focused on the individual risks or rewards of each security, the theoretical objective being to isolate the assets that offered the greatest reward whilst presenting the least risk. From these, an investor would construct their portfolio. Markowitz solidified what investors had intrinsically thought by crystallising it in a quantitative model. This put form to thought and illustrated that portfolio composition mattered.

This theory, called 'modern portfolio theory' (MPT), also endorses the idea that an investor can create an 'efficient frontier'. This strand of Markowitz's theory states that it is possible to calculate the Vol and expected return of a portfolio once you have allocated the individual securities correlations, expected values, and standard deviations. In turn, it is then possible to rank these portfolios in order of which best balance Vol and expected return. Therefore, one could choose the most efficient portfolio for whatever risk profile one is willing to accept.

Taking MPT one step further, James Tobin scoped out Markowitz's work by including risk-free assets in the analysis,[1] which resulted in the concept of the capital market line and the super-efficient portfolio. This is where leverage is incorporated into MPT, resulting in a risk–return profile which is better than a portfolio on the efficient frontier.

In 1964, six years after Tobin's work, William Sharpe built on his theory by solidifying the capital asset pricing model. This model is used to ascertain what the theoretical rate of return from an asset should be, so as to inform an investor whether to add an asset to a well-diversified portfolio.

Fast forward to 1993 and 'post-modern portfolio theory' (PMPT) arrived. This theory uses the downside risk of returns (an assessment of a security's chance of decreasing in value if the conditions of the market change) as opposed to the mean variance analysis used by investors in

MPT. Essentially, the theories differ in how they define risk and to what extent that definition of risk impacts expected returns.

PMPT was, in part, driven by a key criticism of MPT, i.e. that MPT is based on the assumption that the risk, return, and correlation measures used by this approach are founded on 'expected values'.[2] Ergo, they are 'mathematical statements about the future'[3] – which in practice is not always what happens. Investors will actually replace predictions derived from past events with these values in their analysis. These expected values[4] will often fail to incorporate the possibility of variances that have not existed before. '*Post hoc ergo propter hoc*' is just the Latin way of saying mean-variance analysis relies on expected values derived from historical events.

The financial crisis brought a further resurgence in the criticism of MPT. Bob Rice made the point succinctly when he wrote MPT 'recognizes neither duration nor geopolitical risks'.[5] These two factors have influenced capital markets far more over the past ten years than they did in 1952. It is unlikely, therefore, that a manager will be successful if they base their allocation purely on Markowitz's model, despite the fact that he won a Nobel Prize.

MPT assessed the risk of the financial crisis as a one in 10 000-year occurrence,[6] which sounds obviously bonkers. This suggests that either we as a generation are particularly unfortunate, or the assessment of risk by the model is fundamentally flawed. Equating risk with realised Vol (historical behaviour) and nothing else, is too narrow. As an example, the impact of politicians on the markets (US–China trade war) who do not take into consideration historical behaviour of assets when making all their decisions is growing. The MPT model that quantifies risk by reference to past Vol, considers asset correlations to be static, and assumes outcomes will be in line with a normal distribution shape appears to be out of step with current trends.

For the investor who is using a robo-adviser or putting money into a passive fund that bases its allocation on MPT, this should be a concern. The world, as outlined in Chapters 1 and 13, is changing, as citizens around the world reject their conventional politics and embrace more extreme positions. Investors and managers who react to these changes will undoubtedly fare better than those who do not.

## STRATEGIC ASSET ALLOCATION

The objective of strategic asset allocation is to maximise the risk return characteristics of a portfolio to an investor's objective. These objectives differ from investor to investor. A younger individual investor may be more inclined to take on risk in comparison to someone approaching retirement.[7] This will manifest in the relative weightings the differing investors place on asset classes. For example, the younger investor may be willing to allocate more to equities (an objectively riskier asset class then most) than to bonds (an objectively less risky asset class than most) in comparison to someone much older. This approach changes according to the type of investor. A family office, for instance, may wish to preserve wealth for the future generations or it may need to create extra returns to fund the new ventures proposed by the current generation. As mentioned in the introduction, we all make asset allocations in our own lives. Each person goes about this differently depending on their objective and time frame. Professional asset allocation by institutional asset owners is equally varied and we will discuss the priorities of different asset owner types in this section.

Strategic asset allocation is designed to be the long-term strategy of an investor. Strategic asset allocation structures its approach through specifying a percentage allocation for differing asset classes and then rebalancing accordingly when this goes out of kilter. This allocation is premised on a variety of factors, namely – risk appetite, time horizon, and the objectives of the investor. How quickly the rebalancing occurs is determined by the degree of deviation that occurs from the original target allocation.

This approach of setting long-term strategic asset allocation as the core of an investment policy originated in the 1980s, when Gary P. Brinson, Randolph Hood, and Gilbert L. Beebower argued cogently that it was investment policy rather than investment management that drove returns. This is not to say, nor was it necessarily their argument, that active management does not have a crucial role to play in maximising alpha for investors. Rather that, when looked at objectively, it is the asset allocation that generates the major differentiation between portfolios. This is an important point to make, as often these authors' arguments are misrepresented.[8] The statistic often used is that asset allocation provides 90% of returns.[9] These are two different, but often interchanged, claims.

Underlying their approach is the premise that the percentages of assets that compose the portfolio can realise anticipated rates of returns. When the correct percentages are combined, the returns generated will meet the overall target for the portfolio.[10] This method follows one of the key principles of investing – maximising portfolio returns whilst minimising risk. Although this approach has its criticisms, one way of mitigating them is to adjust leverage with cash flow, as John Y. Campbell and Luis M. Viceira explain expertly in *Strategic Asset Allocation: Portfolio Choice for Long-Term Investors*.[11]

The main limitations of the methods of determining strategic asset allocation are centred on the assumptions that are made around various asset classes, the wrong assumptions can lead to a 'garbage in, garbage out' problem. For example, proponents of strategic asset allocation often uses historic Vol and long-term risk premiums as a starting point for their models. In principle, this works fine if the historical trends are resolute and carry on as expected. The danger, of course, is that they do not. Over a period of 100 years, one can see a trend but in the short-term the level of Vol increases significantly – calling into question the utility of using assumptions based on historical trends.[12] This issue is not just limited to Vol but can be found in assumptions based on returns and correlations. Another key assumption that strategic asset allocation makes is that asset classes retain the same structure over time. This is clearly not the case and can be evinced by the evolution of hedge funds over the past 40 years. In the 1990s, global macro was *en vogue*, but by 2006, they comprised just 11% of hedge fund strategies.[13] As the liquidity, risk, return, and Vol of these asset classes can change it is important to not treat each class as set in stone. This is especially important when investing over a long period of time – which is a key factor in strategic asset allocation.

**Strategic Asset Management for Pension Schemes** Pension schemes – and their needs and modus operandi – are discussed earlier in the book, but the following is a brief recap of the two basic types of scheme. The first type of fund offers 'defined benefits', which is where the benefits paid out to the investors are based on a predetermined formula. The second type of fund offers 'defined contribution', which is essentially where each investor has their own fund and they receive the total benefit. Given the metronomic nature of the death rate and retirement age, it is easier for defined contribution funds to accurately predict the need of their fund using relatively simple calculations. However, both types of fund are trying to provide inflation adjusted returns for their investors at some point in the future. This section will illustrate some of the factors pension schemes take into account when deciding how to allocate their assets.

First, pension schemes by definition are concerned with the future. The objective necessitates a long-term view on creating wealth. Traditionally, this meant a significant proportion of pension funds in the UK investing heavily in equities, as they married well with long-term inflation matched liabilities. Although short-term Vol would be a concern, in the long run (ten years plus), equities will almost always increase in value. Moreover, this risk could be reduced by holding a percentage in non-correlated assets. This is why pension schemes historically employed an orthodox strategic approach, as this method is future-centric. Were pension schemes to be worried about the present, their asset allocation may be more tactical in nature in order to mitigate more prescient swings in the market. Over time, the pension fund would reallocate to less risky assets in order to preserve the wealth needed for an investor later in life. This was seen as a proactive and secure way to ensure pension schemes meet their liabilities.

**This was the theory.** However, the pension fund 'strategic approach' contains some inherent flaws. The most significant being time – 'time is not what it used to be' (I will bag that quote). People now live longer and many of the life patterns so modelled especially in the US (also around the much discredited life settlements acquisitions) do not now hold, thus destroying the patiently built-up pension funds past planning. In addition, by the time a member retires, reducing the percentage of equities in their fund considerably may not be the best option. For example, by increasing the percentage make up of bonds in your fund to 50% from 20% you are diversifying and potentially de-risking, but you are also eroding one of the main advantages of accumulated wealth – compound growth. This 'lifestyle strategy'[14] is often automated by pension schemes to protect investors in the later stages of their careers. This approach reduces the cost to the pension scheme for managing your fund by giving each investor a ready-made de-risking package. Indeed, given that this knowledge is open source, an investor could implement this process themselves. For example, if they are able to, by cashing in their pension that is now more tax efficient than it used to be in the UK – rather than paying a fee to a pension scheme. This is not to say that it is risk-free. Indeed, by maintaining a higher percentage of equities in a portfolio an investor is leaving themselves open to the impact of events and risks out of their control, such as geopolitical and market risks. HMRC released figures in January 2019 revealing that GBP 23.6 billion had been taken out of pensions since pension freedoms were introduced in 2015.

**Strategic Asset Management for Family Offices** Family offices differ dramatically from each other when it comes to their investment goals. This is partly because family offices are hugely affected by personal whims. Theoretically at least, for a family office, 'long term' is the watchword, as cash needs should be easily maintained with a small percentage of the assets. Preserving wealth and ensuring that future generations benefit from previous generations' wealth is typically the unifying factor. In 2016, the EY Family Office Guide showed that there are over 10 000 single family offices worldwide.[15] They are used as the key tool for the ultra-wealthy to protect their assets and ensure future generations can enjoy them.

The cultural, social, and economic norms that influence families also influence their offices and in turn where those offices invest. For example, there was a recent trend for Russian and South American family offices to invest in RE (often statement properties) in American cities such as New York or Miami. Family offices based in emerging markets have also been known to heavily invest in London – which has been heavily publicised in the capital's papers. Looking at the Latin American and Asia-Pacific regions, it is easy to see how the increasing wealth in these areas will necessitate better, more sophisticated family offices. More established brands will try to tap into these areas to offer the services that are growing in demand.

More generally, over the past ten years and as a consequence of slowing markets and low growth, family offices have divested from traditional asset classes. For example, offices have tended to move into areas such as alternative energy, climate change, food security, and agriculture.[16] As markets improve and there is significant recovery, family offices will most likely take advantage of this and shift away from conservative investment strategies. Whilst still maintaining the preservation mandate of their fund, family offices can start looking at investment into RE, PE, and other alternative assets.

**Strategic Asset Management for SWFs**  Sovereign wealth funds (SWFs) are discussed in more detail in Chapter 6, but the following is a brief recap. The owner is the sovereign power, which employs an investment team to manage the assets. Typically, their governance structure is organised by a finance ministry or a central bank. The start-up wealth will often be derived from commodities, an excess reserve, or perhaps state-owned real assets.

Their investment goals can broadly be split into five categories:

1. Savings
2. Stabilisation
3. Pensions
4. Management of reserves
5. Development (although this is often an additional factor for SWFs).

SWF growth has been considerable since the early 2000s and today they make up a considerable percentage of global assets. This has been criticised, for example, with decisions taken in Norway having the potential to impact the capital markets around the world.

Importantly, like other investors, the varied purposes of SWFs have implications for the types of asset allocation they pursue. The differing purposes will undoubtedly mirror the liability structure of each fund and will dictate their individual investment horizons. Moreover, the range of purposes found across SWFs is indicative of a wide scope in terms of objectives. The asset allocation strategies that these SWFs then employ will comply with the original purpose of the fund, but often will have flexibility to match the risk profile.

The difference in asset allocation strategies can be seen when comparing stabilisation SWFs with pension SWFs. For obvious reasons, a stabilisation SWF will have an investment horizon which is far more short term than a pension SWF. As such, it would be unlikely to see a stabilisation SWF with an allocation to alternative assets. In contrast, a pension SWF will have a different liability structure, which will be less explicit and therefore will likely have a considerable portion of its wealth allocated to alternatives. This is, however, not always cut and dry. For example, the largest SWF (and investor) in the world – the Government Pension Fund of Norway – suffers from political, external, and internal bias, that has led it to determine frankly quite strange investment themes, such as a low allocation to alternatives and almost nothing (for its size) to PE or VC.

Going forward it is clear that SWFs will grow in importance, with their ability to meet national policy requirements. Moreover, their increasing influence amongst emerging technology is vital for the world as a whole. As more nations create their own funds, it is likely that we will see an even more diverse range of purposes and consequently asset allocations.

## DIFFERENT APPROACHES TO STRATEGIC ASSET ALLOCATION

**Tactical Asset Allocation**   Tactical asset allocation is, in effect, a subset of strategic asset allocation. It can be employed as an overlay on top of a strategic allocation or on a portion of a portfolio. For example, in a generic 40:40:20 split (with the 20 being allocated to the dull end of fixed-income – 'cash in the bank' and similar) a tactical approach could be taken on the 20. As this process can be siloed to one part of the fund, it can also be outsourced to an individual manager, or more traditionally, kept within the in-house investment management team.

This approach is nicely summed up by Don Phillips and Joan Lee who state, 'tactical asset allocation uses quantitative models of asset value to determine short-term portfolio allocations within the framework of strategic asset allocation'.[17] In part, this is a response to the challenges presented by a strategic asset allocation methodology. Given that a strategic approach is often associated with a long-term viewpoint (e.g. pension funds) the short-term can present a material risk that might not be sufficiently mitigated. What the tactical approach does is try to maximise short-term gains by taking a more active approach in the immediate term. By folding this into a strategic approach, a manager is trying to offset the geopolitical factors that can have a significant impact on the markets. This is a post-Markowitz approach that acknowledges that risk is not just about historical performance. It enables investors to have their money invested into riskier assets, whilst also ensuring a long-term approach is maintained.[18]

At their core, asset allocation strategies will necessitate some form of rebalancing. At the portfolio level a tactical approach will try to improve the short-term gain by actively managing the assets, using the weightings of short-term assets as a crutch for the long-term asset section. A tactical approach is therefore clearly an active approach (although Loistl[19] maintains it is a relatively moderate active strategy, as once the short-term goal is achieved the approach is reverted to the long-term). By shifting from a more passive position (i.e. invest and wait) managers have the opportunity to exploit opportunities in the market such as pricing anomalies or differing strengths in market sectors. Kaplan et al. (2011)[20] states that it is the investor trying to orientate a portfolio towards equities, sectors or assets that present that biggest chance of a return. In comparison, a purely strategic approach may look particularly inflexible over the long term.[21] To do this, managers will use regression analysis to construct detailed equations to pre-empt short-term movements in the markets. This enables them to be more flexible and react rapidly to changing circumstances through adjusting their portfolio to take advantage. It is therefore more common to see a tactical manager, within a strategic investment team, make more decisions and at a faster rate than his colleagues.[22]

There are roughly four stages when constructing a portfolio[23] following a tactical asset allocation model. First, the investor must decide what types of asset should be included and therefore, by proxy, what to exclude. Second, the investor will need to make a decision on the weighting for each of the asset classes which they have included within the portfolio. Third, in keeping with this method, strategically changing the investment combination weights away from normal to take advantage of excessive returns from short-term changes in asset class prices. This suggests that market timing and tactical allocation follow a broadly similar approach. However, tactical asset allocation uses quantitative methods to assess the value of assets to make short-term allocations within an overarching strategic approach, whereas market timing uses quantitative methods to predict fluctuations in the market, which they will then, in theory, take advantage of.

Darst and David[24] argue that it is crucial for a strategic approach to deviate through tactical movements to make the most of opportunities that are irregular or perhaps unusual.

Although the liability profile of each fund will dictate the asset allocation – ultimately the investor wants to see a good return. There is always the risk versus reward debate but within a mandate there should be the flexibility to capitalise when the opportunity presents itself. Although this raises the ghost of market timing, it is again important to point out that the processes used are different. Moreover, it is the exception not the rule, with the long-term perspective still being maintained. It requires significant discipline, as Ryland et al (2003)[25] point out, to employ an overlay of tactical asset allocation onto a strategic approach. One must know how to spot the opportunity, if it is worthwhile, when they have run their course, and then ultimately rebalance the portfolio in line with the original mandate. To do this requires considerable skill and effort.

**Constant-Weighting Asset Allocation**  Constant-weighting asset allocation is similar to a strategic approach but deviates from the long-term buy and hold perspective. For example, if the portfolio is structured 40:40:20 (equities, bonds, and cash) and equities increase in value so that they comprise 50% of the portfolio the fund will automatically rebalance by selling the additional 10% to invest in the other two asset classes. The underlying objective it to make sure that the fund will never deviate from the original composition by more than a certain percentage (often 5%). Indeed, as Kaplan points out[26] the rules as to when to rebalance are not set in stone.

This technique is used by investors as a subset of a strategic approach. Similarly, to a tactical approach Lustig et al. point to its active tendencies.[27] Although, often automated and used by mutual funds as well as smaller managers[28] it is inherently concerned with the performance of individual assets. It is also similar to a generic strategic approach in that it has a 'base policy mix'[29] which is the percentage of the portfolio to be allocated to any one class.

Ostensibly, this is similar to the rationale behind the tactical approach. Constant weighting is trying to take advantage of the short-term opportunities that present themselves in the market. What is happening is that a fund is buying in a dip and selling at a peak. The fund then rebalances and pursues its long-term goal. This, like a tactical approach, is particularly understandable when markets are volatile. It is especially so when viewed from the investor's perspective, who may wish to increase the risk slightly at points but does not want to maintain that level of exposure in the long run. Indeed, behavioural economics has shown us that investors are particularly bad at making decisions when markets move. They attribute their success to their decisions but often their losses to external factors. Often decisions are made too frequently, and not with the best insight. What constant weighting does is provide the investor with the knowledge that their allocation is being managed in response to these market events but prevents any significant changes occurring outside the predetermined range of movement. Ultimately, this strategy provides a more active position for a manager to take on top of their strategic approach, whilst offering investors comfort in the knowledge that their fund can react to market swings.

**Dynamic Asset Allocation**  Typically, dynamic asset allocation would not be used by an institution. However, it might be by a fund manager or endowment. A good example of this is Standard Life's Global Absolute Return Strategy. This form of strategy could be characterised as a more militant form of tactical allocation. Although it has the same objective as a strategic approach it takes a very different angle. For example, if equities were increasing in value dramatically, the dynamic approach would be to purchase more of them. Loistl[30] submits that this approach makes dynamic asset allocation the direct opposite of constant-weighting.

The example he gives is that in the situation of a market slump, the dynamic asset manager would sell off their equities to prevent further losses. Underlying this process is a similar thought process to the broader philosophy found in strategic asset allocation. Managers who practise this approach believe in the principle that what an investor buys are more important than when they buy it.[31]

## ASSET ALLOCATION CONSIDERATIONS

**The State of Capital Markets**   I know it is obvious, but at a basic level, it is important for investors to establish which asset class will perform better compared to others. Not just in the immediate future, but also in the medium- and long-term. If this is established, it simplifies the process of recalibrating a portfolio when changes in the market occur (depending upon your strategy). From this stand-point an investor that expects the equities market to perform better than the bond market should weight their portfolio to include more equities. Conversely, if the bond market was predicted to do better, then the opposite would be true.

**Current Evidence vs. Past Performance**   It is a common approach for investors to examine current asset classes' performance in comparison to their historical results. This is a useful metric, as it is a proven indicator for how well an asset may do in the future. For example, it is a common occurrence that an asset class that has performed well below its historical average will see a correction and upcoming returns will improve. This is known as mean reversion, i.e. a return to its trend growth line. However, it is important to remember the FCA's words of wisdom that past performance is not always a reliable indicator of future returns. It is still a prediction, which may or may not have included factors that were not present historically. For example, there may have been recent or upcoming structural changes to a sector that could significantly hamper the performance of said company. This may have a large impact and render the previous performance figures unreliable when considering future growth.

**Valuations**   By examining market prices, investors will be able to gain an insight into how their competitors and the market at large are valuing various asset classes. There are industry standard methods for this, for example, when considering the returns from equity markets a manager will look at the price/earnings ratio, price to book ratio, dividend yields, and expected earnings growth rates (amongst other things). In the bond market, managers will look at the credit spreads and the 'real' rate of interest. The objective for investors here is to ascertain if the asset class they are considering investing in is priced appropriately. The mere fact an asset class is over- or under-valued will elicit information on future performance and therefore the potential returns on offer if they invested. Moreover, for certain strategies, undervalued assets are considered a perfect opportunity to invest if they have strong fundamentals or significant growth potential.

**The Direction of the Business Cycle**   Understanding the machinations of the business cycle is a useful skill for an investor. Because it provides the opportunity for a savvy investor to take advantage of cyclical events. For example, in a 'normal' market, interest rates tend to lower just after the peak and during the recession. This is to prevent inflation as the market over-heats as the cycle extends. The objective is to create a standard prosperity/depression sine wave without too much damage being done. An investor might, if they believe this to be a truism, decide to increase the percentage of bonds in their portfolio to take advantage of this predictable event.

This being said, current interest rates have been reduced for a considerable period of time and have not been mirroring the economic cycle. Mostly, this was because of the 2008–2009 recession with central banks like the Federal Reserve keeping interest rates low with a resultant liquidity trap. As the US has recovered, the Federal Reserve has incrementally increased interest rates, potentially signalling a return to the standard business cycle. What is important to remember is that timing the market can be difficult. In the long-term, it may be possible for a skilled investor to take advantage of the variations in a business cycle – but this is not guaranteed. We also have been sat in (what I call) the Long Sideways for nearly 20 years in the Western world – more on that in the concluding chapters.

**Macro Factors**   There are significant exogenous factors, for example, political change (Brexit, mid-terms, populism), economic growth/decline (financial crises), demographics (ageing populations, migration) that can have a significant impact on the expected returns from an asset class. Investors will most likely be aware of these trends, although some pay closer attention than others depending on their strategy.

**Diversification**   Diversification is considered a favourable strategy within the asset allocation sphere – albeit it has its limitations. The key is the level of correlation an asset class has with another within the portfolio. For example, RE is often used as a diversifier as it tends to perform in a different way to bonds and equities under 'normal' market conditions. The objective is to prevent Vol, which should help ensure an expected rate of return.

Diversification does not just have to happen at the asset class level. Within the asset allocation process, it is possible to diversify within each asset class. For example, it is possible to hold multiple types of equities within the portfolio or vary the length of time you hold on to bonds. A manager may also consider different sectors or geographies when diversifying – all in an attempt to reduce Vol.

## THE CHALLENGES OF ASSET ALLOCATION OVER TIME

**Cost of Transactions**   When shifts in assets are processed, there is an increase in the cost.[32] This is because a cost is incurred when the asset class percentage is sold to another manager and then another cost is created when the selling manager uses the new funds to purchase different assets. These costs can quickly add up, especially if the manager is rebalancing the portfolio frequently. This undermines the value to the investor as the returns from the portfolio are diminished further and further. From the perspective of the investor, it is very important to consider whether rebalancing the portfolio actually achieves a net gain, or it is just being done to enforce a preordained strategy. This is a criticism of asset allocation generally but specifically it questions the value of tactical asset allocation. Especially with so much geopolitical uncertainty (see Chapters 1 and 13) it is understandable why most investors or managers will only reallocate when there is a genuine possibility of making a significant gain. Making decisions based around a concrete set of parameters also makes sense as it prevents managers from consistently shifting their assets with little to no long-term gain. A good example of a manager with a long-term perspective is a pension scheme (discussed further in Chapter 6). Some pension managers have used futures contracts to essentially mirror bond and equities portfolios. This prevents transactions costs from running out of control, but is not an available strategy for most managers.

**Missed Opportunities**  Like most commercial decisions, there is always the danger that the opportunity is missed. The nature of capital markets means that the potential upside of a decision may not last for very long. In order to take advantage of a situation, it is often needed to move quickly, which may not always be a possibility.

**Pernicious Precedents**  As discussed in the upcoming technology chapter, there is now a huge wealth of data available to investors from which they can draw predictions about future performance. The risks associated with gathering that data and processing it (i.e. if data starts from an incorrect presumption it will lead to a false conclusion) rings true especially when considering asset allocation. The majority of investors will use quantitative models to understand and elicit information which they will base their predictions on. When the data that is used for these models is incorrect or contains bias then this can lead to ill-informed decisions and poor asset allocation.

**Varying Conceptions of 'Risk'**  There are, depending on the type of investor, varying risk profiles and conceptions of risk. For example, a private client may consider risk to be associated with the loss of capital. In contrast, an institutional investor may perceive risk to be the potential to miss the benchmark return. The knock on impact when allocating assets is the need to understand the investor's objectives clearly. Unless this is done, you will be unable to match their risk appetite with the appropriate asset allocation. As has been indicated in the rest of this chapter, the composition of a portfolio can be safer or riskier depending on the choices made. It is important for a manager and a client to be on the same page.

**Liquidity Concerns**  The liquidity of the asset classes being invested in must be considered. Depending on an investor's risk appetite and investment horizon – with cash at one end of the spectrum and RE near the other end – the composition of the portfolio will be dictated by this consideration.

Illiquid assets have their benefits, as they can create uncorrelated returns and are not so susceptible to short-term market movements. A manager of illiquid assets is not forced to sell if times get rough for his investors and they can ride through tough markets. Hence the move in 2018–2019 – and as Vol and interest rates rises have returned – towards more investment in private equity, private markets, and private debt. 'Private' anything generally means the securities do not have a listed price.

## RISK CONSIDERATIONS

**Scenario Testing**  Underlying the strategic asset allocation model is that Vol is a short- or medium-term issue. Over the long term, it is argued, these risks level out and can be predicted by looking at historical trends. Future gazing is a tricky science and can be more of an art than is advertised. It is therefore important to apply a robust approach by considering as many possible economic scenarios that could impact the portfolio that has been created. There are many advantages to doing this before the final allocation is finalised. Namely, it may prompt an investor to hold on to certain assets that perform well in multiple scenarios.

Rather than just choosing an allocation that will only excel in one situation. If the allocation only succeeds in one core scenario (albeit one that has historically proven to be consistent) it may be advisable to hedge the risk in case this does not occur. This is especially true when considering the differing objectives of investors. A family office may not have as high a risk appetite as other forms of investors and may want to take a more cautious approach. This can be achieved by examining all the possible scenarios rather than just the favourable one.

**Taking a Global Approach**    There is a danger created when conforming to rigid asset allocation benchmarks that are dictated by domestic or foreign assets that a nationalistic bias comes through. It is important to be rational about choices and not base them on what is accepted both generally and locally. There may be a very good reason to have a local weighting but it is also very important for this to be rational and thought out. By exploring options at a global level there is the potential to create value that otherwise may not have been achieved.

**De-Risking**    Depending on your investment objectives, there are different methods where a portfolio can be de-risked. These can vary depending on what you are trying to accomplish. For example, a private family may wish to invest primarily in structured products or derivatives in order to protect their wealth. In contrast, institutions may be able to take a riskier approach in order to guarantee any liabilities they have taken on. However, should the desired funding level be reached following a bull run in the markets an institutional investor, such as a pension fund may well look at de-risking their portfolio by shifting the allocation away from riskier equities towards lower-risk bonds.

**Liability-Driven Investing**    Liability-driven investing (LDI) seeks to resolve the differing risk profiles of investors. The orthodox approach to investing for pensions plans centred on ensuring the maximum possible returns. LDI takes a new approach by placing risk at the centre of the decision-making process. In this sense, LDI does not measure performance by an external benchmark (peer group or otherwise) but instead aims to keep in step with the changing value of the given liabilities. The overriding objective is to increase stability in terms of balance sheet impact, funded status and required contributions.[33] Over the past two decades LDI has been popular amongst pension schemes in the UK. The 'problem' that LDI is intended to solve is the initial promise pension schemes made to their members to ensure a retirement income. For this to be achieved, they must have enough assets to cover their liabilities. This is considered by splitting the problem into two parts. First, the pension scheme needs to manage their liability risks. Secondly, the pension scheme needs to generate the requisite investment returns.

To achieve the first part a pension scheme will hedge their liability risks. Typically, these risks are changes in inflation or interest rates. Through matching the sensitivity of their liabilities with their choices of investment, the value of these liabilities should rise and fall in tandem with their funding level. To fulfil the second limb, a pension scheme will invest the rest of its assets for growth. Similarly, to other types of investors a pension scheme will make this decision based on the amount of money needed to reduce its deficit and its risk tolerance. This can be achieved through investing in orthodox asset classes such as equities, bonds, and derivatives. There has also been a growing trend for pension schemes to embrace alternatives as a way to boost returns. This has been seen particularly in Japan, a traditionally conservative investment base, as bond allocations have dropped considerably.[34]

Presently, with the potential for interest rates to rise, de-risking through LDI presents a potential hazard. Namely, that rates will rise above what is suggested by the markets.[35] This strategy has almost exclusively been employed within a low-interest environment. If interest rates rise, interest rate swaps which have been used to match liabilities will require pension funds to offer collateral. This will be in the form of cash, which should (in principle) have been set aside by the fund. LDI managers have maintained that they have the correct procedures in place to counter any such rise in interest rates but this scenario has not yet materialised. It is perfectly possible that some funds have not set aside enough collateral to deal with this instance and may find it difficult to satisfy their liabilities. Selling assets in a downturn is never easy and the inevitable discount that will be enforced by purchasers may make this even harder. To counter this a waterfall collateral structure could be put in place where predetermined assets are sold when certain thresholds are breached (i.e. interest rates go above a certain amount). Importantly, this must be done in good time and give the fund ample opportunity to sell off assets they need to generate the collateral required.

**Solvency II**  Solvency II was implemented in the 28 EU member states on 1 January 2016. It harmonises the EU's insurance regulatory regime and brought about significant challenges for operators within this space. Specifically, the Solvency II standard model which the directive requires insurers operating within the regime to use, does not recognise the benefits diversification can bring within a single asset class. For many insurance companies this runs counter-intuitively to the models they employed. This forced a step change in the way insurance firms allocated assets and, in the context of a tricky financial ecosystem, presented significant difficulties.

In effect, Solvency II placed limitations on the way portfolios were designed. The regulation required further capital to mirror the additional risk exposure that in turn has put more pressure on insurance firms who have found it already difficult to operate in an increasingly competitive sector. The capital requirements have resulted in several insurers from the UK remove themselves from the bulk and individual annuity markets. Moreover, insurers have repeatedly removed long-term guaranteed savings products which is a by-product of low interest rates and older business models.[36] The impact in the UK of the risk margin has caused significant disruption in insurance firms' balance sheets. Dr Bruce Porteous from Standard Life Investments suggests that there is a general agreement that the margin is not calibrated correctly and is causing an unintended and unfortunate impact in the UK.[37]

These challenges are set to continue and will undoubtedly lead to further change within the insurance industry. As Dr Bruce Porteous points out, the influx of new regulation will provide opportunities for some but may make it increasingly difficult for others. This space is sure to be influenced by other themes touched on in this book. For example, the regulatory uncertainty surrounding Brexit, wider geopolitical risks, and whether or not interest rates will increase in the near to mid-future.

## RESTRUCTURING A PORTFOLIO

Changing the configuration of a portfolio by selling of unwanted assets or asset types, and replacing them with preferred assets makes portfolio restructuring a dynamic or tactical asset allocation. It is not selling a small number of securities or indeed rebalancing your portfolio following a change in the percentage makeup. Instead, the investor is altering the fundamental structure of the portfolio.[38]

Restructuring a portfolio does not have to be limited to the assets it is comprised of. It can be far more structural. It could be concerned with the processes that are in place that lead to investment decisions or the staff that are needed to implement the decisions themselves. For example, if a portfolio is fundamentally taking a new approach to how it allocates assets it may need a complete overhaul on both the operational as well as the strategic side. In order to realise the new direction, the current asset allocation will need to be divested. The original investment team may not be experienced enough to employ the new strategy so additional hires may be required. The new strategy could need a more quantitative approach therefore necessitating additional equipment as well as intellectual property (IP). Plans would have to be put in place to manage the potential downside of a total overhaul, specifically how to maximise returns in the short term to promote a better recovery for the investors.

Restructuring a portfolio from both an operational and strategic perspective would require significant time, expense, and effort. It is something that smaller managers may struggle to do on their own and so may need to outsource the process to an external party. The costs involved in this would also need to be factored in but the resultant uplift of approaching this properly would be evident.

## THE FINAL STEPS

Once the risk and return characteristics of the desired portfolio have been established and the investor has signed off the investment through their processes and internal governance structure the process begins of selecting and allocating to a fund manager. There are three main steps to follow in this process: manager selection, due diligence, and, finally, the transition of the assets to the manager.

### Manager Selection

Manager selection is at its heart the process of finding the best in breed manager for each asset class and strategy that the investor is looking to allocate to. There are various ways of managing this process and many investors have their approach dictated by regulation; for instance, European public sector funds have to follow the EU's *Official Journal of the European Union* (OJEU) process. Some of these processes approach the market fresh each time, whilst others start with databases of managers. Some of these processes involve one stage at which managers submit information, whilst others narrow the pool of managers down across two. All manager selection processes examine the managers submitting for the mandate with a combination of qualitative and quantitative analysis to reach a conclusion as to which is best suited for the mandate.

This process can be complicated by the esoteric nature of some strategies, making judgement of the manager difficult without expert knowledge. In addition, an investor may well be looking for a number of different managers within an asset/class or strategy or managers running strategies which may overlap. In situations such as this clients can perform combination analysis to ascertain the best mix of clients. How rigorous and complex a manager selection exercise is may depend on the client's preference, budget, the asset class in question and the amount being allocated.

Manager selection is not simply about picking the biggest, baddest (read most established) fund manager on the block or those with the best track record. It must take into account the specific needs of the clients, whether there are new entrants to the market, and how managers have stuck to the desired strategy even if it impacted on returns.

Qualitative and quantitative analysis will take place across more the process as managers are weeded out and more information is gleaned from those remaining. This process will conclude with the most rigorous part of gathering information on a manager: due diligence, which we explore below.

## Due Diligence

Once an investor has selected the manager that they wish to allocate to, they will perform due diligence (DD) to gather a level of detail which it would be overly onerous and impractical to receive during the manager selection process. This detail falls into three key areas: investment, operational, and legal. Due diligence can be done on each of these areas separately or in concert as required. As with manager selection there are obvious areas to enquire into and the investor can follow pro forma due diligence questionnaires, such as Institutional Limited Partners Association's (ILPA) due diligence questionnaire for investing with a PE manager, or AIMA's with a hedge manager. However, the concerns and requirements an investor has often require a bespoke approach and a more extensive back and forth with the manager.

**Investment Due Diligence**  This is the process of gathering information on a fund's current investment strategy and the investment methodology of the fund manager. Investors will need to look at and evaluate the market opportunity set as well as evaluate the manager's track record and performance on both an absolute and relative basis. Investment due diligence (IDD) will also evaluate a manager's risk management functions as well as their approach to portfolio construction and other factors, such as how a manager builds ESG considerations into their investment process.

**Operational Due Diligence**  This is the process of checking a fund manager has in place the best practice operational procedures and structures. This includes reviewing all aspects of a fund's operations and administration including capital calls, movement of cash and investor reporting. Operational due diligence (ODD) will also cover a manager's valuation policies, processes and controls and its corporate functions, including legal, compliance, finance, tax, HR, IT, and business continuity.

**Legal Due Diligence**  Legal due diligence (LDD) involves reviewing all legal documentation provided by the fund including side letter requests, subscription agreements and relevant supplier contracts. This process ensures that the investor's terms are equitable and that the appropriate robust protections are in place. This due diligence can involve advice on key commercial and legal issues, as well as tax. It can even extend to fee negotiation with the manager.

## Transition

Finally, once the agreements have all been signed, the assets need to be transitioned into the target allocation from the legacy position in which they are currently invested. This process has a large degree of operational risk but also risks exposing the investor to the unforeseen and unwanted returns as they transition from the legacy to the target exposure. Transition managers are hired and transition advice sought to ensure that the transition happens smoothly and without incurring undue cost or risk. Once capital is fully deployed in the target asset(s), the new portfolio is in place.

## SOME CONCLUSIONS

**Asset Allocation and Diversification**   Asset allocation is one of the key forms of diversification – it is the diversification of asset categories. This can potentially offer less erratic performance and act as an emotional (and financial) buoy when certain asset classes take a hit. Even if a portfolio is not perfectly optimised every day, allocation over five-plus asset classes can go a long way towards better risk-adjusted returns.[39]

**Future Predictions**   First school of thought: the goals and importance of asset allocation will not change, but the mechanisms by which investors seek to achieve those goals will be new.[40] There will continue to be a need for investors and researchers to scrutinise the assumptions underlying today's models and evaluate whether the model is a sufficient reflection of reality. Undoubtedly, most of today's approaches will be found wanting in the future and new advances will be made.[41]

Second school of thought: asset allocation as a 'free lunch' is over – this decade will likely see the turning point in this narrative. MPT works well in strong markets and over periods of declining interest rates. Many people's predictions on where the markets are heading are the total opposite of this. This will probably force MPT followers to reassess their approach to investing. This will encourage other forms of investing, such as active management and alternative approaches to asset allocation, to gain more appeal.[42]

But with a caveat:

Although the above-described methods come across as straightforward – they are certainly not easy. The precise mix of assets requires considerable analysis of a variety of factors; namely, capital markets, past performance, expected market movements, etc. and therefore necessitates a huge amount of work and intellect. Managers, therefore, have to be fully switched on to the many variables that can influence their decisions. Moreover, these variables are in a constant state of flux, further complicating the situation. Underlying all of this is the need for the objectives of the client to be fulfilled and adhered to by the manager. This is why due diligence is so important, the history of fund management is littered with high profile operational failures and failed investments. With increased public scrutiny on many investors, combined with a general drive towards transparency and the implementation of ESG considerations, we have increasingly been asked to extend and expand our due diligence services at MJ Hudson to include new considerations. It is clear, therefore, that for both managers and investors the task of creating a robust and well-thought-through portfolio of investments has never been an easy one.

## ENDNOTES

1. http://web.uconn.edu/ahking/Tobin58.pdf
2. Ibid.
3. Ibid.
4. Ibid.

5. https://investmentsandwealth.org/getmedia/69e2c4da-936b-4863-98f8-b4400d2f32e9/IWM17Jan
   Feb-UpsideOfDownsideOfMPT.pdf
6. Ibid.
7. Kaplan, P. (2011) *Frontiers of Modern Asset Allocation*. New Jersey: Wiley.
8. www.investorschronicle.co.uk/managing-your-money/2018/06/07/fixed-or-active-which-is-the-
   best-method-of-asset-allocation/
9. www.investorschronicle.co.uk/managing-your-money/2018/06/07/fixed-or-active-which-is-the-
   best-method-of-asset-allocation/
10. www.raymondjames.ca/branches/premium/pdfs/asset-allocation.pdf
11. Campbell, J. and Viceira, L. M. (2002) Strategic Asset Allocation: Portfolio Choice for Long-Term
    Investors. Oxford: Oxford University Press.
12. https://portfolioconstructionforum.edu.au/obj/articles_pcc09/pcc09_DDF_RP_Select-Asset-
    Management.pdf
13. https://portfolioconstructionforum.edu.au/obj/articles_pcc09/pcc09_DDF_RP_Select-Asset-
    Management.pdf
14. www.reevesifa.com/strategic-asset-allocation-pensions/
15. www.linkedin.com/pulse/family-office-asset-allocation-strategies-trends-antonio
16. Ibid.
17. Phillips, D. and Lee, J. (1989). 'Differentiating Tactical Asset Allocation from Market Tim-
    ing. Financial Analysts Journal', 45(2), 14–16. www.jstor.org/stable/4479200
18. https://corporatefinanceinstitute.com/resources/knowledge/strategy/asset-allocation/
19. www.iosrjournals.org/iosr-jbm/papers/Vol17-issue5/Version-1/R01751154163.pdf
20. Ibid.
21. Ibid.
22. https://thephilanthropist.ca/original-pdfs/Philanthropist-13-1-149.pdf
23. www.jstor.org/stable/4478947?seq=1#page_scan_tab_contents
24. www.iosrjournals.org/iosr-jbm/papers/Vol17-issue5/Version-1/R01751154163.pdf
25. http://www.iosrjournals.org/iosr-jbm/papers/Vol17-issue5/Version-1/R01751154163.pdf
26. Ibid.
27. Ibid.
28. https://www.marketbeat.com/financial-terms/asset-allocation-balancing-investments/
29. http://www.iosrjournals.org/iosr-jbm/papers/Vol17-issue5/Version-1/R01751154163.pdf
30. Ibid.
31. https://investinganswers.com/financial-dictionary/investing/dynamic-asset-allocation-5549
32. https://thephilanthropist.ca/original-pdfs/Philanthropist-13-1-149.pdf
33. www.benefitplans.baml.com/Publish/Content/application/pdf/GWMOL/IR_ARDSHKCC_2015-
    11.pdf
34. https://www.ft.com/content/8cafbbd8-810f-11e8-8e67-1e1a0846c475
35. www.ipe.com/investment/briefing-investment/briefing-collateral-challenges/www.ipe.com/
    investment/briefing-investment/briefing-collateral-challenges/10028807.fullarticle
36. www.standardlifeinvestments.com/WP_Asian_Insurance_Survey.pdf
37. Ibid.
38. https://financial-dictionary.thefreedictionary.com/Portfolio+restructuring
39. www.ajc.com/business/wes-moss-what-you-need-understand-about-asset-allocation/6mI1yK9Pm1
    XUKlpBbJT9lL/
40. https://corporate.morningstar.com/ib/documents/MethodologyDocuments/IBBAssociates/
    RoleAssetAllocation.pdf
41. https://corporate.morningstar.com/ib/documents/MethodologyDocuments/IBBAssociates/
    RoleAssetAllocation.pdf
42. www.forbes.com/sites/robisbitts2/2018/08/06/asset-allocation-is-in-serious-decline/

# CHAPTER 8

# Technology

*It's supposed to be automatic, but actually you have to push this button.*

– John Brunner, novelist

**T**his chapter aims to provide an insight into the use of technology in the asset management industry. There have been some incredible technological advances over the last 100 years. The advent of the computer, the internet, the mobile device, and broadband were each seismic for asset management. Ray Kurzweil's law of accelerating returns states that 'fundamental measures of information technology follow predictable and exponential trajectories' which can be illustrated by the mere seven-year gap between Nokia releasing their 3310 model in 2000 and Apple releasing the first iPhone in 2007. Within the last few years, the growth of robo-advisers, blockchain, algo-driven investment and AI-based hedge funds signals the arrival of asset managers into the twenty-first century. No doubt, the cyborg or permanently wired human will be next. For now, strong coffee will have to do for this author.

## THE USE OF TECHNOLOGY

**The Basic Operating Platform** Over a period of more than thirty years, I have been working within or advising the industry, and in this time the way asset managers operate on a day-to-day basis has changed considerably.

PCs, laptops, tablets, mobile phones, and other electronic devices have become staples of modern day living and enable individuals to work anywhere at ever faster speeds. The processing power on our phones is now faster than that of some computers I was using not too long ago. With the growth in technology comes a greater breadth of choice when deciding what tools should be used.

For example, the advent of cloud-based storage facilities clearly marks the beginning of better scalability, as we can be faster to implement and expand. Within this emerging technology, there is debate as to whether private- or public-based storage systems should be used. Orthodox opinion suggests that for companies that are less focused on compliance and governance, public-based storage (for example, Amazon EC2 and Microsoft Azure) is more appropriate. In contrast, private cloud storage affords the purchaser the opportunity to further customise and secure the product. This enables the user to more readily meet their compliance and security objectives as they wish. You are the owner of a private cloud and can take charge even when something goes wrong as opposed to being at the mercy of providers by using public storage, where your priorities or resolutions may not be factored in. However private clouds are very expensive and can get out of date quickly. The public or private cloud debate continues. Some argue that public clouds are the most secure as they evolve with considerably more investment.

Recently, there has been considerable debate around using servers in-house, due to a significant growth in public and private clouds. Those institutions favouring private storage commend it for its adaptability to be tailored according to their business. In part, because of greater control over the standard, application, and users.

**Users** In terms of storage, and especially following the introduction of MiFID II and the General Data Protection Regulation (GDPR) within the EU, personal data must be stored securely and personal data cannot be kept without consent – and especially not used for commercial or other advantage against the user. Technology companies ought to be careful when they crow about the number of users that they 'own'. Google has already fallen foul of the legislation and incurred a fine of EUR 50 million from the French data protection regulator Commission nationale de l'informatique et des libertés (CNIL).[1]

The following are the six core principles that all organisations need to take into account when handling personal data:

1. Data should be processed lawfully, fairly, and transparently.
2. The data should be collected for specified, explicit, and legitimate purposes.
3. The data must be adequate, relevant, and limited to what is necessary.
4. The personal data must also be accurate and up to date.
5. The data needs to be retained by the firm for only as long as necessary.
6. The data should be processed in an appropriate manner to maintain security.

The above principles are also very relevant in the context of security, as I discuss later.

**The Internet** It might seem strange to mention the internet, but the internet (to quote Bill Gates) really did change everything. Hard to remember, but the internet was pretty hopeless in the first dot-com boom and bust (number two bust is coming up – see Chapter 13), and it is only really because of the vast advances in broadband, Wi-Fi, and mobile internet, that the day-to-day life of an asset manager has changed so significantly. This joining of information technology and operational technology that occurred during the turn of the millennium, combined with fibre and faster broadband speed lie at the root of this transformation.

**Ownership or Renting** Adding to the cloud storage debate, asset managers also need to decide whether they want ownership of their IT system, by employing a capital expenditure (CAPEX) system or whether they want to rent it out through operational expenditure (OPEX).

The transition from CAPEX to OPEX is in part attributable to the bottom line, but also the acknowledgement that technology growth has caused greater unpredictability. This uncertainty is characterised by the future cost predictions associated with purchasing technology as well as fast moving obsolete issues. Moreover, this is underlined by the need to future-proof against business and technology growth. Historically, IT services needed employees with the requisite skill set, large amounts of time, and an established set-up. With the advent of subscription-based services and cloud-based technologies additional flexibility for businesses has been created. Therefore, when deciding between OPEX and CAPEX, asset managers usually consider the following:

- **Budget:** OPEX is usually cheaper than CAPEX, principally over the shorter time period.
- **Ownership:** The CAPEX model is owned by the business and not rented.
- **Taxation Allowances:** Having ownership of the CAPEX system means that it is an asset for the firm, and as a result the firm can receive tax allowances and add value to the business by amortising and depreciating the asset.
- **Newer Technologies:** Buying the infrastructure and hardware can be expensive, so the business would want to keep the asset for as long as possible. Therefore, it may not be able to attain emerging technologies readily. By having an OPEX model, the firm is not locked in and can make use of the latest technology on offer.
- **Pay As You Go:** By employing the OPEX model, businesses only pay according to their usage. This is a better option for start-up or fast-moving companies that are unsure as to what model they should use. It also addresses amount of usage and IT future change.
- **Hidden Costs:** In addition to the costs of acquiring hardware and infrastructure, the business will also need to pay for the maintenance of the system and employ staff to monitor it. These hidden costs associated with the CAPEX system may make it expensive to have an on-premise infrastructure.

However, the new expression in town is OPEF, which stands for 'operational efficiency'. An OPEF model aims to deliver 'quality products' and maximum 'resource capabilities' with minimal waste. This is achieved by 'identifying the wasteful processes and resources that drain the businesses' profits and designing a new work process' which will help develop the system's quality and productivity.

**Data Provision**   With the development of open-source software, mobile and cloud-based computing it has become apparent that there is the potential to disrupt the data provider space. There are more rivals now to market leader, Bloomberg – for example, Thompson Reuters, Eikon, Symphony, Slack, Money.net, FactSet, and Markit.

Smaller niche offerings such as NetDania and TradingView may not be considered direct rivals to Bloomberg but perhaps can challenge certain areas. Furthermore, as more platforms are created offering unbundled options, there may be greater co-operation amongst smaller rivals.

Finally, of course, there is masses of free data out there, but providers such as Bloomberg and Thompson Reuters are major consolidators of this information and still incredibly useful.

**Systems**   Technology is essential to asset managers, as it supports them in the decision-making process, primarily by organising up-to-date and critical data on portfolios including whether holdings comply with client-stipulated investment guidelines, risk exposures, and risk analytics. However, technology only helps investment professionals measure their risks relative to the risk and return objectives specified by clients and imputed. The investment managers are the ones with the final say and will need to use their expertise to advise clients on the next steps. Yet, within the investment management space, there is a consensus that technology, data, analytics, and reporting platforms (enabling the integration of risk management and portfolio management) are growing in importance.

The key systems used by managers are the (1) order management systems, (2) risk analytics, and (3) performance and accounting systems.

**Order Management Systems**   These systems typically cover portfolio management, trading and operations, an example of which is the Bloomberg Terminal, the industry leader by a long way in terms of volume. This system provides multi-asset order and execution management solutions and investment cycle analytics that enable buy-side and sell-side firms to turn their trade and order data into a competitive advantage. Using systems like the Bloomberg Terminal, firms can create more efficient workflows, connect to the global capital markets, drive regulatory compliance, and lower their total cost of ownership (so the advert goes).

**Risk Analytics Systems**   Risk Analytics include software such as Citi Yield Book, UBS Delta, and IBM Algorithmics. These software offerings are comprised of advanced analytical tools to measure risk and performance and enable financial institutions and corporate treasuries to make risk-aware business decisions. Modern risk analytics systems can be a powerful tool for an investor, saving time by raising red flags when required and functioning quietly in the background the rest of the time.

**Performance and Accounting Systems**   Accounting systems are becoming ever more sophisticated as software extends beyond the Excel spreadsheets of yore and provides integrated data entry and analysis to funds and fund administrators. These systems range from fairly simple accountancy software to advanced systems allowing performance measurement and monitoring alongside manipulation and management of data to meet a variety of accounting standards and regulatory/reporting requirements.

**Further Systems**   A fund manager also operates different software in the back office (fund admin systems), mid office (governance systems), and front office.

It is, however, important to note that software systems are most likely to be a multi-year commitment. Therefore, it may be advisable for firms to adopt an incremental approach whereby they reduce the risk of paying a large sum up front. This also has the added advantage of improving scalability across the front office and can be done in tandem with investment in new data architecture.

Lastly, some firms are now offering outsourced investment management models (oCIO) to third parties. As the use of data, analytics, and risk management tools are becoming increasingly vital for firms to stay competitive, offering these services to smaller managers or insurers could offset future OPEX costs. According to the Boston Consulting Group, 'for asset managers, offering oCIO services is an opportunity to monetise investments in data, analytics, and risk management capabilities that they already are undertaking on their own behalf.[2]

Consequently, there is an opportunity to mitigate some of the risk of upgrading your own technology through monetising the investments that have already been made.

## FUTURE ADVANCES

Investment management and the asset managers are poised to become even more driven by advances in technology in the coming years, as digital innovation plays a greater role than ever before. With the advent of AI, predictive reasoning, machine learning, and natural language processing the orthodox approach to analysis is set to change. As this technology becomes more mainstream, the competitive advantage gained will diminish. Finding new ways to analyse, present, and utilise data will become in vogue. Furthermore, new technology such as blockchaining, robo-advisers, and robotic process automation (RPA) has disruptive potential. Harnessing these tools to provide cheaper more efficient solutions to clients' objectives will be the hallmark of the technologically forward manager.

**Blockchain**    Blockchain is a secure and effective technology for tracking transactions, and acts as a database, or a giant network known as a distributed ledger. This ledger records ownership and value, and allows anyone with access to view previous transactions and take part. This new system could have the potential to replace centralised systems of record that asset managers have traditionally used. Calastone (a technology company) has said that, under test conditions, it managed to use blockchain to buy and sell mutual funds.[3] The advantage of removing the frictional costs of asset managers is the reduction of costs that are traditionally passed on to the client. This is good news for investors, and it is crucial that asset managers remain forward-thinking to maintain competitiveness.

**Big Data**    Asset management firms are operating within a world that is growing in complexity. Leading firms within this space are combining big data analytics with AI and machine learning to achieve two objectives: (1) providing insight and analysis for investment selection; and (2) improving cost effectiveness by leveraging expensive human analyst resources with scalable technology.

With around 90% of all the data in the world having been created in the last three years[4] the advance of new technology provides an increasingly complicated nexus. To promote the use of advanced analytics and an evolved investment process, asset managers are pursuing a more modernised data architecture. This is often done in tandem with a wider concerted effort to improve front-office technology; for example, order management re-platforming. This will provide a more consistent and efficient stream of data which asset managers can utilise to deliver better results for their clients. Powering this shift is the growing focus placed on big data. It is clear that momentum is with advanced analytics, with over 70% of respondents in a CRISIL survey citing big data investments as important.[5] The value of this information does not always end with superior insights, but includes compliance, risk, sales, and marketing.

Traditionally, quantitative data can be described as structured. This is characterised by a high degree of organisation and an ability to fit that data within pre-existing algorithms that can readily search for the salient information. For example, spreadsheets are typically structured and can be incorporated (or used independently) within a relational database system. In contrast, unstructured data is vast and not easily categorised into one type or the other. Moreover, the sheer volume of data makes traditional methods of data extraction (methods used for structured data) impractical. However, the benefits of developing the correct IT architecture to evaluate and sort big data are invaluable. Investment professionals want access to the layered information big data provides. It can create a wealth of intelligence that will help improve efficiency and decision-making processes.

Big data mining of items such as analyst reports, regulatory filings, e-mails, satellite imaging, and even the tone detected in the language can all be valuable inputs for managers. This information can be sorted, analysed, and then used by data scientists to give managers an edge. Not only is this information useful for analytics and portfolio construction, but it is used in operations as well. Combined with automation, platforms can highlight which trades are most likely to succeed and fail. This can then be examined by a human employee who can correct the trade. The combination of human and computer is more valuable than the output of a solo computer. Going forward, it may be that a manager can create a large enough data set to correct possible errors in the system by itself. For now, it appears that technology will give an advantage, but not the whole answer.

The incorporation of big data into an asset manager's strategy is not completely seamless. It may be tempting to look at BlackRock, Vantage, or others and assume that a large outlay on new technology will result in immediate financial gains. However, there are several important factors to consider before any expenditure is made. First, honing in on the right sources of data is not straightforward. The volume of data means asset managers will need to validate any source they think can contribute to their intelligence. Moreover, conducting the requisite DD on the providers of information is also important. Just because the data you collate is accurately and legally sourced does not mean data from other sources is. Second, although the value of big data is that it gives an asset manager an edge over competitors, this only lasts for a period of time. The strategies firms use, which are determined by the intelligence from big data must be revisited and altered if necessary. Once a competitor, or competitors, catch on to the same insight its value lessens. Third, there is a danger to becoming overly reliant on the data and run the risk of not being able to see the wood for the trees. Therefore, individuals who are using this information would ideally be trained in statistics in order to understand the limitations of big data.

One way to mitigate the risks (and costs) posed by incorporating big data is to implement it incrementally. Not all firms need to have their own version of Aladdin (operated by Black-Rock). Taking time to develop a strategy through using external providers and consultants, as well as internal appraisal, could prevent a misstep. Moreover, this gradual approach will help with scaling the technology later and preserve resources for a later date. Data is worthless without analysis.

## Robo-Advisory

> The future of asset management will be dominated by several themes including robo-advisory which is touted to ultimately replace much of the human investment selection element. Thus far it has had more impact on distribution through the formation of platforms where there is effectively one-stop shopping where many propositions are available but the selection still remains by the investor and not by a machine.
>
> **– Richard Novack, founder of Alpha Hawk**

There will be a likely rise in the deployment of robo-advisers to help provide online investment management services to clients. A typical robo-adviser collects information from clients regarding their financial situation and future goals through an online survey, and then uses the data to offer advice. They can even be used to automatically invest client assets. Improvements in computing power are making robo-advisers more viable for both retail and institutional investors. In addition, some cutting-edge robo-adviser firms could emerge with AI-supported investment decision and asset allocation algorithms.

These services have been perceived as an example of wealth management democratisation. Indeed, some commentators have suggested that using them is as easy as ordering a pizza.[6] They enable members of the public to engage in their own investments and many of the providers have zero or very low entry fees for their services. By 2020, it is suggested that robo-advisers will manage around USD 8 trillion.[7] The cost, accessibility, and growing trend amongst younger clients to trust automated services is behind the growth in this space.

Broadly speaking, it is more accurate to describe the service they offer as 'simplified advice'[8] regarding a specific product based on the information you provide them. It will not, unlike a more sophisticated financial adviser, look at the wider picture. Although it must be noted that certain robo-advisers offer full financial advice. Consequently, it is common for the majority of robo-advisers to only offer advice on a limited pool of products. Despite this, it is clear there is a strong appetite for these services, which is most likely grounded in the unintended consequences of the Retail Distribution Review 2012 (RDR) – a review of the UK market for retail investment products conducted by the FCA's predecessor, the Financial Services Authority (FSA).

The RDR had the objective of solving the problems associated with advisers receiving commission from fund managers. Criticism levelled at advisers ranged from conflicts of interest, bad value, and mis-selling. In banning the payment of commission, large numbers of advisers left the industry. For the current investor, who does not have extensive finances, their access to an adviser is limited. Prior to the invention of robo-advisers, this type of investor would have to do it themselves through online fund services and take responsibility for the whole process (investment goals, risk, and choice of investments). Robo-advisers have the potential to fill this gap, and the plan is for them to do so.

However, as a warning to the European market, robo-advisory services in the US have struggled recently. Competition is proving to be too great for some providers, with leading firms (for example, Betterment, Wealthfront, Ellevest, and TD Ameritrade) having to pay upwards of USD 1000 to acquire new customers.[9] Indeed, Victor Basta's comments in the *Financial Times* that the developed nature of the market means competition will create diminishing returns[10] appear prescient.

More recently, there has been acknowledgement that robo-advisers need to have more of a human feel about them.[11] This is an appreciation that not everyone is ready to trust their investments with a machine just yet. Indeed, the idea that one form can be filled out, a choice made, and everything set, can be intimidating for an investor. In order to attract more customers and perhaps prevent the issues of competition found in the US market, Scalable Capital (backed by BlackRock) has launched a new over-the-phone and face-to-face package. Nutmeg is soon to follow suit with a new service and it looks likely that other robo-adviser companies will too.

So, add a human to a robot and read Isaac Asimov.

## ADOPTING TECHNOLOGICAL ADVANCEMENTS

Arguably, the extent to which asset managers stay competitive will, in part, be determined by their proficiency in advanced data, analytics, AI, and machine learning. It is vital that managers continually upskill by adopting and mastering these evolving technologies. By adopting these technologies into their processes, managers will gain an edge and those who do not will face the threat of being undermined. Asset managers will have to grab the opportunities that technology affords them today in order to succeed tomorrow.

Asset managers have identified that there is a market for sophisticated automated advice for retail clients, or the type of people who are not usually inclined to employ wealth managers for their investments. Despite its use for exploiting the advice gap and target the mass affluent, AI is also a valuable tool to help client advisers. According to PricewaterhouseCoopers,[12]

26% of asset and wealth management firms globally use artificial intelligence to inform their next 'big decisions'. BlackRock has an artificial intelligence engine called Aladdin, which uses natural language processing (this allows computer programs to understand human speech) to read thousands of documents, such as news articles and broker reports, and produce a sentiment score on a particular company or entity. Similarly, Morgan Stanley has a platform called 3D Insights, which analyses research, information, and products, and matches them to the relevant client portfolios and financial advisers.

Bridgewater Associates, a large hedge fund manager states that they have invested heavily into technology to be used for back office functions and is building a piece of software to automate the day-to-day management of the firm, including hiring, firing, and other strategic decision-making. With regards to the investment side of their business, Bridgewater Associates have created Bridgewater Associates' Book of the Future, or Principles Operating System (PriOS), which is a technological platform driven by data designed to make investment decisions more effectively. The platform is a giant algorithm that can provide GPS-style directions for how staff members should spend every aspect of their day, down to whether an employee should make a particular phone call or not. It differs from traditional algorithms in that most algo-traders are using a systematic approach to make investment choices.

AI is also being used by hedge funds, with Numerai being a recent notable example. Numerai is a fund that aims to bring network effects to capital allocation by providing data scientists with financial data (redacted stock market information to remove bias) which they then use to create financial prediction models and submit this to the hedge fund. The models are built using machine-learning algorithms and are pieced together by the fund in order to allow the meta-model they use to grow and learn.

Lastly, more and more investment management firms are looking to employ sophisticated RPA tools to streamline both front- and back-office functions. Using RPA technology is efficient as it can carry out tasks that require a significant amount of time, such as client onboarding and regulatory compliance in less time than when performed manually. This technology has the ability to make a significant impact on how business is carried out and undoubtedly offers strategic and financial benefits.

Where the process is typically repetitive and routine, RPA can replace an individual who would ordinarily fulfil that role. This frees up the individual to do more nuanced tasks that would require innate human qualities (for example, emotional intelligence) that a machine does not possess. It has the added advantage of ensuring that there will be fewer mistakes in the work, which is a risk when repetitive tasks are carried out by humans.

## CYBERSECURITY

The sweeping changes to the technological landscape have not just benefited asset managers. With new developments in artificial intelligence the threat of cyberattacks is growing. According to Accenture's High Performance Security Report 2016, many firms have faced 'cybersecurity breaches'. Wiki Leaks, Luxembourg Leaks, Panama Papers, and Paradise Papers are just a few examples of high-profile incidents that have kept the fourth estate busy and the rest of the world fascinated.

In December 2006, a website named 'WikiLeaks' uploaded a document that claimed to be a decision to assassinate government officials. The authenticity of the document was questioned by both the media and WikiLeaks itself. What followed over the next 12 years became front page news globally. From Tibetan dissent to US intelligence, WikiLeaks has released documents covering a vast range of subject matters. Along the way, individuals such as Edward Snowden, Chelsea Manning, and Julian Assange (the founder of WikiLeaks) have become household names. Their behaviour has been scrutinised from a legal and ethical perspective. Whether their actions are treasonous or part of a wider effort to hold governments around the world to account has been debated consistently in the media since the first upload. What is undeniable is that the world, and the way in which we understand privacy, has changed forever.

The most recent hack was the release of the so-called 'Paradise Papers', in which 13.4 million[13] financial documents were leaked from the law firm Appleby and corporate service firms Estera and Asiaciti Trust. Not only were famous faces such as the Queen of England, Lewis Hamilton, and members of President Trump's administration exposed, but multinational companies such as Apple and Nike were also given honourable mentions. This leak culminated in a combined effort from 96 media partners and 381 journalists operating from 67 countries to break the story. Originally obtained by a German newspaper (Süddeutsche Zeitung), the information was disseminated at the International Consortium of Investigative Journalists. Afterwards, a co-ordinated release was planned, with the news breaking simultaneously across the world. These papers raised questions concerning the moral and legal strength of these schemes and shed light on how they operate.

It is, of course, important to highlight that this act was a breach of data privacy. Data was extracted without the owner's consent, a spokesperson from Appleby summing this up by stating that their 'firm was not subject to a leak but to a serious criminal act'.[14] Some may argue that this is a matter of public interest, i.e. the public should be aware of these individuals and big corporations using tax mitigation techniques. Against a global backdrop of slow economic growth and, closer to home, imposed austerity measures, many commentators were asking – although illegal, was this fair? Is the 'elite' taking advantage of the small guy? Indeed, as Barack Obama pertinently put it, 'The problem is that a lot of this stuff is legal, not illegal'.[15] The morality of these schemes has also sparked a debate over ethical hacking.

It is assumed that those firms dealing with multinational companies or HNWIs are more susceptible to hacking as opposed to other businesses. Recent years have seen offshore firms being targets of such attacks as illustrated by the Panama, Luxembourg, and Switzerland leaks.

Unlike the Panama Papers leak, the Paradise Papers did not reveal too overtly any 'corruption' or 'dirty money'; instead, it was just exposing a lot of tax planning. In contrast, the Panama Papers revealed widespread corruption which resulted in Brazil's largest ever bribery scandal. The investigation was launched by the International Consortium of Investigative Journalists (ICIJ), which relied on its network of over 200 investigative journalists operating in more than 70 countries to break this story. In the roughly 11.5 million files, 140 politicians from over 50 countries, who were involved with offshore companies operating in 21 offshore havens, had their financial dealings revealed.[16] Hailed as one of the largest blows to the offshore world ever seen, the darker side of these findings revealed how blacklisted individuals could still conduct business without being traced. The extent of the ramifications of this leak are still not certain.

We have also seen in the previous years, breaches of data where personal data records have been leaked. Examples of this would be the Yahoo breach or even the more recent Equifax leaks. The Equifax cyberattacks signalled a change in the mindset of many executives, who now believe that information-related risks are the key concern.[17] Around 143 million US citizens had their personal data compromised by the attack.

When speaking of leaks and cyberattacks asset managers should now also be aware of the new GDPR guidance, according to which breach reporting is now mandatory. The incoming regulation replaced the EU Data Protection Directive 95/46/EC and aims to update and harmonise the differences between member states privacy laws. In the event of a data breach, the GDPR states that the controller should notify the supervisory authority (the Information Commissioners Office or ICO in the UK) immediately and where possible within 72 hours of the controller becoming aware of the breach. The controller must also communicate the breach to the data subjects effected 'without undue delay' and this must be direct communication, i.e. the controller cannot simply post a notice on their website. The content of the GDPR will affect the operators within the alternative asset space in a number of ways (for example, compliance, business model, selection of technology, and the integration of data protection throughout the business). In real terms, this will require alternative asset managers to place a far greater emphasis on data protection. One solution is to encourage digitisation and promote new technologies, which will manage the data in a compliant way. This will fulfil the purpose of the GDPR, which is to reformat personal data protection as an inherent right, thus creating greater demonstrable transparency. The introduction of mandatory breach reporting requirements, fines of up to 4% of global turnover, and the removal of the DPA's threshold for the 'right to erasure' means the GDPR will inevitably become a catalyst for change in this space.

In terms of cybersecurity, there are increasing numbers of software systems out there to defend your data. Also there are consultancies to hire to try and hack your systems, and then fill in the holes. Cybersecurity is only growing and increasingly needed.

## SOCIAL MEDIA

Studies have shown that the use of social media also influences decision-making. Take, for instance, the impact the US government can have by its continuous use of Twitter. Within the finance sector, many investors increasingly make an investment decision or recommendation based on social media. The use and influence of social media has been associated with the location of the asset managers. Apparently, European institutions prefer LinkedIn, whereas US asset owners prefer Twitter, and those in Asia-Pacific prefer YouTube.[18]

Even though they have a social media influence, a study has shown that asset managers are not necessarily using social media as effectively as they could be. Whilst 80% of asset managers have a Twitter account, with 60% posting daily, just 23% of investors engage with this content. Similarly, YouTube had the highest level of investor engagement, at 58%, even though only 9% of asset managers provided content via the platform on a weekly basis.[19]

Twitter, whilst growing as a news source, is not really a professional tool used by investors. LinkedIn attracts a different audience than that found on Twitter or Facebook. All asset managers should make it their priority not to ignore social media – especially with on-going generational changes – as they will be missing out on a large number of potential investors. Many of the asset managers who have excelled at using social media to their advantage have employed the following methods:

- **News Updates:** Posting latest industry news
- **Career Opportunities:** Posting job opportunities
- **Region-specific Filtering:** Having country specific pages
- **Segmentation:** Segmenting audience with specialised company affiliated pages.[20]

Social media influences investment decisions. Therefore, asset managers should consider social media strategies given its impact on investment decisions and usefulness in distributing messages.

## COMPETING WITH SOCIAL MEDIA AND TECHNOLOGY GIANTS

PwC's white paper, 'Asset Management 2020: A Brave New World', argued that some fund managers' failure to keep up with technological change will create opportunities for groups like Google, Apple, Twitter, or Amazon to break into the market.

Facebook has set up Libra, as a form of "money" for its billions of users. What would set Google apart if it accelerated its foray into the financial services industry is its advanced analytics capabilities from Google keyword search volume to its advanced satellite imagery that could be leveraged to predict macroeconomic and company trends, which could ultimately be applied to developing highly advanced investment strategies.

For example, Google's acquisition of Skybox Imaging, which has created a system of sub-meter resolution Earth observation satellites. These provide high definition video, analytics, and imagery which is of sufficient quality that one can monitor the movement of goods and people. This could ultimately lead to satellite imagery being used to determine inventory for car manufacturers or the amount of traffic coming through seaports. It could also be used to analyse the progress of mining operations and infrastructure development, or to study the supply chains of multinational companies like Apple.

More to the point on these giants entering asset management, is that whatever they turn their hand to (note Amazon's entry into new markets) they do it on a massive scale, and they aim to disrupt. They also have access to near limitless funding, and can – through scale – provide very cheap or free (free is in their DNA) access.

So watch out, these social media and tech giants could hit fund management big time!

Supported by billions of users that trust the brand, they could completely disrupt asset management. There would be little cost of customer acquisition, and they could use their platforms to provide easy access for a customer or user to acquire units in equities, bonds, hedge, RE, etc. Not only easy access, but also likely with smaller denominations – and with complete liquidity to owners of units. Thus, at the same time turning illiquid asset classes liquid. It is almost mind-boggling, the possibilities here. Any such market entry would also rub out intermediaries and the friction of trading. The trading would be done further down the organisation, funds or pools of units could be made – liquidly – available. To a traditional fund manager, this last paragraph could represent its worst nightmare.

## MARKET DISRUPTION

There are some clear new competitors using technology to drive down costs and improve access to information.[21]

**Wealth Managers and Broking**  There has been significant growth in online platforms since the early days of Charles Schwab and online banking/broking, and the term 'robo-adviser' is now much used.

They utilise methods such as:

- **The use of index funds:** Clearly, technology and passive investing go hand in hand.
- **Low cost and small minimums:** This is also where the social media giants could play, so that someone anywhere could invest a few dollars at the flick of a finger.
- **Online brokerages:** These allow investors to invest in stock and bond portfolios built around everyday ideas and broad economic trends.
- **Algorithm-driven:** The use of algorithms to optimise portfolios.
- **Automated data configuration:** Tools to gather and analyse all of the investor's financial data.
- **Low-entry requirements:** Platforms with no minimum investment.
- **Robo-advice:** In addition, with extremely low costs to customer owing to the lack of people, and the use of AI, selling passive funds, and with robo-advice.

**Retail Funds** The introduction of online financial portals and apps which enable retail investors to have a better handle on the investment process is indicative of how emerging technology is changing the market. It is clear that for the retail investor this provides a previously unheard of level of communication between themselves and a fund. In reverse, funds now have, through these apps and portals, increasing access to their investors. In order to attract and retain their clients a greater emphasis is being placed on the relationship that is cultivated through these channels. In short, communication is vital for the relationship between the investor and fund to flourish. Best practice and market expectations are being changed by the introduction of new technologies.

**Apps** For the investing millennial, there are a number of apps that provide financial information cheaply and intuitively straight to your mobile device. Prior to the invention of the 'app', using your phone to invest would typically have meant calling your financial adviser.[22] However, the creation of the App Store and the technology to support it means that your phone can now provide you with the information you need to make an 'informed' investment decision. iBillionaire, Feedly, Bloomberg app, and TheStreet app, all provide information for the retail investor. Amongst other options, financial news, analysis, and stock-picking insights are part and parcel of the services that these apps offer. For example, in the Bloomberg app it is possible to tailor the information you receive depending on the sector you are interested in. TheStreet app aggregates the news from a variety of sources in an attempt to provide the most up-to-date and accurate stream of information for investors. The development of these informational apps has created readily accessible data and analysis. This has inevitably increased expectations amongst investors, who expect better value for money from the funds they are dealing with. One of the ways this can be mitigated is through the use of investor portals for client level information.

**Investor Portals** The facility to communicate between investor and fund has changed remarkably since the advent of the internet. More recently, sophisticated investor portals are being used so investors are able to access information. Companies like eFront, InvestorFlow, and Investing.com offer funds the opportunity to supply information to their clients in a secure and accessible way. These portals can be customised to match the formatting and branding of the fund they are for. Moreover, they provide document and data management, dynamic data visualisation, and multi-device capabilities. This enables clients to access the information they want around the world and in a format that is informative and intuitive.

For the retail investor, this is particularly welcome and provides an opportunity for the fund to offer reassurance and value for money. Indeed, the FCA highlighted how investors felt value for money could be achieved through better and timely communication between themselves and their fund. This, it is argued, can be achieved through multiple avenues with one of them being the ability to access their investments online.[23] Within the FCA report, it is noted that there is a general resistance to reporting underperformance and clarity surrounding charges within the UK market. There is a clear advantage here for technology forward retail funds to differentiate themselves from their competitors by being open with their communication channels.

**Private Funds** Traditionally, the formal modes of communication between funds and their investors would have been through investor reports and memos to stakeholders and an annual meeting. The frequency, format, medium, and accessibility was arguably not given the level of consideration one would expect today. The consumption of information is radically different now than it was ten years ago and the expectations have changed too. With the increasing ease in which individuals can access information in many areas of their lives, there is a growing expectation that this should apply to their financial lives as well.

There are now many providers of bespoke communication products that provide managers a platform for disseminating information to their clients. Services include data feeds, digital communication, and document production all in pursuit of a clearer understanding between the investor and the fund. The creation of transparency to enable a better understanding for the investor will form better relationships between the parties.

**Have These Applications Made Market Disruption Easier?** Automated investment advice firms may accelerate the disruption of traditional markets for investment advice and the market for asset management and institutional intermediation. Automated investment advice firms may reshape wealth and asset management, as a result of which traditional firms providing wealth management services may struggle to preserve their profit margins whilst competing against automated investment advice firms. Automated investment advice firms may disrupt these markets and put downward pressure on fees by providing asset allocation assistance at a fraction of the cost of more traditional firms.

However, the rise of automated investment advice does not mean that human advisers will stop serving clients. Instead, competitive pressure will mostly likely drive human advisers to embrace these automated investment advice tools in order to provide a wider variety of services. Advisers that do not embrace technology may struggle to compete against those advisers that do turn to technology to manage client portfolios, from which the time saved can be used to assist clients with other financial decisions.

Robo-advisers may, therefore, not be the direction the industry transitions to. Indeed, they are more likely to be the thorn that pricks the intent of human advisers. Reinvestment in financial technology and an acceptance that the industry needs to evolve is perhaps the real consequence of this initial disruption. Technologically equipped human advisers are already in a better position to help clients and are likely to outpace their rivals. As Peter McGratty writes, 'an outright "arms race" of technology is emerging amongst financial adviser custodians and broker-dealers all seeking to be the future platform of choice'.[24]

**Regulatory Concerns Related To Market Disruption** Balancing the benefits of automated investment advice against its risks will require cautious regulatory engagement. Effective regulatory responses will require independence, as well as financial and technological literacy – the latter two skills often found lacking in this generation's politicians. The exponential growth and potential scale of automated investment advice firms has significant systemic implications. For example, if increasing numbers of consumers allocate their assets using the same or similar automated investment algorithms, the previously out-priced members of the population could experience highly correlated losses. Dominant automated investment advice firms controlling massive market shares may also introduce new cybersecurity risks. If a hacker caused an automated investment advice firm to suddenly sell substantial assets, it could significantly disrupt markets.

However, despite these potential future risks, regulators need to strike a fine balance when adopting new regulations and should not be too overbearing and subject automated investment advice firms to higher standards than those currently applied to natural persons. For now, the standard against which automated advisers should be compared is that of humans, whom we know are less than perfect, other than the author of course (just to show that this is a human writing this) – like the CAPTCHAs ('completely automated public Turing test to tell computers and humans apart'), one of the more interesting acronyms I have come across of late – we get asked to enter online to prove we are humans, unless robots have developed humour by the time this book goes to print. Instead, regulators need to grow their expertise and capabilities to provide effective oversight for automated investment firms by devoting resources to developing as digital regulators also.

## SOME CONCLUSIONS

The introduction of emerging technology has provided greater competition throughout the asset management space. Amongst others big data, blockchain, cybersecurity, robo-advisers, and biometrics are all hot topics. However, it is not just what is new that is interesting. How this technology effects pre-existing processes and influences the dynamic between investor and fund is fascinating. Below are just a few of the issues this chapter has raised.

Even though AI may bring out competition with the traditional asset management firms, when it comes to HNWI clients and the complexities which grow as wealth accrues, that personal touch is still in demand. This is evident in the types of services that are now being floated by BlackRock, State Street, and Vanguard. Smaller robo-advisers have acknowledged that they will need to provide a human and more tailored approach to their product if they wish to stay competitive.

Although Bloomberg has dominated the operating platform market for years, it may finally be facing more competition. With Blackstone having acquired a majority in the financial and risk business of Thompson Reuters[25] and the creation of unbundled solutions and newer niche providers, this space looks ripe for disruption.

The rise in cybercrime and the growing importance of cybersecurity for both commercial entities and governments is a key issue of our time. Unprecedented levels of attacks across the world have made the front page of newspapers. Wikileaks, Panama Papers, Paradise Papers, and the Luxembourg Leaks are but a few of the high-profile incidents we have seen in recent years. As technology develops the risk of these attacks increases. In response, businesses are focusing their efforts on innovative solutions to protect their systems, and by proxy, their clients.

There are a number of competing macro themes around technology, data and its impact on asset managers. Is full transparency always a good thing? KYC and AML require full disclosure, but what about concerns of piracy, kidnapping, theft, bribery, and on- or off-line bullying. If there is full transparency, can I therefore expose personal data of other people?

Is everything on, all of the time, a good thing? Is it bad for our health? Does technology lead to the breakdown of human interaction? Will it create wars through misinterpretation, or HAL, or the Terminator machines working out that the world is better without humans? Is the author becoming overly alarmist?

All news is essentially immediate with social media and wireless internet. A revolution in the Middle East is seen immediately in a kitchen in Dursley, Glos.

Can one disappear anymore? Can one's data vanish, or be vanished, if I want. Even worse is faking of data – which is a lot easier now – so photographs and film can be completely falsified (using a technique known as 'deepfake') – and this new notion of fake news.

In general, there is a concerted effort to keep up with the technology curve. Those that embrace the opportunities (and risks) that this sector presents can look to gain an advantage over their rivals, disrupt old practices, and potentially create better or cheaper products for investors. Of course, there are potential pitfalls that businesses may stumble into and undoubtedly, some will. However, the risk of not evolving with the times is to become reactive. For businesses this means they will become uncompetitive and unattractive to their clients, although I am sure a few Luddites – and proud to be so – might retain a certain retro-cool and a certain 'screw this' cache with certain investors.

## ENDNOTES

1. www.bbc.co.uk/news/technology-46944696
2. 2016
3. Mooney, A. (2018) *Financial Times*, Feb 22 2018. www.ft.com/content/b6171016-171f-11e8-9e9c-25c814761640
4. Julie Segal, J. (2016) 'BlackRock Is Making Big Data Bigger', *Institutional Investor.* www.institutionalinvestor.com/article/b14z9p1z99mmlg/blackrock-is-making-big-data-bigger
5. CRISIL (2017). www.crisil.com/content/dam/crisil/our-analysis/reports/gr-a/whitepapers/big-data-in-asset-management-may2017.pdf
6. Kate Beioley, 'Robo-Advice Revolution Comes At A Cost', FT, 22 November 2017. www.ft.com/content/4488fdd0-cde9-11e7-b781-794ce08b24dc
7. Andrew Meola, 'Is Robo Investing Better Than Traditional Investing? See The Pros And Cons', Business Insider, 9 January 2017. http://assets.businessinsider.com/4-reasons-robo-investing-growing-2017-1
8. Myron Jobson, 'How To Find The Best Robo-Adviser To Invest With – And Do They Really Offer Financial Advice?' This is Money, 3 July 2017. www.thisismoney.co.uk/money/investing/article-4577798/How-best-robo-adviser-invest-with.html
9. Michael Kitces, 'The B2C Robo-Adviser Movement Is Dying, But Its #FinTech Legacy Will Live On!' www.kitces.com/blog/robo-advisor-growth-rates-and-valuations-crashing-from-high-client-acquisition-costs/
10. Victor Basta, 'Digital banking: a tough way to make money', FT, 29 November 2017. https://ftalphaville.ft.com/2017/11/29/2196236/digital-banking-a-tough-way-to-make-money/
11. Kate Beioley, 'Robo advisers recognise the need for human touch', FT, 29 December 2017. www.ft.com/content/f9b8fda4-e1c1-11e7-a8a4-0a1e63a52f9c
12. Yoosof Farah, 'How AI could transform wealth management'. https://citywire.co.uk/wealth-manager/news/how-ai-could-transform-wealth-management/a1006508
13. Pierluigi Paganini, 'Paradise Papers Were The Result Of The Hack Of External Attackers'. https://securityaffairs.co/wordpress/65247/data-breach/paradise-papers-data-leak.html

14. Christopher Burgess, 'Paradise Papers: Data Leak Shines A Light On The Monies Of The Elite', 17 November 2017. www.csoonline.com/article/3237670/paradise-papers-data-leak-shines-a-light-on-the-monies-of-the-elite.html

15. Rupert Neate, 'Obama Calls For International Tax Reform Amid Panama Papers Revelations', The Guardian, 5 April 2016. www.theguardian.com/news/2016/apr/05/justice-department-panama-papers-mossack-fonseca-us-investigation

16. International Consortium Of Investigative Journalists, 'The Panama Papers'.

17. Caroline Binham, 'Cyber Attacks Push Corporate Fraud To All-Time High', FT, 22 January 2018. www.ft.com/content/d67e920c-fd48-11e7-a492-2c9be7f3120a

18. Taha Lokhandwala, 'Social Media Influences Investment Decisions, Shows Research', IPE, 17 April 2015. https://www.ipe.com/news/asset-managers/social-media-influences-investment-decisions-shows-research/10007592.fullarticle

19. John Harrington, 'Which Asset Management Firm Is Best At Social Media – And Why Does The Sector Fall Short?' PR Week, 17 January 2017. www.prweek.com/article/1420938/asset-management-firm-best-social-media-why-does-sector-fall-short

20. Taha Lokhandwala, 'Social Media Influences Investment Decisions, Shows Research', IPE, 17 April 2015. www.ipe.com/news/asset-managers/social-media-influences-investment-decisions-shows-research/10007592.fullarticle

21. Kate, '14 Companies That Are Leading Online Investment Platforms'. https://gomedici.com/14-companies-in-online-investment-platform/

22. Lou Carlozo, '10 Investing Apps To Supercharge Your Portfolio', 25 February 2015. https://money.usnews.com/money/personal-finance/mutual-funds/articles/2015/02/25/10-investing-apps-to-supercharge-your-portfolio

23. Financial Conduct Authority (2016) Asset Management Market Study, June 2017, MS15/2.3. www.fca.org.uk/publication/market-studies/ms15-2-3.pdf

24. Michael Kitces, 'The B2C Robo-Adviser Movement Is Dying, But Its #FinTech Legacy Will Live On!' www.kitces.com/blog/robo-advisor-growth-rates-and-valuations-crashing-from-high-client-acquisition-costs/

25. Pamela Barbaglia, 'Blackstone In Talks To Buy $17bn Stake In Thomson Reuters Unit', The Independent, 30 January 2018. www.independent.co.uk/news/business/news/blackstone-thomson-reuters-deal-financial-and-risk-business-a8184676.html

# CHAPTER 9

# Regulation in the Asset Management Industry

*If it moves, tax it. If it keeps moving, regulate it. And if it stops moving, subsidize it.*

– Ronald Reagan

This chapter will be broken down into four geographical sections when discussing the regulatory environment. It will consider asset management regulation in the main blocs of the UK, EU, and US, as well as considering certain compelling regulatory themes throughout the rest of the world.

Chapter 10 will consider the growing area of risk and compliance, as well as containing some thoughts on the future direction of regulation within the industry. Clearly, Brexit will also be a theme in Chapter 10.

Since Lehman Brothers went down, it is clear that regulators have been focused on the existential threat to capitalism – the systemic risk of bank failure. However, it feels like now the regulators are very much turning their attention to asset management.

## UK REGULATORY ENVIRONMENT

Prior to April 2013, the Financial Services Authority (FSA) was responsible for the regulation of the financial services industry in the UK. However, the FSA then became two separate regulatory authorities known as the Financial Conduct Authority (FCA) and the Prudential Regulation Authority (PRA). The FCA and the PRA work together, forming a 'twin peaks' regulatory structure in the UK.

The PRA is now part of the Bank of England (BoE) and is responsible for the prudential regulation and supervision of banks, building societies, and various other institutions presently totalling around 1500 financial firms. Using a twofold approach, based on regulation and supervision, the PRA is judgement-based, forward-looking and forward-focused. It is not set up to prevent all failure that is impossible. Instead, it aims to minimise the risk posed to critical financial services by the failure of financial firms. This long-term approach is born out of the impact the financial crisis had on households and businesses.

The FCA is a quasi-governmental body, which is responsible for the regulation of the financial services industry in the UK. The FCA is now responsible for conducting the regulation of all UK-based retail and financial services firms. In addition, the FCA is the regulator of the UK Listing Authority (UKLA). The statutory powers to regulate the financial services industry were conferred on the FCA by the Financial Services and Markets Act 2000 (FSMA) as amended by the Financial Services Act 2012. The FCA is accountable to the Treasury, including the Chancellor of the Exchequer, as the Treasury appoints the board of the FCA. However, the FCA does not receive any government funding. Instead, it is funded by charging fees to the firms which it regulates and to other bodies such as investment exchanges. At the time of writing, the FCA supervises the conduct of around 26 000 financial firms.

**Financial Conduct Authority**   The Financial Conduct Authority (FCA) has three statutory objectives under FSMA:

1. to protect consumers;
2. to enhance the integrity of the UK financial system; and
3. to help maintain competitive markets and promote effective competition in the interests of consumers.

The FCA operates within its own 'principles of good regulation' when they carry out their work. Broadly, these principles can be categorised into efficiency and economy, proportionality, sustainable growth, consumer responsibility, senior management responsibility, recognising the differences in the businesses carried on by different regulated persons, openness and disclosure, and transparency. Moreover, the FCA mandates that businesses follow a separate but similar set of principles, including integrity, skill, care and diligence, management and control, financial prudence, market conduct, customers' interests, communications with clients, conflicts of interests, customers, relationships of trust, clients' assets, and relations with regulators. The FCA argues these principles represent a framework which, when worked within, can provide a financially healthy system.

More specifically, under FSMA, any person who carries on a 'regulated activity' must either be authorised by the FCA or fall within one of the statutory exemptions. The Financial Services and Markets Act 2000 (Regulated Activities) Order 2001 (RAO) sets out these 'regulated activities', which include (for our purposes):

- **Dealing:** Dealing in investments as principal or as agent, both of which include buying, selling, subscribing for or underwriting securities or investments.
- **Arranging:** Arranging deals in investments for another person, whether as principal or agent.
- **Managing:** Managing investments or assets belonging to another person whereby a degree of discretion is involved.
- **Safeguarding:** Safeguarding and administering of investments.
- **Collective Investment Schemes (CISs):** Establishing, operating or winding up a CIS, or acting as trustee of an AuT scheme, or acting as the depositary or sole director of an open-ended investment company.
- **Advising:** Advising on investments.

For each regulated activity, an applicant for FCA authorisation must identify which investment types their activities concern. The RAO describes these as shares, instruments creating or acknowledging indebtedness, government and public securities, instruments giving entitlements to investments, certificates representing certain securities, and options to acquire or dispose of a security or contractually based investment.

Persons exempt from FCA authorisation include:

- **Firms:** Professional firms such as solicitors and accountants that carry on certain of the above listed activities that are incidental to their main business.
- **Local Authorities:** Local authorities or housing bodies which carry on insurance mediation or mortgage activities.

A person must be FCA authorised, or have an 'authorised' person approve the content of a 'promotion' being made to would-be investors. A 'promotion' is generally regarded as communicating an invitation or inducement to engage in certain investment activities. Under FSMA, this is defined as, 'entering or offering to enter into an agreement, the making or performance of which by either party constitutes a controlled activity; or exercising any rights conferred by a controlled investment to acquire, dispose of, underwrite or convert a controlled investment'.

The FCA monitors and regulates firms according to the risks they present. For this purpose, the FCA places firms into four different categories. The first category applies to the largest firms with the most customers and those firms are subject to continuous assessment over rolling two-year periods. The assessments in the other three categories are less stringent, as these firms will have fewer customers and/or pose fewer risks. Firms in the fourth category are subject to FCA assessment every four years.

An 'approved person' is an individual that has been approved by the FCA to perform one or more 'controlled functions' on behalf of an authorised firm. Under FSMA, in order to obtain approval, the FCA must be satisfied that the candidate is 'fit and proper' to perform the relevant controlled functions.

When determining fitness and propriety, the FCA considers honesty, integrity, reputation, competence, capability, and financial prudence. The supervision of individuals performing controlled functions is integrated with the FCA's regulation of the authorised firm for which the approved person acts. An individual cannot be approved before the firm is authorised but both applications can be performed simultaneously.

The FCA updated their philosophy in 2017 and provided an outline on their new decision-making process, including the prioritising of certain issues, styling it as the 'FCA Mission'. According to Megan Butler during a speech at the FT Investment Management Summit (Europe) 2017, the mission now 'sets out a fundamental switch by concentrating on "harm" to customers and markets', taking an externally focused approach to regulation.

The FCA Asset Management Authorisation Hub was set up to assist start-up managers moving between pre-authorisation, authorisation, and then regular supervision.

There are four principal objectives:

1. to clarify expectations and provide better guidance to firms on regulations and processes by providing dedicated case officers and offering pre-application meetings;

2. to provide easier access to information through a dedicated portal for investment managers;
3. to foster more positive personalised engagement between FCA and market entrants; and
4. to provide end-to-end support for firms moving through start-up cycle.

Going forward, personal accountability is fundamental to financial services, with good governance as a central theme of asset management. With this in mind, the Senior Managers and Certification Regime (SM&CR) was rolled out in March 2016 to all firms offering financial services. Regulated by the FCA, it is comprised of three elements:

1. the Senior Managers Regime;
2. the Certification Regime; and
3. the Conduct Rules.

The Senior Managers Regime is applicable to most individuals who have key roles (senior management functions) within an organisation. This is defined in more detail within the FCA Handbook and the PRA Rulebook. In general, the responsibilities of these individuals must be set out clearly with the firms having to certify the suitability of the individuals to perform their roles annually.

The Certification Regime encompasses any individual who has the capacity through their role to cause significant harm to the firm or its customers. The FCA will not inspect these individuals, but the firms that employ them must do this at least once a year.

The Conduct Rules apply to practically everyone within the banking sector. Some senior managers will be subject to specific additional conduct rules. It is the firms' responsibility to train their employees so they are knowledgeable about the rules that apply to them. Moreover, they are responsible for reporting to the FCA when these rules are breached. The FCA is currently proposing an additional requirement that a senior manager is appointed by every firm to ensure that that firms employees are trained.

The aim of the FCA remuneration codes is to ensure greater alignment between risk and individual reward, and to discourage excessive risk-taking and short-term thinking via more effective risk management. In essence, the initiative supports positive behaviours and a strong and appropriate conduct culture within firms. This will, it is hoped, prevent harm and encourage more responsible and appropriate action by the firms that are regulated. A detailed account of the FCA remuneration codes can be found on the FCA website.

**Prudential Regulation Authority**    Under Financial Services Act 2012, the Prudential Regulation Authority (PRA) has a general objective of promoting the safety and soundness of PRA-authorised persons. It achieves this core goal by:

- **Ring-fencing businesses:** It aims to ensure that the business of PRA-authorised persons is carried on in a way which avoids any adverse effect on the stability of the UK financial system.
- **Minimising Failure:** It also aims to minimise the adverse effect that the failure of a PRA-authorised person could be expected to have on the stability of the UK financial system.

There is an additional objective to ensure that policyholders of insurance companies are protected appropriately. Underlying this is the PRA's general intention to ensure effective competition within the markets it regulates. This should be pursued, when appropriate, when the PRA conducts its primary role.

Firms are required to apply for authorisation to accept deposits, elect or carry out contracts of insurance and manage the underwriting capacity of a Lloyd's syndicate as a managing agent of Lloyds, as they are all PRA-regulated activities.

There is no definition of 'bank' under the PRA. However, banks incorporated in the UK, outside the EEA but authorised to accept deposits through a branch in the UK, or in the EEA but entitled to accept deposits through a branch in the UK are listed as banks regulated by the PRA.

To carry on one of the above activities without authorisation from the PRA may constitute a criminal offence. Firms that seek to carry on activities other than those listed above need to apply to the FCA for authorisation as well.

As in the case of the FCA, the frequency and intensity of supervision which the PRA applies to the firms it supervises is decided through the division of firms into specified categories. Category 1 is subject to the most frequent and intense supervision, whilst category 5 is subject to the least supervision:

- **Category 1:** Significant deposit-takers, designated investment firms, or insurers with the potential to cause very significant disruption to the UK financial system; and insurers with a certain type of business with the potential to cause significant disruption to the interests of a substantial number of policyholders.
- **Category 2:** Significant deposit-takers, designated investment firms, or insurers with the potential to cause some disruption to the UK financial system; and insurers with a certain type of business with the potential to cause some disruption to the interests of a substantial number of policyholders.
- **Category 3:** Deposit-takers, designated investment firms, or insurers with the capacity to cause minor disruption to the UK financial system, in the event difficulties across the whole financial sector arise; and insurers with a certain type of business with a minor capacity to cause disruption to the interests of a substantial number of policyholders.
- **Category 4:** Deposit-takers, designated investment firms, or insurers with very little capacity to cause disruption to the UK financial system, but which have the potential to generate disruption in the event difficulties across the whole financial sector arise; and insurers with a certain type of business with very little capacity to cause disruption to the interests of a substantial number of policyholders.
- **Category 5:** Deposit-takers, designated investment firms, or insurers, with almost no capacity to cause disruption to the UK financial system, but which may cause some disruption in the event difficulties across the whole financial sector arise; and insurers with a certain type of business with no capacity to cause disruption to the interests of a substantial number of policyholders.

Under section 59 FSMA 2000, individuals who are to carry out controlled functions on behalf of a firm must be approved by the PRA. An individual cannot be approved before the relevant firm is authorised, but the applications can be formed simultaneously. Those who perform controlled functions include the CEO, all directors, and partners.

Individuals who apply to carry out a controlled function are assessed by the PRA in respect of their reputation and financial soundness, and in addition, they must be deemed to be competent and capable of carrying out the role. However, it is also the responsibility of the relevant firm to ensure that the individual is fit and proper to take on a controlled function.

## US REGULATORY ENVIRONMENT

**The United States Securities and Exchange Commission**  The Securities and Exchange Commission (SEC) was established in response to the Great Depression and stock market crash of 1929 by the Securities Exchange Act of 1934 which, along with the Securities Act of 1933, set out to restore market confidence by providing more reliable information and setting out clear rules for legitimate financial dealing. The SEC's primary role is to protect investors, which it does in essence by requiring companies that publicly offer securities or have more than 2000 shareholders (or at least 500 that are not accredited investors) and have total assets in excess of USD 10 million to register the applicable class of stock be open and honest about their business, any securities being offered, and the risks involved, and by obliging those that sell and trade securities (brokers, dealers, and exchanges) to treat investors fairly and honestly, putting investors' interests first. The SEC's remit also encompasses the maintenance of the markets as well as facilitating capital formation with a view to macroeconomic growth.

In the US, the rules governing the securities industry derive from one mantra – full and fair disclosure of all material facts to all investors. In light of this, the SEC obliges public companies to disclose financial and other information to the public. Based on this publicly available information investors can make an informed judgement on their investment – whether to buy, sell, or hold the same.

As a regulator, the SEC constantly samples the opinions of market participants in order to gauge concern and learn from their experiences in an attempt to maintain this information flow. Aside from the investors themselves, which the SEC is charged with protecting, it regulates the major participants in the market such as exchanges, brokers, dealers, investment advisers, and mutual funds. The SEC's dealing with such entities is dual, in so much as it tries to aid the market by promoting the disclosure of information whilst protecting investors through the policing of such bodies.

In its role as an enforcement authority, the SEC can and does bring civil actions against those (whether individuals or companies) in violation of the securities laws. Typical causes of action include insider trading, fraudulent accounting, and providing false or misleading information about securities and the companies that issue them. The SEC relies heavily on investors providing information in order to bring actions. Moreover, the SEC is responsible for maintaining the database of disclosures that public companies are required to file.

The SEC is part of a wider regulatory network in the US and whilst its primary responsibility relates to securities, it works closely with other bodies and institutions. Furthermore, the Chairman of the SEC serves on the President's Working Group on Financial Markets along with other institutional heads such as the Chairman of the Federal Reserve and the Secretary of the Treasury.

The SEC is headed by five presidentially appointed commissioners of which one is appointed chairman. In order to maintain impartiality and prevent tribalism, no more than three of the commissioners may belong to one political party.

The SEC has approximately 4200[1] staff, who are responsible for interpreting federal securities laws; issuing and amending rules; overseeing inspection of securities firms, brokers, investment advisers and ratings agencies; overseeing private regulatory organisations in the securities, accounting and auditing sectors; and coordinating US securities regulation with federal, state, and foreign authorities (such as the FCA). The SEC is divided into five divisions, each responsible for a different area of the securities industry:

1. The Division of Corporation Finance is responsible for overseeing the provision of obligatory information to public investors. Public companies are compelled to disclose information that must be made when stock is initially sold and then on a continuing and periodic basis. The information disclosed is reviewed on an ongoing basis. The division also supports companies by providing guidance on the rules and regulations. By extension, it recommends rules to the SEC for adoption.
2. The Division of Trading and Markets is charged with maintaining an efficient market. It provides oversight of the major market participants. The division also oversees the Securities Investor Protection Corporation, which is a private, non-profit corporation that provides insurance to member firms for the securities and cash in customer accounts against the failure of those firms (such insurance does not extend to market decline or fraud).
3. The Division of Investment Management protects investors and promotes capital formation by overseeing and regulating the investment management industry in the US. This important part of the market includes mutual funds, professional fund managers, analysts and advisers to individual customers. As this division's remit involves a high concentration of individual investors, the division focuses on ensuring that disclosures are useful to retail customers and that the regulatory costs borne by consumers are not excessive.
4. The Division of Enforcement recommends the instigation of investigations and the bringing of civil actions, and prosecutes any such cases on behalf of the SEC. The division works closely with law enforcement agencies in the US and around the world to bring criminal cases when appropriate.
5. The Division of Risk, Strategy, and Financial Innovation was established in September 2009 to analyse and identify emerging risks and growing trends in the market. The division then makes recommendations as to how any developments or trends affect the regulation of the markets. This division also provides support to the other divisions by way of research, analysis, and training.

**The Commodity Futures Trading Commission** Another significant regulator is the Commodity Futures Trading Commission (CFTC). Congress created the CFTC in 1974 as an independent agency with exclusive jurisdiction over futures trading in all commodities. Similar to the SEC, the CFTC's mission is to protect investors. The regulatory scope of the CFTC has expanded significantly since its formation, as certain swaps now also fall under the regulatory authority of the CFTC.

There are five commissioners of the CFTC, which are appointed by the US president, with the advice and consent of the US Senate. The commissioners serve staggered five-year terms. The CFTC has several divisions that oversee and enforce the regulations.

The Division of Market Oversight (DMO) oversees trade execution facilities and data repositories, conducts surveillance, reviews new exchange applications and examines existing exchanges to ensure compliance with applicable core principles. The DMO also evaluates new products to ensure they are not susceptible to manipulation, as well as rule filings by exchanges to ensure compliance with core principles.

The Division of Swap Dealer and Intermediary Oversight (DSIO) oversees the registration and compliance of intermediaries and futures industry self-regulatory organisations, including US derivatives exchanges and the National Futures Association (NFA). The DSIO is also responsible for developing and monitoring compliance with regulations addressing registration, business conduct standards, capital adequacy and margin requirements for swap dealers and major swap participants.

The Division of Clearing and Risk (DCR) oversees derivatives clearing organisations (DCOs) and other market participants in the clearing process, including futures commission merchants, swap dealers, major swap participants and large traders. The DCR also monitors the clearing of futures, options on futures and swaps by DCOs; assesses DCO compliance with CFTC regulations; and conducts risk assessment and surveillance. The DCR makes recommendations on DCO applications and eligibility, rule submissions, and which types of swaps should be cleared.

The Division of Enforcement investigates and prosecutes alleged violations of the Commodity Exchange Act and CFTC regulations. Potential violations include fraud, manipulation and other abuses concerning commodity derivatives and swaps that threaten market integrity, market participants, and the public.

**The Dodd–Frank Wall Street Reform and Consumer Protection Act**  The Dodd–Frank Wall Street Reform and Consumer Protection Act (the Dodd–Frank Act) was signed into US federal law by President Obama on 21 July 2010 and was passed as a response to the credit crisis. The Dodd–Frank Act brought significant changes to financial regulation in the US that affect all federal financial regulatory agencies and almost every part of the US financial services industry. It is an important consideration for all fund managers who deal with (or may deal with) US investors.

The 2008 market crash was in part fuelled by the bursting of the housing bubble in the US. In an attempt to prevent this in the future, the Dodd–Frank Act (named after Senate banking committee chairman, Senator Christopher J. Dodd, and the House of Representatives financial services committee chairman, Barney Frank) includes provisions to protect borrowers against predatory lending and to prevent abusive mortgage practices. The Dodd–Frank Act aims to achieve this by establishing US government agencies to monitor banking practices and oversee financial institutions. It also restricts the types of trading activities that certain financial institutions, such as banks, are allowed to practise, increases the registration requirements of financial institutions in the PE and hedge fund industries, and increases the oversight and supervision responsibilities of the SEC and the CFTC, particularly in the swaps and derivative markets.

The Dodd–Frank Act created the Financial Stability Oversight Council (FSOC) to oversee financial institutions and fill the regulatory gaps created by the numerous agencies responsible for regulating the various corners of the financial markets. In a broad sense, the FSOC identifies and responds to risks to stability and promotes discipline by reducing bailout expectations. Whilst creating this and other new agencies, the Dodd–Frank Act introduced a swathe of reforms to the mandates and procedures of existing agencies such as the SEC and the Federal Reserve.

Under the Dodd–Frank Act, the rules regarding credit risk retention were tightened, obliging an increased retention of risk including a prohibition on the transfer of the same. The disclosure requirements in this area have also been strengthened, including an obligation on the securitiser to perform due diligence (DD) on products and provide this to investors.

While the substantive law dealing with this element of the Dodd–Frank Act is developed by other agencies such as the CFTC and the SEC, the legislation itself does provide a set of objectives. A key development is that no federal government assistance (subject to conditions) will be provided to non-bank institutions engaging in 'swaps'. Moreover the proposed regime includes provisions for the regulation of those participating in the derivatives market such as swap dealers.

What the financial crisis revealed was a broad lack of investor knowledge with regard to the complex financial products in which they were investing. With respect to this, the Dodd–Frank Act proposes greater investor protection through imposing fiduciary duties on those providing investment and related advisory services to investors. Moreover, the prevention of malpractice has been partly addressed by proactively offering rewards to whistle-blowers.

The Dodd–Frank Act seeks to build on the reforms introduced by the Credit Rating Agency Reform Act of 2006. The Dodd–Frank Act attempts to achieve reforms in this area by extending the liabilities and penalties similar to those applicable to accountancy firms as well as increasing the burden of proof on the agencies by requiring them to demonstrate quantitative and qualitative reasoning for their publications. Moreover, certain activities are now restricted or prohibited, such as the requirement to separate rating activities from sales and marketing activities, and that each agency must establish an effective internal control structure for which it is accountable to the SEC.

Introduced by Title VI of the Dodd–Frank Act, the 'Volcker Rule' relates to certain speculative trading activities. Important distinctions are made between activities that may be conducted by banking entities and by non-bank financial companies supervised by the Federal Reserve. The rules set out explicitly permitted activities and services as well as capital requirements and restrictions on transactions with affiliates. The prohibitions specifically apply to 'banking entities' which include insured depositary institutions, the controlling company and any foreign bank with operations in the US including parents, affiliates, and subsidiaries of the foreign bank.

The Volcker Rule prohibits a banking entity from engaging in 'proprietary trading'; acquiring or retaining any equity, partnership, or other ownership interest in a hedge or PE fund; and sponsoring a hedge or PE fund. These prohibitions apply to US banking entities, regardless of where the trading or activities are conducted. For non-US organisations, the rules will only apply if the trading or activities take place in the US or if they involve the offering of securities to a US resident.

The Dodd–Frank Act defines 'proprietary trading' as engaging as a principal for the trading account of a banking organisation or supervised non-bank financial company in any transaction to purchase or sell, or otherwise acquire or dispose of any security, derivative, futures contract, option on any such security, derivative, contract, or any other financial instrument so determined by the regulators. A trading account is defined as any account used for acquiring or taking positions in the proprietary trading of securities and instruments principally for the purpose of selling in the near term, and other accounts as determined by the regulators.

Conversely, the Volcker Rule also explicitly permits certain types of trading, such as in government securities and on behalf of customers. The rules also permit certain hedging that is undertaken to mitigate risk, investments in small business investment companies, and public welfare.

As mentioned above, banking entities are prohibited from having ownership interests in a fund. This prohibition is subject to an exception for seed investment. In order to take advantage, the organisation must comply with the same conditions allowing 'sponsorship' in certain cases and that within a year of the fund having been established, the banking organisation's interest must be no more than 3% of the total ownership interests. Moreover, where the seed investment amounts to more than 3% of the ownership interests in the fund, the banking entity cannot dilute its interest by divesting interests to an affiliated organisation. Additionally, the aggregate of all such interests may not exceed 3% of the banking entity's Tier 1 capital.

In relation to 'sponsoring' of hedge and PE funds, it should be noted that this has not been taken to mean simply advising. The Dodd–Frank Act defines 'sponsoring' as serving as general or managing partner or trustee of a fund; selecting or controlling a majority of the directors, trustees, or management of a fund; or sharing the same name of the banking organisation or any affiliate or a similar name with the fund. However, subject to certain conditions, in certain circumstances, banking entities may be able to organise and offer a hedge or PE fund.

A particularly topical item on the Dodd–Frank Act's agenda deals with corporate governance and executive remuneration. Shareholders now get a non-binding vote on the compensation of executive committee members. A new set of standards promoting independence have also been applied to compensation committees. Moreover, executive compensation must now be linked to financial performance. Companies are now obliged to operate policies designed to recuperate any compensation that falls out of line with a restatement of accounts. In addition, the Dodd–Frank Act imposes much tighter regulatory capital requirements on financial institutions. The Dodd-Frank Act and the Volcker Rule did much during the financial crisis to push asset management and especially alternatives and hedge funds, out of banks and into independent asset management groups. Since these rules, banks are barely involved any more in asset management, although is creeping back into private banks servicing high net worth clients. Holding companies still own banks and asset managers (Goldman Sachs, Morgan Stanley) but they are ring-fenced. Banks' prime brokerages have shrunk dramatically. Hedge leverage is semi-toxic to banks' balance sheets. The 'integrated' bulge bracket bank meets investment bank, or the earlier 'merchant bank' of the late twentieth century, with its model of banking, asset management and trading is shackled. Note the recent Deutsche Bank retreat of 2019.

**The Foreign Account Tax Compliance Act**    The Foreign Account Tax Compliance Act (FATCA), was enacted by the US congress in 2010 in an effort to address non-compliance by US taxpayers. This is achieved through a reporting mechanism that mandates foreign (external to the US) financial institutions to report to the Internal Revenue Service (IRS) information about the accounts of US nationals. This process enhances cross-border tax compliance through the creation of an international standard for the automatic sharing of information concerning US taxpayers. Underlying this process is a targeted movement towards greater transparency.

Under FATCA, the relevant withholding agent may be required to withhold 30% of any interest, dividends, and other fixed or determinable annual or periodical gains, profits and income from sources within the US, or gross proceeds from the sale of any property. This will not apply if such a foreign financial institution agrees to verify, report and disclose its US accountholders and meets certain other specified requirements, or a non-financial foreign entity that is a beneficial owner of the payment unless such entity certifies that it does not have any substantial US owners or provides the name, address, and taxpayer identification number of each substantial US owner and such entity meets certain other specified requirements.

Thus, non-US investors could be subject to the FATCA withholding tax if they do not provide information to the fund in which they invest so that the fund is able to comply with the FATCA information reporting rules. In such case, the partnership agreement of, say, a PE fund will often require the investors whose failure to provide information resulted in the FATCA withholding tax, to indemnify the PE fund for the tax and associated costs, treat the FATCA withholding as an amount deemed distributed to such investors for purposes of calculating the carried interest threshold and/or seek other remedies.

**Report of Foreign Bank and Financial Accounts** A US person (including a US tax-exempt investor) is required to file a Report of Foreign Bank and Financial Accounts (FBAR) with the IRS with respect to their financial interest in or signature authority over certain classes of foreign financial accounts for each calendar year when their aggregate value exceeds USD 10 000 at any time during the year. The FBAR reporting requirement generally does not apply to a US person's ownership of an equity investment in an offshore hedge fund. The FBAR reporting requirement, however, applies to:

- **Offshore Hedge Fund:** Any foreign financial account of an offshore hedge fund if the US person owns, directly or indirectly, more than 50% of the value or voting power (or, if partnership, profits or capital) of all classes of equity investments in the fund.
- **Other Entities:** Any foreign financial account of any corporation, partnership, other entity or trust (other than the fund) if the US person, directly or indirectly (including through the investment in the offshore hedge fund), owns more than 50% of the value or voting power (or, if partnership, profits or capital) of equity investments in such entity or trust.

# EU REGULATORY ENVIRONMENT

## AIFMD

The Alternative Investment Fund Managers Directive (AIFMD) provides a framework for the regulation of Alternative Investment Fund Managers (AIFM). For the purposes of this legislation, an Alternative Investment Fund (AIF) is broadly a structure which falls within the description of collective investment undertakings, including investment compartments thereof, which raise capital from a number of investors with a view to investing it in accordance with a defined investment policy, for the benefit of those investors; and which do not require authorisation pursuant to the Undertakings for Collective Investment in Transferable Securities (UCITS) Directive 2009.

Certain structures fall outside of this definition, such as managed accounts, but the definition of an AIF is wide. It includes, for example, closed-ended company structures which were not subject to fund regulation in the UK before implementation of the AIFMD.

The legislation is largely indiscriminate towards the asset class or structure of a fund and therefore applies to the managers of any AIF. The AIFMD defines an AIFM, for the purposes of the directive, as a legal person (i.e. a company or other legal entity, distinct from a natural person) whose regular business is the management of one or more AIFs. For further clarity, this has been defined as performing at least portfolio or risk management functions. Therefore, advisers providing only advice to an AIFM are not within the remit of the legislation. An AIF must have a single AIFM, which is responsible for compliance with AIFMD.

Where an AIFM does fall within the scope of the AIFMD, the applicable regulator is that in its home state, which for EU AIFMs means where it has its registered office (for example, the FCA for AIFMs whose registered office is in the UK). Areas covered by the AIFMD include:

- **Being, Appointing, and Delegating Rules:** Such as an obligation to appoint a depositary, conditions relating to being an AIFM and authorisation, and restrictions on the ability to delegate functions to third parties.
- **Finance:** Regulatory capital, financial resources requirements, and remuneration requirements for senior executives.
- **Organisation and Governance:** Requirements pertaining to the organisation of the AIFMD including internal governance and requirements for independent valuation of assets.
- **Reporting Requirements:** Reporting, such as annual reports, disclosure to investors, and regulatory reporting.
- **General Rules:** Rules relating to investors including conflicts of interest, fair treatment, and risk and liquidity management.
- **Special Rules:** Rules relating to listed and unlisted companies in the portfolio including 'asset stripping' restrictions on dividend payments and other actions after acquiring stakes.

These requirements do not, however, apply universally to all AIFMs and are in particular relaxed for small AIFMs.

**Authorisation Requirements for AIFMs**   An AIFM will need to obtain authorisation from its home regulator, unless it is subject to one of the exemptions. In the UK this is known as 'Part 4A Authorisation' in reference to FSMA 2000. When applying for authorisation, the AIFM must provide information relating to the AIFM as well as information relating to each AIF it intends to manage.

The information required includes the credentials of the people conducting the AIFM's business, shareholders with 10% of the voting rights or with an ability to exert 'significant influence' over the management of the AIFM, the organisational structure of the AIFM, a plan on how it intends to comply with the AIFMD, the remuneration regime of the AIFM, and arrangements regarding delegation.

In terms of the AIF, the AIFM is required to provide information about investment strategies, information about the master fund (where the AIF is a feeder AIF), the fund's governance documents, the AIFM's plan for appointing a depositary and the proposed information that is to be disclosed to investors investing in the AIF (as prescribed by the AIFMD).

It should be noted that the home regulator may qualify any authorisation granted by limiting its scope such as by placing restrictions on the investment strategy.

**Authorisation Requirements for Small AIFMs**   A 'small AIFM' is a manager that operates one or more AIFs with aggregate AuM below one of two thresholds as below. The relevant threshold depends on whether the fund uses leverage or not to acquire its assets. Note that this does not include the portfolio assets (for example, shares in unlisted portfolio companies) of PE funds where the fund is not exposed to the borrowing of such portfolio assets. The thresholds are:

- **EUR 100 million:** AuM across all AIFs managed of no more than EUR 100 million including any assets acquired through the use of leverage.

- **EUR 500 million:** AuM across all AIFs managed of no more than EUR 500 million when the assets acquired by the fund(s) are unleveraged and the AIFs have no redemption rights exercisable during a period of five years following the date of initial investment in each AIF.

A small AIFM complies with a lighter regime than other 'full-scope' AIFMs – although it is not entitled to the EEA marketing passport available to full-scope AIFMs. This includes an option for member states to introduce a registration regime for small AIFMs, which is less onerous than requiring full authorisation. The AIFMD sets out the following minimum requirements for a small AIFM:

- **Registration:** The AIFM must register with the competent authority of its home member state.
- **AIF Identification:** The AIFM must identify the AIFs that it manages to such authority at the time of registration.
- **Investment Strategies:** The AIFM must provide information about the investment strategies of the AIFs that it manages to the competent authority at the time of registration.
- **Instrument Reporting:** The AIFM must regularly provide information to the competent authority relating to instruments in which it trades and the most important concentrations of the AIFs managed in order to allow effective monitoring of systemic risk by such authority.
- **Notification:** The AIFM must notify the competent authority where it no longer meets the conditions for being a small AIF.

A small AIFM can also opt in to the full-scope compliance requirements of the AIFMD in order to obtain the rights granted therein (i.e. the right to passport the fund across the EU without relying on private placement regimes).

In the UK, a distinction is drawn between 'small authorised AIFMs' and 'small registered AIFMs'. A small authorised AIFM is a small UK AIFM (i.e. it has its registered office in the UK) which meets the threshold test and has not opted into the full-scope regime. A small registered AIFM is a small UK AIFM which meets the threshold test and is one of the following three options:

- **Option One:** The internal AIFM of an AIF which is a body corporate and not a CIS under existing UK law.
- **Option Two:** The external AIFM of AIFs which are CISs under pre-existing UK law (and not an AUT, an OEIC, or an authorised contractual scheme) and hold the majority of their assets as land, provided that the AIFs are established or operated by a firm which has regulatory permission for this activity under pre-existing UK law.
- **Option Three:** It has applied for registration as a European Social Enterprise Fund Manager or a European Venture Capital Manager and meets the necessary criteria.

Small AIFMs which are not eligible for registration must obtain authorisation from FCA.

An internal AIFM is an AIF with a legal structure that permits the management of its assets by its governing body or other internal body. In such a case, the fund is both the AIF and the AIFM. An external AIFM is a separate legal person from the AIF that has been appointed to manage the AIF.

Both small authorised AIFMs and small registered AIFMs may be subject to pre-existing UK requirements (including in effect those applicable to CISs under pre-existing UK requirements).

**Marketing of AIFMs**   Marketing is defined by the AIFMD as 'a direct or indirect offering or placement at the initiative of the AIFM of units or shares of an AIF it manages to or with investors domiciled or with a registered office' in an EEA state. As with the definitions of AIF and AIFM, the definition is wide. However, in this case it will capture third parties, such as placement agents. The marketing restrictions do not apply to an offering or placement of units or shares made at the initiative of the investor in question – also known as 'reverse solicitation'. In general, full-scope AIFMs must obtain regulatory consent to market specific EU AIFs in their home member state.

Where a full-scope AIFM with its registered office in an EEA state is authorised to provide its services in one member state, it may provide and market EU AIFs throughout the EU under a passport (on a similar basis as under the UCITS regime). The passport for EEA AIFMs to market non-EEA AIFs will not be available until sometime in the future, and presently such funds can only be marketed (if at all) in accordance with national private placement regimes (NPPRs). The concept of the passport means that an authorised AIFM can market to non-retail investors in other member states without having to comply with local regimes regarding private placement. The AIFMD also regulates non-EU managers that, for example, manage an EU AIF or market a non-EU AIF within the EU.

The marketing passport is provided by the home state regulator once satisfied that the AIFMD has been complied with. It only allows direct marketing to 'professional' investors, i.e. those who are 'professional clients' for the purposes of MiFID, which includes credit institutions, investment firms, and pension funds. It is worth noting that 'professional' may not include high-net-worth individuals or family offices, even if they are sophisticated investors, although individual member states may permit this in accordance with their own rules. The AIFMD does allow for retail marketing under certain circumstances but this is separate to the passport and local private placement rules would apply.

**National Private Placement**   The private placement regime permits EU member states to allow the marketing of AIFs to professional investors within an EU member state without a passport, but in limited circumstances, and at the discretion of the member state in question. In the UK, the private placement regime in place allows for the marketing of a non-EEA AIF by a UK or EEA full-scope AIFM; the marketing of a UK or EEA AIF managed by a UK or EEA full-scope AIFM that is a feeder vehicle in a master/feeder structure where the master vehicle is either an EEA AIF managed by a non-EEA manager or a non-EEA AIF; and the marketing of a UK EEA, or non-EEA AIF by a non-EEA AIFM (small or not).

An EU AIFM wishing to market in the UK under the private placement regime is required to notify the FCA that it will comply with the directive (with certain exceptions), that there are sufficient cooperation arrangements for the exchange of information between the UK and the relevant country or countries, and that any relevant non-EEA state is not listed as a Non-Cooperative Country and Territory by the Financial Action Task Force (FATF).

A small non-EEA AIFM wishing to market will be required to comply with certain information requirements with the FCA. A non-EEA AIFM that is not a small AIFM wishing to market must give a written notification to the FCA confirming that:

- **FCA Rules:** The non-EEA AIFM in question is responsible for compliance with the FCA's rules.
- **Reporting and Leveraging:** The AIFM complies with the directive in respect of reporting obligations, managing leveraged AIFs, and the acquisition of control of non-listed companies and issuers (and the FCA rules relating to implementation of the same).
- **Cooperation Arrangement:** There are sufficient cooperation arrangements for the exchange of information between the UK and the relevant country or countries, and that any relevant non-EEA state is not listed as a Non-Cooperative Country and Territory by the FATF.
- **Depositary:** Certain other requirements apply (in particular, if there is no depositary, information must be provided as to appropriate custodial arrangements).

The EC said that it would review the operation of the passport after two years under the AIFMD, and it may recommend that it be extended to non-EEA AIFMs. If the passport is extended to such managers, they will then have to be subject to the full provisions of the AIFMD in order to obtain the right to do so. More on this in Chapter 10.

**Delegation** The delegation provisions have an impact on an EU AIFM's ability to delegate functions to third parties or group companies, particularly with reference to those outside the EU and where investment management responsibilities are delegated. It should be noted that seeking advice without providing any discretion to said adviser is unlikely to amount to delegation.

A full-scope UK AIFM may not delegate its functions of portfolio or risk management for an AIF to an undertaking (or an undertaking may not sub-delegate, etc.) unless that undertaking is authorised or registered for the purpose of asset management and is subject to supervision in respect of that asset management function.

The specific provisions provide that:

- **Advance Notification:** Advance notification to the relevant regulator is required.
- **Delegation:** Delegation must be justified with reasoning.
- **Authorisation/Registration:** Authorisation or registration will be required in the delegated jurisdiction where the delegation involves portfolio or risk management.
- **Liability:** Liability to the fund will not be affected by the delegation.
- **De Facto Manager:** The delegation cannot be so extensive that the result is that the entity to which the functions have been delegated has become the de facto manager.

**Depositaries** The AIFMD requires the AIFM to appoint, in writing, a single independent depositary. Under the AIFMD, the depositary must be appointed to perform certain functions including overseeing the fund's cash flows, holding the fund's financial instruments in custody, verifying the ownership interests in any assets of the fund, and various overseeing functions in relation to the units and shares in the AIF. Marketing of non-EEA AIFs under national private placement regimes is subject to broad equivalence requirements in respect of depositaries.

For example, in the UK, authorisation of the marketing of any third-country AIFM requires, amongst other things, that where a depositary is not appointed, a custodian is appointed to carry out certain functions of a depositary. Use of a depositary is not a formal precondition to marketing of any AIF by a third-country AIFM, although a level of compliance with the directive is still required. Consistent with the lighter touch regime for small AIFMs, small third-country AIFMs seeking to market AIFs in the UK are subject to more limited notification requirements with no formal requirement for a depositary or custodian.

**Capital Requirements**  There are various minimum capital allowances depending on the manager's relationship to the AIF. However, if so permitted by member states, the percentage of funds under management requirement can be reduced by up to 50% if the AIFM is guaranteed by a bank or insurer.

Notwithstanding the requirements of the AIFMD, the Capital Requirements Directive IV (CRD) may also apply where a firm is subject to its requirements.

AIFMs must also have professional indemnity insurance or sufficient funds to cover professional negligence and that of the third parties (if any) to which any functions have been delegated.

It should be noted that AIFMs authorised under the UCITS Directive need not comply with the capital requirements under the AIFMD.

**Code of Conduct**  In addition to specific rules, the AIFMD contains a wide-ranging set of general principles. These principles include acting in the best interests of the fund and investors.

As well as following a set of principles regarding conflicts of interest and treating investors fairly, AIFMD requires (subject to issues of proportion and scale) AIFMs to have a permanent risk management function and that risk management is 'functionally and hierarchically' separated from operating units, including the portfolio management function. The principles also call for appropriate liquidity management protocols allowing for the accurate monitoring of the liquidity risk of the fund. The FCA requires a programme of activity to be submitted with the application for permission to manage an AIF, which details compliance with these requirements. Additionally, the Commission Delegated Regulation introduces further compliance measures.

**Transparency**  Certain information must be provided to investors and the regulator during the marketing process and on an ongoing basis. Before investors make an investment, the manager must disclose to the investors information including the investment strategy, the legal implications of the investment contract, and the identities of the manager, depositary, and other third-party service providers. An audited annual report must be disclosed in respect of each EU AIF within six months of the end of the financial year. AIFMs must also regularly report trading information and information regarding the portfolio to regulators. The frequency upon which such disclosures to regulators must be made is determined by reference to the amount of funds under management.

**Leverage and Asset Stripping**  In order to monitor risk, AIFMs are required to report to the regulator the level of leverage employed in a fund, the make-up of the leverage as between borrowed cash and securities and other elements, as well as provide any information requested by the regulator in order to monitor the risk to the fund.

**Remuneration**  The AIFMD prescribes certain principles for AIFMs, which relate to the remuneration policies for staff who exert influence on the risk profile of the AIFM and/or the AIF under management. Broadly, the rules aim to prevent policies that promote risk-taking, avoid conflicts of interests, and keep policies and practices in line with the investors' best interests.

It was at first felt by the industry that the remuneration rules would be the main off-putting aspect of AIFMD and would force managers to seek to skirt around AIFMD if possible. However, their impact have been much less severe and restrictive than first thought.

**Valuation** Under the AIFMD, managers are directed as to who can value the assets of a fund as well as the method for making such a valuation and the manager's liability to investors for valuations. The applicable rules pursuant to the AIFMD will be according to the laws of the member state in which the fund is incorporated and/or has its registered office.

**Reporting** Annex IV of AIFMD sets out the documentation and information that needs to be disclosed by AIFMs making use of or intending to make use of the AIFMD marketing passport. AIFMs must provide this detailed information to the relevant national competent authorities, for example, the FCA in the UK.

## MiFID II

The Markets in Financial Instruments Directive (MiFID) was applicable in the UK from November 2007.[2] Over ten years later MiFID II was finally introduced in January 2018, much to the apprehension of market participants. Amongst others, the new legislation greatly affects asset managers and pension funds, many of whom spent 2017 ensuring they would be compliant with the new directive as it was introduced into national law. Perhaps the more pressing updates to regulation for the asset management industry include the unbundling of research, taping of telephone conversations, how clients are categorised, and how transactions are reported. MiFID II is discussed in much more detail in Chapter 10.

## UCITS V

Prior to UCITS legislation, legal diversity had made it difficult for European investors to buy into funds domiciled in other European countries. The first UCITS directive was introduced in 1985[3] as an initial framework to harmonise the management and sale of mutual funds across the EU. The regime applies to open-ended CISs that invest in listed securities.

In principle, the first UCITS directive enabled any fund that had valid authorisation in its home state under the directive to market its units in other EU member states. The fund would have to notify the reciprocal EU member states of its intention to do so, but would not have to go through the individual registration process for each state.

A second UCITS directive was never actually adopted but, in 2002, UCITS III was adopted. This package was composed of two separate directives, which amongst other things, reduced restrictions on index tracker funds and created minimum standards for a UCITS management company to comply with (such as rules of conduct and risk control).

UCITS IV introduced substantial reforms from the previous directive in 2011. The focus of this directive was on:

- introducing a passport enabling a UCITS funds to be managed in a member state other than its home member state;
- simplifying the cross-border distribution procedures;
- introducing the master-feeder structure to help asset-pooling;
- introducing the key investor information document in replacement for the simplified prospectus; and
- the consolidation of UCITS funds through a framework for the domestic and cross-border mergers of UCITS funds.

Most recently, UCITS V came into force across all 28 EU member states in March 2016, with the general aim of bringing the regime for traditional CISs more into line with the policies of AIFMD. It focuses on three main areas, being:

- **Depositary Regime:** Introduction of new depository regime (enhancing rules of responsibility).
- **Remuneration Policies:** Rules governing remuneration policies of management and investment companies managing UCITS funds to be applied to key members of UCITS fund managerial staff.
- **Administrative Sanctions:** Harmonisation of the minimum administrative sanctions regime across Member States.

UCITS funds are popular investment vehicles amongst investors because they are so tightly regulated and tend to offer favourable tax treatment. They can also be redeemed very regularly (some even daily), so they are attractive for their liquidity. For managers, regulation is a burden, but the ability to reach investors across the EU (and the attractiveness of UCITS funds to investors) makes UCITS fund structures popular amongst managers too.

## MAR/MAD II

In July 2016, the Market Abuse Regulation (MAR) officially supplanted the Market Abuse Directive (MAD) and associated FCA rules. Clearly, being just MAD was not enough! The increasingly global flavour of financial interactions necessitated a more developed approach to combat market abuse. Off the back of the LIBOR scandal – it was deemed appropriate that a new framework would be created to prevent financial abuse. The original MAD legislation required signatories to commit to an equivalence regime that mandated a close working relationship and transparency. However, rapid technological advancement has facilitated more sophisticated forms of market manipulation that in turn demanded improved legislation.

MAR extends the scope beyond individuals who are producing recommendations as part of their day-to-day business to include anyone producing or disseminating a recommendation.

Information must be objectively presented and firms must disclose any conflicts of interest concerning the financial instrument to which the recommendation relates. Firms will be required to record all investment recommendations made at the issuer and security level and make 12 months of this data available when making new recommendations.

In short, MAR aims to improve and align the EU regime on market abuse. It widens the remit of existing offences and introduced new offences, for example, manipulation of benchmarks and attempted insider dealing.

## Basel

The Basel III framework is the latest in a line of international agreements that regulate the conduct of banks, with particular regard to their capital adequacy. Capital adequacy is the holding of capital to cover liabilities owed to the bank. Capital adequacy is commonly expressed as a ratio of liquid assets to the sum of liabilities owed to the bank, with different weighting given to various liabilities. The overall purpose of capital adequacy rules is to ensure that banks are sufficiently liquid to reduce the risks of default-inspired contagion spreading through the banking system, by forcing banks to hold sufficient capital to honour their own debt obligations (whether to other lending banks or to retail depositors). Many commentators have suggested that due to perceived over-complexity with Basel III, there is a need for a fourth framework with clearer drafting.

Banks are required to also improve the quality of their capital. A greater proportion of capital is required to be made up of common equity and retained earnings rather than debt instruments (or debt-like instruments, such as convertible loan stock). Another measure to increase capital adequacy is to require banks to increase the short-term liquidity coverage of the bank's high-quality liquid assets against expected cash outflows measured over a 30-day period. This is commonly referred to as a 'stress test', examining and proving a bank's ability to meet its obligations during a time of market difficulty. Many banks have previously and publicly failed such tests. The liquidity of assets held is weighted (an issue of some contention) where assets such as government bonds are considered the highest quality assets for a bank to hold when valued in the context of a stress test.

These measures and other ancillary provisions have dramatically affected banking activity in the markets. Many banks have retreated from certain asset classes and instruments, due to either their long-term illiquidity or the risk weighting that they are apportioned for the adequacy ratio and rules. This retreat has given rise to both the shadow banking sector, as well as significant increase in private debt funds amongst more traditional PE managers.

## Solvency II

The Solvency II directive aims to impose coordinated rules to supervise insurance groups, with the objective of protecting consumers by increasing the chances that insurance payments are made following a claim. The deadline for implementation of the directive in all 28 member states was 1 January 2016, thereby harmonising individual insurance regulatory regimes into a singular EU version. Most EU insurers are covered by the directive, and only the smallest insurers will be excluded from the scope of the directive.

The directive imposes the following requirements on EU insurers:

- **Information Divulgence:** To provide greater information to consumers in relation to their business, including providing details of their group structure, and demonstrating that they have sound financial health.
- **Effective Governance:** To demonstrate that they have put in place an effective system of governance to provide for the sound and prudent management of the business.
- **Key Personnel Qualifications:** To fulfil certain 'fit and proper' requirements in respect of key personnel, including ensuring such members have adequate professional qualifications, knowledge and experience, and they must also be of good repute.
- **Minimum Capital Requirements:** To satisfy minimum capital requirements (MCR) and solvency capital requirements (SCR). The MCR is the minimum level of security below which an insurance company's resources should not fall. The SCR is the solvency margin, which an insurance company must hold to cover the risk that their assets will not meet their liabilities.

Solvency II has had the effect of preventing insurance companies from investing anything like as much as they did pre-crisis in traditionally illiquid funds, such as infrastructure and PE funds, because the underlying assets in these types of funds are held for a fixed period of time. This may be contrary to sound and prudent management, which requires a certain level of liquid assets to satisfy liabilities.

## GDPR

The General Data Protection Regulation (GDPR) is intended to overhaul and harmonise data protection throughout the EU. The deadline for firms to comply with the GDPR was 25 May 2018 and the UK government confirmed that its implementation into the law of England and Wales will not be affected by the UK's decision to leave the EU. In fact, the UK government has passed the Data Protection Act 2018, which received royal assent on 23 May 2018. This transposed many of the provisions of the GDPR into free-standing English law, negating the potential impact of Brexit.

The GDPR has a broad geographical scope and will apply to the processing of personal data of individuals in the EU regardless of whether the processing of such data happens in the EU. This captures almost all multinational corporations.

**Controller or Processor?**   When considering how the GDPR might affect fund managers, it is important to categorise the manager as the 'controller' of the data processing, or the 'processor' (in some cases the manager may occupy both of these roles).

A controller is defined in the GDPR as 'the natural or legal person … which, alone or jointly with others, determines the purposes and means of the processing of personal data'. A processor is defined as 'a natural or legal person … which processes data on behalf of the controller'. In the context of a usual fund, the manager will likely outsource their IT functionality to a third party provider, but will inevitably control the type and source of the data which they collect from third parties, for example in subscription documents. However, processing is defined broadly to include operations 'such as collection, recording, organisation, structuring, storage, adaptation or alteration, retrieval'. It may be that managers are therefore both controllers and processors of data.

The minimum level that authorities can impose for data protections breaches is EUR 10 million, or in the case of an undertaking, up to 2% of the total worldwide annual turnover of the preceding financial year, whichever is higher. However, for breaches of certain provisions the level of fines are increased to EUR 20 million, or in the case of an undertaking, up to 4% of the total worldwide annual turnover of the preceding financial year, whichever is higher.

This is far above the fines that were previously being levied under the UK's Data Protection Act 1998, under which the Information Commissioner's Office (ICO) could impose a fine of up to GBP 500 000. The implications of making data protection errors have therefore now become extremely severe.

**Lawfulness of Processing**   There are a number of lawful reasons for processing data, one of which being that the data subject consents to the processing (see below). Others include that the processing is 'necessary for the performance of a contract' or that it is necessary 'for the purposes of the legitimate interest pursued by the controller'.

The latter of these two lawful reasons, legitimate interests, covers a situation where there is a 'relevant and appropriate relationship' between the controller and the data subject, such as that of service provider and client. This could include the relationship between a general partner or fund manager and an investor (if professional) in a fund. However, it is likely that it will not cover marketing the fund to investors in the first place.

The former of the above reasons could cover initial communications with potential investors before a 'relevant and appropriate relationship' has arisen.

Certain information, such as that collected in subscription agreements, is clearly necessary for the performance of a contract. Firms should, however, be cautious not to collect additional information, which is not required for the purposes of allowing investment into the fund. The

GDPR explicitly indicates that where the performance of a contract is conditional on the processing of data, which is not necessary for the performance of the contract, consent may be deemed not to have been freely given.

**Data Subjects' Rights**  The GDPR intends to make individual's rights to their data the paramount focus of firm's data protection regimes. As such, it expands on the rights that data subjects have in relation to their data. A large amount of the coverage of the GDPR has focused on the 'right to be forgotten' that data subjects hold. This right fits with a number of others under the regulation, many of which existed previously in some form or another, including the right to data portability and the rights to object and to rectification. The takeaway point is that firms will need to institute a system whereby all of the data collected and processed in relation to a data subject is easily accessible, searchable, and secure.

It should be expected that firms already have a system that maintains secure and accessible databases of data subjects' information. The additional rights under the GDPR require that this information is communicated to the data subjects efficiently, in plain language, so that they can exercise their rights should they choose to.

Fund managers will have to consider the means in which they collect and store data subjects' information, ensure that the information that they hold and how they hold it is communicated clearly with the data subjects, and have in place a system whereby data can be easily retrieved, modified, exported and, if necessary, deleted. The right to be forgotten above is not an absolute right and there are instances in which Article 17 of the GDPR states that the right does not apply, such as a situation where the controller has a legal obligation to retain data or it is required for the controller to establish, exercise, or defend a legal claim.

**Principles Relating to Processing**  The fact that the right to be forgotten is not absolute does not negate the need to implement a system in which the process of deleting data is possible. However, there are other means of retaining data in a way which satisfies the data subject's wish to be forgotten and other legal requirements to maintain data.

The GDPR set out a number of principles for processing, one of which is that data is 'kept in a form which permits identification of data subjects for no longer than is necessary for the purposes for which the personal data are processed'. Anonymising data might be a means by which controllers can comply with both the terms of the GDPR and any other legal obligations.

A further principle is that data must be 'accurate and, where possible, kept up to date'. Breach of this principle is sanctioned under the higher tier of possible fines and as such, the repercussions for not maintaining accurate data records could be severe. Fund managers and general partners will have to maintain a continuous dialogue with investors, representatives of investments, and parties to transactions in order to maintain the controllers' data records and avoid potential sanctions. Thought will have to be given to creating a system that allows for easy and practical updates.

We all remember the mass panic of cleansing data and contacts list at the start of 2018. How many emails did you get asking for your consent? Holding personal information just became very restricted. If you do not need it, delete it.

GDPR will have a large impact on technology as well as asset managers and might help see off the future social-media based threat of disruptive asset or wealth managers. That said, it might also stand in the way of healthy innovation and, along with MiFID II, the ability to offer quality investment advice and management to the many (not the few) to quote a certain UK politician right now.

## European Market Infrastructure Regulation

European Market Infrastructure Regulation (EMIR) came into force in August 2012, with the objective of reducing the risk, which derivative contracts may pose to the financial system. The regulations came into effect in stages during 2013–2014 and impose certain conditions upon entities entering into any form of derivatives contract. There are five key obligations imposed under the EMIR, which are:

1. certain eligible OTC derivatives are subject to clearing by a central counterparty (CCP);
2. authorisation and supervision of CCPs;
3. reporting obligations;
4. imposition of risk management techniques for non-CCP cleared OTC derivatives; and
5. application of organisational, conduct of business and prudential requirements for CCPs.

The EMIR regulations restrict the market in derivatives, often a core element of some alternative asset investment strategies, or part of an underlying strategy in relation to RE or commodities. Limiting these strategies has affected the gearing strategies of funds. It may also have unforeseen knock-on effects in the market, such as funds moving offshore to avoid restrictions if they prove too unworkable.

## Anti-Bribery Legislation

The UK Bribery Act 2010 was created to answer the requirements of the 1997 OECD anti-bribery Convention. In essence, the UK Bribery Act 2010 improves the previous UK law and represents one of the most stringent global regulatory frameworks. This is in part because of the creation of a strict liability offence for partnerships and companies who fail to prevent bribery. Importantly, the UK Bribery Act 2010 represents an increased liability risk for companies that operate or are incorporated within the UK.

The four primary offences that the UK Bribery Act 2010 creates are as follows:

- two general offences covering the offering promising or giving of an advantage, and requesting, agreeing to receive or accepting of an advantage;
- a discrete offence of bribery of a foreign public official; and
- a new offence of failure by a commercial organisation to prevent a bribe paid to obtain or retain business or a business advantage (should an offence be committed it will be a defence that the organisation has adequate procedures in plan to prevent bribery).[4]

## Anti-Money Laundering

The Money Laundering, Terrorist Financing and Transfer of Funds (Information on the Payer) Regulations 2017 came into force on 26 June 2017 and transposed the Fourth EU Money Laundering Directive into UK Law. The objectives of the regulations can broadly be described as follows:

- to prevent new types of terrorist financing, for example, using e-money and prepaid cards;
- to improve transparency of beneficial ownership of companies and trusts;
- to change the approach to customer due diligence; and
- to enforce sanctions effectively.

Importantly, the scope of the regulation has expanded to include new forms of entity along with the extent of customer due diligence required. Second, the regulation has expanded the definition of a 'politically exposed person' (PEP), thus necessitating firms to re-examine their commercial relationships. Third, there is an increased underlying emphasis on adopting a risk-focused approach. In 2018, MLD4 was updated by MLD5 to harmonise enhanced due diligence requirements for high-risk clients.

## Reporting and Disclosure

The Common Reporting Standard (CRS) requires jurisdictions to acquire information from their financial institutions and automatically exchange that information with other jurisdictions in a reciprocal arrangement on an annual basis. Based on the US system of FATCA, the objective is to prevent tax evasion through reporting.

Importantly, each individual country determines what accounts are reportable. As such Country (X) is perfectly entitled to determine that accounts of its citizens who live in Country (Y) are subject to reporting. The objective is for each country to glean a better understanding of the taxable assets held by their citizens abroad. As a process, it requires a concerted effort by all 96 countries involved in the reporting scheme, but has a wider scope than the equivalent FATCA provision created by the US.

## REGULATION – SOME CONCLUSIONS FOR ALTERNATIVE ASSET FUND MANAGERS

This chapter broadly covers the principal national and supranational regulation affecting alternative asset fund managers.

The changes brought in by Dodd–Frank Act and FATCA have had far-reaching effects on the alternative asset management industry. The provisions of Dodd–Frank Act significantly reduced the scope for small private fund managers to market in the US to private investors without SEC approval. This has increased costs and time delays for fund managers outside the US who wish to source US investors. FATCA has also increased the burden on alternative asset managers who have accepted US investors into their funds. They are required to report to the IRS information regarding their US investors in order to avoid a 30% withholding charge on income sourced from the US.

The extensive Banking Act of 1933 in the US (following the Great Depression) is often referred to as the Glass–Steagall Act, which over time came to be further condensed in the public imagination to refer to two provisions of that legislation restricting affiliations between commercial banks and securities firms. Starting in the early 1960s, federal banking regulators interpreted provisions of the Glass–Steagall Act to permit commercial bank affiliates to engage in an expanding volume of securities activities. In 1999, the Gramm–Leach–Bliley Act finally repealed these two provisions. The Volcker Rule seeks, in part, to reinstate the division between retail and investment banking.

The Volcker Rule is the most controversial plank of all the reforms that have emerged from the credit crisis. It has led to an exodus of top proprietary traders from large banks to form their own hedge funds or join existing hedge funds. Prevailing industry sentiment is that it may prove difficult under this new regime to distinguish banned proprietary trading from its bona fide counterpart – the buying and selling of securities on behalf of clients. Industry participants also contend various unwanted adverse consequences of the rules, for example, that market liquidity will be negatively impacted, that transaction costs will rise, that trading volumes will be driven to other jurisdictions, and that the US economy will suffer. They also point out that these effects are likely to be extraterritorial in that, if the analysis is correct, these consequences will extend to overseas funds and bank subsidiaries. President Trump seems to agree.

Meanwhile, AIFMD has had a widespread effect on asset managers that are based in, or wish to market in, Europe. In order to market across borders, managers have had to comply with new capital requirements, information standards, standards of disclosure to regulators, requirements to use certain functionaries such as depositaries, and a plethora of other obligations. There is a Euro threshold limit for the 'full scope' of the AIFMD regulations, but the implementation of this threshold varies across member states of the EU. In the UK, for example, asset managers operating under the threshold are still required to seek authorisation from the FCA, which entails compliance with a significant proportion (but not a majority) of the AIFMD rules.

The overarching impact of these rules is to introduce higher costs to the operation of an investment manager, in terms of both money and time. Such regulation was clearly targeted at Ponzi schemes and other frauds, as well as to otherwise protect the public through greater transparency. In addition, it was an attempt to reduce systemic risk in the financial markets by limiting the investment activities of fund managers. From the industry's point of view, although regulation, which protects against fraud, is welcome, the increasing regulatory landscape of the industry can sometime be a sledgehammer to crack a nut. In addition, regulation does not usually catch the real crooks. It did not catch Madoff.

As can be seen, since the start of the financial crisis, there has been a considerable amount of reform. Much of this reform is new and untested. It is feasible that the new regulation will be diluted or be more narrowly defined over time. Indeed much of it will only be properly understood by its implementation.

On the broader policy front, asset management firms are recognising that regulation will lead to a restriction on liquidity available to their clients. We have already seen some direct effects, for example, of the Volcker Rule impacting affiliates of US banks, when Citi (and others) announced its withdrawal from alternative asset funds. In general, there has been a tendency for banking institutions to retrench and to re-focus on core activities. We have to recognise that asset management firms are likely to experience the higher costs of debt and equity capital because of this resultant lower liquidity.

Since the financial crisis, the regulatory 'assault' on the banking industry has arguably created a stronger, more robust, less risky, more transparent banking backbone to our capitalist society. However, with the banks retreating from investment, the investment needs of pension plans and you and I have been squeezed more into wealth management and asset management funds and platforms. Perhaps this is a good thing – as now the experts are doing it.

However, more and more debt, as of 2019, is now unregulated, despite the demolition job by regulators on the more aggressive 'doorstep' lenders a couple of years back. In addition, much of the services that the banks provided managers, not just leverage, through prime brokers (PBs) or sponsor desks, have now vanished. Hence the increase of 'mini-primes'. Recent news though, is that Citi (having effectively been a hedge fund pre-crisis) has now retreated even further from these PB services and supporting hedge teams.

## OTHER REGULATORY ENVIRONMENTS

For comparison, I have mentioned three other interesting jurisdictions below.

**China – Asia's Powerhouse**   The regulatory framework in respect of Chinese funds is set out under the 'Law of the People's Republic of China on Funds for Investment in Securities' (FIS Law) and a number of administrative regulations have been made pursuant to the same. The China Securities Regulatory Commission (CSRC) is responsible for the regulation of both open and closed-ended retail funds, and fund supervision is conducted by a branch of the CSRC known as the Department of Fund Supervision (DFS). The DFS has a number of responsibilities, including the following:

- **Securities Investment Funds:** Examining securities investment funds, the establishment of securities investment fund management companies, and supervising the business activities of the same.
- **Senior Officers:** Reviewing the qualifications of the senior officers appointed to fund management companies.
- **Foreign Fund Management:** Verifying the branch established by a foreign fund management company.
- **Supervision:** Supervising the sales and the operations of investment fund management companies.

Further to requirements set out under the FIS Law, fund management companies are subject to requirements under 'the measures for the administration of Securities Investment fund management companies', such as:

- **Company Capital Requirements:** The registered capital is not less than CNY 100 million and a company must have capital and net assets of more than CNY 100 million.
- **Company Governance Requirements:** corporate governance and internal monitoring rules;
- **Shareholder Requirements:** In relation to major shareholders with more than 25% of the registered share capital of the fund management company, major shareholders must have a registered capital of more than CNY 300 million and have a good business performance track record.
- **Fund Management Company Dissolution:** A fund management company may not be dissolved until the CSRC has cancelled its fund management qualification.

**Brazil – South America's Powerhouse**   The financial markets of Brazil are supervised by three regulatory institutions, each of which seeks to uphold the parameters defined by the Securities Law 1976 and the Corporations Law 1976. The Central Monetary Council issues regulations applicable to all participants within the Brazilian financial system and is responsible for the coordination of credit, budget, fiscal, debt, and monetary policies. These monetary policies are executed by the Brazilian Central Bank (BCB), an institution that ensures 'the stability of the currency's purchasing power and a solid and efficient financial system' and which is responsible for the control of foreign capital flow and the credit risk of the markets. The CVM engages in securities, derivatives, and investment fund regulation, and has additional duties that involve supervision of the stock exchange. The Council of Appeals of the National Financial System is an appellate body, which reviews decisions of both the BCB and the CVM.

**Australia**   In Australia, the regulations and regulatory bodies relating to investment funds apply to both open-ended and closed-ended retail funds, and to a lesser extent to funds restricted to wholesale investors. The Corporations Act 2001 sets out a number of requirements in respect of the retail funds. A managed investment scheme must be registered with the Australian Securities and Investments Commission (ASIC) if it has more than 20 members, or if it is promoted by a person whose business involves the promotion of managed investment schemes, or as otherwise determined by the ASIC. In addition, the trustee of such schemes is referred to as a 'responsible entity' and must hold an Australian financial services licence that authorises the entity to operate the fund. A manager (if one is appointed by the responsible entity) may also need to be licensed to deal in fund assets and to provide financial product advice to the beneficiaries/investors. The Corporations Act 2001 further imposes obligations upon entities, and the relevant officers responsible for the management investment scheme, whereby they are under a duty to exercise care and diligence, and act in the best interests of the members of the fund.

Where funds are restricted to investment by wholesale investors, the fund registration requirement does not apply. Wholesale investors include persons investing more than AUD 500 000, persons controlling more than AUD 10 million for investment in funds (including through trusts or by associates) and other types of professional or sophisticated investors. The trustee, however, may still require an Australian financial services licence unless they are exempted or authorised as a representative under another person's licence to provide the financial services in respect of the fund.

ASIC is an independent Commonwealth governmental body. It is empowered to regulate under the Australian Securities and Investments Commission Act, and oversees the compliance with the Corporations Act 2001. Regulation by the ASIC extends to Australian companies, financial services organisations, professionals who deal and advise in investments, and trustees who operate retail funds, or provide custodial or depositary services for a fund.

The powers of the ASIC include registration of companies and managed investment schemes, and the granting of Australian financial services and credit licences.

## SOME CONCLUSIONS

Asset management is a regulated industry. However, a recurring theme in this book is my view that, despite President Trump's 'bonfire of red tape', regulation globally is on the up. Protectionism leads to greater regulation. Brexit could force the UK to strip back regulation. More in the next chapter.

## ENDNOTES

1. www.sec.gov/spotlight/sec-employees.shtml
2. www.fca.org.uk/markets/mifid-ii
3. www.alfi.lu/setting-luxembourg/ucits/historical-overview-and-upcoming-changes
4. www.transparency.org.uk/our-work/business-integrity/bribery-act/

# Risk, Compliance, and Regulatory Trends

*Risk comes from not knowing what you're doing.*

– Warren Buffett

This chapter will explore the importance of risk in an asset manager's decisions. We will review how a manager measures their portfolio risk, the procedures they implement to deal with those risks, and the different types of risk that managers are wary of. We will also ask asset managers why they have chosen the risk profile they currently employ with their funds.

Following their pivot from banks to the investment communities, global regulators, including the ECB and FSB, have begun to classify fund managers and their investment activities as systemically important. Leverage is interesting. Within the banks, assets can be leveraged up between 10–30 times the amount of the original asset, whereas leverage used in funds is generally much lower. That said, leverage in funds is on the rise.

This chapter will also be reviewing upcoming regulation not yet in place, especially in light of Brexit, President Trump's plans to deregulate the market in the US, and the continuing fusion/federalisation of the 'United States of Europe'.

## UK REGULATORY ENVIRONMENT

Regulators are looking at the asset management industry with more scrutiny now they have cauterised the systemic risk of mass bank failure. Beyond this more stringent regulatory approach, Brexit permeates a large portion of any discussion on future risk. In Andrew Bailey's speech at the 2018 Future of the City dinner, he highlighted operational risks as well as the need to ensure an efficient regulatory system was in place. It is important, as Bailey states, to point out that London has been (and still is) the pre-eminent financial centre. These are, of course, interesting times politically. However, it is also important to remember that, with disruption comes opportunity.

## Brexit

The broad issues of the Brexit saga are as follows.

**Withdrawal Agreement**   Before we know what the future relationship between the EU and UK will be, the divorce settlement must be agreed – this (if adopted) will be the withdrawal agreement. Some of the key points covered by this agreement will be how much money will be paid by the UK to the EU on leaving, what will happen to UK citizens living in other EU countries and citizens of other member states living in the UK, and border arrangements between Northern Ireland and the Republic of Ireland (the only UK land border with the EU and a politically sensitive issue for Ireland and the UK). The agreement will also provide for a 'transition period', during which we can expect minimal change as the UK and EU prepare for the actual departure of the UK from the EU.

Since the UK government is struggling at the time of writing to get a withdrawal agreement through parliament, the issue will likely be resolved following one or a combination of the following: another referendum, a general election, a 'crashing out' with no deal, and/or the agreement of an extended negotiation period. The outcome of the political process will eventually be one of the following: the UK leaves the EU without a withdrawal agreement, the UK leaves on the terms of a withdrawal agreement, or the UK remains within the EU.

**Future Relationship with EU**   The future relationship of the UK with the EU will only be negotiated after the withdrawal agreement has been finalised. Currently there are a few notes on future arrangements. If the UK leaves without a withdrawal agreement, until a new arrangement is agreed, the UK's relationship with the EU will default to World Trade Organisation (WTO) terms. Any future agreement will likely model an existing relationship between the EU and a third country such as Canada, Norway, Switzerland, or Turkey. The options receiving the most airtime at the time of writing are Canada- and Norway-style arrangements. The Canada option involves full withdrawal from the EU's single market and customs union and a new comprehensive trade agreement entailing 'mutual recognition' of certain regulations; whilst the Norway option would entail staying in the EU single market and customs union (and having no say on the EU rules to which the UK would remain subject).

**No Deal**   The following points represent key operational issues in the event of the failure to agree a deal and a default to WTO terms.

- **Contract continuity:** There is the potential that when the UK removes itself from the EU, certain contracts (notably derivative and insurance contracts) may not be serviceable. There are, as at the beginning of 2018, GBP 26 trillion in derivative contracts and around 36 million EU and UK insurance policyholders.[1] The ecosystem that is built up around these contracts would be impacted significantly unless this is resolved. This has been disputed by the EU[2,3] but is nonetheless a component of both the FCA[4] and BoE's warnings.
- **Central Counterparties:** If there is not an agreement in place when the UK departs from the EU, then either side may be in breach of regulation if they facilitate clearing services in each other's jurisdiction. This is applicable in either providing new clearing services or continuing with previous arrangements.
- **Data:** The importance of data and how it is utilised is growing (discussed in Chapter 8). Moreover, how that data is handled, the regulation governing this, and the services offered

to do the above is also widening. The UK and the EU exchange an extraordinary amount of data. More than this, the UK exports a significant number of data services and is currently used as an entry point to the EU by many businesses.

▪ **Delegation and passporting:** A no-deal Brexit could lead to a breakdown in cross-border delegation models and shut down cross-border marketing activity for AIFMs and UCITS funds. However, the FCA has recently agreed memoranda of understanding with ESMA and member state regulators which promises to allow for delegation to continue post-Brexit in a no-deal scenario.

**No Brexit** It is also possible that the UK will not leave the EU at all. Alternatively, we could leave in some sense, but not entirely. For example, the UK could remain in a customs union. In any of these scenarios, passports to market and substance to manage will be part of a negotiated agreement. As I have said throughout this book, it is best to plan as if the UK is leaving in its entirety, with loss of marketing passports from the UK to the EU and from the EU to the UK a substantial risk. Building substance within the EU or using a third-party EU platform are options.

Prior to the referendum on the future of the UK's membership of the EU there was a lot of talk about how leaving could result in deregulation. This was championed by various members of both sides of the campaign. For Leavers, it was seen as an opportunity to 'take back control' (how I disliked that line) and create a more business-friendly, entrepreneurial environment that valued invention over stagnation. For Remainers, it was used as a sign that the UK would become a breeding ground for unscrupulous activities and encourage bad business practice. The commercial reality is, of course, far more practical than the political discourse. The UK has historically gone further than what much of the EU regulation requires. Especially within the context of cyberattacks and advancements in technology, the UK has taken a very strong line in relation to risk. It is unlikely, therefore, that we will suddenly see a bonfire of regulation post-Brexit.

**MiFID II – Impact Since Implementation** Following the successful rebuke of the introduction of MiFID II by the industry, pushing the date for implementation back a year, MiFID II was finally introduced in January 2018, much to the apprehension of market participants. Amongst others, the new legislation greatly affects asset managers and pension funds, many of whom spent 2017 ensuring they would be compliant with the new directive as it was introduced into national law.[5] Perhaps the more pressing updates to regulation for the asset management industry include the unbundling of research, taping of telephone conversations, how clients are categorised, and how transactions are reported.

From an asset management perspective, there has been little impact in the UK since MiFID II has been introduced. Indeed, for many operating in this sector, the introduction of the directive was greeted with relief. At least the past seven years of back and forth discussion about policy, with intermittent delays thrown in, could finally stop. However, there have been a few noticeable changes that should be highlighted. First, brokers have started to notice a fall in commissions as the rules designed to prevent inducements have been introduced. Prior to the directive, brokers may have offered research for no cost in an attempt to entice managers to use their services for trading. Second, the policymakers behind MiFID II had intended to reduce the amount of equity trading in private venues run by independent operators, exchanges, or banks. This has fallen from roughly 9% of the market to around 0.15%[6] indicating that at least one objective of the directive was being felt considerably. Yet, despite these changes, the departure of the UK from the EU may have an impact that is yet not easily quantified. The assumption during the policy's creation was that the UK would remain part of the EU – with the resultant calculations of its impact made on this basis. Any future changes, which may or may not impact the UK, will also be made with a new set of policymakers as the EU's elections will result in wholesale changes in 2019.[7] This confluence of variables indicates that prior predictions may not be indicative of future outcomes.

On the UK broking and asset management side, since the implementation of MiFID II, there have been grumblings in the city. At its core, MiFID II holds transparency and the protection of consumers paramount. However, in its attempts to ensure this happens it has accepted compromise on multiple fronts. One of those compromises is the need for fund managers to pay for their investment research separately. Undoubtedly, this has made managers more aware of how they spend their money and questions how useful the research they are using is. Moreover, it has not helped that larger banks have put pressure on the market as a whole by reducing the price of the research they provide. Inevitably, this has had an impact on smaller and mid-cap managers, with some predicting a significant reduction in the number of UK analysts. (In addition, small to mid-cap public companies are losing their coverage, so what is the point of being listed if there is no trading in the stock?)

I discuss in more detail in the EU section of this chapter, the impact of MiFID II. However, Brexit could present an opportunity to roll back the impact MiFID II has had on areas such as equity research. Indeed, Prime Minister Theresa May's appearance at the Bloomberg Global Business Forum in September 2018 was notable for her perspective on future regulation for the city. She articulated that Britain should 'deliver an economy that is knowledge rich, highly innovative, highly skilled and high quality, but with low tax and smart regulation'.[8] This presupposes that a post-Brexit Britain will focus on regulation that aims to achieve intelligent objectives that promote a competitive world leading financial centre. Yet, despite this optimistic response, there is concern that after Britain leaves the EU the most obvious solution to a lack of a deal on financial services would be an era of equivalence. This is not quite the rollback on regulation that many who have been impacted by MiFID II would like. That being said, it must be remembered that with change comes opportunity. Although there may not be a bonfire of regulation, there will certainly be an opportunity at some point to take a more outcomes-based approach on financial services legislation.[9]

**AIFMD**   As with MiFID II, Brexit offers an opportunity to roll back some of its provisions. Brexit also begs questions of how EU managers will pitch their funds to UK investors and whether the UK will continue to be a global meeting place for international managers and investors. More on the future of AIFMD below.

## US REGULATORY ENVIRONMENT

**GDPR – Impact in the US**   The impact of the General Data Protection Regulation (GDPR) on SMEs and larger companies in the US has not been as strong as first thought. Most companies have not been energetically proactive. Whilst those that have are traditionally strong on data security (for example, Fortune 50 companies). This is in part due to the lack of personal liability for senior employees in these companies. Although GDPR increases this chance, no corporate officer has yet been found personally criminally liable. Until this happens, it may be the case that companies do not implement the policies needed under GDPR with any real urgency.

Undoubtedly, however, GDPR has raised the public awareness of cybersecurity and the dangers of cyberattacks. Within the commercial sphere, there has been an increase in risk-management and internal policy assessments.[10] Although this may be in response to GDPR enforcement action, what this demonstrates is that by hook or crook the commercial world will eventually comply (even if it takes longer than initially anticipated). Within the political sphere, the impact of GDPR has perhaps been felt most by the increased legislative activity of state level government. The California Consumer Privacy Act[11] has been passed, which will go into effect on 1 January 2020. Other states are considering introducing similar legislation, which undoubtedly is due to the influence of GDPR.[12] This mirroring of European legislation may be perhaps the biggest legacy in the US and indicates how prescient a topic data protection is.

**Bonfire of Regulation**  A key part of Donald Trump's election strategy was his attack on regulation. His approach was to endorse change and reduction at any opportunity. Whether this was through the visual aid of cutting red ribbons[13] wherever he went or comparing one small pile of documents to another much larger one[14] – he tried it all. On his first day in the White House, President Trump made a promise to reduce regulations by 75% or more.[15] Indeed, President Trump later announced Executive Order 13771[16] – which said that for every new regulation introduced, two previous regulations must be cut. President Trump was literally doing a two for one deal. His supporters are proud of his war on red tape grounded on a belief that government is too freewheeling with taxpayer's money. Indeed, the assumption is that the removal of red tape is good for the average worker. However, critics have indicated they feel President Trump's war on regulation could have a significant detrimental impact on the US economy – leading to poor performance of companies and eventually job losses.

## EU REGULATORY ENVIRONMENT

There have been significant developments in EU legislation in the wake of the financial crisis. The updating of legislation that is not fit for purpose is likely set to continue with EU financial institutions operating in an increasingly global world. To remain competitive and provide the security that the public demands, more changes will inevitably be made. Creating a safer financial system is at the core of much of the legislation that has been implemented within the EU over recent times and this no doubt will remain a key tenet. Prior to the financial crisis the orthodox opinion on financial regulation amongst academics was that it is bad for growth. Post-credit crisis this has been re-evaluated[17] by the EU. It is likely that we will see further regulation – which will certainly add costs but perhaps not value.

On 13 December 2018, the ECB ended its eurozone QE stimulus programme.[18] The programme relied on the ECB purchasing around EUR 30 billion worth of bonds every month. By keeping interest rates incredibly low for a significant period the ECB argues that it has prevented deflation and stopped an even worse financial crisis from occurring. The ending of this programme marks perhaps a political rather than economic watershed. Prior to the programme being implemented, it was not particularly popular. Moreover, the funds that the ECB believed made a large impact in boosting activity where argued to be too focused on assets held by the wealthiest. Given economic growth across the eurozone is cooler than it was, this decision by the ECB perhaps may not be permanent as interest rates remain low.  Expect European QE to be turned up again.

Underlying these regulatory and political shifts lies three broader aims for the EU. Completing the financial union, improving integration regarding the fiscal and economic union, and shoring up democratic accountability and eurozone institutions.

I am assuming when I discuss the EU regulations below, that they still apply to the UK. Post-Brexit, all EU laws will be the subject of a large piece of UK law applying them all to the UK. After which, many of these rules will – piecemeal – be amended.

**AIFMD**   AIFMD is not the finished article. Indeed certain EU states do not recognise NPPRs (see below), and states interpret pre-marketing and reverse solicitation differently. Just as MiFID I never really happened, AIFMD I has a somewhat pre-birth ghostly appearance.

**Delegation – Threats to Portfolio Management Strategies**   Under the AIFMD, fund managers can choose between two strategies for portfolio management decisions made on behalf of an EU-domiciled fund:

a) portfolio management decisions can be delegated in their entirety to a UK- or US-based (for example) investment manager (the 'delegation model'); or

b) decisions can be made at the fund level, under advice from a UK- or US-based investment adviser (the 'investment advisory model').

The current regulatory regime explicitly permits managers to use either one of these strategies.[19]

There have been concerns from the EC and ESMA that the current regime is a bit soft-touch. This view has been expressed in particular concerning the position of the UK following the decision to leave the EU. The UK is the largest asset management market in the EU, with around 36% of the managed assets in the EU being managed from London.[20] At the end of 2016, around GBP 900 billion was being managed in funds domiciled in Dublin and Luxembourg with portfolio management decisions being delegated back to the UK.

Currently, national regulators are charged with ensuring that managers comply with the spirit of AIFMD, and the EC has concerns that certain national regulators may loosely interpret the regulatory guidelines around the delegation model in order to pick up business from UK managers who are looking for an EU base when the UK leaves the EU, by permitting managers to effectively delegate all management decisions to a non-EU third country.

In other words, their concerns are that EU member states are fighting for post-Brexit UK business in the event that the UK loses its AIFMD passports, by encouraging UK managers to move to their country and imposing too light a regulatory or taxation touch. Then the portfolio management piece (i.e. the delegated piece) would be delegated back to the UK.

The threat to cancel the delegation model is though not just about Brexit. Putting an end to the delegation model will also impact other countries, and especially the US. The US was unhappy with the threat to the delegation model, as it is relied on for many of its European funds. The US kicking up a fuss was a more powerful rebuke than the UK complaining in a Brexit-minded EU-culture of UK punishment.

**Delegation – What Has ESMA Said?**   ESMA published an opinion in July 2017 which, although not going so far as to say that the delegation model will be dismantled in its entirety, was a warning to national regulators that may have been flexible to UK managers making use of EU structures post-Brexit. This opinion seeks to harmonise the implementation of the AIFM regimes on delegation across EU national regulators and delegation arrangements are likely to come under additional scrutiny in the run-up to and post-Brexit. Although they remain a viable option, it will be important to ensure sufficient substance in terms of management functions remain in an EU state.

The emphasis remains on national regulators to police the organisational procedures that authorised entities (i.e. AIFMs) have to ensure that they do not fall foul of the delegation requirements in AIFMD. Further, the delegation and any risk management policies and procedures must detail all functions (listed at Annex I of AIFMD) which are not performed internally and are subject to delegation requirements.

National regulators must be satisfied that there are objective reasons for delegation based on detailed descriptions from the authorised entity. Objective reasons could include, but are not limited to, optimised business functions, saving costs and benefitting from additional expertise. Again, special consideration should be given to delegation models that involve non-EU entities.

ESMA highlighted that national regulators should give 'special consideration' to the appointment of investment advisers to ensure that the delegation rules are not circumvented. Further, where authorised entities appoint an investment adviser and do not carry out their own 'qualified analysis' (which is left suitably vague) of any investment advice, this amounts to delegation of portfolio management activities and so can only be to an undertaking which is authorised/registered for asset management.

Further, authorised entities cannot delegate portfolio management functions to an extent that exceeds a 'substantial margin' of those functions performed internally. This analysis should take place at the level of each individual fund and will require funds to have people on the ground in the country of domicile to avoid being seen as a mere letterbox company. Further, sufficient internal resources must be maintained by the authorised entity in order to monitor delegated function. National authorities should apply additional scrutiny where an authorised entity does not have at least three locally based full-time equivalents monitoring portfolio and/or risk management functions.

Much of the above is already contained in the AIFMD. However, there is a shift in focus on which entities can carry out investment decisions, with more emphasis being placed on the manager rather than investment adviser. Any delegation arrangements will need to be structured with this in mind to avoid infringing the investment management rules. This does not make the delegation model impossible; however, managers may have to consider setting up EU-domiciled management companies and adopt a system of portfolio management more akin to the investment advisory model to avoid regulatory scrutiny.

This opinion has, unsurprisingly, divided regulatory authorities, with the French and British authorities taking different lines. The Autorité des Marchés Financiers (AMF), the French markets watchdog, has welcomed the move, stating 'we are vigilant that entities based in France or in Europe wishing to delegate will have sufficient means to control all investments delegated. In that respect, we welcome the opinion released by ESMA'.[21] Meanwhile, the FCA in the UK has questioned the need for any changes to be made to the current regime, with Andrew Bailey saying 'This is a model that works effectively. There is no need for it to change. I would put the question back to my ESMA colleagues, "Why do you think Brexit requires these changes?"'.[22]

**National Private Placement Regime Under AIFMD** The National Private Placement Regime (NPPR) gives member states discretion to allow non-EU AIFMs to market EU AIFs and AIFMs based anywhere in the world to market non-EU AIFs in that Member State. A Member State that chooses to implement a private placement scheme must apply at least the AIFMD rules in their placement scheme, but can add additional requirements.

When AIFMD was created, it was said that the NPPR would only be short-term. In other words, it was intended that eventually only EU AIFs managed by EU AIFMs should be able to market in the EU (except so far as third country passporting was made available). In 2018, ESMA was supposed to be advising on the future of NPPR, but we are yet to hear from them.

That being said, many EU member states have not even implemented a private placement scheme anyway.

**Third Country Passports**  The Eurovision Song Contest notably allows countries from outside Europe an opportunity to participate. In a similar fashion, AIFMD makes provision for 'third countries' to access the EU's alternative investment fund market. Unlike the song contest however, the EU authorities are concerned to ensure that everyone who participates in the EU's alternative investment fund market is singing from the same hymn sheet.

The AIFMD regulates the management and marketing of alternative investment funds, such as hedge funds, private equity (PE), and real estate (RE) funds, in the EU. It provides for a 'passport' which allows AIFMs to manage and/or market AIFs across the EU, on the basis of a single authorisation by their local regulator. Currently, only EU authorised AIFMs managing and/or marketing EU registered funds can avail of the passport.

Non-EU AIFMs wishing to manage or market AIFs in the EU, and EU AIFMs marketing non-EU AIFs, do not have a passport, so any marketing of such AIFs may only be carried out in compliance with the private placement rules of each EU country into which the AIF is sold. The problem here is that private placement rules differ from one EU country to the next. Indeed, some EU countries are effectively closed to non-EU AIFs since they do not permit marketing to investors in their jurisdiction without the AIFMD passport. The disparity in treatment between EU and non-EU AIFMs has led to criticisms that the AIFMD has created a 'fortress Europe' in the AIF industry.

However, the AIFMD, which came into effect in 2013, envisages the extension of the passport to AIFMs and AIFs from third countries, and mandates ESMA to advise the EC, EP and European Council in this regard.

ESMA has so far assessed 12 different non-EU countries to determine the suitability of granting AIFMD passporting rights to those countries' AIFMs and AIFs. ESMA assessed each country on the basis of a standard set of criteria, which includes a consideration of the effectiveness of the cooperation arrangements between the supervisory authorities in the EU and the relevant third country and whether there are any significant obstacles to extending the passport on the grounds of investor protection, market disruption, competition, and the monitoring of systemic risk.

In July 2015, ESMA issued its initial advice on the extension of the AIFMD passport, followed by its second set of advice in July 2016. Here is a summary of ESMA's findings:

- **Canada, Guernsey, Jersey, Japan, and Switzerland:** ESMA issued a positive assessment to extending the passport to these countries.
- **Hong Kong, Singapore, and Australia:** ESMA indicated there are no significant obstacles to extending the passport to Hong Kong and Singapore when the assessment is based on those jurisdiction's AIFs alone. ESMA gave a largely positive assessment of Australia. However, for all three jurisdictions, ESMA qualified its endorsement by highlighting a lack of full reciprocal access for EU funds marketing in these third countries.
- **United States:** ESMA found no significant obstacles to extending the passport under the criteria of investor protection and monitoring of systemic risk. However, under the criteria

of competition and market disruption, ESMA highlighted that extending the passport might result in an uneven playing field between AIFMs in the EU and US. US funds accessing the EU through the passport would be faced with less onerous rules than would apply to those EU funds choosing to market in the US by way of public offer.

- **Bermuda and Cayman Islands:** ESMA stated that it is as yet unable to give definitive advice on the extension of the passport to these jurisdictions as each are in the process of implementing new regulatory regimes.
- **Isle of Man:** ESMA stated that in the absence of an AIFMD-like regime, it was difficult to carry out a full assessment.

The AIFMD's approach to third country entities can be contrasted with other EU directives which grant access to the EU single market to firms from those third countries which are assessed as having a regulatory regime equivalent to that in the EU. The AIFMD is not concerned with equivalence per se, since non-EU AIFMs which are granted the AIFMD passport will in any event be required to sign up to substantially all of the AIFMD by obtaining authorisation in their 'member state of reference', i.e. the member state with which the non-EU AIFM is most closely connected based on certain criteria set out in the AIFMD.

The extension of the AIFMD passport is now dependent on the EC adopting rules extending the passport to those third countries which have received a positive assessment from ESMA, and such legislation not being objected to by the EP and European Council. However, ESMA suggests that the EU institutions might wish to wait until ESMA has advised on a sufficient number of non-EU countries before it legislates for the extension of the AIFMD passport, bearing in mind the market impact of extending the passport. In the meantime, ESMA will continue its assessment of other non-EU countries which have a presence in the EU funds sphere. In other words, third country passports are off the agenda for now.

**Implications for Brexit**  ESMA's advice on the extension of the AIFMD passport will be of interest to UK asset managers. Currently, UK AIFMs can manage and market EU AIFs across the EU on the basis of authorisation by the FCA. However, if the UK is outside the EEA post-Brexit, UK AIFMs will be considered as third country AIFMs and will lose their passport, subject to any transitional relief.

The position of UK UCITS funds is also relevant – they stand to lose their status as UCITS, and consequently their passport, post-Brexit. Such funds will presumably then be categorised as AIFs. whilst UCITS are designed for sale to retail investors, many are sold exclusively to professional investors. The third country AIFMD passport would thus enable UK UCITS to be continued to be marketed to professional investors across the EU on a passported basis (with the UK UCITS perhaps re-branded but nonetheless adhering to UCITS-compliant investment strategies).

The granting of the AIFMD passport to the UK post-Brexit would, we expect, require ESMA to undertake a review of the UK regulatory regime. ESMA is unlikely to be in a position to advise on the extension of the AIFMD passport until the UK has put in place a replacement AIFMD regulatory regime post-Brexit (in much the same way as they were unable to adjudicate on Bermuda and the Cayman Islands in their most recent advice). Whilst that regime may look largely the same as that in place at the moment it will not be identical and that may inevitably result in delay in ESMA's adjudications. Any delay could be very disruptive for the asset managers unless a transitional arrangement is in operation.

In this regard, the UK may have some concerns with the speed and transparency of the AIFMD passport extension process, i.e.:

- ESMA's assessment of a third country can take several months to complete and resource constraints on ESMA may hinder the chances of a speedier review. Furthermore, if ESMA delivers a qualified approval of a third country, it may result in a further delay if the Commission has to consider different policy options regarding the conditions under which the passport is granted, e.g. in the case of its advice on extending the passport to the US, ESMA suggests three different ways in which the passport may be extended.
- There are no clear timelines. whilst the AIFMD envisages the EC taking steps to extend the passport within three months of ESMA issuing positive advice on a third country, this timeline has not been complied with so far.
- Even where a third country receives a positive assessment from ESMA, it may have to wait until a sufficient number of third countries have been recommended for the passport before the EC will act.
- The process is somewhat politicised, since the EC has previously specified to ESMA which particular third countries should be assessed. The UK will hope that it is at the top of the queue for ESMA assessment if and when the time comes.

As the AIFMD approaches its fourth year in operation, a review of the directive, involving a public consultation, is scheduled to begin. It will be interesting to hear the views of industry on the extension of the passport to third countries and to see how the review is impacted by Brexit considerations. It is all a moving political feast.

**A New Directive?**   The EC followed ESMA's Opinion with draft legislation in September 2017 proposing an overhaul of European Supervisory Authorities (including ESMA). The proposals provide that national authorities will have to notify and obtain an opinion from ESMA if a market participant (i.e. AIFMs) intend to significantly outsource, delegation or transfer risks to non-EU countries 'in a way that would allow it to benefit from the EU passport whilst essentially carrying out its activities outside the EU'. This proposal is likely intended to supplement the ESMA Opinion; however, does indicate that the EC believes closer regulatory oversight of AIFMs is required at an EU level. This is likely to prevent any national regulators taking a light touch to the delegation model.

A prospective timeline for implementation is not clear; however, the takeaway point is that delegation, in particular to non-EU countries, is going to be increasingly difficult.

**AIFMD Review**   AIFMD objectives are to ensure appropriate risk management; strengthen investor protection; prevent systemic risk, as well as shore-up risk management processes; establish common rules for the organisation, supervision and authorisation of asset managers; and establish a single market for these funds in the EU.

In March 2017, the EC issued a tender for a market study into AIFMD. Under the tender documents, the contractor was to carry out a survey into the functioning of AIFMD focusing in particular 'on how effective, efficient, relevant and coherent the AIFMD rules are in achieving their objectives'.[23] The study was led by KPMG and the final report was published on 10 December 2018.[24]

The report concludes that 'AIFMD has played a major role in helping to create an internal market for AIFs and a harmonised and stringent regulatory and supervisory framework for AIFMs.' The report suggests that AIFMD has been largely effective in achieving its objectives but that some amendment is desirable. Some of the key findings are listed below.

- **Reporting requirements.** The report highlights that AIFMD reporting requirements are troublesome – some of the data required from AIFMs is not necessary, whilst some additional useful data should be reported, and some of the reporting requirements are duplicated under other EU legislation. Furthermore, the study found that there is not a clear understanding within the industry of what needs to be reported.
- **Valuation.** The report suggests that valuation rules under AIFMD (which expose external valuers to unlimited liability and require AIFMs to either employ an external valuer or run the valuation process in-house) have led to an increase in internal valuation by AIFMs. There is now an insufficient supply of external valuers, which is pushing fees up. The overall result is a decrease in independent valuations.
- **Leverage.** The report notes that leverage is rare in AIFs, but that it would be useful to harmonise calculation methodologies for leverage across all UCITS and AIF legislation.
- **Depositaries.** The report notes that there has been an increase in the costs of depositary services since AIFMD's introduction. It also highlights that AIFMD depositary rules are interpreted differently in different member states, particularly in relation to cash monitoring duties. The report notes a feeling among market participants that there is a one-size-fits-all approach that does not accommodate differences in asset class and geography.
- **Separation.** The report notes that PE and RE players doubt the necessity of full functional and hierarchical separation of risk and portfolio management, and find it challenging because of the nature of their asset classes and a lack of resources.
- **Disclosures to investors.** The report notes that the disclosure requirements under AIFMD are excessive. As a result, they 'are ignored or prevent investors from obtaining a clear understanding of the AIF's investment proposal'. Additionally, it was noted that disclosure of fees and costs is inconsistent and often insufficient.
- **Investments in non-listed companies.** The report finds that rules relating to investment in non-listed companies are seen by the industry to be arduous and unhelpful – AIFMs find the administrative burden of reporting to NCAs time and cash consuming and it is not clear what use is made or could be made of the information provided.
- **Passport regime.** The report notes that the management passport has been particularly successful but that the marketing passport 'is lagging behind and is suffering from the different approaches taken by NCAs'. In addition to legal heterogeneity, uncertainty around the definition of marketing and pre-marketing is problematic. The report also notes a demand for third country passports to be introduced.

While the position of the EU's most dominant player in the asset management market hinges upon political negotiations, it seems foolish to take any further legislative action in response to this report that may not fit into the final picture. This of course leaves UK-based managers in a state of limbo until any political negotiations are finalised.

## Substance

'Substance' is important from both a tax and regulatory perspective. 'Substance' refers to the substantive activities of a business, which, in a funds context, means activities such as portfolio management, risk management, investment analysis, trading, fundraising, valuation, and compliance.

Substance affects where a fund and its participants are taxed. Funds generally aim for tax neutrality in their structure, and a common approach to this is to use a tax-transparent vehicle in a low-tax country (such as Guernsey). Such structures can result in the manager, the fund, and the investors being based in different countries. In order to receive the tax treatment desired, substance in the right places is required. The OECD's BEPS project looks set to make this a more pressing concern for the industry.

Substance also affects where a fund is regulated. Wherever a manager is based, they will have to report to the EU authorities if they market services in the EU (under AIFMD) and the US authorities if they manage funds for US investors (under the Advisors Act of 1940).

Therefore, when considering the structure and operation of a fund, managers should be aware that legal fiction is not always able to save them. Real people in real offices doing real things is the new now.

## Solvency II

Solvency II Directive (2009/138/EC) (Solvency II) is a review of the regulatory requirements for the European (re)insurance industry. A number of the features of Solvency II will have an impact on asset managers. The new rules ensure that insurers and reinsurers consider the risks to which they are exposed and attempt to manage those risks with increased transparency.

Similarly to the Basel regulations (below), Solvency II requires insurance undertakings to hold a certain amount of capital, known as the Solvency Capital Requirement (SCR), in order to face unexpected events. The new regime's requirements are more closely linked with the asset side of the insurers' balance sheet, hence why they impact asset managers.

In particular, insurers must consider certain risks. The most pressing of which, for asset managers, being market risk and third-party default risk. This in turn will affect the way in which the insurer calculates the amount of SCR they will have to hold. Managers will have to liaise with insurers to construct portfolios that work with the insurers risk appetite with a view to the amount of SCR that an insurer is comfortable holding.

**Solvency II – Where Next?**   Solvency II was implemented with relative ease by most member states – although it must be noted that it was not seamless, but then these things never are. As most regulation, there are snags and it is important not to be disproportionate in response to potential disconnects between the legislative intention and the commercial outcome. Importantly, the EC set out a timetable for various reviews of Solvency II. By 31 December 2019, there will be an assessment of the benefits of enhancing group supervision and capital management within a group. In addition, there will also be a review of methods, assumptions and standard parameters used when calculating the SCR with the standard formula. By 31 December 2020, there will be a follow up to the assessment of the SCR calculation along with the annual report until 1 January 2021. These reviews were specifically kept in mind when Solvency II was designed. It is partly why the regime itself is based on principles, which it must be said reflect the sometimes intense but undeniably valuable debate that occurred during its creation. It is unlikely that Solvency III will arrive any time soon and any rush to do so would seem unnecessary given the extensive review that has occurred throughout the creation and implementation of Solvency II.

## Basel IV

On 7 December 2017, the Basel Committee released a document that finalised the Basel III reforms. Due to the extensive nature of the reforms and the extensive capital requirements, these changes are informally referred to as Basel IV.

One of the core objectives of Basel III was the reform of regulatory capital. The follow up to this is a different approach to calculating risk-weighted assets (RWA), which are used to assess the minimum level of capital that a bank (and other institutions) must hold to minimise the risk of insolvency. The change introduced new rules on the standardised approach for credit risk, the standardised measurement approach for operational risk, and a further two new approach for the credit valuation adjustment (CVA) risk capital charge.[25] As a whole, these changes combined with the 2016 updates will necessitate banks (and other institutions) to renew their assessment of capital consumption throughout their organisation – with the knock on impact potentially being felt in pricing and product offerings. Impact will be felt in other areas, with the potential for capital to be redistributed and smaller institutions needing to examine their processes and whether they need technological and infrastructure updates to cope with the new complexities.

## GDPR Impact

Since 25 May 2018 to March 2019, only a small number of companies are facing fines due to non-compliance with GDPR. One prominent example is the Centro Hospitalar Barreiro Montijo in Portugal, which was fined twice. The first fine of EUR 300 000 was a consequence of failing to protect patient confidentiality and prevent access to patient data. The second fine of EUR 100 000 was for not ensuring 'the confidentiality, integrity, availability and permanent resilience of treatment systems and services'.[26] Although only a small number of companies have been fined – some larger more well-known tech companies have come under greater scrutiny. Microsoft has had trouble with the Dutch government for gathering data from users of their Office suite[27] and Facebook suffered badly post the Cambridge Analytica scandal after a huge data breach that impacted around 50 million accounts.[28]

What is clear, however, is that the average size of fine for a data breach has doubled since the introduction of GDPR,[29] showing the need for businesses to take this regulation seriously. Although SMEs are unlikely to be targeted as much by regulators, the rate of cyberattacks is increasing (see Chapter 8). It is highly likely that, going forwards, we will continue to see GDPR enforcement agencies be inundated with complaints from EU citizens.[30] It is vital, therefore, that data privacy and cybersecurity are taken seriously – especially by large tech companies or tech-enabled retail-facing asset managers that will be in the spotlight.

## MiFID II

**Research Unbundling** Traditionally, banks and brokerages bundled research into those costs charged to fund managers for the execution of trades. This model hails from the days of fixed commission, whereby brokerages had to offer more than simple trade execution to attract buy-side business. However, there were concerns amongst lawmakers that such pricing was effectively equivalent to offering inducements to managers in order that they placed trades with the bank or broker. MiFID II effectively ends this practice by banning inducements, save for 'minor non-monetary benefits'. Generally, research will not be included in this exception.

The FCA has approved this particular regulation and confirmed that it will extend to cover AIFMs.

As such, research must now be priced separately from fees for trade executions. There are a number of ways in which managers might pay for research to ensure that it does not fall foul of the MiFID II rules, including:

- **Profit and Loss Method:** The manager paying itself out of its own resources (the P&L method).
- **Research Payment Account:** Through a research payment account (RPA) controlled by the manager and funded by a pre-agreed research charge to the fund.

The P&L method may in fact not be an option for some smaller managers, with reports suggesting that this will cost around 10 basis points of AuM[31] and could lead to the equivalent of a 4–7% profit reduction.[32]

As such, it seems likely that managers will have to engage with clients at an early stage in the relationship in order to agree a capped research fee to be deposited in the RPA from time to time. Managers will also have to be active in reviewing the nature and quality of the research they receive to ensure that it is useful and comply with transparency and disclosure obligations. Even with an RPA arrangement, research unbundling will push additional burdens on to managers in terms of MiFID II compliance.

I fear that any regulation that restricts access to research and data, is both contrary to the increasingly transparent and immediate world we live in, and negative to consumers and their managers that will not be able to access quality information. It is also negative for public companies, especially the smaller ones, if information thereon is now being restricted.

**Telephone Taping** The FCA removed the exemption for discretionary investment managers to record conversations in relation to portfolio management activity. The FCA has said that this decision was based upon 'our supervisory and enforcement experiences' and that they had particular difficulties relying on sell-side records – i.e. on 'those who may not have been the subject of the investigation'.[33]

MiFID II requires that managers record calls which relate to the 'reception, transmission and execution of client orders'.[34] Not only this, but calls which 'are intended to result in transactions concluded ... even if those conversations or communications do not result in the conclusions of such transactions' must also be recorded.[35]

Whilst managers may have previously had systems to record fixed, landline telephone calls, mobile calls will present particular challenges and it might be that managers have to rely on a policy of banning mobile calls for trading-related calls. Further, managers will have to maintain records of 'electronic communications', which could include a wide variety of potentially messenger services, including Bloomberg mail, SMS, and other instant messaging services. Again, it might be that managers decide to limit trading conversations to a particular medium to ensure compliance.

There is some respite, owing to pressures on the FCA from the PE industry, as the FCA has included an exclusion to the telephone taping provisions for discretionary portfolio management activities in relation to unlisted securities.

**Client Categorisation** The new client categorisation provisions under MiFID II affect managers that deal with local public authorities and municipalities (and their pension schemes). Such clients will no longer be categorised as per se professional clients or eligible counterparties, but instead as retail clients, with the result that they will have increased investor protection under the new regime.

Local authorities will have the opportunity to 'opt-up' to professional client status, subject to passing the qualitative and quantitative tests below:

- **Qualitative Test:** The manager must undertake an adequate assessment of the collective expertise, experience, and knowledge of the client to give reasonable assurance in light of the nature of the transactions or services envisaged that the client is capable of making his own investment decisions and understanding the risks involved.
- **Quantitative Test:** The size of the client's financial instrument portfolio, defined as including cash deposits and financial instruments, exceeds GBP 10 million; and the client has carried out transactions, in significant size, on the relevant market at an average frequency of ten per quarter over the previous four quarters; or the client works or has worked in the financial sector for at least one year in a professional position, which requires knowledge of the transactions or services envisaged; or the client is an 'administering authority' of the Local Government Pension Scheme (LGPS).

In light of the new rules, managers have now had to review their current client categorisation procedures in order to ensure compliance. Further, any current local authority clients should be 'opted-up' if appropriate to professional client status to avoid any additional burdens on the manager.

**Transaction Reporting and LEIs**  The FCA has confirmed that the increased transaction reporting obligations will not apply to AIFMs. However, they will still be applicable to MiFID investment firms. Such firms will have to be aware of the broader scope of reporting obligations that MiFID II implements, which applies to equity and non-equity transactions, including shares, ETFs, bonds, and derivatives.

Further, the obligation to report under MiFID II has also been expanded to apply to financial instruments, which reference other financial instruments that are traded on a trading venue, or references a basket or index of such financial instruments, which are referenced on a trading venue. The report will need to include the legal entity identifiers (LEIs) of the counterparties to the transaction.

An LEI is a 20-digit alphanumeric code, which is generated to identify parties to a transaction. Currently, counterparties have been using LEIs as part of the reporting obligations under EMIR, but MiFID II expands the entities, which require an LEI to a 'decision maker' in relation to a transaction. This includes investment firms, which execute financial instruments on behalf of clients and investment managers acting under a discretionary mandate on behalf of their clients.

## Capital Markets Union

The Capital Markets Union (CMU)[36] is a plan of the EC to 'mobilise capital in Europe'. The plan is to establish a single capital market in the EU where investors can invest and raise funds across borders without hindrance and from a diverse range of sources. The idea is that this will provide businesses with a greater choice of funding at lower costs, offer new opportunities for savers and investors and (hopefully) improve resilience of financial system. The aim is for it to be in place by 2019; however, with Brexit dominating the current agenda it may end up being pushed back to 2021 or beyond.

Indeed, as recently as August 2018 the EC vice-president, Valdis Dombrovskis, pointed out that the goal of implementing the project by 2019 is unlikely to be reached. Several important bits of legislation that form the foundations of the project have been postponed. These include, but are not limited to, the development of an EU-wide pension fund, a cross-border market in covered bonds,[37] and a much simplified process for bankruptcy proceedings. Indeed, only three of the thirteen legislative tests released by the EC since 2014 have been adopted despite it being a signalled as a priority for several member states.[38] A greater concerted effort may be made, however, in light of the UK's departure from the EU, as member states will feel the need to strengthen the financial conditions within the EU to replace the UK as the financial centre.

The CMU project was also started to combat the risk of another financial crisis by putting European savings to a productive use under a more stringent and centralised form of EU-supervision. Moreover, there is the potential to reduce inequality at a macro level by using the savings of individuals from wealthy member states to invest in projects elsewhere within the EU.

**ESMA Supervisory Convergence Standing Committee**    The supervisory convergence standing committee helps with the common supervisory culture amongst NCAs to ensure that each NCA that has adopted EU regulations adopts them consistently.[39] The Committee is what coordinates this task, ensuring that a level playing field is not only implemented but also maintained through correct supervision between member states. The implementation is not done through a one-size-fits-all, however, the idea is for NCAs to take an adequately similar approach to upcoming risks in order to achieve comparable regulatory results.

## RISK

Well 'Risk' could be a whole book, not a short section. However, I will attempt to summarise the main areas.

**Banks**    Different types of risk are identified by banks, including credit risk, market risk, liquidity risk, operational risk, and systematic risk. These types of risk are well understood within the banking sector, because risk is a big deal for banks (especially post-crisis). Banks have developed sophisticated risk departments and they continue to grow.

**Asset Management**    Risk is less developed in asset management than in banks. That said, risk officers/departments are more advanced in hedge fund management than in PE or RE. This would be largely because hedge managers have traditionally come from the banks.

Asset managers are now building larger risk functionality. A risk officer and their team have to understand many specific, as well as more generalised macro, strategy, and investment risks.

I will break this section down into four categories of risk, which I will be calling (1) strategic risk; (2) risk for fund investors; (3) risk for managers in their portfolio and assets; and (4) manager operational risks.

## (1) Strategic risk

### Strategic or macro

This is more out of the hands of managers. However, this is an area that must be monitored closely. Strategic risks can be 'out there' or 'in there'. Outside a portfolio per se, such as geo-political shifts or climate change or in a portfolio, such as a specific industry undergoing structural changes.

### Market risks

Clearly listed or market investments can be hit by the 'market'. This means that political, environmental (storms and 'Beasts from the East' for example), and social developments can have major impacts on returns. Volatile markets, or large surges or dips, can lead to significant risks to portfolio weightings and returns.

## (2) Risk for fund investors

### Strategic risk

This covers the risk inherent in investing, including covering capital at risk, fund, liquidity, and market risks.[40]

### Market risk (unrealised values)

This category poses conceptual issues especially in the illiquid classes. Many managers report as net asset value (NAV) on a quarterly basis. An alternative way of valuing an asset could be to take the present value of the predicted future cash flows. In a listed market, liquidity and the constant buying and selling of assets usually force these two valuation methods to give close figures. In illiquids, the figures these valuation methods produce divergence. This makes it difficult to assess how market fluctuations impact the assets. It is often the case that the impact of market events is not felt by the underlying assets until the fund exits the assets and seeks to realise its value. For example, following the financial crisis, seasoned PE investors, who typically used distributions from older vintage funds to fund their capital calls in younger funds, found themselves short of liquidity as distributions dried up. 'Over commitment' was caught short. This and the double fee squeeze devastated the fund of funds model in the financial crisis. In addition, the NAVs of the underlying assets were only gradually adjusted in the face of the rapid deterioration of their assets performance, leading to a huge disparity in sellers' and buyers' expectations in the secondaries market.

### Funding risk

The typical structure of PE, RE, and credit funds, is such that investors make a commitment to pay a certain amount into the fund on day one, but the commitment is not drawn down by the manager in one tranche. Over the fundraising phase of the fund, the manager calls on the investors to make payments of segments of their committed capital. The fundraising phase can last for a number of years and often overlaps with the investment phase, during which the manager starts investing investors' capital into new deals. As an investor does not need to provide the entire committed capital upfront, this capital can be placed into other investments or assets. This cash management strategy carries the risk that the investors will overcommit themselves across their portfolio, be unable to liquidate other assets quickly enough, or be exposed to market downturns which lead to them being unable to pay their capital calls to the fund when due. This represents the funding risk – the risk of a default.

The funding risk that the investors carry also affects managers. If an investor, or multiple investors, cannot meet their commitments to the fund, the managers may be unable to invest in certain opportunities. This creates a risk to all investors in that fund. Whilst heavy penalties can be levied against investors, the problem still arises that managers may have to deal with a hole in their anticipated funding, which is a situation best avoided. The question remains how managers can ensure that LPs do not overcommit themselves to the point where capital calls are missed.

## Liquidity risk

Especially for illiquids like PE, RE and credit, the lead time to realisation is longer than that in hedge funds for example, where securities are being traded. As such, LPs are locked in for the life of the fund.

A secondary market for investor fund interests has developed in an attempt to introduce some liquidity into the industry. The limited number of secondaries participants, and the difficulties with pricing PE holdings means that quarterly NAV is often used to price a holding and a discount applied when it comes to selling. As a result, the secondaries market does not always allow an investor to 'cash out' as such.

This risk does not materially affect managers in the same way as funding risk might. However, it is important to note that these risks do not operate individually in a vacuum. If an investor is overcommitted across their portfolio, the liquidity risk affects the investor's ability to meet capital calls by liquidating assets. This in turn causes the funding risk to materialise for a manager. In short, if an investor runs an investment strategy that places a high percentage of their portfolio in illiquid asset classes, such as PE, the liquidity risk is such that it makes it more likely that the funding risk materialises.

## Capital risk (realised values)

Capital risk is exactly what it says on the tin – the risk that an investor might lose, or at least not recover, the value of their invested capital over the lifetime of a fund. A further consideration could be capital risks relationship with liquidity risk, as there is the potential that liquidity constraints can result in an investor losing their committed capital. Managers retain the right to force an LP to sell at the wrong time if the LP defaults.

Arguably, the manager has the most impact and level of direct control over the capital risk that an investor takes on. Manager performance is an important factor in realising profit on an underlying investment through operational development of the company. The ability of a manager to identify a potential investment, analyse and improve the company's strategy and exit an investment at the right time has a large impact on an investor's capital risk. It is for this reason that manager reputation and past performance is so important to LPs investing in a fund.

However, as good as a manager is at the above, capital risk will always be partly influenced by external factors outside of the manager's control. Factors such as interest rates and refinancing terms can affect a manager's ability to improve the operations of an investment as it was envisaged or may affect the value of the company and the equity the manager has invested. Future market conditions might be such that, although the manager has added significant value to the company, a buyer cannot be found unless a discount is applied. Exit conditions such as these affect the capital risk that accrues to investors.

**(3) Risk to portfolios and assets** Managers' incentives to implement good risk-management practices are a function of a number of fund characteristics:

## Leverage

Higher borrowing increases the fund's exposure to changes in asset values. Large losses can lead to margin calls from lenders and redemptions from investors, both of which can require the manager to liquidate the portfolio at low prices. In addition, as the portfolio company level, large leverage can lead to 'wipe-outs' or covenant resets and equity cures.

## Market risk

The risk of losses in the market prices of the portfolio companies held by a fund. Market risk is captured by using a value-at-risk (VaR) approach, which has become the standard measure used by financial analysts to quantify this risk. Generally, VaR is defined as the maximum potential loss in value of a portfolio of financial instruments with a given probability over a certain horizon. In other words, it is a number indicating how much a financial institution can lose with a given probability over a given time horizon.

In PE, RE, and private debt funds, the VaR measure is based on the assumption that an investor can at any time sell their position in the fund at the fund's current NAV. In reality, stakes in PE funds are highly illiquid and can typically only be sold at some discount on the secondary PE markets. In order to account for this form of liquidity risk, the VaR calculation can be extended to a liquidity-adjusted VaR (LVaR). A comparison between the simulated VaR and LVaR measures highlights that the effects of illiquidity on the investor's risk exposure over the life of a fund can be substantial. However, the numerical results also show that illiquidity only increases the investor's risk exposure if the time horizon under consideration is shorter than the fund's total remaining lifetime, as liquidity risk is fully resolved with the final liquidation of a fund.

## Liquidity of the portfolio

The strategy and portfolio instruments traded must be in line with the manager's liquidity parameters and, more broadly, with the fund's investor-redemption or fund exit terms. For hedge or open-ended funds, there are often gates and lock-ins to protect ongoing investors from the adverse valuation effect of a forced selling of positions in the market.

## Fund size

Can a manager fund suitable investments, and within the time constraints expected from their funds?

## Alignment of interest

Managers with a substantial portion of their liquid net worth invested in their funds are likely more risk-averse. This can be called alignment, or a risk.

## Reputation

Managers of established managers want to protect reputations.

## Traditional risk-management tools

This includes mean-variance analysis, beta and the various iterations of VaR. However, VaR does not always help so much for hedge or PE strategies which are less linear and relatively uncorrelated with equity market indices. Risks can also be idiosyncratic and some strategies target relative value relationships that are complex.

## Concentration

A concentrated portfolio of securities could pose a liquidity risk to the portfolio. Hedging techniques, if any, should be examined. Does the manager hedge at the portfolio level and/or the individual position level? What types of exposures does the portfolio face: interest rate, credit, currency, event, or liquidity risk?

## Currency

Should the manager hedge the currency risk fully, partially, or not at all?

## Stress testing

To what extent is the fund's portfolio tested? What are the scenarios and exposures tested, and are they realistic?

## Measuring Risk

Reviewing the fund's position data on a regular basis. Risk management aims to eliminate – or at least partly mitigate – the potential tail risk events.

## Other risk tools

Risk measures are often developed further by using Monte Carlo simulations. For PE funds, patterns in VaR dynamics show for example that VaR initially rises sharply up to some fixed time horizon, but then peaks and decreases to zero over the fund's lifetime. This behaviour is consistent with the typical life cycle of PE funds. As the fund gradually draws down capital and builds up the investment portfolio, the investor's risk exposure increases markedly. After the maximum level has been reached, the fixed-horizon VaR decays rapidly toward zero as capital distributions of the fund decrease the investor's risk exposure stepwise.

**(4) Operational Risks**   Operational risks are those which fund managers face day-to-day as a result of running a business, and includes (amongst others) technological, third-party, reputational, cyber, and compliance risk. Operational risk would also include the risk of regulatory upheaval, the type of which is covered earlier in this chapter.[41]

## Technological risk

This category does not merely cover information security, but is broader and, in particular, covers the risk that managers face in being left behind technologically. This may manifest itself in managers not being able to keep speed with their competitors as they have not proactively invested in their own technological systems. It may, perhaps more tangentially, mean that managers, depending on their investment strategy, fail to spot opportunities in the high-growth technology industry or those companies where technology has a large impact. There could be a risk of missing upside, in addition to the risk of realising a loss.

The potential downsides associated with technological risk are more prevalent following the introduction of the GDPR. Managers are at risk of being exposed to far greater fines for data breaches, whether they be as a result of technological or cyber risk.

Under GDPR, fund managers are likely to have to appoint a person as their data protection officer. This allows for real-time identification and response to any issues that might arise.

## Third-party and reputational risk

This risk covers themselves, as well as the service providers that fund managers might typically outsource to, as well as the companies in which managers invest.

Risk to the manager brand – or returns – risks the ability to raise further funds, find good deals, or stay in business.

Risks also apply if a manager outsources some functions, including to reduce costs, utilise specific expertise, and to reduce the ever-increasing regulatory burden. However, third party arrangements bring with them the risk that those third parties might not be operating to the same standards as the manager. Further, the use of a third party to undertake certain operational activities does not absolve the manager of overall responsibility for those activities. Again, a pertinent example is in the context of the GDPR. Where a manager outsources their IT functionality to a third party provider, that third party must have a GDPR compliant system. If they do not, even if the manager does, the manager could be liable to hefty fines and potential lawsuits from their end clients. It is for the manager to ensure that investors' personal information is kept safe.

## Cyber risk

Where technology risk could be described as a 'hardware' risk, cyber risk is very much a 'software' risk. Firms must ensure that they have appropriate cybersecurity measures in place and governance structures to allow the firm to react efficiently to any cybersecurity breach.

One of the first steps in addressing any cyber risk is to undertake a data mapping process, whereby all of the sensitive data held by a manager is located and any security measures identified. Once the data is located, any potential weaknesses and the cybersecurity framework can be identified and steps taken to rectify this. It is important to identify any particularly sensitive sources of data, whether personally or commercially, and focus on ensuring that these are secure before attempting to overhaul any security system.

Beyond data mapping, managers can take precautionary measures to prevent these attacks, by identifying possible threats. Some firms remain unaware of such threats and may not even realise that their security has been breached, requiring them to take a longer time to build up their security mechanism or to react to the threat. Indeed, often these attacks are based on the premise that the victim is unaware they are being targeted. A high-profile example being the 2016 presidential election in America. The Democratic National Committee (DNC) was targeted by a variety of cyber weapons, but the innocuous phishing e-mail addressed 'Best, the Gmail Team' convinced one employee to reply. This resulted in free rein being granted to hackers who were attempting to influence the election's outcome. From a security perspective, it is clear that more needs to be done to stay ahead of the game so that further developments in technology do not lead to greater vulnerability. From a financial perspective, research shows that cybercrime costs organisations approximately USD 450 billion a year, with an estimated 200 000 attacks worldwide.[42] Despite these colossal figures, there are some routine processes that firms can employ to prevent attacks.

Firms should take reasonable steps to protect their client's sensitive information. This can be achieved through employing the following methods:

■ **Passwords:** Creating strong passwords and changing them frequently (i.e. every three months). According to a study, only 1 in 7 companies are using strong passwords.[43]

- **Training:** Providing employees with cybersecurity training and informing them of good cyber hygiene practices.
- **Penetration Testing:** Phishing emails containing attachments with malware and viruses are the common methods used by hackers, as seen in the German steel plant hack. Therefore, it is of upmost importance that the businesses send out fake phishing emails to their employees as part of the cybersecurity training process. Other than this, if the IT team detects any phishing email, they should immediately inform all employees the details of the email with a warning message not to open the phishing email.
- **Encrypting:** Asset managers should make sure that all important documents are security protected, ensuring that there are no large scale downloads or copying of data.
- **Log Out:** Ensure that all work computers are automatically logged off after 10–15 minutes of inactivity.
- **Get it right:** Employees should be educated in cybersecurity to the extent that they can go home and protect their personal data and devices.
- **Software:** Ensuring that the cybersecurity software is up to date.
- **Internal Threat:** Most firms are more concerned about internal threats rather than external threats, as it may be comparatively easier for an employee to leak sensitive information. Therefore, it is important that client information is only accessed by authorised users, i.e. only those people who need the information.
- **Planning:** Despite it occurring randomly, firms should ideally be prepared for these attacks so that they can immediately start putting procedures in place without further delay. This will help minimise the damage done. If left too long then it may cause more harm to firm, its reputation and the business may be fined according to the GDPR.

## Compliance risk

Regulatory scrutiny of funds is increasing. This can be seen through the statement of ESMA and the EC discussed above, and is unlikely to slow down. Not only this, but there is an increasing regulatory burden on funds, with more rules to comply with.

As a result, managing a fund's exposure to regulation is important, especially in light of the proposed changes to the asset management regulatory landscape. It is advisable for funds to appoint a compliance officer to ensure that that this is upheld.

## SOME CONCLUSIONS

**Platforms** I can see increasing use of platforms. Investors would prefer to see the use of industry-strength platforms rather than managers doing it badly themselves. Using a platform does not make the manager look young, small, or stupid. Not using a platform when you really should as you do not have the skills or resources in-house, makes you look young, small, and stupid, or just risky.

**Compliance** Never has the role of compliance and risk been more important than today. The increase in technological, third-party and cyber risk intensifies the need for the correct structures and people to be in place. Having the right technical knowledge, and keeping up with it, is critical. The growing utility of data for managers also brings with it new challenges under GDPR and other regulation that both protects and requires information to be shared (e.g. KYC, AML, and anti-bribery). Regulation is growing and bound to continue to do so.

Being ready for regulatory changes and having a proactive culture is vital pursuing and maintaining comprehensive compliance and risk systems. Being reactive will not suffice in a rapidly changing regulatory landscape. By giving your firm time and putting the right people and processes in place, you are de-risking both yourself and your investors. The days of tossing a coin to see who will be compliance officer that week or finding a retired lawyer or accountant to 'cover the back office' doesn't work anymore (if it ever did). Three to four full-time people in compliance and risk is a bare minimum I would say.

From both a regulatory and a taxation perspective, substance is important. Having some friendly farmer as your Channel Islands representative does not (again, if it ever did) cut it. Both front and back offices need real trained professionals that work for you on the ground or otherwise a highly skilled large professional umbrella can be used.

From a UK (and EU) perspective, Brexit poses fundamental risk and compliance issues that asset managers and investors need to be prepared for, including the potential loss of passporting and delegation capabilities.

Many of these risks pose new challenges to managers but these can be mitigated with proper processes and strong compliance structures.

# ENDNOTES

1. www.fca.org.uk/news/speeches/future-city
2. https://uk.reuters.com/article/uk-britain-eu-finance/eu-and-boe-clash-over-fate-of-financial-contracts-after-brexit-idUKKBN1K11MX
3. www.insurancejournal.com/news/international/2018/07/12/494918.htm
4. www.fca.org.uk/news/speeches/future-city
5. Treasury legislation implemented MifiD II through the following statutory instruments: Financial Services and Markets Act 2000 (Markets in Financial Instruments) Regulations 2017 ('MiFI regulations'), SI 2017/701, The Data Reporting Services Regulations 2017 ('DRS regulations'), SI 2017/699 and Financial Services and Markets Act 2000 (Regulated Activities) (Amendment) Order 2017 ('RAO Amendment Order'), SI 2017/488.
6. www.ft.com/content/8c7e9ef0-996e-11e8-88de-49c908b1f264
7. Ibid.
8. www.fnlondon.com/articles/do-not-expect-a-brexit-bonfire-of-regulation-20181116
9. Ibid.
10. https://threatpost.com/gdprs-first-150-days-impact-on-the-u-s/138739/
11. https://www.caprivacy.org/
12. https://threatpost.com/gdprs-first-150-days-impact-on-the-u-s/138739/
13. https://edition.cnn.com/2017/12/14/politics/trump-deregulation-in-gifs/index.html
14. https://www.marketwatch.com/story/cutting-red-tape-isnt-as-positive-or-as-easy-as-trump-says-2018-02-01
15. https://www.telegraph.co.uk/news/2017/01/24/donald-trump-sets-alight-bonfire-waste-red-tape-first-full-day/
16. https://money.cnn.com/2018/06/05/news/economy/trump-executive-order-red-tape/index.html
17. www.ecb.europa.eu/press/key/date/2017/html/ecb.sp171109.en.html
18. www.bbc.co.uk/news/business-46552147
19. Article 20 of the AIFMD and section 8 of AIFMD Delegated Regulation expressly allow managers to utilise the delegation model.
20. 2015 data from Asset Management in Europe, 9th Edition, EFAMA, May 2017.
21. See www.independent.co.uk/news/business/news/brexit-latest-news-london-fund-management-business-eu-guidance-1-trillion-euros-a7862266.html

22. Ibid.
23. http://ted.europa.eu/TED/notice/udl?uri=TED:NOTICE:113303-2017:TEXT:EN:HTML
24. https://ec.europa.eu/info/sites/info/files/business_economy_euro/banking_and_finance/documents/190110-aifmd-operation-report_en.pdf
25. www.pwc.com/gx/en/financial-services/assets/basel-iv-big-bang.pdf
26. www.itgovernance.eu/blog/en/portuguese-hospital-appeals-gdpr-fine
27. www.theregister.co.uk/2018/11/16/microsoft_gdpr/
28. www.zdnet.com/article/facebook-could-face-billions-in-fines-under-gdpr-over-latest-data-breach/
29. www.information-age.com/data-breaches-fine-123475976/
30. https://threatpost.com/gdprs-first-150-days-impact-on-the-u-s/138739/
31. Christopher Dearie, 'Mind iF I Don't, too?'
32. Oliver Wyman (2017)
33. Financial Conduct Authority (2017)
34. Markets in Financial Instruments Directive II [2014] OJ 2 173/397
35. Ibid.
36. https://ec.europa.eu/info/business-economy-euro/growth-and-investment/capital-markets-union/what-capital-markets-union_en
37. www.ft.com/content/937c4388-90a4-11e8-bb8f-a6a2f7bca546
38. Ibid.
39. Review Supervisory Convergence Work Programme 2017.
40. BVCA – Risk in Private Equity, New insights into the risk of a portfolio of private equity funds (October 2015).
41. KPMG – Safeguarding private equity firms: Six key risk management strategies to head off trouble (March 2017). https://assets.kpmg/content/dam/kpmg/us/pdf/2017/03/us-private-equity-safeguarding-private-equity-firms.pdf
42. Matthew Martindale, 'The Evolving Cyber Threat For Asset Managers'. https://home.kpmg/uk/en/home/insights/2018/01/the-evolving-cyber-threat-for-asset-managers.html
43. '5 Tips To Protect Your Organisation From A Cyber Security Attack'. https://cbscreening.co.uk/news/post/5-tips-to-protect-your-organisation-from-a-cyber-security-attack/

# CHAPTER 11

# Taxation

*Every tax ought to be so contrived as both to take out and to keep out of the pockets of the people as little as possible, over and above what it brings into the public treasury of the state.*

– Adam Smith, *Wealth of Nations*

This chapter provides an overview of the key tax considerations for asset managers seeking to establish or currently operating an investment management business in the UK or US, with a commentary on the EU and offshore jurisdictions.

The core revenue stream for an asset manager is its management fees, although its executives typically also share in the profits of the investments managed through a performance element such as a performance fee (typical for hedge fund managers) or carried interest (in the case of PE-type funds). It is important for asset managers to optimise tax treatment of these fees and incentives. Investors want as much growth as possible, and both asset managers and their executives need to be suitably incentivised to deliver such growth. In addition to fees, managers will sometimes also seek to sell stakes in their management group or indeed list their management companies to raise capital. Tax plays a key part in all of this.

One trend I have seen affect management group structures – particularly those operating management entities in different jurisdictions – is the global move toward 'economic reality' or 'substance' requirements when it comes to allocating operating cost and profit. This development has been driven to a significant degree by the OECD – with prominent input from the UK.

## UK

The UK has the second largest asset management industry in the world – only the US is bigger. A key factor in this development has been the commercial and regulatory environment in the UK – particularly London. However, alongside these factors, the tax regime has also played a major part in the UK's success. One important contributor is the so-called 'non-dom regime' which allows UK tax residents who are domiciled outside the UK (i.e. broadly, who come to live in the UK from abroad) to avoid paying tax on all non-UK source income so long as the monies are kept outside the UK. Whilst HMRC has significantly reduced the ambit of the non-dom regime, it remains available for non-UK domiciled managers during their first 15 years of residence in the UK.

Looking specifically at the tax regime for fund managers, two tax concessions have played a significant role.

The first is the investment manager exemption (IME), which has for a long time encouraged hedge fund managers to base themselves in the UK. The IME enables offshore trading funds (hedge funds) to use a UK-based investment manager, that takes all the investment decisions for the fund in the UK without the risk of the fund or its non-UK investors being subject to UK tax themselves. Under normal OECD 'permanent establishment' principles, this is often not possible because a manager entering into trades on behalf of an offshore fund will create a taxable permanent establishment of the fund where the manager is based. This is the reason why hedge funds never took off in Germany (apart from the general hostility towards them).

In order to qualify for the IME, the manager must meet the following conditions:

- **Investment Management Business:** The business undertaken by the UK-based manager on behalf of the non-UK investors must be investment management services.
- **Ordinary Course of Business:** The transactions must be undertaken in the ordinary course of business.
- **Dealing at Arm's Length:** The dealings between the UK-based manager and the non-UK investor(s) must be carried on as independent businesses dealing with one another at arm's length. One example where HMRC believes dealings at arm's length to be satisfied requires that the services provided by the investment manager to the non-UK investor do not make up more than 70% of the investment manager's business. Start-up managers have an 18-month period during which to satisfy this test.
- **20% Rule:** The UK-based manager (and any persons connected with them) must not be entitled to more than 20% of the fund's income.
- **Receipt of Customary Remuneration:** The UK-based manager must receive remuneration for the provision of the investment management services that is not less than is customary for that class of business.

Second, in 1987 HMRC (the UK tax authority, then called 'Inland Revenue') and the British Venture Capital Association (BVCA) agreed a beneficial tax regime for the taxation of carried interest held by managers of PE funds (the '1987 MOU').[1] Principally, the 1987 MOU provided that PE fund managers who receive carried interest in the fund are not taxable on receipt of the carried interest and any gain when the carry is paid out is taxed as capital gain, not income. (Capital gains are taxed more favourably than income.)

The IME and the 1987 MOU (as supplemented in 2013) still form the basis for the taxation of hedge fund and PE managers, although HMRC have legislated extensively in the last few years so that the landscape has become considerably more complex to navigate.

### Taxation of the Investment Manager: Company or LLP

One of the first decisions that an asset manager seeking to establish a UK management business must take is to decide whether to establish the UK management operations as a UK limited liability company or a UK LLP. Whilst there are important operational considerations (for example, an LLP offers great flexibility for its partners – termed 'members' – to vary income and capital shares), in practice, tax is often the key factor in deciding which entity is better suited to a particular manager.

Looking at some of the commercial factors first, companies and LLPs both have legal personality, which means that they are legally separate from their members (members being shareholders in the case of a company and partners in the case of an LLP). Both companies and LLPs can enter into contracts and hold assets in their own name, sue and be sued, and, importantly, confer limited liability status on its members so that they are not liable for its actions (save for certain strict liability matters and circumstances where, for example, authority is exceeded). Companies are formed usually when the manager believes they can create a valuable, sell-able operating entity. LLPs usually when the management vehicle is merely perceived as cashflows.

**Taxable Entity vs. Tax Transparency** A key distinction between companies and LLPs is their tax treatment. Companies are taxable, whereas LLPs are tax transparent.

As taxable entities, companies pay UK corporation tax on their profits at 19% (presently – the rate is scheduled to go down to 17% in April 2020, although in the current volatile political environment it is difficult to predict whether the reduction will happen). Salary and bonus payments to employees and directors are generally taxable to the individuals and tax deductible for the company. Specifically, any salary and bonus paid by a company to its employees, officers, or directors are subject to income tax and national insurance contributions (NICs) in the hands of such employees, officers, or directors at up to 45% income tax and 2% NICs (the rates depend on the individual's applicable tax band). The tax is normally collected by the company via Pay As You Earn (PAYE), the UK's employment payroll tax system. In addition to the personal income tax and employee's NICs liability, the employer is subject to an employer's national insurance charge at 13.8%. To illustrate, a salary or bonus payment of GBP 100 to an employee therefore costs the company GBP 113.80 (although the employer's NICs are deductible, so if the company is profitable, the cost is only around GBP 112). The imposition of the 13.8% employer's NICs is often a key factor in deciding whether to use a company or LLP as management vehicle (the 13.8% do not apply to payments of partner profit, as discussed later).

Any surplus profit earned by the manager can be kept in the company, reinvested in the fund or extracted via dividends. Dividends are taxable to shareholders and can only be paid after the company profit has been taxed at the corporation tax rate – so that the effective rate for dividends includes the corporation tax payable by the company declaring the dividend and the dividend tax for shareholders. The rate of tax an individual must pay on dividends varies depending on the income band that the individual is within. At the time of writing, individuals within the additional rate of tax (earning GBP 150 000 and above) are subject to 38.1% tax on dividends. Combined with the 19% corporation tax that companies will have suffered on the profits out of which the dividend is paid, the combined corporation and dividend tax paid on profit of a company including when it reaches the hands of an additional rate shareholder by way of a dividend is effectively 49.86%. For every GBP 100 of profit a company makes, additional rate shareholders will therefore receive GBP 50.14 if distributed by way of a dividend.[2] However, UK corporate shareholders are generally exempt from tax on dividends paid by UK companies. Use of a personal investment company is therefore sometimes an attractive option for managers when extracting profit.

With certain limited exceptions,[3] LLPs are not subject to tax themselves. Instead, LLPs are normally transparent for UK income, capital gains, and corporation tax purposes. Generally, each member of the LLP is therefore treated as if he or she has personally received any income or capital gains realised by the LLP in proportion to his or her profit share in the LLP.

An individual member of an LLP is subject to income tax on their share of profits, whilst a corporate member of an LLP is subject to corporation tax on its share of LLP profits. This is the case regardless of whether or not that profit share is actually distributed.

Due to the tax transparency, profits realised by an LLP are only subject to a single layer of taxation: corporation tax in the case of a corporate member (presently 19%), and the individual marginal income tax and NIC rate for individual members (of up to 45% and 2% respectively), leading to an aggregate maximum tax charge of 47% for partnership profit. The allocation of these profits and losses is normally calculated in accordance with the profit sharing arrangements detailed in the constitutional documents of the LLP – typically the LLP agreement.

As a body corporate, the LLP can also have employees (and officers/directors) who are taxed in the same way as employees and officers/directors of companies.

**Which Entity to Choose**  In practice, the key distinction between LLPs and companies is that individual members of an LLP are only subject to personal income tax and NICs. Unlike for employees (but subject to the anti-avoidance provisions discussed below), the 13.8% employer's NICs are not applicable to LLP profit distributions to members. This feature makes the LLP particularly attractive for investment management businesses that are expecting significant levels of income distributions to its members as they will want to access the 47% tax rate. However, LLPs are subject to certain anti-avoidance laws discussed below.

A UK company potentially offers similar tax efficiency to an LLP to the extent earnings are not paid out by way of salary but by way of dividend – contrasting 49.86% against 47%. This will, however, only work for those individuals who are shareholders of the company – in practice, this is generally only a small number of individuals. It should also be noted that there are restrictions under English law on the payment of dividends, such as the requirements for distributable reserves to be available. Payments of salary or bonus to employees, officers, and directors attract the 13.8% employer's NICs which are not applicable to profit distributions for LLP members.

Since the recent changes, and in particular the mixed member rules described below were enacted, managers who want to reinvest their profit, rather than take it out, prefer companies as management vehicles.

**Working Capital and Reinvestment**  A significant benefit of companies lies in the ability to create working capital at the 19% corporation tax rate. Thus, to the extent that a company has 'excess' profits (i.e. earnings not distributed to UK resident employee shareholders) these can be stored up within the company at a tax cost of only 19% with further tax being deferred until the company declares a dividend or pays salaries or bonuses to such UK resident individuals. Equally, such excess profits can be reinvested in the fund.

By contrast, the LLP is likely to be the more attractive vehicle where substantial current year income is envisaged to be paid out to UK resident taxpayers – i.e. resulting in 45% income tax rate and 2% partner NICs (i.e. a total of 47%) – compared to the combined corporation tax and dividend rates of 49.86% for corporate structures, and – crucially – the 13.8% employer's NICs that apply to salary and bonus payments for employees, officers, and directors. Over the last 15 years, I have seen many investment management businesses move away from a company model towards the LLP route due to the lower NICs obligations. However, more recently the mixed member rules below have created a reverse trend.

Due to perceived abuse, HMRC enacted a raft of anti-avoidance rules, which means that UK-based managers now need to navigate the tax environment with considerable care.

**LLP – Salaried Member Rules** In certain circumstances, an individual member of an LLP can be considered an employee of the LLP for tax purposes, notwithstanding his or her status as a partner under partnership law and in particular the Limited Liability Partnership Act 2000.

As mentioned above, a principal benefit of LLP membership was the absence of the 13.8% employer's NICs that were payable on salaries and bonuses of employees and directors. This different tax treatment led to the wide take-up of LLP member status in circumstances where individual members were not regarded by HMRC as true 'partners' of a business – the argument being that, but for the NIC saving, such individuals would not have been appointed as 'partners' and are really only partners in name, rather than genuine co-owners of the business. There were circumstances where HMRC had a point – but the law was clear and firms were within their right to establish themselves as LLPs.

Thus, before April 2014, individual members of an LLP could only be treated as employees of an LLP if they would have been treated as an employee under general partnership law in the same circumstances (member status was, in fact, almost automatic – if the individual was a partner under the LLP agreement and registered as such with Companies House, his status was secure). The possibility of a member also being treated as an employee of an LLP was therefore remote.

HMRC labelled these tax-driven relationships as 'disguised employment',[4] and in April 2014, introduced complex anti-avoidance legislation deeming individual LLP members to be salaried members (essentially employees) unless certain conditions are satisfied. Broadly, the salaried member rules apply to treat members as employees who do not exercise 'significant influence' over the LLP (as specified by HMRC guidance), have high levels of predetermined income from the LLP (generally, at least 80% of their compensation is fixed), or whose capital contribution to the LLP is less than 25% of their 'disguised salary'.

The principal effect of the salaried member rules is to treat such members for tax purposes as employees or 'salaried members', rather than genuine partners, adding the 13.8% employer's NICs on the relevant member's profit allocations and generally applying employment income principles. And under the law of unintended consequences, carried interest became an employment related security where the salaried member rules applied (see further below).

Generally, the salaried member rules are unlikely to apply to LLPs with a small number of members, or the founding members of an LLP but this will need to be considered with respect to each member to ensure that the individual is indeed recognised as a partner for tax purposes.

As it is not common for fund managers other than the founders to provide significant levels of capital, and base compensation is fixed, the most contentious test has become the 'significant influence' condition. The purpose of the rules is to determine which individuals 'have a real say in the business' – an inherently nebulous question, in my view. For example, HMRC guidance provides that a key portfolio manager will have significant influence – how is this measured? Unsurprisingly, the salaried member rules caused friction between HMRC and the investment management industry in recent years following the opening of enquiries by HMRC into asset managers where individual LLP members were relying on HMRC guidance that such members were exercising 'significant influence' by being, for example, members of the manager's executive committee. One disputed question was the number of individuals who could exercise significant influence.

The position is not completely clear and careful structuring is required.

**LLP – Mixed Membership Rules** Until the 'mixed member rules' were introduced in 2014, it was common for LLPs with 'mixed memberships' (i.e. LLPs with both corporate and individual members) to apportion annual profit between individual and corporate members to benefit from the differential in personal and corporation tax rates. For example, individual members could extract LLP profit at personal income tax rates, whilst retained profit could be allocated to corporate members and taxed at the lower corporation tax rate (thereby maximising the amount of profit available for reinvestment).

The 'mixed member' rules were introduced to counter tax avoidance schemes involving individual and corporate partnership members where planning went one step further and individual partners were able to extract profit allocated to corporate members themselves without paying further tax, thereby effectively extracting income profit at the corporation tax rates. Rather than countering the perceived abuse, HMRC reacted by disallowing profit allocations to corporate members in a wide set of circumstances. The new rules reallocate the distribution of profits of mixed membership partnerships for tax purposes where individual partners are allocated less profit by the LLP than the legislation determines has been earned through their efforts. What this means in practice is that, where an individual is a personal member of an LLP and his efforts lead to profit being earned, then such profit will be taxed at the individual tax rates, even where part or all of such income is allocated to a corporate member. As a result, any allocation of LLP profit to corporate members has to represent an arm's length return on the corporate member's investment (or other contribution) to the LLP in order for such profit to be taxed at the corporation tax rate. This would be the case where the corporate member provided working capital, and receives some allocation of profit in return for his capital contribution. However, any profit earned by an individual member's contributions will now otherwise need to be taken out at the personal income tax rates.

The introduction of the mixed member rules thus created a significant tax inefficiency of LLPs in respect of reinvestment of profit – except where an arm's length amount is properly allocable to a corporate member, all profit must be taxed at the higher income tax rates of present 47% – leaving a comparatively small amount of net profit for reinvestment only.

### Reinvestment into Business or Funds

As mentioned previously, the mixed member rules opened up the choice of management vehicles which UK-based investment managers utilise. Asset managers do not always wish to extract earnings from their management entity immediately. They may prefer to reinvest earnings into the management entity to spur growth, or a fund that the management entity manages, for example, which is typical for PE managers. By reinvesting into a fund it manages, managers demonstrate commitment to their investment strategy by having (or increasing) 'skin in the game'. In fact, our research at MJ Hudson[5] suggests that the majority of PE managers account for between 2% and 2.99% of total committed capital in the funds that they manage[6] – although a larger proportion will normally have been committed at launch.

The choice of management vehicle has a significant bearing on the amount of net profit that is available for reinvestment into the management business of the fund. See the example below, which shows the different levels of tax cost for companies and LLPs following GBP 1 million of gross (pre-tax) profit. For the purposes of this demonstration, it is assumed that members of an LLP are individuals and they are additional rate taxpayers with an effective tax rate of 47%.

**Tax on reinvestment comparison**

| Company | Corporation tax @ 19% | Net reinvestment |
|---|---|---|
| GBP 1 million reinvestment | GBP 190 000 | GBP 810 000 |

| LLP | Income tax and NICs @ 47% | Net reinvestment |
|---|---|---|
| GBP 1 million reinvestment | GBP 470 000 | GBP 530 000 |

Therefore, a manager intending to reinvest net earnings would normally prefer to use a company, rather than an LLP as a UK management vehicle. The amount of profit available to reinvest is almost 53% higher for a company than would be available for an individual LLP member, thus being the more tax efficient vehicle in such circumstances. What this means in practice is that a manager must decide at the outset whether his or her preferred fee strategy is optimum income tax for profit payments (LLP) or profit reinvestment (company).

## Executive Incentivisation

The tax treatment of performance fees and carried interest – the two principal management incentives for sharing in PE and hedge fund's profit – differs fundamentally.

**Performance Fees**   Performance fees, payable primarily by hedge funds, are typically payable annually where the fund's returns available to investors are above agreed performance levels. The standard performance fee has historically been 20% of the fund's profit above watermark, although this can vary.[7]

As the name suggests, the performance fee is a 'fee' – payable in return for investment management or advisory services provided to the fund. As such, it is normally payable to the manager and will constitute income which is liable to corporation tax or income tax – depending on whether the recipient is a management company or the individual member of an LLP. Either way, income treatment is generally accepted. Where the manager receives performance fees annually, it is difficult to treat such fees as anything other than income for tax purposes.

Where a management group comprises non-UK management vehicles with genuine local operations (for example, local personnel, offices, etc.), it may be possible to apply a fee profit split between the different management vehicles – so that not all income is taxable in the UK. This can be helpful for UK managers that are non-UK domiciled and able to benefit from the remittance basis of taxation. However, the classic Cayman offshore manager without genuine local substance is unlikely to be helpful in this regard (there may be other benefits).

**Carried Interest – A Hot Topic**   Senior executives of PE funds are normally awarded carried interest to incentivise them. Carried interest is essentially a share of profits generated from the fund's investments (typically 20%).[8]

Carry arrangements are reasonably standard but can nonetheless be complex. For example, it is common for asset managers to place limits on when carried interest vests in executives. Also, executives are typically unable to retain carried interest if they leave their position in 'bad leaver' circumstances.

Under the 1987 memorandum of understanding (MOU), carried interest holders received the carried interest free of tax and paid capital gains tax on carry gains (this was derived from the capital nature of the investments). The treatment followed the general principle that partners in a partnership are for tax purposes considered to be notionally carrying on the trade of the partnership. Therefore, if the partnership receives profit of a capital nature, then the partners' receipt of such profit is also capital in nature.[9]

For many years, the headline carried interest tax rate was the 10% capital gains rate available for the sale of business assets. Deductions available under the capital gains tax regime, including the so-called 'base cost shift', provided that the effective rate was often lower. Various changes to the capital gains tax and carried interest regimes meant that the capital gains (and therefore carry) rate increased to 28% in 2010. In July 2015, this rate was entrenched as a separate carried interest regime. The purpose was to differentiate the tax rate for carried interest from that for general capital gains. In fact, in 2016, this was precisely what happened. Then UK Chancellor of the Exchequer, George Osborne, reduced the higher rate of capital gains tax from 28% to 20%, but retained the 28% rate for carried interest (and for the sale of secondary homes). Further, parliament also removed the ability for managers to benefit from the 'base cost shift' for carried interest – the tax deduction previously available which significantly reduced the effective tax rate payable by managers.

Even though carried interest is now taxed at 28% – significantly more than the 10% or less which applied until the credit crunch, it is still a significantly lower tax rate than the 47% which executives would have to pay if carried interest were treated as income.

Similarly to LLPs, carried interest also received its fair share of anti-avoidance legislation when HMRC targeted the investment management industry.

**Carried Interest Bifurcation: Two Regimes Emerge** For tax purposes, treatment of carried interest in the hands of a manager now effectively depends on whether the individual is a self-employed partner of a manager set up as an LLP, or whether the individual is an employee or director of a UK manager established as a limited company.

Contractually the carried interest is usually an interest in a limited partnership that acts as the 'carry partner' of the fund and into which executives are admitted as partners. The partnerships are often Scottish limited partnerships or offshore vehicles. The carry partnership receives a proportion of fund profits after the hurdle has been met, and in turn passes on such profits to its partners, in accordance with the waterfall provisions in the fund limited partnership and the profit sharing ratios of the carried interest partnership.

**Carried Interest Received as an Employee** Under UK employment tax legislation, the carried interest is considered an 'employment related security' for carry holders who are employees or directors of the manager. This is the case for employees or directors of a manager established as an English limited company, but, importantly, also for members of LLPs who are deemed employees for tax purposes under the salaried member rules discussed above. Where the managers are, or are deemed to be, employees, the employment tax provision govern the tax treatment of the managers.

The first question is whether the carried interest is 'restricted'. As mentioned above, carried interest is usually subject to vesting provisions for good and bad leavers and other contractual restrictions. Carried interest will, therefore, be a 'restricted' employment related security where such provisions are present – which is almost always the case. What matters for tax purposes is that restrictions can depress the market value of the security compared to non-restricted securities.

The rules on restricted employment related securities provide that executives are charged to income tax on their receipt of restricted carried interest to the extent they do not pay full market value for their interests. The income tax payable in this case is calculated by reference to the restricted market value of the carried interest – i.e. the depressed value because of the restrictions. Any subsequent lifting and/or variation of restrictions on carried interest are then further chargeable events to the extent value is said to be released. When such chargeable events occur, additional value is deemed unlocked. Executives are charged to income tax on such value where, for example, value may have increased because vesting provisions enable the individual to benefit from the performance of investments.

The continuous income tax charges are obviously undesirable (and difficult to quantify). To avoid these chargeable income tax occasions, executives in practice always elect to disregard the restrictions on their carried interest for tax purposes at the time the carried interest is awarded. This is known as a section 431 election, because that is the legislative section that permits the election.[10] By making a section 431 election, executives are taxed upon receipt of carried interest by reference to its unrestricted market value, i.e. as if all restrictions had been lifted. In consequence, the subsequent lifting or variation of restrictions are no longer taxable events so that the individual is then only taxed when the carried interest pays out – usually to capital gains.

Given the complexities of the new restricted securities regime which came into force in 2003, the BVCA agreed a further memorandum of understanding with HMRC in 2003 concerning treatment and valuation of carried interest under typical PE structures (the 2003 MOU). In the 2003 MOU, HMRC accepted that the unrestricted market value of the carried interest is equal to the nominal amount paid for it by the carry holders provided the fund and managers meet pre-agreed conditions, particularly that the carry holder is fully compensated through salary and bonus payments, and that the fund and carried interest structures are substantially the same as the structure envisaged within the 2003 MOU.

Where the 2003 MOU applies, regardless of a section 431 election, the award of carried interest will therefore not give rise to a tax charge upon receipt nor upon the lifting or variation of any restriction. In that case, tax liability will only arise when the carry comes into money and actual payments are made to carry holders.[11]

Where the underlying fund investments from which the carry gains are derived have a non-UK source, UK managers who are non-UK domiciled or deemed domiciled may be able to avoid tax on carried interest altogether so long as carry proceeds are kept outside of the UK.

**Income-Based Carried Interest** In response to political pressure and perceived short-termism by some managers, HMRC in 2016 introduced a new carried interest regime for carried interest holders who are partners of the manager but not employees or directors (so that the carried interest is not an employment-related security). In those circumstances, carried interest will be subject to the 'income-based carried interest' (IBCI) rules.

Under the ICBI regime, the question whether carry proceeds are subject to income tax or capital gains tax depends on the average investment-holding period of the fund. Specifically, if the average investment holding period is at least 40 months, then the entirety of an executive's carried interest will be subject to capital gains treatment at the 28% carried interest rate. Conversely, an average holding period of less than 36 months (i.e. three years) will result in the executive being charged in full to income tax on any gains arising from his carried interest.

The government's aim in introducing this test was to ensure that carried interest was available only in respect of 'long-term investment activity'.[12] The key here is that it is the average holding period of the fund's investments, not individual investments.

For holding periods between 36 and 40 months, the proportion of carried interest subject to income tax progressively decreases by 20%. Thus, 80% of carried interest is subject to income tax if the average holding period is at least 36 months (and 20% subject to capital gains); 60% of carried interest is subject to income tax if the average holding period is at least 37 months; 40% of carried interest is subject to income tax if the average holding period is 38 months, and 20% of the carried interest is subject to income tax for average investment holding periods between 39 and 40 months. Where the carried interest wholly or partly falls within the IBCI regime, the income is treated as trading income of the manager and the income source depends on where the services where provided.

I have two principal observations here:

The idea that tax treatment changes from income to capital over a five month period is obviously nonsensical, but represents the compromise position negotiated between the PE fund industry and HMRC who had initially argued for a longer vesting period. Theoretically, the timing difference also creates misalignment between the managers and investors – where the fund's average portfolio holding period is 36 months, and a sale is possible, managers may well prefer to sell four months later. However, in practice the investment holding periods for many PE funds or similar funds is well in excess of three years.

Perhaps more poignantly, the fact that the carried interest tax treatment of a manager now depends on whether he receives the carried interest as partner or employee creates a curious distortion.

**Disguised Investment Management Fees**   Separate wide-raging anti-avoidance rules were introduced in 2015 in the form of the Disguised Investment Management Fees (DIMF) legislation.

The disguised investment management fee rules prevent capital gains treatment of performance-related remuneration in a wide range of circumstances. The rules were enacted in response to a number of managers attempting to structure management fees as capital receipts rather than the expected income treatment. The legislation is extremely widely drafted and essentially provide that any fees payable to executives for the provision of investment management services in connection with a fund are subject to income tax, unless they fall within three permitted categories which are excepted. The most important exception is carried interest.

Broadly, for these purposes, carried interest is subject to a number of requirements. It must not be guaranteed, be variable, and calculated substantially by reference to the profits of the fund. Returns to investors must also be determined by reference to those profits. If there is no significant commercial risk that carried interest will not be paid, it will not be taxable as capital gains.

Carried interest payable under standard PE arrangements can normally be done without difficulty, but bespoke or hybrid fund structures do not always fall within the exception and can create difficulty. The other two exceptions which lead to capital gains treatment are repayments of coinvestments to managers and any profit made on such coinvestments.

The disguised investment management fee rules are part of a raft of anti-avoidance measures aimed at the investment management industry such as the IBCI rules and form part of a gradual shift by HMRC of taxing asset managers more aggressively in the UK. Until recently, executives had less difficulty securing capital gains treatment as opposed to income, but the recent wave of legislation has made structuring more difficult. Nevertheless, typical managers of PE fund structures should be able to secure beneficial carried interest treatment under the DIMF rules.

**Value Added Tax** When looking at the setup of UK asset managers, an additional tax that needs consideration is Value Added Tax (VAT). VAT is a tax on the supply of goods and services, and was assigned to the remit of HM Customs and Excise originally, whose aggressive anti-smuggling culture meant that the 'VAT man' was much feared. Since the merger of HM Customs & Excise and Inland Revenue in 2005 to form HMRC, the 'fear' factor has reduced, but VAT remains an important issue for UK managers.

VAT law is complex, at times counter-intuitive, and at 20% can add significantly to the operating cost of UK fund managers where the tax is not recoverable.

The starting point under UK VAT legislation (which is based on EU law) is that the performance of investments management and advisory services by a UK manager is in principle subject to VAT. A UK-based manager will therefore have to register for VAT once the annual turnover threshold – presently GBP 85 000 – has been exceeded, although voluntary registration may also be possible. However, whether or not UK VAT is actually chargeable on the investment advisory or management fees depends on the nature of the services and where the recipient of the service is based. VAT can therefore be a significant consideration in deciding where to locate a fund.

Broadly, if the recipient of the service is in the UK, then UK VAT applies and must be charged as so-called 'output' VAT by the manager. Where a UK PE fund is set up as an English limited partnership and the general partner (GP) is based in the UK, then UK VAT applies on the services to the fund (with English limited partnership funds, the partnership is ignored and it is the location of the GP which matters for VAT purposes). As the GP is not VAT registered, the GP cannot recover the VAT so that it represents a real cost. However, there is a solution to this VAT tax leakage. Two or more companies (or LLPs) can register as a UK VAT group which is then treated as one taxable person. In practice, the manager and the UK GP of the LP fund will, in many cases form a VAT group. This works because all transactions amongst members of the same VAT group are disregarded – so that no VAT applies on the services from the manager to the GP. However, services provided to portfolio companies based in other jurisdictions can impact the overall VAT recovery for the management group.

Where the recipient of the services is based in a jurisdiction which is located outside the UK – for example, a Cayman Islands-based corporate hedge fund, or the Guernsey-based GP of a Guernsey limited partnership fund – then no VAT is chargeable because the recipient is located outside the EU so that the services are out of scope. However, the manager is still entitled to register for VAT and receive full input credit for services performed (i.e. it can recover its own VAT cost on rent and other items).

Where the recipient – the overseas manager or fund – is based in another member state of the EU, the analysis is more complicated. The UK manager or adviser has to 'zero rate' the services it provides – effectively issuing a VAT invoice which is showing 'zero' VAT. It is then the VAT regime of the recipient EU jurisdiction which determines the VAT treatment of the services. Broadly, under the 'reverse charge' requires the recipient to treat itself as if it had provided the relevant services – to itself. It is then local law which determines whether the services are vatable or VAT exempt. For example, in Luxembourg, investment management of a Luxembourg PE fund established as a Luxembourg partnership such as the société en commandite spéciale – the most popular PE vehicle in Luxembourg – are exempt. This means that no VAT is payable on these services in Luxembourg, but the exempt nature of the services creates some VAT leakage in respect of fund costs which are non-exempt.[13]

**VAT and GPS**   In a closed-ended limited partnership structure, the fund's GP has primary responsibility for the management of the partnership fund and in return receives a priority profit share. The priority profit share, also known as the GP share (GPS), sits at the top of the waterfall (i.e. it is distributed first) and is the GP's share of fund profits which is used to pay the management fee to the fund manager. This profit share usually represents around 2% of fund commitments and does not attract VAT as it is not a fee for services, but a share of profits. In response to recent loss restrictions under revised corporation tax rules that came out in 2017, PE funds have started to restructure the GPS so that they are no longer paid to the GP and treated as a profit share, but instead paid as a fee directly by the limited partnership to the manager. Given that the limited partnership benefits from the tax treatment of the GP that will be grouped with the manager, no VAT applies to the services.

**Brexit**   At the time of writing, it is still unclear what form Brexit will take, and when or if it will happen. While the regulatory implications outweigh any tax threats in the asset management sector, there are a number of tax implications regarding Brexit that could impact UK-based asset managers.

First, VAT (and customs duties) are key areas affected by Brexit. The UK is part of the EU VAT regime which, as set out above, has different rules for dealings with non-EU members than those that apply to EU member states. It is therefore crucial to know how the UK will be treated post-Brexit – will it remain in the EU for VAT purposes, or become a 'third country', which seems more likely?

The draft Withdrawal Agreement expressly sets out the finite applicability of EU VAT legislation once the UK departs the EU. However, under the Withdrawal Agreement the UK will implement all EU law into UK law – including VAT. Most EU VAT law is already incorporated into UK tax law, so that that existing VAT laws will continue to apply in the UK after Brexit. Thus, the UK would leave the EU, yet continue to implement a parallel VAT regime.

The principal question is whether the UK will remain in a customs (and VAT) union with the EU. If it does, there will be no immediate change. However, if it does not – as is likely – then one consequence would be that services supplied by UK managers to funds or vehicles located in EU member states will become services provided to 'third countries'. The net tax effect for the manager is likely to be limited as the VAT analysis would change from 'zero rated' to 'out of scope'. In neither scenario would UK VAT be payable; however, the local (EU) VAT would need considering where the services are provided to EU member states. There will, of course, be other VAT consequences.

Secondly, some UK managers may be forced to establish or engage an AIFM based in another EU jurisdiction in order to continue to avail themselves of the marketing passport for AIFMD purposes. In these circumstances it is crucial to structure any change in operation carefully to avoid or minimise any risk that the introduction of a non-UK-based manager into the manager structure could be a UK taxable transaction (for example, care must be taken to avoid the taxable transfer of management contracts). Extensive meetings have been held between HMRC, HM Treasury, and industry which considered key Brexit-generated tax issues, including VAT and the impact of any restructurings. Somewhat surprisingly, HMRC were guarded in their approach and did not feel able to make formal Brexit-related concessions. This does not mean that there will invariably be tax – but rather, that ordinary tax rules will determine the extent to which Brexit-related restructurings will give rise to tax charges. From a practical perspective, Brexit is not necessarily seen by HMRC as different from any other business transaction. Nevertheless, in practice HMRC may well be more helpful.

# US

The US is famous for the concept of charging all of its citizens on their worldwide income.

Clearly, as in other Western countries, the US has corporation taxes, personal income taxes, and personal capital gains taxes. The US has separate federal, state, and local government taxation imposed at each of these levels. Thus, companies sometimes avoid being in New York to avoid its extra local tax charges on residents. Taxes are levied on income, payroll, property, sales, capital gains, dividends, imports, estates, and gifts, as well as various fees.

I discuss a number of relevant US taxation matters in this section. At the end of the section, we come to President Trump's Tax Cuts and Jobs Act, a hugely interesting and provoking piece of legislation that actually impressed me as much as the Trump trade wars have had the opposite effect on me.

**A Summary**  Citizens and residents are taxed on their worldwide income and allowed a credit for foreign taxes. The only other country that taxes its non-resident citizens is Eritrea.

There is wide variation in the tax rates set at federal level and between states and local tax jurisdictions.

Given the multi-layered tax regime, state taxes are generally deductible when calculating federal tax liability. However, a USD 10 000 limit applies to this practice, known as state and local tax (SALT) deduction. This limit hits the wealth-generating hubs of California and the tri-state area of New York, New Jersey, and Connecticut the hardest, of course.

Taxes are levied on employment income at both state and federal level, such as social security and Medicare taxes (which both employers and employees must pay). Taxes are also applied to the sale of goods and services. These sales taxes vary not only from state to state, but also within states depending on the type of taxable good or service.

Tax rates in the US are surprisingly high for a country that does not have free healthcare – so what are they spending their taxes on? (I am really trying hard not to say The Wall!).

**Corporates and Repatriation**  Until recently, many US companies gamed the system by holding billions outside the US. This also led these companies to acquire more non-US companies, or even cleverer, reverse into non-US companies. President Obama tried to stamp down on this by further taxing these offshore profits, as well as not allowing the reverse method. However, President Trump passed legislation that allowed them to bring this money back into the US at a reduced tax rate of 15.5% (for cash – only 8% for non-cash assets), which has given a large and immediate economic bump upwards for the US, with hundreds of billions of USD being repatriated already.

**Management Fees – Some Variations**  Management fees attract income-style tax.

Generally, US PE investment funds pay the management fee to a management company that is separate from the GP entity. Occasionally, the management fee is paid by the fund to the GP entity, which typically pays the fee (net of expenses) to the management company. The management fee is normally taxed as ordinary income. Another alternative often used to achieve a more favourable tax position is to receive a lower management fee and instead receive a larger carry interest. This position may be subject to change. US tax laws are promulgated by the US congress. All legislative action originates in the US House of Representatives Ways and Means Committee. This committee has visited and may revisit the character of the income of the carry interest and require that it be recognised as ordinary income. In addition, the IRS has the authority to require that the substance of the transaction and not the mere form control the recognition and character of the income. One alternative that is often used by PE funds and hedge funds is to not charge a management fee by the investment amount contributed by the management team. This prevents a circular cash flow that would result in the recognition of income (the management fee).

If the management company is organised as a fiscally transparent vehicle (such as a limited liability company or a 'Subchapter S corporation'), the management fee, along with any expenses of the management company (including salaries), will be allocated to the owners of the management company and included in the calculation of their taxable income.

If the management company is organised as a corporation which is not fiscally transparent the management company will be taxed on the receipt of the management fees. Generally, this fee income, net of any expenses of the management company, will be paid to the managers as compensation which the managers must include in their taxable income at ordinary income rates. Double taxation may be avoided where the compensation payments to the managers remain at a reasonable level because the corporation should receive a tax deduction for these compensation payments. The use of a non-fiscally transparent corporation where the deduction is unavailable is not tax efficient. The Internal Revenue Code (IRC) and the applicable regulations include certain rules regarding the appropriate or reasonableness of compensation. It is unlikely that a corporation can merely 'wash' the income through compensation and such structure would merely result in structure that is substantially equivalent to using a fiscally transparent vehicle. Using a corporate structure could be useful, at least in the near term, if the amount of the fees is expected to be reinvested in the fund, for example due to a clawback, or used to support other businesses. The structure should also consider state and local tax regimes.

Income received by a management principal from management fees is taxed as ordinary income. It is sometimes the practice of PE fund managers to channel a principal's share of the management fees into the fund to contribute towards their required investment, known as the management fee waiver. This converts the tax liability from that of ordinary income to long-term capital gains. Recent investigations begun by the IRS and state prosecutors into this practice suggest that it is in question.

**Carried Interest**  Like the UK, carry is subject to capital gains tax, within certain parameters. Otherwise, it is income tax. Again, like the UK, there has been much political discussion around the capital nature of carried interest (only 'enhanced' by having a PE guy run for President – Mitt Romney from Bain Capital).

The carried interest paid by US PE investment funds is normally structured as an allocation of fund profits to the GP of the fund. The GP (normally a partnership or a limited liability company) then allocates the carried interest amongst its members, the fund managers. To the extent that such profits represent long-term capital gains realised by the fund, those profits will be taxed at preferential capital gain rates when allocated to the managers (provided that the managers are treated as 'partners' of the GP entity for US federal income tax purposes).

Carried interest is the portion of an investment fund's returns eligible for a capital gains tax rate of 23.8% instead of the ordinary income tax rate up to 27%. Following campaign promises by President Trump that he would do away with it, carried interest was one of the lightning rods during the tax reform debate. Yet, instead of an outright repeal, the final outcome required that a fund's GP holds the relevant investments for three years, instead of one, starting in 2018.[14] This came as somewhat of a relief for VC and PE operators – with the impact not being as severe as previously thought.[15]

US tax reform under President Trump is discussed in more detail below.

**Variations for Open-Ended** Like the UK, open-ended funds mostly do not have the capital advantages for their performance fees. The clue is in the word 'fees'.

Open-ended funds are often structured as mutual funds (which themselves are not exclusively open-ended). The fee structure of a mutual fund is typically divided in two: fees which are owed by the investors to the fund and the fees owed by the fund to the investment manager. The latter fees are indirectly owed by the investors but the distinction is important in its tax implications for the manager.

The fund typically pays the manager management fees out of the pooled assets of the fund on an annualised basis to cover the cost of providing portfolio management and other related services. This income is taxed as ordinary business income and the person who bears the tax liability depends on the structure used – if it is a company that is not fiscally transparent it is corporation tax, and if it is a partnership it is borne by the individual members.

Other fees paid by the fund to the manager include those that cover expenses such as legal and accounting costs, and as they are directly attributable to those expenditures, there is a small likelihood that such fees will generate profit that is taxable.

Broadly speaking, performance fees for hedge fund managers are charged to tax as income.

Hedge side pockets though have the opportunity to create capital.

**Fees for Services** Where a manager receives fee income such as directors' fees, consulting fees, monitoring fees, or any other fees for services provided, such income likely would constitute effectively connected income (ECI) (discussed further below). It is common for such fee income when paid by investee companies of a fund to be received by the managers of the fund and not by the fund directly to avoid this treatment, and to reflect the reality that the management of the fund is providing these services. Funds may provide for a reduction of the management fee to a specified extent that such fees are received.

**The Tax Cuts and Jobs Act** Following intense rhetoric during his campaign, President Trump signed into law the Tax Cuts and Jobs Act (the 'Tax Act') in December 2017. The new tax reform, aimed at allowing people to file their taxes on a postcard (supposedly), undoubtedly affects asset managers too. The Tax Act had in fact been based on separate legislative proposals from US Democrats and Republicans, but for political reasons never been put forward until then.

Below is set out some of the relevant changes to asset managers.

**Carried Interest** Although several legislative proposals had been introduced in prior years that would have eliminated any tax benefit to carried interest, the Tax Act retains the treatment of carried interest. However, the Tax Act states that, and similar to the IBCI rules discussed earlier in the chapter, American asset managers are now required to hold their investments for a minimum of three years, lest they incur income tax rates on any gains made from an investment. This new requirement brings the previous minimum holding length up from just one year.

Capital gains rates in the US vary depending on the income tax bracket a person falls into, however, for those in the highest income tax bracket, the capital gains tax rate is still only 20%, a much more attractive rate than the 37% faced from income tax.

The three-year holding period will be determined based on the holding period of the asset giving rise to the gain and will apply irrespective of whether a section 83(b) election was made for the carried interest.

Capital gains not satisfying the three-year holding period requirement will be treated as short-term capital gains, which are taxed as ordinary income rates but can be offset by long-term capital losses.

**Corporate Taxes**  One of the more headline-grabbing changes to regulation was the scrapping of the tiered corporate tax rate system, which was replaced by a 21%.[16] This reduces the corporate tax rate permanently from 35% to 21% for tax years beginning after 31 December 2017. This reduction in corporate tax rates may impact the decision by fund managers to structure portfolio companies as corporations rather than pass-through entities, such as LLCs, and will have implications for the use of US 'blocker' corporations often established by funds for investment by non-US and US tax-exempt investors.

A corporation's ability to use net operating losses will be limited to 80% of its annual taxable income. The Tax Act disallows the carry-back of losses but allows for an indefinite carry-forward of losses.

**Effectively Connected Income**  Under the Tax Act, when a non-US person is engaged in trade or business in the US, all US-sourced income in relation to that trade or business is considered to be 'effectively connected income' (ECI) – i.e. effectively connected to the US and therefore taxable by the US. A non-US recipient of ECI will normally be taxable on such income. The issue principally arises where a fund directly holds US trading businesses.

Where a non-US person sells an interest in a partnership engaged in trade or business in the US, the proceeds of such a sale will be considered ECI to the extent that the non-US person would have had ECI had the partnership sold its assets for fair market value. In addition, to support the collection of tax from non-US sellers of interests in partnerships receiving ECI, the Tax Act imposes a 10% withholding requirement on the amount realised from the disposition of the interest.

Many funds have established US corporate 'blockers' to shield non-US investors from ECI and the resulting US tax filing and payment obligations. This approach entails investors investing into a US corporation, which pays US corporation tax and which invests into the main fund vehicle. The non-US investors then receive returns on their investment in the form of dividends instead of US income, and are therefore not liable to US income tax.

Under the Tax Act, non-US investors will increasingly likely use US blockers, especially with the decrease in the corporate tax rate from 35% to 21%.

**Unrelated Business Taxable Income**  Section 501 of the IRC grants tax-exempt status to certain organisations. In 1950, the concept of 'unrelated business taxable income' (UBTI) – which is any income that does not fall within a tax-exempt organisation's exemption – was introduced, meaning that tax-exempt organisations would have to pay tax on UBTI (if any was due). This move was designed to avoid unfair competition between taxable and tax-exempt entities. Before the Tax Act, however, expenses or losses from one UBTI activity could offset UBTI from another activity. The Tax Act now requires that tax-exempt organisations calculate their tax returns separately for each unrelated trade or business – which means a bigger UBTI tax hit for tax-exempt entities.

Tax-exempt investors often choose whether to participate in a fund that is expected to generate UBTI directly or through a blocker. The blocker works because certain forms of passive income are not considered UBTI, such as rent, interest, capital gains, and dividends. The elimination of the ability to offset UBTI gains and losses may encourage tax-exempt investors to invest through blocker corporations.

**Controlled Foreign Companies**  Many jurisdictions have a controlled foreign companies (CFC) regime, which brings the income and gains of foreign entities, onshore. CFC rules are designed to stop shifting profits to low-tax offshore jurisdictions, by bringing the profits of such entities back onshore.

The US CFC regime provides that a non-US corporation is a CFC if 'US shareholders' own, directly or by attribution, more than 50% of the non-US corporation. The Tax Act expands the definition of 'US shareholder' to include US persons who own 10% or more of the total value of shares of all classes of stock, voting or non-voting. The Tax Act says that stock owned by a non-US person in a non-US corporation can be taken into account for the purposes of determining whether a US person is a US shareholder.

These changes are likely to result in more non-US portfolio companies being treated as CFCs.

# EU

Trade is at the forefront of the EU's agenda, which is hardly surprising given its origins as the European Coal and Steel Community. In fact, the Treaty of Lisbon signed in 2007 expressly identifies the establishment of an internal market and the sustainable development of Europe as one of the EU's core objectives. The free movement of goods, services, capital, and persons within the EU, known as the four freedoms, are integral to EU project from the perspective of community-building and economic growth.

**Corporation Tax**  Taxation is not harmonised across the EU, which provides both difficulties and opportunities. The power to tax is in the hands of each EU member state, with the EU having only limited oversight and influence over such rates.

The rates set by each member state differ widely. For example, at the time of writing, the corporate tax rate is 29% in Greece, 25% in Spain, 22% in Denmark, 19% (soon to be 17%) in the UK, 12.5% in Cyprus, and just 9% in Hungary.

The discretion to set corporate tax rates is caveated by EU principles concerning competition and the internal market. For example, the four movements – and in particular, the freedom of establishment and free movement of capital – were also instrumental in shaping UK tax law.

Given the size and appeal of the EU market, member states compete to be seen as the most attractive jurisdiction for companies to base themselves in. Beyond corporation tax, indirect taxes such as VAT, national insurance, and most of all income taxes are also key measures in each member state's armoury.

Although the EU cannot directly set each member state's corporate tax rate, it has proven that it takes its oversight role seriously and will enforce EU tax and state aid legislation when looking at specific measures. In September 2018, for example, Apple was compelled to pay the Irish government EUR 14.3 billion after the EC ruled that tax breaks given to the company by the Irish government were illegal and amounted to unlawful state aid. Indeed, it was the EU's threat of legal action against Ireland that brought about this outcome.

Despite the friction that divergence between tax rates can create between member states, it does provide opportunities for asset managers to use cross-border corporate structures for tax efficiency without moving any operations too far from home.

**Personal Taxes**  Personal tax rates are also the remit of individual member states. There are no EU-wide rules that say how EU nationals who live, work or spend time outside their home countries are to be taxed on their income. However, the country where you are resident for tax purposes can tax your total worldwide income, earned or unearned. This includes wages, pensions, benefits, income from property, or from any other sources, or capital gains from sales of property, from all countries worldwide.

In some cases, two countries could consider a person tax-resident at the same time, and both can require them to pay taxes on total income. The problem of double taxation tends to be solved in one of two main ways. One approach is for the home tax jurisdiction to unilaterally exempt foreign-sourced income or give credit to tax-payers for foreign taxes already paid. The other option is to enter bilateral agreements with foreign tax jurisdictions known as a 'tax treaties'.

Luxembourg is a tax treaty champion. It has built a niche for itself as a centre for cross-border trade and investment within the EU. Many financial services providers, investment funds and holding companies are established in Luxembourg. At the time of writing, Luxembourg is party to more than 70 tax treaties. Counterparties to Luxembourg tax treaties include not only every member state of the EU, but also the US, Canada, Japan, Russia, Brazil, and China. Tax treaties allow for more tailored solutions to double taxation.

There is a cold war within the EU on personal taxes. Brexit has exasperated this even more, with states pitching for wealth creators, whilst at the same time behind their back and in direct contradiction, sound off against oligarchs and international tax ne'er-do-wells.

A number of member states offers their own incentives to entice wealth creators to live and work within their tax jurisdiction. For example, in Portugal, for 'non-habitual residents', a 20% flat rate applies to certain Portuguese-sourced income, whilst foreign-sourced income is tax-exempt. Meanwhile, in Italy, 'non-domiciled residents' pay ordinary taxes on Italian-sourced income, but a fixed EUR 100 000 in relation to non-Italian income.

**VAT**  The European Union value added tax (or EU VAT) is a value added tax on goods and services within the EU. The EU's institutions do not collect the tax, but EU member states are each required to adopt a value added tax that complies with the EU VAT code. Different rates of VAT apply in different EU member states, ranging from 17% in Luxembourg to 27% in Hungary. The total VAT collected by member states is used as part of the calculation to determine what each state contributes to the EU's budget.

Value added tax collected at each stage in the supply chain is remitted to the tax authorities of the member state concerned and forms part of that state's revenue. A small proportion goes to the EU in the form of a levy ('VAT-based own resources'). The co-ordinated administration of value added tax within the EU VAT area is an important part of the single market. Cross-border VAT is declared in the same way as domestic VAT, which facilitates the elimination of border controls between member states, saving costs and reducing delays

## OFFSHORE

Offshore taxation is a very contentious topic. I might as well have written 'plastic in oceans'. A bit like the term 'terrorist', the terms 'offshore' or even worse 'tax haven' are thrown about and are often in the eye of the beholder or used defensively to cover up one's own guilt. Thus, the US and UK criticise illegitimate use of tax havens, yet harbour their own either in their country (Nevada, Delaware, Montana, South Dakota, Wyoming) or just outside (the Cayman Islands or Guernsey).

Today, offshore jurisdictions and tax are usually about two aspects: (i) minimising the amount of tax payable on relevant income; and (ii) confidentiality. Both items face immense pressure.

The 2016 Panama Papers and the 2017 Paradise Papers caused great damage to the public's view of the use of offshore jurisdictions. In both, millions of confidential documents were stolen from offshore law firms and published. The offshore affairs of numerous high-profile individuals and businesses were made available to the public, and the ramifications have been extensive. In many instances, no attempt was made at distinguishing perfectly legal offshore conduct from illegal hiding of monies.

Also, you would have thought someone might have attacked the data thefts with GDPR or other data protection rules. Hardly ever is the hacking of such offshore data described as theft or criminal damage.

The opening line from the *Guardian*'s report on the Paradise Papers best captures the mood of the nation: 'The world's biggest businesses, heads of state and global figures in politics, entertainment and sport who have sheltered their wealth in secretive tax havens are being revealed this week in a major new investigation into the UK's offshore empires.'

Whilst this chapter is concerned with tax, it should be noted that confidentiality is and should be paramount for lawyers across the globe. Yet, such confidentiality was not necessarily respected here. In particular, under UK law a breach of confidentiality can be permitted by law if the breach is in the public interest. Indeed, it was key to the *Guardian* and the BBC's argument in litigation (now settled) following the Paradise Papers that their publication of leaked documents was justified on this ground. Whilst I do not wish to overtly opine on this, I do point to the fact that there is a difference between what is in the public interest and what the public are interested in.

Many offshore jurisdictions are well-established for investment funds and generally reputable – take Jersey, Guernsey, and the Cayman Islands, for example of established, reputable jurisdictions.

From a tax perspective, the use of offshore vehicles does not avoid UK taxation per se. Where a revenue stream is taxable as employment income, then it may make no difference if it is paid to an offshore entity. Further, anti-avoidance provisions may apply. Thus, careful tax structuring is normally required and offshore havens may not always be the answer.

However, in an asset management context, it is very common to use offshore jurisdictions – precisely because of the no-tax position. Broadly there is little or no corporation tax (other than for certain financial entities), capital gains tax, VAT, or inheritance tax offshore. Income tax is limited to lower levels.

Thus, not only are hedge and private equity funds often established in jurisdictions such as the Cayman Islands or the Channel Islands, but often offshore management vehicles or general partners (in the case of limited partnership funds) can be located in these jurisdictions.

However, these jurisdictions are undergoing significant changes. Similar to developments in taxing jurisdictions, the leading offshore fund jurisdictions are starting to introduce substance and disclosure requirements to ensure that they will remain competitive and avoid blacklisting by the onshore jurisdictions.

## Some Interesting Trends

**More Transparency Between Taxpayers and Tax Authorities**   The EU, with its Savings Taxation Directive, and more recently the US with FATCA have sought to enhance intergovernmental information exchange between tax authorities.

Increasing retaliation against President Trump's federal tax reforms could launch a global trade war that undermines international trade agreements. The reforms are designed to spur future investment in the US and bring back trillions of dollars in offshore US profits, though they are viewed by some countries as an attack on the global tax consensus and the balance of global investment. These countries could make a referral to the WTO court, leading to a US retreat on international trade cooperation.

For over 30 years, the US has stayed out of the race to the bottom on corporate tax rates, leading to significant international investment by US companies that have helped underpin the economies of many trade rivals. However, the new US reforms make the US far more attractive to multinationals that are able to shop around the world for the most favourable tax environments.

The key reforms tabled include cutting the US federal tax rate from 35% to 21%, a one-off tax charge of 15.5% on historic earnings sheltered offshore and now repatriated to the US and an imposition of a minimum tax on earnings held offshore from technologies and related IP.

**Disclosure**   Since the credit crisis, there has been a big move toward transparency globally from a regulatory perspective. But transparency is also important to governments from the perspective of tax collection. In an increasingly globalised economy, tackling international schemes of tax avoidance and evasion and maintaining robust tax treaty arrangements calls for high levels of disclosure by taxpayers, not only to their local taxman, but to and between foreign tax authorities.

Measures implemented as part of this trend include FATCA and the CRS promoted by the OECD (and inspired by FATCA). There is no doubt that openness around tax matters is increasingly expected by law, but interestingly it has also fast become a reputational risk. If it feels like a convoluted legal fiction to avoid paying a level of tax that the average taxpayer would consider 'fair', it probably is. Companies and individuals now have to consider whether the risk of being called out for overly ambitious tax planning is worth the tax savings.

**Substance**   'Substance' is an important tax consideration. Substance refers to the substantive activities of a business, which, in a funds context, means activities such as portfolio management, risk management, investment analysis, trading, fundraising, valuation, and compliance. The concept of substance over legal form has been pioneered by the OECD to crack down on tax avoidance. The principle is that tax authorities should be able to look at the commercial reality of how and where a business is being run so that tax cannot be avoided by clever use of multi-jurisdiction group/fund structures without business operations actually being carried out in the relevant jurisdictions.

Substance is in vogue with tax authorities and regulators, and will continue to be a major consideration in asset management. The OECD's BEPS project looks set to make this a more pressing concern for the industry.

**BEPS recommendations** Base erosion and profit shifting (BEPS) refers to tax planning strategies designed to shift profits from high tax to low tax jurisdictions, essentially exploiting mismatches in tax regimes across different jurisdictions. The OECD estimates that between USD 100 billion and USD 240 billion is lost per year as a result of BEPS, so the impact is significant.[17] In particular, the OECD considers developing countries to be at a significant disadvantage as a result of BEPS, though its key goal is to demonstrably restrict tax avoidance. The OECD is of the view that tax avoidance by large multinational corporates damages perceptions of tax regimes for smaller taxpayers, which is potentially harmful.

The BEPS project was launched in 2012 by the OECD and the G20. In 2013, the OECD and G20 published an Action Plan on BEPS comprising 15 recommendations, which remain the core principles of the BEPS project today. Over 115 different jurisdictions have signed up to the implementation of the Action Plan on BEPS, accounting of for over 93% of global GDP.[18]

## ENDNOTES

1. www.bvca.co.uk/Policy/Tax-Legal-and-Regulatory/Industry-guidance-standardised-documents/Agreements-between-the-BVCA-and-the-UK-tax-authority/The-Use-of-Limited-Partnerships
2. If the corporation tax rate does reduce to 17%, the effective tax rate will be 48.623%, meaning that additional rate shareholders will receive GBP 51.377 for every GBP 100 distributed by way of dividend.
3. LLPs are taxable entities for value added tax (VAT) purposes and required to withhold the income taxes and NICs for its employees and directors under PAYE.
4. See HMRC's Summary of Responses dated 10 December 2013, in respect of 'Partnerships: A review of two aspects of the tax rules.
5. See the fourth edition of MJ Hudson's Private Equity Fund Terms Research. www.mjhudson.com/wp-content/uploads/2018/07/MJHudson_PE-Fund-Terms-2018-Report_Part_1.pdf
6. See p. 21 of that report.
7. However, the classic 2/20 model is diminishing in the hedge fund industry – the move is towards smaller management fees and a larger performance share.
8. The name '*carried interest*' originates from profit sharing arrangements between ship captains, crewmen and the merchants whose cargo they transported. The crewmen and the captains had an interest in what they *carried*.
9. With this also came the ability to use costs of acquisition as losses for carried interest partners (this was known as the base cost shift).
10. Section 431 of the Income Tax (Earnings and Pensions) Act 2003.
11. It is, however, customary for managers to make protective section 431 elections in case of future HMRC challenge.
12. See p. 4 of HMRC's Summary of Responses dated 9 December 2015, in respect of 'Taxation of performance linked awards paid to asset managers'.
13. It should be noted that EU legislation provides that the management of '*special investment funds*' is exempt from VAT. Member states are given discretion in defining '*special investment funds*'. In

the UK, this broadly equates to funds that are specifically regulated by the FCA (OEICs, AUTs, and trust-based schemes). Whilst this is useful for managers of certain authorised or regulated funds in the UK, many other assets managers cannot rely on this exemption. PE and real RE funds, for example, are not within the definition of special investment fund. Management services in these types of fund are standard rate supplies. However, other EU jurisdictions such as Luxembourg have applied the exemption more widely.

14. https://uk.reuters.com/article/us-usa-tax-carriedinterest/u-s-treasury-to-close-carried-interest-loophole-in-new-tax-law-idUKKCN1GD5YE
15. www.pionline.com/article/20180319/PRINT/180319865/carried-interest-lives-on-despite-tax-reform
16. http://klgates.com/tax-reform-and-investment-management-initial-observations-12-29-2017/
17. OECD: Policy Brief October 2015 – BEPS update Number 3.
18. Inclusive Framework on BEPS: Progress Report July 2016 to June 2017, p. 1.

# CHAPTER 12

# Regional Trends

*The fundamental delusion of humanity is to suppose that I am here and you are out there.*

— Yasutani Roshi, Zen master

As globalisation continues to shrink the world, it has never been more important to have an understanding of one another – being global but local. Every region across the globe suffers or is bolstered by its own unique combination of religion, culture, geography, sociological, and political factors, as well as its relations with its neighbours and those it trades with. This combination forms trends that influence the way asset managers do business as well as the very form of the asset managers themselves. The asset management landscape is continually adapting to the changing trends across the globe. A European asset manager will not experience the same issues an asset manager based in Africa will and an American asset manager certainly does not share the same advantages or disadvantages afforded to a Chinese or Korean manager.

Whilst it may be easy for managers to focus on their own regions, an understanding of how their competitors on the other side of the world operate is relevant if they wish to achieve recognition as a global brand, find new investment opportunities, or attract international investors.

This chapter covers relevant points impacting a region's asset management industry. So far, in this book, we have focused on the UK, US, and Europe, and therefore this chapter contains an overview of the asset management market in each of Africa, South America, the Middle East, and Asia. The next section compares the changes in pension systems and investment between developed and developing nations as we look at the big institutional investors. We also examine the effect a few trends are having on the asset manager's world that are not exclusive to certain jurisdictions. The final section considers the offshore jurisdictions and their use by asset managers following the stripping back by global tax authorities and news reporters of concealed client information and investments, as described briefly in the last chapter.

## AFRICA

As is similar with South America (discussed below), Africa is on the receiving end of increasing levels of investment, as parts of the continent are becoming wealthier and experiencing significant growth within its young working age population. According to the World Bank bi-annual report, Africa's Pulse, Sub-Saharan Africa's growth is projected to reach 3.6% per annum in 2019–2020.[1] A growing middle class with growing spending power has heightened economic advancement and encouraged businesses to flourish. Increased demand for financial services, electricity, consumer goods, and housing, coupled with a stronger commercial case for infrastructure spend, has triggered growing interest in the underlying demographic and economic changes in the region. We are therefore observing an emergence of strong, local and international fund management brands investing in Africa. Crucially, there is a sense amongst fund managers that Africa is a worthwhile investment space, with untapped potential. That said, as with part of Asia and Central and Eastern Europe, there is still concern about the lack of exits and low liquidity.

In South Africa, since 1994, the working age population increased by 11 million and, as of 2015, comprised 65% of South Africa's total population of 54.9 million. It is thought that the working age population will grow by another 9 million in the next 50 years.[2] There is a 'demographic window of opportunity'[3] for Africa to propel and grow, promoting the notion of the 'demographic dividend'.[4] This is the idea that this kind of significant demographic transition can lead to rapid economic growth. Africa's expanding working population and treatment of education as its greatest priority has spread prosperity throughout the region. Getting basic schooling is crucial to ensuring that school leavers and graduates have the fundamental skills to perform in the modern workplace. This in turn expands Africa's working middle class, which is key to accelerating its growth. Nonetheless, the region has some way to go before realising its full potential. In particular, there is a high number of unemployed youth, which better educational attainment and vocational training, coupled with policy action, would tackle. Having a large number of workers per capita can give the economy a significant boost, provided there are sufficient jobs. If the growth of job creation does not match the growth in those able and willing to be employed, more of a country's spending will be allocated towards assisting those not able to fend for themselves, rather than creating opportunities for the population as a whole. After a period of stagnation, the take-off in economic growth in Africa over the last 15 years creates great optimism for the future. A rise in foreign direct investments is compensating for weak domestic savings.

South Africa has, for some time, been attractive to investors. Being a gateway to the rest of the continent, its market of about 1 billion people, and it being a member of (the now infamous) BRICS (Brazil, Russia, India, China, and South Africa), has made it a hub for investment projects in the last couple of years. Even though the main focus is still South Africa, there have been a few successful fund managers who have instead focused on establishing funds in Kenya, Nigeria, Botswana, and other African countries. Contrary to Europe, which is home to many single-country funds, it is more challenging to raise capital for individual African markets from investors outside of the region. As such, it is suggested that fund managers ought to look towards pan-continental and regional strategies. Successful managers typically are those that ignore borders and instead choose to invest across the continent. The larger amounts raised be these managers exemplify the preference of investors for such funds. Hesitation towards single-country funds in Africa has commonly been due to concerns about the quality of deal flow and the concentration risk associated with an African portfolio that is not sufficiently diversified.

Despite political unrest, there is significant appetite and interest in assets in northern and western Africa. This should provide investors in countries such as Angola with far greater confidence than before and deal flow should remain moderate to high hopefully given economic growth. However, fund managers must remain vigilant regarding quality and bankability due to the inescapable financial, structural, and political instability in Africa. Growth trends will require that fund managers initiate highly specialised teams with expertise and experience as well as a thorough understanding of the region's markets. Moreover, a new manager relationship trend is emerging due to investors spending more time on pre-investment due diligence than they would do with a European, Asian, or US fund proposition. This is as a result of the unfamiliar geography, deals, and team executives. Such increase in vigilance from potential foreign investors necessitates a stronger team framework and careful marketing from fund managers.

Fund managers in Africa have received increased support from development finance institutions (DFIs), who often put a stress on the importance of environmental, social, and governance (ESG) factors when allocating capital. DFIs are specialist banks or subsidiaries set up to support private sector development in developing countries. Fund managers in Africa will observe that the support of DFIs, even if only a soft commitment, is crucial. Beyond providing direct support, DFIs are also actively engaged in creating enabling environments to tackle regulatory and institutional challenges. With many DFIs looking to invest capital in developing emerging economies, these investors provide an important source of capital for Africa and the private capital fund managers looking to raise funds there. International Finance Corporation (IFC), an independent arm of the World Bank, which aims to finance private sector investment in emerging markets such as Africa in the hopes of encouraging economic growth is a prime example of a DFI. If investors can see that a fund has the backing of DFIs, they will be reassured that not only are their investments socially beneficial but they can expect stronger capital returns as DFIs often set a high benchmark for asset managers to hit before releasing their capital. More importantly, if fund managers do not have this backing, potential investors are likely to be wary. The African Venture Capital Association (AVCA) notes that DFIs, which catalysed commercial PE investment in Africa, maintain high standards for ESG in Africa and have diffused the practice throughout the PE industry. FMO, a Dutch DFI, has observed that fund managers who incorporate ESG practices into their business have enjoyed stronger financial results and long-term viability.[5] The positive effects of ESG are heightened by its contribution to better financial outcomes as, without PE investment, it is arguable that the level of engagement with ESG considerations in Africa would be lower.

The ESG trend in Africa has improved the investment climate and assisted Africa on a social level. Environmental policies that require firms to improve how they manage everyday issues such as waste disposal have a positive impact on public health. Other examples of ESG include investing in housing and agriculture that not only generates healthy returns, but also averts environmental issues further down the line. For example, by installing incinerators that reduce toxic emissions and new treatment tanks to treat wastewater from agricultural production sites. Sensitivity to issues such as the education crisis in Africa coupled with the provision of safe and secure management of African portfolio holdings, means that a future of increased protection and diverse investment opportunities certainly looks more hopeful than before.

In the developing markets across the continent of Africa, where labour laws may not meet developed world standards and corruption is a prevalent issue, investors must take care to ensure that their fund managers have 'clean hands'.[6] In developing jurisdictions, it is important to ensure that the complexities of a deal or fund structure are not complex for the purpose of concealing inefficient or even corrupt practices. As mentioned previously, a strong and experienced team that can clearly demonstrate a robust governance policy being implemented is key in combatting such doubts from investors. Fortunately, in contrast to many European or US managers, African managers consider well-documented ESG policies a fundamental component of the operation of fund and portfolio companies. However, despite ESG being a fairly well-entrenched concept in African fund management, managers must ensure that their ESG and business integrity procedures can be implemented in practice.

The necessity for a good track record, strong team composition, infrastructure, budget, and successful execution are not issues confined to Africa as a region. However, considering Africa's position as an emerging market, these factors become possibly more necessary for the consideration of fund managers seeking to attract foreign investors. Exits for managers are still weak in Africa. The underdeveloped African stock markets are also not helpful to alleviate this issue. Fund managers can look forward to Africa becoming an increasingly rewarding market, but they must nonetheless adopt careful and informed measures to reassure foreign investors and tackle a multitude of challenges. Despite this being a largely optimistic period for Africa as a region with record levels of investment, investors still need and want confidence and surety, as well as good returns.

## SOUTH AMERICA

South America as a region is susceptible to frequent changes in administration, which bring with them disruptive changes to markets and regulations. This political risk and the accompanying currency Vol are the two main concerns for the majority of investors (both domestic and foreign) hoping to invest into South America (83% and 62% respectively as of 2018).

Notwithstanding the political fervour and economic risks, South America's asset management industry is expected to grow to nearly USD 7 trillion, at a rate of 12.5% from 2004 to 2020, the highest growth rate across the globe.[7] A large portion of this growth will be coming from pension funds, for which the asset pool is expected to experience nearly 10% growth in South America by 2020, again, making it the highest growth rate compared to other regions across the globe. In the next 12 months, 68% of South American investors are preparing to increase their allocations to the overall alternative asset market, and the same number of investors will be increasing allocations in PE funds.[8] Despite the perceived risks in investing in South America, these figures represent confidence in South America's markets and asset managers over the next 5–10 years, especially given the illiquid nature of private capital investments.

**Brazil** Currently, the two countries within South America vying to become the focal point for investment funds are Brazil and Chile. Brazil has a clear lead, being the third largest mutual fund marketplace in the world, slightly ahead of the US, with over USD 1.2 trillion in assets under management (AuM).[9] A majority of international investors have indicated that within the next three years they expect to invest into Brazil-focused PE funds, even though only 23% of South American investors are expecting to do the same.[10]

Following historically low inflation rates in the first half of 2018, Brazil's inflation rate has only recently picked up, although it is still far below levels previously seen in the twenty-first century.[11] The Central Bank of Brazil brought interest rates up to 14.25% for nearly two years in order to check the rising inflation and has only recently, since January 2017, reduced the interest rate to 8.25%.[12] These significantly high interest rates are perhaps one of the main reasons, therefore, that the funds industry in Brazil is so intensely concentrated in the fixed-income space, with roughly 53% of federal public bonds being held by investment funds.

Brazil's Brazilian Securities Commission (Commissao de Valores Mobiliarios or CVM) introduced a raft of new legislation as part of a modernisation drive with the aim to facilitate investment into funds at both national and international levels. For example, CVM Instruction No. 555, which, as well as dealing with the management, incorporation and operation of funds, permits Brazilian funds to increase their allotment into foreign products. The same regulations have reclassified what used to be seven different investment funds on offer to Brazilian investors into just four, which are (i) fixed-income funds, (ii) equities funds, (iii) foreign exchange funds, and (iv) multimarket funds.[13] The Brazilian government is hoping to create an environment for its fund industry to grow through a process it sees as simplification of what was perhaps a previously splintered market. CVM Instruction No. 555 also permitted, for the first time, the communication by fund managers with their investors through electronic means. The concept of a professional investor was introduced in CVM Instruction No. 554 and also changed the definitions of existing categories of investors. With these basic changes only having happened fairly recently, it is impressive that Brazil's asset management industry has been able to grow to such an extent without them.[14] Currently, however, there is an aversion shared by Brazilian investors of investing in foreign markets, the outcome of which being that Brazilian managers tend only to invest locally. CVM Instruction No. 555 has helped to make changes to this mindset but, unfortunately, the possibility of currency instability eating away at returns is still keeping local investors (and consequently their managers) from investing in foreign jurisdictions on a large scale.[15]

**Chile**  While Chile may be losing out to Brazil in the overall size of its funds market, there are certainly many aspects of the Chilean sociopolitical landscape that intimate that it may become a bigger hotspot for asset managers than Brazil in the future. The Association for Private Capital Investment in Latin America (LAVCA) publish a bi-annual report scoring the PE/VC market within each of the relevant Latin American jurisdictions. The scoring takes into account tax treatments, investor restrictions, capital markets, perceived corruption and entrepreneurship (amongst others).[16] Even though Chile has received a slight downgrade since 2015, it still sits at the number 1 spot when compared against the likes of Brazil, Argentina and Mexico.[17] According to LAVCA, Chile has a high average amongst all 13 categories and is noted as a Latin American country where the level of corruption is perceived to be low. The concept of entrepreneurship is heavily promoted as well, with accelerators like Start-Up Chile, created by the Chilean Economic Development Agency, providing capital (between USD 15 000 and USD 60 000) to young companies.[18] This type of programme is to be expected in a country where more than a third adults between the ages of 18 and 64 declare themselves to be entrepreneurs.[19]

Unfortunately, recent changes in the Chilean local law have created uncertainty and have meant that some pension funds (administradoras de fondo de pensiones or AFPs) have, at least for the moment, withheld investing in certain PE and VC funds.[20] The Chilean AFPs do however enjoy other liberal laws when compared to other Latin American jurisdictions. Current regulation permits AFPs to invest up to 80% of their assets in foreign assets (even though in reality this leads to about 40% foreign investment), compared to Brazil's limit of 10% (which in reality is only around 1%).[21] A major component of overseas investment is through ETFs, with, for example, USD 8.3 billion invested into BlackRock's iShares.[22]

**Argentina**  Argentina is not as popular a hub in Latin America as Brazil and Chile are, but that is slowly changing. Reforms introduced in 2017 by President Mauricio Macri created the role of 'Asesor Global de Inversiones' (AAGI), the global investment adviser, which for the first time, allows an investment adviser to advise clients with regards to both their onshore and offshore funds.[23] Prior to the introduction of the new role, clients had to receive advice from separate advisers. Even though this was lauded as a huge step in the right direction, as of early 2019 there have only been five licences issued.[24] Due to a combination of slow processing by the Comisión Nacional de Valores (CNV), the regulator of the AAGI, and more attractive tax rates in the neighbouring capital city of Montevideo, the new licence has not proven to be particularly popular. Combine those factors with a turbulent macro-economy and Argentina's bid to attract foreign asset managers (and grow its own local asset managers) appears to be going slow.

**Mexico** Mexico's go at introducing new regulations has had a much more positive effect on its asset management industry than Argentina's attempts, and it remains a key market for US asset managers wanting to expand into the Latin American asset management industry. In 2018, Mexican pension funds (Administradoras de Fondos para el Retiro or Afores), were able, for the first time, to invest in foreign mutual funds, having previously been restricted to investing in ETFs and separate managed accounts.[25] These new rules follow earlier changes to regulation allowing the Afores to invest 20% of their AuM in foreign assets. The relaxing of regulations by Mexico's pension regulator (Comisión Nacional del Sistema de Ahorro para el Retiro or Consar) has helped Mexican private capital vehicles raise USD 2.1 billion in 2015, a significant increase from USD 152 million in 2008.[26]

## THE MIDDLE EAST

The Middle Eastern investment landscape is dominated by its large sovereign wealth funds (SWFs). SWFs are established and managed by an investing arm of a country's government (as discussed in Chapter 6).

The investment objectives are flexible, which allows SWFs to adapt and react to economic or political factors. Middle Eastern SWF reserves and liquidity were affected by the recent oil price collapse. This resulted in some governments having to adjust their investing strategies and withdraw some assets in order to counter the sort of public deficits observed in Saudi Arabia and Qatar. However, SWFs in the region are still expected to grow albeit at a slower rate.

As one might expect, Sharia compliance tends to be a central tenet in the investment strategy of Middle Eastern SWFs. Although conventional investments still attract SWFs, there is still a preference for investment in Sharia-compliant financial products to satisfy all investors as it encourages the parties to a transaction to be just, fair, and ethical, in line with the Qur'an (the holy book of Islam) and the Sunnah (social and legal practices within the Islamic community). Asset managers abroad are increasing their offering of Sharia-compliant financial products in order to attract the higher liquidity of wealth from the Middle East.

The number of Islamic funds across the globe is growing rapidly. Back in 2008, there were 802 Islamic funds with a collective AuM of USD 47 billion. These numbers have now shot up to 1535 funds managing USD 70.8 billion as of early 2017.[27] However, when one compares these figures to the size of the overall Islamic finance universe (this includes Islamic banks and Sukuk), which is valued at around USD 2 trillion, the Islamic funds world seem small.[28]

The highest concentration of Islamic investing is found in equity, real estate(RE), and commodity funds. Investment funds that operate in accordance with Islamic principles are called Sharia-compliant funds. In order for a fund manager to operate a Sharia-compliant fund, there are certain fundamental rules that the manager needs to keep in mind. First, there cannot be any interest (riba) charged solely on the basis of money being lent from one person to another – this applies to the borrower, who is not allowed to pay it, and the lender, who is not allowed to receive it. Second, asset managers aiming to operate their fund as Sharia-compliant will have certain investment restrictions placed on them. The usual restrictions include producers of alcohol, tobacco, pornography, casinos or places of gambling, and banks. These restrictions are often requested in any event by non-Sharia investors, especially following the rise in ESG policies amongst asset managers. The final fundamental requirement deals with the contracts between the individuals involved and is the prohibition of gharar, which is the concept of unacceptable uncertainty. There is major emphasis placed on transparency in contracts and there cannot be contingency in a contract, meaning instruments such as derivatives where there may be a promise to sell a good that may not exist yet, are not Sharia compliant.[29]

Asset managers who wish to run Sharia-compliant funds will also need to appoint a panel of experts, known as a 'Sharia advisory board' that will consist of Sharia scholars who will provide a fatwa, a religious ruling, on the underlying investments made by the asset manager. The panel will ensure that the investments comply with fundamental Islamic principles but will also provide annual audits to ensure that returns from any previous investments made by the manager are still within the range for what scholars consider Sharia-compliant. In equity funds for example, if more than 5% of returns can be shown to be generated from small loans that may only be a small portion of a company's business, the Sharia advisory board will rule that the entire investment is not acceptable. If this amount is below 5%, however, (and is not an investment into a company focusing on the products listed above), then the investment might be Sharia-compliant. That 5% that was traced back to profits from loans will nevertheless be charitably donated, as it does not conform to Sharia principles, thereby 'purifying' the proceeds. This process is known as zakat and will be undertaken by the Sharia advisory board.[30]

The two countries leading the way for Islamic fund domiciliation are Malaysia (with 388 managers managing USD 22.6 billion) and Saudi Arabia (with 209 managers managing USD 25.2 billion), as these two countries have a steady supply of investors who are restricted in their investments to Sharia-compliant investment funds only.[31] Perhaps more surprising is the fact that there are 44 Islamic funds domiciled in Jersey, that between them manage USD 8.3 billion, which represents 11.8% of the total global Islamic AuM.[32] Due to the fact that the Islamic fund market is still relatively focused on smaller regions (although growth and the general upward trend in the area proves that that will not be the case for much longer) the distribution of assets to fund managers is slanted heavily towards smaller funds, especially those with an AuM of USD 50 million and below.[33]

**Gulf Cooperation Council**   Asset managers in the Gulf Cooperation Council (GCC) have benefitted greatly from the increasing popularity of Sharia-compliant funding and AuM of managers in the region is forecasted to grow to USD 110 billion by 2020 (from USD 45 billion in 2016).[34] These figures pale in comparison however to the total wealth held by participants of the GCC, which was estimated at USD 8 trillion in 2015 and is expected to be USD 11.8 trillion by 2020, the growth of which outpaces the global average by over 2%.[35] This growth is due to a combination of evermore high-net-worth individuals (HNWIs) in the region and capital-rich SWFs. A lack of foreign investors and participants in the GCC's markets is hamstringing growth in the region. However, changes are being implemented to boost the slow growth. Reforms to the Saudi Stock Exchange (which, at approximately USD 480 billion is the largest exchange in the GCC[36]) now allow foreign investors to hold assets through a global or local custodian bank rather than relying on local stock brokers.[37] This, as well as the inclusion of Saudi Arabia within the Emerging Market index in the MSCI will mean that Saudi Arabia's market will attract more foreign capital and it might cease to be the lowest foreign-held emerging stock market.[38]

**Dubai** The Dubai International Finance Centre (DIFC) is a 110-acre special economic zone, established in 2003 to become a pre-eminent financial centre across the entire region of the Middle East, Africa, and South Asia. The DIFC is run by three separate bodies:

- **DIFC Authority:** The main entity, the primary role of which is to plan the strategic development of the DIFC.
- **Dubai Financial Services Authority (DFSA):** The independent regulator of the financial services companies based in the DIFC.
- **Dispute Resolution Authority (DPA):** The body in charge of enforcing justice within the DIFC, it incorporates the courts, wills and probate registry and the arbitration centre. The laws are based on the English common law.[39]

A fund manager within the DIFC will be classified either as a 'domestic fund manager' or an 'external fund manager'. A domestic fund manager will be incorporated within the DIFC and be regulated by the DFSA in order to be able to manage a collective investment fund. An external fund manager is a foreign fund manager who may manage a domestic fund within the DIFC without the need to establish a registered office within the DIFC.[40] The external fund manager must be regulated by a regulator in a recognised jurisdiction (which includes, amongst others, the UK, US, Switzerland, and Hong Kong) and must also appoint a DIFC-based fund administrator to act as its agent when communicating with investors.[41] The DIFC has created a transparent and simple system for registration of different types of funds in the hopes of attracting asset managers to its centre.

The DIFC (and the rest of Dubai) have created an environment supportive enough of the financial system that it was ranked as number 25 in the 2017 Global Financial Centres Index (GFCI), which measures business environment, financial sector development, infrastructure factors, human capital, reputation, and other general factors.[42] It ranks three places above Abu Dhabi, its closest Middle Eastern rival.[43] The DIFC's ease of doing business (discussed in the paragraph above), as well as its lack of income and corporate tax, has created a desirable jurisdiction that has taken business away from Bahrain, previously the go-to fund jurisdiction in the Middle East.[44]

**Abu Dhabi** The Abu Dhabi Global Market (ADGM) is a similarly established onshore financial hub, based in the United Arab Emirates' (UAE) capital city. It is also run by separate authorities that run a separate legal system and regulatory framework. With the continued low price of oil, the UAE has concluded that by using its existing wealth, it can begin to diversify away from its primary resource of oil and instead build its financial sector's offerings and expertise. Abu Dhabi currently accounts for 75% of the UAE's total AuM, through the creation (and continued investment by) institutions such as the Abu Dhabi Investment Authority (ADIA), Mubadala, and the Abu Dhabi Investment Council (ADIC).[45] ADIA alone is estimated to be managing nearly USD 1 trillion and has been recently named as the world's biggest RE investor, with USD 62 billion of RE AuM.[46] The list of largest RE investors is usually dominated by US and European pension funds, but as the UAE moves further away from their dependence on oil, they should begin to dominate the 'top ten' lists.

# ASIA

Asia is a rapidly developing region, aided by double taxation treaties, growing entrepreneurship, greater access to financing options, a large and growingly educated population, and an increase in HNWIs and SWFs. Asia is quickly becoming a targeted hotspot for asset managers around the world, who do not want to miss out on the opportunity to tap into the region's increasing wealth. The increased offering of robust fund investment products as well as significant updates to regulations are allowing hubs such as Hong Kong and Singapore to challenge New York and London for top spots in the eyes of the asset manager.

However, whilst the Asian region has been developing, its asset management landscape is still lagging behind those of Western economies. There have been a variety of Ovum surveys carried out highlighting that management confidence in their current systems across different regions varies enormously. One Ovum survey[47] asked asset management firms how well they believed their systems' ability to support expansion into new geographies, introduce new asset classes, and to comply quickly with new regulations would be. The response of European investment management firms averaged at 38.2%, with Asian firms falling far behind at 21%.

**China**   China is predicted to have the highest assets under management growth-rates in Asia. China's current assets under management sits at around USD 3.2 trillion but predictions have the 2030 figure sitting at USD 17.1 trillion, overtaking the UK shortly and coming in second only to the US.[48] This is a stunning achievement given that the Chinese asset management market did not really exist until the early 1990s.[49] Following a sluggish start throughout the 1990s and early 2000s, the market really began to open up in the earlier part of this decade as the various Chinese regulators began to relax their financial regulations.

The relaxation of financial regulations may be one of the reasons behind the explosive growth in the number of mutual funds on offer to Chinese investors. In June 2013, there were only 1345 mutual funds offered in China, whereas by June 2017 there were 4419.[50] Accordingly, the average size of each mutual fund has not increased. It may be that we see a change in this, whereby the number of mutual funds on offer slows and the average assets under management grow as the market matures and (as has happened in the UK and US) competitors consolidate to preserve costs.

The growth of the asset management industry in China was previously bottlenecked by the Chinese state. The Chinese Securities Regulatory Commission (CSRC), only in late September of 2017 granted approval to six different asset managers for the establishment of fund of funds.[51] Further, at the beginning of 2018 the Chinese government introduced a new 3% tax on certain investment returns in China, part of a wider movement in how companies will need to pay their tax. This tax will impact hedge and equity funds significantly more than other asset managers as the traditional strategies they employ are more vulnerable to the new rules. Indeed, competitors in this space, such as mutual funds, are partially exempt. Underlying these new rules may be an attempt by China's Ministry of Finance to slim down the hedge fund industry in China – in which there are thousands of lightly regulated firms currently operating.[52]

Cross-border regulation has been monitored carefully in different jurisdictions and regions for many years, and the cross-border fund passport, initially borne out of Europe spread rapidly to other funds and regions. This passporting trend carried formidable strength and was naturally aligned to the increasing reputation and size of the financial services. However, within Asia, there are now obstacles appearing to this trend, questioning the future regulation of cross-border business. In China, three passports have been in use, but not all have reached their intended purpose. The China Mainland-Hong Kong Mutual Recognition of Funds (MRF) has experienced strong 'southbound' activity, but much less in the 'northbound' trading area. Southbound trading refers to Chinese mainland investors who 'have access to Hong Kong shares through either Shanghai or Shenzhen brokers'.[53] Whereas, northbound trading refers to 'foreign investors from Hong Kong buying and selling shares in Shanghai and Shenzhen under the "Connect" scheme, as part of Beijing's efforts to open its markets more widely for foreign investors'.[54] As such, only a handful of Hong Kong funds over the past few years have been approved for distribution into mainland China. In addition, the Asian Region Funds Passport (ARFP) had been slow to reach any formalised agreements, but has slowly gained participation. Also, the Association of South-East Asian Nations Collective Investment Scheme Framework (ASEAN) has seen very little activity, but still keeps Singapore as a strong influencer and supporter of the passport.

However, despite all three passports being somewhat disappointing in recent times, there has been major take-up of a range of bilateral agreements. In December 2016, the People's Bank of China granted Ireland an RMB 50 billion quota under the Renminbi Qualified Foreign Institutional Investor (RQFII) scheme,[55] and the purpose of this is to allow Irish-domiciled funds to purchase securities in local Chinese markets. This ultimately provides an opportunity to further enhance the Irish funds' ability to gain access to Chinese mainland markets, and the Chinese Central Bank stated that it would begin to accept applications for investments through Shenzen Connect, in which Irish funds were first granted access in early 2015. Additionally, Swiss funds can now be sold in Hong Kong, and vice versa following an agreed understanding between Hong Kong's the Securities and Futures Commission (SFC) and the Swiss Financial Market Supervisory Authority (FINMA).

**Japan**   Prime Minister Shinzo Abe's introduction of economic reforms in Japan has been dubbed 'Abenomics'. Against the backdrop of Abenomics and Japan's economy, the Japanese asset management has undergone some serious regulatory reforms in an attempt to open up the Japanese asset management industry. People over the age of 60 hold a staggering 70% of household financial assets, many of whom experienced heavy losses during the bursting of Japan's bubble in the 1990s.[56] Understandably, the losses instilled an incredibly conservative 'investing' nature in the population of Japan, with 52% of this wealth being held in bank accounts generating eye-wateringly low returns, compared to the US, where only 13% of household financial assets are held in the same manner.

The Japanese asset management market is one that has already been penetrated by foreign asset managers, especially in the institutional sector. Of the JPY 96.9 trillion managed through toshin (domestic registered investment vehicles such as investment trust funds) in Japan by asset managers, foreign asset managers account for JPY 10.2 trillion, or nine out of the top 20. Whilst the top ten managers benefit from being household names and are able to utilise their existing networks of banks and intermediaries, the bottom half of the top 20 is dominated by foreign managers who offer a more customer-centric service and are also unencumbered by the large conglomerate-like size of the domestic managers. This growing in popularity of foreign managers is also prevalent when studying the pension asset market where four of the top ten managers are foreign (a total of JPY 27.9 trillion out of 140). The reasoning behind this growth are twofold. First, domestic investors are (albeit slowly) beginning to allocate more assets towards foreign funds and investments, which oftentimes is outside of the domestic asset managers' capabilities and therefore allows foreign managers to step in with their own offerings, or acting as sub-advisers to the domestic manager. The other point to highlight is that the Tokyo Metropolitan Government has gone on a large-scale offensive to woo foreign managers – even setting up a 'Financial One-Stop Support Service'[57] to provide comprehensive support to foreign businesses setting up shop (or expanding) in Tokyo. Advice given by the Tokyo government includes avoiding crowded domestic long-only equities that many domestic managers already offer and instead offer new classes of investment such as PE and VC opportunities.

One cannot mention pension funds in Japan without mentioning the Government Pension Investment Fund (GPIF), more commonly known as the 'Whale'. The GPIF is the world's largest pension fund with an AuM of USD 1.4 trillion, truly a mover of markets.[58] Over 90% of the Whale's holdings are split between equities and bonds, both domestic and foreign, and active and passive, whilst the remaining amounts are split between infrastructure (JPY 1967 trillion), PE (JPY 82 trillion) and alternative RE (JPY 81 trillion) –'tiny' in comparison.[59] GPIF has recently undergone some aggressive changes in order to brace for the inevitable cost of having an increasingly elderly population. At the rate that Japan's population is shrinking, by 2040, more than one in three people in Japan will be over 65, the highest proportion of over 65s in the world.[60] An old colleague and friend of mine, Hiromichi Mizuno, the last CIO of the Japanese pension fund recognises that these challenges exist and has been pushing for changes in a very positive way with how GPIF interacts with its external asset managers. By producing its 'Stewardship Principles', GPIF have forced its external managers to incorporate ESG investment policies within their investment process and provide explanations as to why the asset manager has not done so.[61] GPIF are also signing their equities managers onto long-term mandates to allow them to focus on a longer investment horizon, rather than short annual investment cycle normally seen in the market.[62]

**India**  On 8 November 2016, Indian Prime Minister Narendra Modi introduced a new 500 rupee note and cancelled the circulation of the old 100 rupee note in an attempt to fight money laundering and introduce more cashless transactions to the Indian economy, whether these objectives will be achieved we do not know yet. It is clear that many new bank accounts have been opened. Now, 80% of Indians have bank accounts, compared to 53% in 2014 – a huge increase.[63] This is expected to help move more Indian savers towards investing, whereas before most saving was held via cash or gold – a new wave of bank accounts is expected to provide a boost to the domestic asset management industry. Other steps recently taken include regulation introduced by the Securities and Exchange Board of India (SEBI) which stated that each asset manager must ring-fence 2 basis points of their total expense ratio to be spent on initiatives for investor education and awareness.[64] The initiatives then need to be disclosed to SEBI in the asset manager's half yearly trustee reports that are made to SEBI. One of the goals of this initiative is to educate would-be investors who live in the B15 cities, a term coined to describe those cities ranking below the top 15 cities (T15) in terms of GDP per city. Research has found that the B15 cities only provide roughly 14% of AuM compared to 72% of the T15 cities (the rest being split the remaining cities in India) and SEBI and the Indian government are keen to unlock the potential of the B15 cities.[65]

Very similar to managers targeting millennials through investing apps on smartphones, asset managers in India are utilising the Indian population's access to mobile phones as a chance to reel in new investors. Impressively, the share of trading undertaken on the National Stock Exchange of India (NSE) by mobile phone users more than doubled, from 3.3% in 2016 to 7.7% in 2018 – meaning that there is plenty of opportunity for further growth.[66] Giving mobile phone users the chance to trade via apps or even through normal SMS should help to tap into the populations of the B15 cities. Finally, if managers made it simpler for investors to submit the required know-your-client documentation through apps or photos taken on their phone, they would be able to open the market to people who previously had difficulty opening even basic accounts, a large number of whom live in B15 cities.

**Singapore** Singapore is a key hub for the financial sector – its strategic location and proximity to other Asian capital cities, early embrace of technology, and skilled English-speaking workforce, supported by robust infrastructure and a business friendly government, mean that foreign investors are keen to part with their capital in Singapore's favour. Singapore is also the only country in Asia with an AAA credit rating from all three ratings agencies (S&P, Moody's, and Fitch), further illustrating its stable nature.[67] This stability has allowed Singapore's asset management industry to grow to USD 2.4 trillion in 2017, 78% of which originated from outside of Singapore, with 67% of total AuM invested into Asian Pacific countries, underscoring Singapore's position as the gateway for Asian investment.[68] The AuM growth is seen in both the traditional investment types as well as alternatives such as PE and hedge funds.

The Monetary Authority of Singapore (MAS) continues to target alternatives as a growth area for the Singaporean asset management industry, currently comprising 21% of Singapore's total allocation to investments. In order to develop these areas, MAS has introduced multiple initiatives over the last few years in order to capture the growing deal activity ongoing in Asia Pacific (USD 158 billion in 2017).[69] One of these initiatives was to create a simplified regulatory regime for VC fund managers that aims to greatly lower their compliance costs and make more capital available to them. For example, VC managers will no longer be required (as other fund managers do) to have directors with at least five years of experience in fund management, nor will they be required to adhere to the same capital requirements as other fund managers.[70] MAS even established a platform called MATCH (Meet ASEAN's Talents and Champions) that facilitates investments from investors into ASEAN enterprises. A short survey was required to be completed by start-up companies whereby participants would provide certain information, which amongst other things included how much capital they were hoping to raise and what types of business activities would this funding be used for (technology, marketing, infrastructure, etc.). Investors would complete a similar survey asking how much they typically allocate to ASEAN investments, what their typical deal range was and their top sectors of interest.[71] This platform hosted 380 participating investors who will now invest USD 6 billion in 2019 and a further USD 6 billion during the course of 2020–2021.[72]

**Hong Kong** Hong Kong is often compared with Singapore and the two are seen as regional competitors for the financial hubs in Asia. Hong Kong, too, has a strong regulatory framework, impressive infrastructure, and deep talent pools of educated service providers who speak English. Whilst comparisons between the two often see Hong Kong slightly trailing behind Singapore (especially following 'independence') Hong Kong has perhaps a (not so) secret weapon – unrivalled access to the Chinese mainland. Co-ordination between regulators of the Hong Kong and the rest of China should increase Hong Kong's standing as a hub for asset managers looking to invest in China. However, this access may also be causing over-reliance on mainland China and its influence. Another local Asian hub could challenge this unrivalled access and China's financial industry itself could grow to challenge Hong Kong's expertise.

The Hong Kong asset management industry is littered with regulators: the Securities and Futures Commission (SFC), the Hong Kong Monetary Authority (HKMA), the Mandatory Provident Funds Authority (MPFA) and the Office of the Commissioner of Insurance

(OCI). According to surveys, 73% of asset managers enjoy a healthy relationship with these regulators; however, 53% are growing more concerned as to the possible negative impact of increased regulations in the asset management industry over the next five years.[73] An even larger number of asset managers are worried about their growing compliance costs. In order for a fund market in any given jurisdiction to grow and become world leading, it needs an understanding regulator that lays out clear guidance as to what is to be expected from those it regulates. Unfortunately, for Hong Kong more managers perceive that the current regulatory framework for asset management is slightly stifling as it was developed originally for banks. If it wishes to grow and become a more diverse industry, the regulators will have to recognise that more overarching changes are needed if more complex products are to be successfully managed or marketed in Hong Kong. This bank-led origin though is not unique to Hong Kong. Other jurisdictions such as Italy and Ireland also suffer from the same bank-led origin.

**Southeast Asia** I define this region here as Brunei, Cambodia, Indonesia, Laos, Malaysia, Myanmar, Philippines, Thailand, and Vietnam. Growth in the Southeast Asia (SEA) region is expected to be significant, reaching nearly USD 4 trillion by 2025 and it will become the fourth largest market in the world (although these figures includes Singaporean AuM, representing a significant chunk).[74] Key trends being witnessed within the SEA region are shared with those that managers are seeing in India and China, namely that changes in demographics on both ends of the age spectrum are producing more growth and investors are becoming more interested in a variety of products.

Currently, the much-cursed millennials make up 27% of SEA's population, leading to a high degree of smartphone usage in the region.[75] Meanwhile the makeup of elderly people (aged 60 and above) within the population's region will range between over 25% in Thailand, to only 8.1% in Laos.[76] Both of these scenarios require separate solutions that asset managers should note. Whilst the younger generation demand increased use of digital platforms when investing, the growing elderly population will require pension funds and insurance providers to account for increased life expectancy (meaning larger liabilities) and allocate their capital accordingly. Some changes to regulation will need to come from governments, however, as many in the SEA region do not have access to a pension fund and have savings far below those that they need when they retire. In Thailand, for example, more than 50% of working-age people do not have access to a pension fund, and the country is not an anomaly – Vietnamese, Indonesian, Malaysian, and Filipino lack of access varies from just under 40% to over 20%.[77]

Whilst active strategies in the SEA region are still the most popular strategy amongst mainstream asset managers, investors have started to look beyond traditional strategies in order to find more alpha-generating opportunities. The demand for alternative assets and Sharia-compliant products has doubled in the years between 2012 and 2017, and is unlikely to slow down as local managers begin to provide more innovative products.[78] Asset managers will need to weigh up the decision between offering a multi-product range or delve into specialist products.

One of the more positive trends as of late has been the popularity of impact investing in the area. State-backed lenders in Indonesia, the Philippines, and Vietnam were key reasons for a growth of 90% of impact investing over the past ten years.[79] More than 60% of the capital was deployed across the three countries, of a total of USD 12.2 billion between 2007 and 2017.[80]

Another common theme amongst all of the Southeast Asian countries is the opening up its financial markets to foreign investors. The largest of these economies, Indonesia, is predicted to have a middle class of over 140 million by 2020 with consumer spending to grow alongside that to over USD 800 billion.[81] Previous caps that limited the allocation of Indonesian asset managers to overseas investment at 15% have recently been repealed, permitting 100% of assets to now be invested outside of Indonesia.[82] Further opening up has taken place in Vietnam, where a previous lack of liquidity was solved when foreign ownership restrictions on public companies was lifted, allowing foreign investors to purchase 100% shareholdings of public companies that have not been deemed nationally strategic.

**Australia**   The key to Australia's asset management market is the sheer size of their pension funds, known as 'superannuation' funds (discussed in Chapter 6).[83] In September 2017, the total size of Australia's pension funds was estimated to be AUD 2.5 trillion by the Australian Prudential Regulation Authority (APRA) which equates to an 8.7% increase from the previous year.[84] This leaves Australia with the fourth largest pension pot globally and one of the fastest growing resources for local asset managers. The superannuation's industry asset allocation is noted in a quarterly report, with equities being allocated 50%, whereas hedge funds have only been allocated 2%.[85] The amounts allocated to 'other' (which includes hedge funds) have stayed relatively level, indicating that alternatives have not yet experienced much of an increase in popularity amongst pension fund managers in Australia.

The size of the superannuation and its growth since its introduction in 1992 is the main driver behind the growth of Australia's managed funds industry. Australia's assets totalled only AUD 255 billion at the end of 1991 but have subsequently experienced a 10.1% compound annual growth rate (CAGR).

## OTHER TRENDS

**Population**   Different population trends around the globe will all have their own unique impact on the asset management industry in the future. As the composition of a population changes, whether it be the median age becoming older or younger, or the median income growing, fund managers will have to change to adapt to their new markets. In almost every country in Europe, the demographic is shifting to an older generation, with fewer people left to replace them, illustrated by the dependency ratio, which is the number of people aged 65 and over as a proportion to those between 15 and 64.[86] This issue is not split between north and south or east and west Europe, with Germany's ratio rising from 24% in 2000 to 59% in 2050, for Spain from 25% to 59%, and for Slovenia from 20% to 54%.[87]

Worryingly, this comes with the possibility of putting European pension systems under significant stress. If governments are not at the forefront, they will need to protect savers whilst still allowing for flexibility amongst the pension funds to generate sufficient returns for the growing elderly population. Savvy asset managers will be those that develop products that cater towards pension funds that now have stakeholders living much longer lives than previous generations. There will also be a significant passing-on of wealth from the Baby Boomer generation to Generation X and their kin, with questions needed to be answered on wealth accumulation.

Whilst Europe will struggle with an ageing population (and at the same time, declining overall), Africa is projected to have three times the population of Europe by 2050, even though their populations were level in 2000.[88] This phenomenal growth in population will see a massive increase in the demand for investment products that asset managers will be able to offer, some of which are likely not yet on offer. As the dependency ratio falls in Africa, more capital will be freed up for the newer generations. The largest benefiter of this will be retail investment products, as they will see a huge upswing in demand as levels of disposable income grow.

The concept of the 'Asian Century' has been self-heralded so that the twenty-first century will be dominated by Asian culture and politics, much as America dominated the twentieth century. However, I believe the twenty-first century will still belong to the US. But with Asian shifts in population, its cities alone may hold up to 3 billion people by 2050, meaning significant investment in infrastructure will be required by governments and their investing arms.[89] As discussed in the section below on pensions, Asia will need to quickly upgrade its existing pension landscape in order to provide a safety net for its rapidly ageing population. In 2015, the share of the Asian population over 65 was 7.8%, but by 2040 this will have more than doubled to 16% and as the working age population shrinks in some countries, asset managers will need to find a way to exploit the 'silver dividend'.[90] By staying in jobs for longer, the elderly population are supressing the younger generation from advancing into more senior roles. Eventually the older generation will have to secede their jobs, but instead of being removed altogether from their positions, there may be a way to keep them employed as advisers and supporters to the younger generation.

The speed at which this ageing occurs will also be something that asset managers and investors need to be mindful of. France took 115 years to go from being an ageing society to becoming an aged society, whereas China will make that transition in a quarter of a century, again, presenting the need for urgent pension reform across the region.[91]

**Pensions**   A study undertaken by Willis Towers Watson of the P22 (countries whose pension funds manage the most assets) show that levels of pension fund capital have hit USD 41.35 trillion as of 2017.[92] Where these managers allocate their assets therefore has a massive impact owing to this enormous amount of capital, with governments frequently changing a central pension fund's mandate in order to invest where the government of the day believes there to be a need for funds.

In some areas of the world, where pension systems are only beginning to be established and fleshed out, governments are hoping to learn from mistakes made by those countries with more established systems. One common theme, however, across the globe (admittedly more so in certain jurisdictions) is that it is obvious that more capital is being moved into alternatives (hedge funds and PE). Whilst this move may be more related to the recent low interest rates in many parts of the world, another aim of this new policy is to get more money flowing into areas of infrastructure, which has been sorely underfunded in recent years due to government policies of reducing spending.

**Developing Countries' Pensions**   Although already firmly established in the European, Australasian, and North American regions, middle classes in parts of Asia and Africa have not yet reached their full potential. The population of the middle class in countries such as China and South Africa will grow exponentially over the next few decades. As of 2015, middle class spending in Asia-Pacific had already reached 36% of the world's total amount, outstripping Europe (at 31%) to become the region with the highest spending amount of the middle class.[93] A growing middle class in any country in the world is important as demands from people in the class cascade across multiple sectors to help shape a country's economy. For example, as an individual's disposable income increases they will be able to allocate more towards saving, which often takes the form of pensions.

Within Asia's 12 key markets, the impact of an ageing population is felt across both retail and institutional investors. For example, the number of people aged 50 and over is likely to exceed 1 billion in Asia by 2025. Public pension funds will therefore need to ensure that they adjust and react to these demographic factors. The uncertainties caused by early retirement and improvements to people's way of life in Asia is causing pension funds to ensure risk-management procedures mitigate any future cash flow volatilities, whilst ensuring satisfactory returns.

China's pension assets are expected to grow astronomically. Between 2015 and 2025, there will be an estimated CAGR of 18% as the total pension assets grow from USD 1.33 trillion to USD 7.04 trillion.[94] Hopefully, this asset growth will be enough to support the country's growing elderly population, which will have grown to around 300 million by the same time.[95] Unfortunately for China, its public pension fund that currently manages around 65% of China's total pension assets is currently generating very low returns due to its conservative investment attitude. The three governing pillars of China's pension system are the PFF and NCSSF (discussed below), enterprise and occupational annuities and individuals' private pensions, with the majority of the focus being on the first pillar. A centralisation of the management of the two pension systems and a reallocation of surplus funds in the provinces to the NCSSF should in the long term produce better returns.

Previously, the PFF could only allocate its assets towards cash and Chinese government bonds, the main factor behind the return rate being only 2.5%. However, through 2016 and 2017, these restrictions have begun to be lifted, allowing the PFF to begin allocating assets to managers that invest in PE and RE, along with other alternative asset strategies. The NCSSF (the National Council for Social Security Fund) currently only manages slightly over 10% of China's pension assets, but will be estimated to manage closer to 30% by 2025. In 2017, the chairman of the NCSSF, Lou Jiwei, outlined five key strategies that the NCSSF will aim to focus on, two of which were fund of funds and overseas PE. The new key strategy points, along with the ability for asset managers to now pitch for external allocation from the pension funds will provide more opportunities for the asset manager market, alternatives and mainstream alike.[96]

As of 2017, South African pension assets accounted for USD 258 billion, which represents a slow growth of 2.8% 10-year CAGR from 2007 when total assets were USD 195 billion. Whilst this may be sluggish growth, the ratio of total assets managed by pension funds to GDP is 75.1%, which is well above the average of the P22 which is currently 64.5%.[97] South Africa's largest pension fund is the South African Government Employees Pension Fund that is a defined benefit scheme with nearly 2 million members and USD 124 billion of AuM.[98] The other two large public pension funds in South Africa are Eskom Pension and Provident Fund and Telkom Pension Fund, both trailing behind with USD 48.5 billion and USD 36.6 million each.[99]

According to the South African Government Employees Pension Fund's latest annual report, the government employee's fund is reallocating capital, shifting nearly USD 5 billion to 'developmental, infrastructure, renewable energy, economic transformation and other unlisted investments'[100] in order to invest long term in such a way as to create a sustainable future. The fund invests both directly into infrastructure assets and indirectly, through jointly owned funds such as the Pan-African Infrastructure Development Fund. The strategy of the pension fund follows a liability-driven approach that is able to take into consideration any future payments to members, a strategy discussed more in-depth in Chapter 7. As discussed elsewhere in this book, there is a growing need for pension funds to invest in their country's infrastructure projects.

It appears that South African pension funds have awoken to demand for infrastructure spending and are reacting accordingly.

ESG considerations are also at the heart of the fund's investment strategy, being a signatory to the UNPRI as well as the Code for Responsible Investing in South Africa and ensuring that they consider South African society as a whole rather than just their members. The amended regulation 28 of the Pension Funds Act 1956 implemented in 2011[101] introduced responsible investing into the fiduciary duty a pension fund has to its members. The amendment specifically cited the ESG characteristics of an investment that should be taken into account when pension fund managers deploy capital. This was a blanket-wide amendment, applying to all possible categories of assets.

**Developed countries' Pension Systems**  Europe, in contrast with developing countries, has enjoyed an elderly population for years, and the effects as such will not be felt in the same way as changes in the Asian population. Instead, one argument is that the rapid ageing of Western populations will cause stock markets to sink. The reason for this is that as wealthy, older investors retire, they will sell their shares and move the proceeds into cash or spend their wealth during retirement. Additionally, this argument also suggests that younger generations, who perhaps have not had a chance to save as much (generation rent), will comparatively not have as much capital to allocate as the generations before them. The younger generation may therefore feel that in the case of riskier assets such as shares, they may be out of reach for the average younger investor. In some cases, they may feel that they are barred entirely from markets such as alternative assets.

On the other hand, many have argued that an ageing population is leading to certain sectors, such as health care, insurance, pensions, and leisure, enjoying greater investment. In the case of the financial crisis for example, the unfortunate and indebted nature of a plethora of Western governments was highlighted when investment was cutback across the board. This in turn has emphasised the problems with severe, continued austerity measures and individuals are now perhaps more aware that when the government provides less investment to public services such as health care and public transportation, individuals will be required to pay for more. Expert reports and global pensions fund managers have agreed with this latter argument, and stated that, 'over the medium to longer term, the demographics of ageing populations are likely to collide with rising and unsustainable public-sector debt levels in many areas of the world'.[102]

## NOTABLE CHANGES ON A GLOBAL SCALE

**Consumer Spending**  The change of spending habits by the global middle class will create further opportunities for asset managers. The behavioural changes in the middle class will see the creation of certain markets that did not exist before (i.e. the sharing economy) and also the growth in popularity in other markets that may have previously been out of reach whilst in the lower-income thresholds (e.g. luxury goods).

**English Language as an Asset**  The types of goods and services will differ between developing and developed nations; nonetheless, both sets of countries will witness a change in attitude in the middle class. Two separate trends predicted by Partners Group amongst emerging markets is the increase in spending on higher quality foods and English language education.[103]

The British Council predicts that, by 2020, more than one in four people in the world will be using English, and indeed will need to use English as a tool to develop their business on a global stage.[104] Across the developing world, the middle class see English as a tool to improve their employment opportunities and thus fuel their income growth. In China, for example, the value of the market for English language education is set to grow by roughly 15% over the coming years.[105]

This growth of a lingua franca can be seen throughout history with the growth of empires, from Greek, Latin, and French, to English. Indeed, Greek was the very height of sophistication two to three thousand years ago (noting, for example, its use by Saint Paul in spreading the Christian word through 'Greek' cities). However, it is the internet and the entertainment industry that has, in recent years, forged English as the language of business and mass communication (even better when you can rap to it – a small nod to Carlyle).

**The Sharing Economy**  In more developed countries meanwhile, the middle class is changing its spending habits through the increase popularity of the sharing economy. The massive increase in popularity of open platforms such as Uber and Airbnb highlights the changing in attitudes to the consumption of goods and services. In the US, although this phenomenon is not restricted to the middle class, nearly 60% of those that provided a service or goods were part of the middle class.[106]

**Breaking Down Investing Barriers**  New generations of investors also have different priorities when investing, many are more ESG-conscious than their predecessors and look to invest only in impact funds (see Chapter 4 on governance). Many in the new generation also feel barred from the investing world for a multitude of reasons, including lack of income to invest, lack of knowledge of the subject, desire to save rather than invest, or even that their parents never gave them advice on the subject. Certain asset managers have learnt that the best way to break down these barriers is to tailor their investment approach to the younger generation through, for example, applications on smartphones. The concept of a 'round up' has been transposed into investing and the concept has recently been heavily marketed to the younger generation of investors. Round ups work simply by rounding up an investor's latest purchase on their card to the nearest full unit of currency. A coffee for GBP 2.75 will include a roundup of GBP 0.25 that will be allocated towards an index fund. Whilst this is an effective method for getting younger generations interested in investing at an early age, the amounts invested each time are arguably too small, depending on the personal goals of the younger investor. Smartphone growth and use is monumental in regions such as Africa and India where costs of expensive computer equipment means that smartphone reliance is heavier in these regions.

**Growth of Technology and Digital Natives**  Whilst there are concerns surrounding the asset management industry, it is certain that asset managers are keen for the implementation and trialling of technology. Technological innovation is enabling asset managers to access upgraded and integrated systems whilst lowering overall operating costs. Asset managers are seeking to adopt cloud-based delivery models in order to ensure agile operating models amid downward market pressures (see Chapter 8 on technology). Younger generations that are being raised in a digital and technological world are typically perceived as being capable of handling such technologies. Whilst previously jobs in asset managers may have been allocated to those of an older generation, successful asset managers will be those who convince new entries to the jobs market that working in the asset management industry will prove to be a fulfilling career. Otherwise, the brightest and best will seek careers in technology. Instead of fully immersing themselves in the latest tech, asset managers would also benefit from partnering up with technology or software companies to enhance their offerings. These partnerships should also cater to the need for newer generations to receive more frequent updates and become more immersed in their investments.

**Increased Drive for Risk**  As super-low interest rates have become the new social norm during and following the financial crisis, a return to higher interest rates over the coming years would slowly reverse the changes undertaken by asset managers in order to generate returns for investors. Larger institutional investors especially have been pushed to move more money into riskier bond portfolios and alternatives such as PE and hedge funds. The move back to 'normal' (I would argue) interest rates may reverse some of these changes in investor appetite; however, especially in the case of alternatives, it is not always easy to quickly unwind an investor's holdings. It may be that having had a taste of riskier products producing better returns that pension funds and other institutions stick with their now riskier portfolios. It is still the case that outside the US and Canada, the allocation by institutions to alternatives is still too small. As the alternatives market becomes more mainstream and government policies change, we will see more capital moved into the alternatives space. However, I do not see a return to normal interest rates for years to come.

**Changing Pricing Structures**  It is undeniable that the traditional fee structures in mainstream assets are on their way out. This is due to a combination of the rise in index trackers that charge brutally competitive low (or zero) fees and the increase in the number of millennial investors. Fee structures do need to change to adapt to the new type of investor. In 2014, only 39% of global AuM was invested through active products, which was a huge drop from 59% in 2003.[107] More on the existential risk of the size of the passive market later in this book.

This is forcing managers to come up with increasingly complex fee structures and move away from the more basic options of charging a percentage of the value of the AuM and charging on the performance of the fund. So, for example, index and tracking managers can make enough base management fee from renting out their holdings to shorting hedge managers.

## OFFSHORE JURISDICTIONS: THE GOOD, THE BAD AND THE (NO LONGER) UGLY

For the average person, the word 'offshore' has become synonymous with the phrases 'tax haven' and 'money laundering'. This has been commonplace since before I started writing this book, of course; however, since the publishing of the Panama Papers and Paradise Papers (see Chapter 8), offshore jurisdictions have since become even more (if possible) vilified in the public eye. As more leaks emerge, politicians are stepping up their calls for transparency amongst the offshore jurisdictions. Queen Elizabeth II has been criticised heavily for having money in offshore holdings, held through the Duchy of Lancaster (the sovereign's private estate).[108,109]

**The Good**  What many people seem to have forgotten, or perhaps did not understand in the first place, is that most people will in one way or another, hold (directly or indirectly) money offshore. Pension funds around the world will often invest through offshore vehicles into PE or infrastructure developments in order to achieve the returns provided to savers. Whilst there are individuals that operate outside of the law, the overwhelming majority of the offshore industry operates within the confines of not only their own legal system, but also within international standards. There are many reasons fund managers choose to establish funds in offshore jurisdictions, not least because of the flexibility and broad offerings established by offshore legal systems. For managers, offshore funds avoid double taxation, at fund and at investor level. Thus, the investor only pays tax once not twice. Is that not fair? This allows the investor to, tax-wise, effectively invest directly. This is a good thing, as it allows investors to invest through professionals, and in a portfolio manner, to allow suitable liquidity and diversification.

Offshore centres also offer a mature marketplace of service providers that has grown to provide for the appetites of fund managers and investors alike. Offshore locations provide access to international investors, both private and institutional. The aim of the offshore jurisdiction, such as the Channel Islands, is to cater to the wider international audience by having a regulatory system essentially built for fund management as well as a legal framework designed for a wide variety of fund vehicle.

The concept of a fund being tax neutral is, however, not one reserved solely for offshore funds – partnerships are specifically legislated (especially the English limited partnership and the Irish ICAV) in jurisdictions such as the UK, US, and in mainland Europe to also be deemed tax neutral.[110]

Many of the commonly known offshore jurisdictions, including the Channel Islands, have had their fund regimes assessed by the European Securities and Markets Authority (ESMA) and were deemed to offer high levels of protections to their investors. Combined with the demolishing of the previous secrecy provisions that limited the transparency and reporting and the new global stance on anti-money laundering, the offshore jurisdictions meet global reporting and transparency standards.

Lastly, the concept of the 'midshore' or 'near shore' is gaining traction. Are Ireland, Switzerland, Luxembourg, Cyprus, and Malta, on- or off-shore? Is Delaware an offshore state? As countries around the world race to push corporation tax down to zero, the distinctions between on-, mid-, near- and off-shore blur.

**The (Once) Bad**   Offshore was once secretive and this was bad. Mind you, so is/was UK RE ownership.

However, following the introduction of the Foreign Account Tax Compliance Act (FATCA) and more recently the Common Reporting Standards (CRS) regimes, secrecy is being abolished. As discussed in Chapter 4 on governance, the implementation of CRS has meant that offshore funds have been forced to report automatically to the individual investor's tax authorities.

The OECD had identified, in the latter half of the 2000s, that large amounts of money were (and still are) being sent offshore in a bid to evade notifying one's local tax authorities and ultimately reduce their tax bill.[111] The CRS was developed by the OECD, after being heavily influenced by the approach taken by FATCA, and initially adopted in July of 2014. In order to be truly effective, the OECD understood that the breadth of data collection had to be extensive with regards to each aspect it collected data on. The gatherers of this information, the 'financial institutions', had to therefore consist of a number of different types of organisations, including banks, custodians, brokers, and certain CISs and insurance companies, all of which collate financial information. The reporters of the information had to include not only individuals but also legal entities behind which individuals often try to hide, which is why the financial institutions are required to look through these entities and identify any beneficial owner. Finally, the financial information itself needed to cover all types of income derived from the investment.

Since its adoption, over 100 countries worldwide have signed up to the CRS, which aims to prevent tax evasion through the facilitation of an investor's information. Within each country that has signed up to the CRS, each financial institution which includes, amongst others, fund managers, is required to gather information on any holder of equity or debt in the fund. The fund manager is then required to report all of the information gathered on its investors to the tax authority in its home jurisdiction. Any information collected on investors that are not also resident in the same tax jurisdiction will be referred to their relevant tax jurisdiction.

For example, a Finnish investor in a fund in Guernsey would provide the fund manager with certain identifying information, such as name, date of birth, bank account details, and relevant tax jurisdiction (often in a document known as a subscription agreement). The fund manager would then provide the tax authority in Guernsey with the Finnish investor's information, who will then pass it on to Verohallinto (the Finnish tax authorities) nine months following the end of the relevant reporting calendar year.

Offshore jurisdictions have since largely complied with CRS and FATCA. Even before the introduction of CRS, an offshore jurisdiction that was either a UK Crown Dependency or Overseas Territory would have been a signatory to the 'UK FATCA', an automatic exchange of information again based on the original FATCA that was announced in 2013. Following the introduction of CRS, however, the UK FATCA will eventually phased out.

More recently, the UK government has passed the Sanctions and Anti-Money Laundering Act.[112] The Act requires its overseas territories (Cayman Islands, BVI, and Bermuda, amongst others) to mandate companies registered within those jurisdictions to maintain registers, made publicly available, of their beneficial owners. The Act states that the public register must be 'broadly equivalent' to what is currently available on the UK Companies House as the PSC ('people with significant control') register. The idea therefore is to ensure that persons (as well as legal entities) who control, either directly or indirectly, 25% or more of a company's shares or who can appoint/remove directors will be caught within this definition. Notably, because Jersey and Guernsey are both Crown Dependencies, they are not covered by this new Act and instead are only mandated to comply with the introduction of the private registers in 2016.

More on registries and beneficial ownership in Chapter 4 on governance.

**And the (Less) Ugly** Arguably, the damage has already been done to the offshore jurisdictions and their choice as a destination for the asset manager. Pension funds are some of the loudest in calling for more of the asset managers to re-centre themselves onshore. Many global asset managers are not considering a favourable tax treatment as the number one priority anymore, rather focusing on service provider capabilities, as well as, clearly, the ability to raise investor money and catering to their fund location participants.

Another threat to the offshore world is the current refusal by the EU to progress the concept of third country passports, following the 2016 Brexit vote. Following this, offshore countries are having to work even harder to justify themselves beyond being a decent pool of talent to hire. Occasionally a bonus comes along, like the USD 100 billion Vision Fund for Jersey, to which EU regulations were irrelevant. Also as mentioned earlier in this chapter, a large percentage of Islamic funds are located in Jersey.

Not only funds, but also managers base themselves offshore. However, with the regulatory and taxation winds blowing toward increased 'substance', managers increasingly face a stark choice. Choose offshore and base yourselves there properly or 'go home'. Very few managers will be able to continue to base themselves offshore in the future, unless they hire more people locally. The UK Investment Manager Exemption (as discussed in Chapter 11) permits managers to reside in the UK and not pollute the fund with UK taxation has always been a significant threat to the offshore manager world.

Personally, I believe there is a role for the offshore world. It is becoming transparent. It has a significant use on avoiding double taxation for investors. It has a fantastic, trained workforce. As of 2019, it is business-friendly, so that, with swirling political winds onshore against business, entrepreneurship, and profit, the offshore world might have the last (capitalist or globalist) laugh.

## SOME CONCLUSIONS

This chapter has been a bit of a whirlwind tour of asset managers on a global, regional and jurisdictional scale, akin to around the world in 80 paragraphs. Whilst I tried to cover a decent amount of what was out there, unfortunately I was not able to include it all and as such have had to leave a few talking points out, such as most of Africa, Russia, and New Zealand, amongst others.

There are a multitude of factors that have influenced the way in which asset management industries have developed – whether that be through the sheer amounts of capital controlled by SWFs in the MENA region or the focus on ESG across African countries. Similarly intriguing is the way in which each region's asset managers face different issues, such as a rapidly aging population in China or political unrest in certain parts of South America. Even though each region faces its own issues, the world we live in is getting increasingly smaller, and as asset managers get larger, they will need to invest heavily in understanding these issues, and how best to resolve them.

## ENDNOTES

1. World Bank Group. 2018. Africa's Pulse, No. 17, April 2018. Washington, DC: World Bank. © World Bank.
2. Ibid.
3. World Bank. 2015. *South Africa economic update: jobs and South Africa's changing demographics (English)*. South Africa economic update; issue no. 7. Washington, D.C.: World Bank Group.
4. Canning, David, Raja, Sangeeta, and Yazbeck, Abdo S. (2015). Africa's Demographic Transition: Dividend or Disaster? Africa Development Forum; Washington, DC: World Bank; and Agence Française de Développement. World Bank.
5. www.fmo-im.nl/en/active-engagement
6. www.mjhudson.com/wp-content/uploads/2017/11/MJ-Hudson-ESG-Factors-in-Private-Equity-Investing.pdf
7. Figure 4: Global AuM projection by region for 2020, 'Asset Management 2020 A Brave New World', PWC.
8. Figure 1: LPs' expected target allocations to alternative assets in the next 12 months, 'Latin American Private Equity Limited Partners Opinion Survey', LAVCA & Cambridge Associates. www.cambridgeassociates.com/research/latin-american-private-equity-limited-partners-opinion-survey-2/
9. www.globallegalinsights.com/practice-areas/fund-finance-laws-and-regulations/brazil

10. Figure 5: Proportion of LPs expecting to access Latin American private equity via particular routes in three years' time, 'Latin American Private Equity Limited Partners Opinion Survey', LAVCA & Cambridge Associates. www.cambridgeassociates.com/research/latin-american-private-equity-limited-partners-opinion-survey-2/

11. https://tradingeconomics.com/brazil/inflation-cpi

12. https://www.wsj.com/articles/brazil-central-bank-cuts-selic-rate-to-8-25-1504732449

13. www.globallegalinsights.com/practice-areas/fund-finance-laws-and-regulations/brazil

14. Brazilian Asset Management Industry Perspective. bibliotecadigital.fgv.br/ojs/index.php/aif/article/download/.../61026

15. Ibid.

16. https://lavca.org/scorecard/20172018-lavca-scorecard

17. https://lavca.org/wp-content/uploads/2017/06/20172018-Scorecard-FINAL.pdf ( p. 10).

18. www.startupchile.org/about-us/

19. http://inbest.cl/chileday2017/wp-content/uploads/2015/09/R.-Castro.pdf

20. https://lavca.org/wp-content/uploads/2017/06/20172018-Scorecard-FINAL.pdf p. 11

21. www.institutionalinvestor.com/article/b14zbj8qk8gcnk/chiles-afps-a-lucrative-market-for-foreign-fund-managers

22. Ibid.

23. https://citywireamericas.com/news/argentina-approves-private-banking-regulation-creating-new-rival-offshore-hub/a1054569

24. https://citywireamericas.com/news/argentina-grants-another-offshore-advisor-licence/a1187805

25. https://citywireamericas.com/news/mexican-pensions-get-green-light-to-invest-in-foreign-funds/a1079485

26. www.empea.org/research/private-equity-in-mexico/

27. Islamic Funds: Gearing Up, p. 1

28. www.imf.org/external/themes/islamicfinance/

29. www.ublfunds.com.pk/individual/resources-tools/learning-center/shariah-compliant-investments/

30. www.ublfunds.com.pk/individual/resources-tools/learning-center/shariah-compliant-investments/

31. Islamic Funds: Gearing Up, p. 1.

32. Ibid.

33. Islamic Investment Funds: An Analysis of Risks and Returns, p. 9.

34. GCC Asset Management by Ento Capital, p. 3.

35. Ibid., p. 17.

36. www.stockmarketclock.com/exchanges

37. GCC Asset Management by Ento Capital, p. 21.

38. Ibid.

39. www.difc.ae/about/difc-district/

40. Dubai Financial Services Authority, 'Frequently Asked Questions for the DFSA Collective Investment Fund Regime', 1 February 2017, p. 3. www.dfsa.ae/CMSPages/GetFile.aspx?guid=6771ff1e-8761-479c-81b3-0c72a4902fb6

41. Ibid.

42. The Global Financial Centres Index 21, p. 8.

43. The Global Financial Centres Index 21, p. 4.

44. Mapping Opportunities in the MEASA Region, p. 29. www.zawya.com/mena/en/ifg-publications/180917121604X/

45. www.adgm.com/about-abu-dhabi/our-vision/

46. www.arabianbusiness.com/banking-finance/398322-abu-dhabi-fund-named-worlds-biggest-real-estate-investor

47. 2016 Ovum ICT Enterprise Insights Survey, www2.deloitte.com/content/dam/Deloitte/au/Images/infographics/deloitte-au-fs-how-you-rate-your-systems-ability-support-following-infographic-230218.pdf

48. Exhibit A: China Assets Under Management; Future Winners in China's Asset Management Industry, p. 4. www2.deloitte.com/ie/en/pages/financial-services/articles/future-winners-China-Asset-Management.html
49. Chen, Zhiwu, Xiong, Peng and Huang, Zhuo (2014) The Asset Management Industry in China: Its Past Performance and Future Prospects. *The Journal of Portfolio Management*. 41. 9–30.
50. www.caseyquirk.com/content/whitepapers/Casey%20Quirk%20-%20Leadership%20in%20Times%20of%20Plenty.pdf – p. 7.
51. www.scmp.com/business/china-business/article/2112036/fund-funds-seen-saviours-chinas-mutual-fund-sector
52. www.bloomberg.com/news/articles/2017-12-27/china-s-new-tax-may-hit-hedge-funds-more-than-investment-rivals
53. DTCC, Trading China Stock Connect Equities, [Accessed at: file://fofp01/London/Users/Home/temp/Downloads/ct683_china_stock_eqt_bps_20180406.pdf]
54. Reuters, [Accessed at: https://uk.reuters.com/article/us-hongkong-regulations/hong-kong-regulator-aims-for-northbound-china-investor-id-system-in-2018-idUKKBN1CF0D4]
55. KPMG, Evolving Investment Management Regulation, [Accessed at: https://assets.kpmg.com/content/dam/kpmg/xx/pdf/2017/06/evolving-investment-management-regulation-fs.pdf]
56. https://web.kamihq.com/web/viewer.html?source=extension_pdfhandler&extension_handler=webrequest_1_autoload_true_user_126182&file=https%3A%2F%2Fwww.seisakukikaku.metro.tokyo.jp%2Fbdc_tokyo%2Fassets%2Fpdf%2Fen%2Fenglish-guidebook%2Feigokaisetsusyo_A4_0908.pdf – p. 6.
57. Ibid., p. 14.
58. The world's 300 largest pension funds – year ended 2017.
59. www.ijapicap.com/blog/the-behemoths-gpif-pfa-maas/ 31 March 2018 value
60. www.ft.com/content/7ce47bd0-545f-11e8-b3ee-41e0209208ec
61. www.gpif.go.jp/en/investment/pdf/stewardship_principles_and_proxy_voting_principles.pdf
62. www.swfinstitute.org/swf-news/chat-with-the-chief-hiromichi-mizuno/
63. https://economictimes.indiatimes.com/industry/banking/finance/banking/number-of-adult-indians-with-bank-accounts-rises-to-80/articleshow/63838930.cms
64. https://web.kamihq.com/web/viewer.html?source=extension_pdfhandler&extension_handler=webrequest_1_autoload_true_user_126182&file=https%3A%2F%2Fwww.sebi.gov.in%2Fsebi_data%2Fattachdocs%2F1347547815927.pdf page 4
65. https://web.kamihq.com/web/viewer.html?source=extension_pdfhandler&extension_handler=webrequest_1_autoload_true_user_126182&file=https%3A%2F%2Fwww.mckinsey.com%2F~%2Fmedia%2Fmckinsey%2Ffeatured%2520insights%2Findia%2Friding%2520the%2520wave%2520of%2520opportunity%2520and%2520optimism%2Friding_the_wave_of_opportunity_and_optimism.ashx page 22
66. www.thehindu.com/business/Industry/mobile-trading-share-jumps-in-2-years/article23885340.ece
67. www.tai.org.au/content/how-many-countries-have-aaa-credit-rating-check-facts
68. https://web.kamihq.com/web/viewer.html?source=extension_pdfhandler&extension_handler=webrequest_1_autoload_true_user_126182&file=http%3A%2F%2Fwww.mas.gov.sg%2F~%2Fmedia%2FMAS%2FNews%2520and%2520Publications%2FSurveys%2FAsset%2520Management%2F2017%2520AM%2520Survey%2520Report.pdf pg 3
69. Ibid., p. 16.
70. https://citywireasia.com/news/singapore-s-new-vc-regime-what-it-means-for-pbs-hnwis/a1084945
71. https://web.kamihq.com
72. https://web.kamihq.com – p. 17
73. https://web.kamihq.com – p. 27
74. Capturing the multi-trillion dollar asset management opportunity in Southeast Asia, p. 1.

75. Ibid.
76. www.thejakartapost.com/news/2018/02/14/how-asias-population-is-aging-2015-2030-scenario .html
77. https://asia.nikkei.com/Editor-s-Picks/FT-Confidential-Research/ASEAN-economies-ill-prepared-for-old-age
78. Capturing the multi-trillion dollar asset management opportunity in Southeast Asia, p. 8. www2 .deloitte.com/content/dam/Deloitte/sg/Documents/strategy/sea-cons-capturing-multi-trillion-dollar-asset.pdf
79. www.asiaasset.com/news/Southeast_Asia_powerhouse_0803.aspx
80. Ibid.
81. www.chinusinvest.com/insights/
82. https://web.kamihq.com, p. 2.
83. Australia's Managed Funds 2017 Update Trade and investment note April 2017, p. 8.
84. Quarterly Superannuation Performance APRA report, p. 7.
85. Ibid., p. 13 – note, this data only includes SuperA's with more than 4 members (or AUD 1.6 trillion of the AUD 2.5 trillion total).
86. Future of the Asset Management Industry: Winning in the New Normal, p. 5. https://www.pwc.lu/ en/asset-management/docs/pwc-future-of-the-am-industry.pdf
87. OECD (2010) Trends Shaping Education, Chapter 2 (2.2).
88. https://wilsonassetmanagement.com.au/2017/10/10/profit-population-growth/
89. Asia 2050: Realizing the Asian Century, p. 6. http://www.iopsweb.org/researchandworkingpapers/ 48263622.pdf
90. www.weforum.org/agenda/2018/05/making-the-most-of-asia-s-aging-populations
91. Ageing in Asia and the Pacific, p. 3. https://www.unescap.org/resources/ageing-asia-and-pacific-overview
92. www.willistowerswatson.com/-/media/WTW/Images/Press/2018/01/Global-Pension-Asset-Study-2018-Japan.pdf
93. www.brookings.edu/wp-content/uploads/2017/02/global_20170228_global-middle-class.pdf, p. 15.
94. assets.kpmg.com/content/dam/kpmg/cn/pdf/en/2017/12/china-pension-outlook.pdf, p. 4.
95. Ibid., p. 3.
96. Ibid., p. 9.
97. www.willistowerswatson.com/-/media/WTW/Images/Press/2018/01/Global-Pension-Asset-Study-2018-Japan.pdf, p. 21.
98. www.gepf.gov.za/uploads/annualReportsUploads/GEPF_2017_AR_2017.pdf
99. www.un.org/en/africa/osaa/pdf/pubs/2017pensionfunds.pdf, p. 47.
100. Ibid., p. 9.
101. http://ww2.oldmutual.co.za/docs/default-source/old-mutual-south-africa/omig/omig-about-us/ responsible-investments/regulation28ofthepensionfundsact.pdf, p. 3.
102. *The Telegraph*, [Accessed at: www.telegraph.co.uk/finance/personalfinance/investing/10191182/ How-to-make-money-from-the-worlds-ageing-population.html]
103. Leveraging the Winds of Change (Partners Group), p. 12. https://www.partnersgroup.com/en/ perspectives/publications/current/
104. The English Effect, The British Council, p. 2. https://www.britishcouncil.org/research-policy-insight/policy-reports/the-english-effect
105. www.esldirectory.com/blog/teaching-english-abroad/changing-face-of-esl-schools-in-china/
106. The Sharing Economy (PWC), p. 12. https://www.pwc.fr/fr/assets/files/pdf/2015/05/pwc_etude_ sharing_economy.pdf
107. www.ipe.com/reports/special-reports/top-400-asset-managers/top-400-trends-in-asset-management-time-for-reinvention/10013544.article

108. www.theguardian.com/news/2017/nov/05/revealed-queen-private-estate-invested-offshore-paradise-papers
109. www.ft.com/content/d26996ea-c57f-11e7-b2bb-322b2cb39656
110. www.aima.org/article/the-truth-about-offshore-alternative-investment-funds.html
111. Standard for Automatic Exchange of Financial Account Information in Tax Matters, p. 9. https://read.oecd-ilibrary.org/taxation/standard-for-automatic-exchange-of-financial-account-information-for-tax-matters_9789264216525-en#page2
112. Passed 23 May 2018: www.legislation.gov.uk/ukpga/2018/13/contents/enacted

# CHAPTER 13

# Future Trends

*The best way to predict the future is to create it.*

– Abraham Lincoln

*If not us, who? And if not now, when?*

– Ronald Reagan (inspired by the words of Hillel the Elder)

This chapter considers trends that could have a major effect on the asset management industry over the next ten years.

Many of these trends I have already touched on in this book, and I see some running and running. Most trends run on too long and overstay their welcome. In markets, momenta tend to overshoot too.

I will make a few bold predictions, slightly mindful of the BBC weatherman, Michael Fish, who in 1987, on the evening before the worst hurricane to hit the UK in over 100 years, said, 'Earlier on today apparently a woman rang the BBC and said she had heard a hurricane was on the way. Well, I can assure people watching, don't worry, there isn't.'

I will be interested to measure myself against this chapter in ten years. Perhaps like Mr Fish, Nick Leeson, or the Wolf of Wall Street, I can have a subsequent career in referencing my worst mistakes.

## MACROECONOMICS

**No Crash**   There will be no crash! Wow, that is a bold assessment. I just wanted to be the opposite of all the economists out there that successfully predicted 11 out of the last 2 recessions. It just seems, with inflation, growth, and interest rates low and tepid, there are no massive bubbles to burst, and no huge shockwaves out there, bar a major war or epidemic. It just does not feel like 1999 or 2006 to me. Sure, there have been market movements, the return of Vol in 2018 – but nothing like dot-com insanity, or mass credit, RE, and securitisation of fraud-fuelled bubbles. Bond markets might be multi-decade churning; equity markets do not feel over-valued; indeed dividends are high with insipid equity growth. There has been speculation about the size of consumer credit following the pumping up of QE, but this is already deflating slightly as QE is gradually replaced with QT. In addition, the digital currency bubble deflated quite calmly, with no real knock-ons to the rest of financial services or the economy.

I suspect there will be some more scandal coming out of digital currencies and the bizarre Initial Coin Offerings (ICOs) that they spawned (what were they about?), but this will be containable. Employment is high. Countries might enter into shallow or brief recessions, but these will generally be foreseen. There is an old joke from the 1990s that a recession is when your neighbour is laid off and a depression is when you get laid off.

**Long Sideways**   Rather, it feels like we are still in the Long Sideways (as I call it – see Chapter 1).

The FTSE 100 stood at 6930 on New Year's Eve 1999, and at the same date in 2018, 19 years later, it stood at 6728.13. Schroders reported, however, over the 19 years, dividends accumulated to 93.5%. However, the point is that in my view, having lived and worked in financial markets during these 19 years, we have never recovered from the hysteria of the end of the last millennium. Sure, there was a fakery imposed credit bubble in the mid-noughties and subsequent implosion, but fundamentally we are in the Japanese-style Long Sideways that I don't see ending for the next 10 years in the West.

Western populations are getting older or shrinking (especially if you factor in anti-immigration countries like the US, UK, and now Germany and Italy). Globalisation is on the retreat, and a digging-up-your-garden-to-grow-your-own-local-turnips mentality is on the rise, with populist leaders shouting louder about 'home grown'. Similarly, and more frighteningly, there is much prejudiced history mis-remembering going on. Older Brits hark back to the Battle of Britain and Winston Churchill, Americans to their GIs at the Normandy landings, the Japanese to the days of Empire, and the French to Versailles; all a very long way of saying that low growth and blinkered thinking is in. I really hope the defamed millennials take over soon!

Thus, not being an economist,  more of a historian, I would predict low growth, low rates, and low inflation in the Western world. Clearly different in the faster and more exciting markets of Asia and Africa. But for the UK, US, and Europe – the Long Sideways continues.

**Dot-Com Bubble II**   However, do look out for Dot-Com Bubble II.

Significant sums of money have been invested in venture capital, both on and off the stock markets, since 2014. There has also been – following a few success stories such as the FAANGs and their Chinese equivalents – a number of investment models where the game is to grow as fast as possible at any cost – land grab and eliminate all other competition with vast cash investment and hundreds of millions in losses. Billions have been thrown at this model, even in some industries with ideas that do not make sense (at least not to me).

This will lead to Dot-Com Bust II. But, as with digital currencies, and high-interest platforms (both of which were marginalised with the help of the regulators), I suspect this will not lead to a broader crash, but a deflation of that particular bubble. In fact, this waste of capital will flow to other areas and people that will catch the cash.

## POLITICS, POPULISM, PEOPLE, POPULATION

Politics has become a little wilder. However, I suspect populism will blow over, and after a questionable leader or two, a calmer more reasonable, statesmanlike one will follow. In the meantime, asset management will be a little at the mercy of politics.

The movement of people – as in the Fall of Rome – will have both positive and negative effects. Most young EU workers I meet in London (and I meet hundreds of them propping up the hospitality and construction sectors) are hard-working, intelligent people that contribute valuably to our economy. Thus, the movement of people, especially young people, can have a positive effect.

It only becomes negative if allowed to go completely unfettered (consider Germany and the fall of Chancellor Angela Merkel) or if it is met by unreasonably disgruntled natives.

**India** There is much talk about China, but the one to watch in the coming years is India. With a population of over 1.3 billion, of which half is under the age of 25, the nation is bursting with potential. India offers both a plethora of alternative investment opportunities as it develops its infrastructure to cope with the world's second largest population, and a mass of skilled and ambitious youths entering the workforce.

Asia more broadly offers a lot of exciting investment opportunities, but with so much focus on the emergence of China as a global powerhouse, and the economic strength of Japan well-established, we should remember to keep our eyes open to prospects elsewhere in the region.

**MENA** Whilst the Arab Spring initially offered great hope for democratisation and freer markets in the MENA region, much of the area has fallen into what has become known as the Arab Winter – the resurgence of Islamic extremism and authoritarianism. The region will continue to offer active managers and risk-tolerant investors exciting opportunities, particularly in oil (at least in the short term) and infrastructure, but political instability (including war and terrorism) looks set to continue for decades to come, and will be a real turn-off for most.

The growing interest in ESG considerations amongst investors makes MENA sometimes unattractive as well, as it can be a complex region to invest in whilst confidently satisfying ESG criteria – adding to the list of reasons for asset managers and investors to avoid the region.

**Europe** In Europe, the consequences of the Arab Spring have been felt in a migration crisis (a consequence also of significant economic migration as well as refugee displacement) and a rise in terrorist threats. This, along with other factors such as wealth inequality and an ageing population, has dramatically impacted the political discourse within Europe and shaken the EU project to a literal breaking point. We have seen the effects in the US and the rest of the world too, as populist politics has become a winning ticket. As austerity measures are lifted, and successful populist movements fail to produce any material change for voters, perhaps we will see the strength of populism wane. Already we have seen President Trump's government shut down by congress in the US and Prime Minister Theresa May's minority government struggling against a defiant parliament in the UK.

However, inequality between the rich and poor and the continued collapse of traditional industries will continue well into the future, and these issues are forming the bedrock of capitalism's twenty-first century existential crisis.

**Ageing populations** Many developed economies are benefiting from high-quality healthcare as well as other social and technological developments which enable citizens to live longer and happier lives. However, this is beginning to place great strain on pension funds and the public purse. As people live longer in retirement, state institutions and private pensions are having to provide for more people for more time. There will therefore be pressure on governments to increase tax revenues (through tax hikes for the wealthy and tax cuts for corporations), to increase the state pension age (making people work for longer), and to look at alternative revenue streams such as SWFs. Defined benefit pension schemes, which pose enormous liabilities that are a struggle to meet, are soon to be a relic of history as contribution-based schemes become the norm.

**The Global Economy**  Regional trends clearly have global impact – and as long as there is trouble in any corner of the globe, there will be challenges and opportunities for asset managers. No one can safely predict the future of global relations between the US, China, Russia, the UK, and the EU. Troops are lined up on the eastern borders of Europe as part of NATO's Enhanced Forward Presence to ward off a neo-imperialistic Russia; China and the US are hitting each other with ever-increasing tariffs as they enter a bitter trade war; and the UK is tangled up in a messy political divorce from its closest trade partners.

**Globalism vs. Populism**  The battle between globalism and populism (an epic worthy of a film to give *Star Wars* a run for its money) may be long fought. Being myself a pro-globalisation lucky baby boomer, I thought we had this battle licked. However, Brexit, Trump, isolationism, trade wars, the Five Star Movement, Le Pen, and Russian aggression have been a whole series of defeats for the globalist. Such stormy weather conditions will continue to rock the asset management boat for some years to come, as the global community establishes a new consensus on democracy, globalisation, and capitalism – the underpinnings of asset management's success in the twentieth century. However, this all seems to be good news for active managers at least (more on that below).

Globalisation will fight back and win, armed with its top weapon of the internet and its immediacy and accessibility. However, under a new name and logo. It might take more than ten years.

# BREXIT

> *Just hedge it, Dad*
>> – Henry Hudson aged 17 in 2016 when MJ Hudson determined to establish a Luxembourg office following the UK referendum

**Timing**  Brexit to me, after the referendum, is just about timing – i.e. the only real question is when will the UK (and EU in reverse) lose financial services passporting rights? The approach for me was to move on and prepare for a time when the UK leaves and to not assume that the UK will ever become a third country with EU passporting rights.

**AIFMD**  AIFMD makes provision for 'third countries' to access the EU's alternative investment fund market and envisages the extension of the passport to AIFMs and AIFs from third countries, and mandates ESMA to advise the European Parliament, Council and the European Commission in this regard. ESMA has so far assessed twelve different non-EU countries to determine the suitability of granting AIFMD passporting rights to those countries' AIFMs and AIFs. In July 2015, ESMA issued its initial advice on the extension of the AIFMD passport, followed by its second set of advice in 2016 and issued a positive assessment to extending the passport to Canada, Guernsey, Jersey, Japan, and Switzerland. However it is 2019, and as of yet no extension.

The AIFMD's approach to third country entities can be contrasted with other EU Directives which grant access to the EU single market to firms from those third countries which are assessed as having a regulatory regime equivalent to that in the EU. The AIFMD is not concerned with equivalence per se, since non-EU AIFMs which are granted the AIFMD passport will in any event be required to sign up to substantially all of the AIFMD by obtaining authorisation in their 'member state of reference', i.e. the member state with which the non-EU AIFM is most closely connected based on certain criteria set out in the AIFMD.

The granting of the AIFMD passport to the UK post-Brexit would require ESMA to undertake a review of the UK regulatory regime. ESMA is unlikely to be in a position to advise on the extension of the AIFMD passport until the UK has put in place a replacement AIFMD regulatory regime post-Brexit (in much the same way as they were unable to adjudicate on Bermuda and the Cayman Islands).

Don't hold your breath. Instead, if you need to access the EU, set up a base there and/or use an umbrella.

**Economy**  I do not wish to be accused of being a Brexit scaremongerer, but the UK and indeed global economy will take a hit from Brexit, just as trade difficulties and wars hit the economy.

Again, best advice – assume the hit. Take it, adapt, and win.

**London Is a World City**  Being a Londoner, I am prejudiced, but London has been a trading city for 2000 years. It aims to be open, honest, and fair. The UK has an amazing legal framework with the best courts and judges in the world. It is for this reason that English law is commonly chosen as the governing jurisdiction for international commercial contracts between non-UK entities. London has built up robust financial trading systems and has thousands of quality professionals. Its exploration and colonial past puts it at the heart of language and communication with the Middle East, North America, and Asia. Prime Minister Margaret Thatcher, deregulation, and the 'Big Bang' in the 1980s cemented London as the number one financial centre in the world.

The UK is the world's largest clearing system. The UK is the number one non-Chinese clearer of renminbi. We are also amongst the best in the world of insurance with the fourth biggest market and the biggest in Europe with a total premium volume of GBP 225 billion in 2018 according to the Association of British Insurers.[1]

The Romans thought the UK had the best weather in their empire too (yes, really) – not too hot, not too cold, and plenty of water.

However, we have to work hard and stay nimble to stay at the top of the pile. Cutting regulation, red tape, and tax, will be important.

**And Be Nice to the Americans**  The US sits at the head of a global cultural and financial empire, having replaced the UK after two devastating world wars (the Americans were especially clever in making us pay them for their help too), and the US will still be the world's great superpower in a hundred years. The China story is overdone, and do not forget that the US navy distinctly rules the waves.

I remember the city pre-Big Bang. The American banks made London the number one financial services city ahead of New York. The Sarbanes–Oxley Act of 2002 could be side-stepped by the Americans by drafting in Brits. The US see the UK as their ally and spy in Europe. Really the 51st state. I write this having established the London offices of two of the largest US law firms from scratch. Banks such as Citi and JP Morgan, and investment banks such as Goldman and Morgan Stanley, are the top of the pops. Europe has nothing approaching them. Look at the sad state of RBS and Deutsche if you need reminding.

So let us keep the Yanks happy and using the UK. I love them.

## REGULATION

**The Regulators are Coming!** Asset management and wealth management have had an easy time of it over the last ten years, whilst the regulators have sought to cauterise the banking system. I would say that the regulators, central banks, and governments over-egged the capital requirements for banks, which has had a negative effect on global growth over the last ten years. Barclays tried heroically to avoid a bailout and look what thanks they got. However, I remember that the credit crisis (as was the collapse of hedge fund LTCM for a few days and the Russian financial crisis in 1998) was very scary, as the end of capitalism was in sight. If banks fail, then where does that leave capitalism?

It is interesting to read the history of financial services over the last 500 years in places like the UK, US, and Italy. The US especially achieved huge amounts in only 70 years from 1850 to 1920. Clearly, it also had a 'good' war in the First World War and came out of it stronger on the world economic stage. However, the national economic and banking system that it rapidly built in those 70 years almost came crashing down in its entirety within a few weeks at the start of the credit crisis. A long way of saying that perhaps the regulators did not overreact to banking. It has, nonetheless, led to lower growth in the last ten years and record beating low interest rates (not really an interest rate at all).

So, for asset managers, expect increased regulation principally aimed at protecting investors.

This will involve:

- Greater transparency
- Greater cost
- More reporting
- More capital adequacy
- More compliance and risk officers needed
- More work around KYC and AML
- More enforcement in the form of fines and shutdowns.

Regulators in the UK have also done a good job on high-interest short-term lending operators and platforms (Wonga an example of effectively being shut down). However, there are still light-touch regulated and unregulated consumer platforms out there, many of which are low due diligence funding platforms. No doubt, we can expect more scandals to be unearthed and brought to the attention of the regulators.

The most immediate change coming for UK-based asset managers is due in December 2019 – the extension of the SM&CR, which initially only covered institutions regulated by both the PRA and FCA (banks and insurers), to solo-regulated firms (i.e. firms only regulated by the FCA, which includes asset managers). This will bring a whole new ream of regulatory challenges for asset managers, requiring them (amongst many other things) to regularly assess the fitness and propriety of their senior managers to perform their roles (at least annually) and to produce statements for each senior manager outlining their personal responsibilities. This is part of a general trend, which we can expect to see more of, toward greater transparency and increased individual accountability within the financial services sector.

In Europe more widely, AIFMD II can be expected in the next decade or so. In its report[2] on the current directive, the EC noted room for improvement on reporting requirements, valuation rules, depositary rules, and the marketing passport (amongst other things). Brexit has probably delayed any progress on third-country passporting, but it is inevitable that AIFMD II will come eventually.

In the US, we have heard strong rhetoric from President Trump about deregulation – he even cut a large piece of real-life red tape strung-up in front of stacks of paper in a symbolic demonstration of his ambitions. To what extent he achieves these ambitions is yet to be seen, but I imagine the reality will not live up to the hype. Current reports appear to agree on this, with many suggesting the deregulatory steps taken by the President's administration so far have been modest in their effect.

**Mid and Back Office**   The reality is that the days of ten or even five to one ratios of front office to back office will become a distant memory for asset managers. In banking, it is already the opposite way around. Expect to pay a fortune for compliance, AML, risk, due process, technology, cybersecurity and similar. Overall, I see regulation (in its broadest sense) increasing and the need for greater mid and back office scale.

This will also lead to more mergers and acquisitions in managers, as well as more scale.

**Platforms**   Increased regulatory demands on managers will lead to an increase in outsourcing and greater use of platforms. Platforms are a good thing. Platforms allow portfolio managers to generate better returns by focusing on investments. Do not be ashamed to use a platform on account of not being big enough to do it yourself. Fund investors demand either top mid and back office or very high-end platforms. It is the middle ground they cannot stand – managers that do it themselves and do not do it properly.

**Closet Trackers**   After an FCA review of so-called 'closet trackers' – passively managed funds that market themselves as actively managed funds and charge the higher fees that an actively managed fund usually attracts – rules were introduced in 2019 to increase transparency and thereby protect retail investors from misleading marketing. Yet another example of the regulators' war against opacity in financial services.

## FEES AND REMUNERATION

Asset managers will continue to be squeezed on fees.

Both regulators and investors are turning ever more scrutinous eyes toward fees. As a result, we can expect continued and increasing downward pressure on fees in both actively and passively managed funds. There are already zero-fee products in the market (Fidelity Investment's zero-fee index fund being the first in August 2018) and we have seen an alarming number of hedge funds cut out external investors and adopt a family-office style approach, at least partially due to the low level of fees they are able to charge investors (2 and 20 is starting to look more like a less catchy 1 and 15).

With suppressed fee income and all too often less than inspiring returns, asset managers can probably expect more of the same in terms of remuneration. Base rate salaries will no doubt continue to creep up as usual, but it seems unlikely that the bonus pool will expand significantly. However, competition for quality ESG and IT professionals will drive up salaries for these specialists.[3] The big winners could be those with advanced skills in artificial intelligence, automation, cybersecurity, and/or data management.

Remuneration models are likely to shift into alignment with investor expectations. Whilst it may be inconvenient for managers, if they manage several different portfolios for different types of clients (e.g. institutional investors and HNWIs), they will have to have separate pay structures. HNWIs will, for instance, expect lower fees, but are likely to be more willing to concede to generous performance-related incentives. Meanwhile, pension funds are likely to be comfortable paying higher fees to managers but less interested in incentivising extraordinary performance, and more interested in seeing sustained and stable returns. Individual managers can expect their remuneration to reflect these structures, with lower base salaries and higher bonuses on the one hand and higher base salaries and lower bonuses on the other.

Most significantly, transparency in respect of manager remuneration will continue to increase in response to rising pressure from regulators (e.g. RDR) and investors for more clarity.

**Debt and Liquidity**   The two pillars of doom. If the 1970s and 1980s were about the bogeyman of inflation, this century might be a constant struggle against debt and liquidity. These two beasts savaged all before them during the financial crisis and they now lurk, growling. Mark Carney, Governor of the BoE recently pointed a shaking finger at illiquidity, that could overwhelm all investors, as deep pools of nastiness fester within illiquid emerging market bond and real estate funds. As the immediate period post the Brexit Referendum showed, 'liquid' real estate funds are illiquid after all. Note also the recent Woodford gating. Open funds are actually therefore all but closed and with secondary markets (at least in private equity) strong, closed funds can actually be 'open'. Debt is a drug the whole world has become addicted to this century. It is also an off and on tap used by Central Banks and Governments (or with QE are they becoming the same thing?). As the private markets show unless debt can become equity it can destroy all before it, or perhaps we just ignore it, like in Italy. I guess the US, the most indebted of all, and with trillions of its dollars in China, could just refuse to repay it and point at its 'big boats'. Debt is a challenge to retail and Governments. There is no immediate solution, other than a couple of decades of cold turkey to wean ourselves off it - think German unification. Growing out of the problem does not currently seem possible, except in India and China.

## TAXATION

**Global Competition**   The challenge facing many governments is how to build a tax framework which attracts investors and wealth creation and actually brings in sufficient tax revenues to cover growing public spending needs (on account of ageing and expanding populations). In simple terms, taxes need to be low enough to bring wealth into the country, but high enough to actually foot the bills. There is a global race to reduce taxes in an effort to encourage immigration of wealth creators. This trend will continue. A bit more honesty from countries would be appreciated as they try to receive tax lost through indirect channels. In addition, there is some hypocrisy in, on the one hand, encouraging wealth creators, and on the other hand berating them for their success or oligarchy status in vote-grabbing one-liners.

Governments and regulators have been working hard to crack down on both tax evasion and avoidance and (with the low cost of air travel and the increasing ease with which businesses and individuals can jurisdiction shop and hop) global co-operation has been seen as an essential component in dealing with this problem. The bigger pressure for managers and investors comes from the fight against (legal) tax avoidance. Tax considerations can really be considered an extension of ESG policy as the reputational risk associated with tax scandals rests heavily on the minds of investors and asset managers, as observed in the reluctance of many managers with European investors to use Cayman fund structures.

We can expect additional measures to be implemented internationally to tackle tax avoidance and the traditional 'tax havens' and offshore or mid-shore jurisdictions (Ireland, Luxembourg, Switzerland, Cyprus, Malta, Gibraltar – the list is long) are likely to continue their public relations campaigns with further tax avoidance policies (such as the Channel Islands have agreed with the EU).

Also expect state-sponsored taxation, or regulation-fine piracy, or just plain revenge attacks from countries or blocs to continue, with large fines, retrospective action or imprisonment by governments or blocs (such as the EU) on the national champions of others. Transparency is key to try and stay out of these fights.

**Investor Tax Expectations** In tension with this changing fiscal landscape, investors will continue to seek certainty in the tax treatment of their investments. As this can never be guaranteed by managers, the key going forward will lie in communication and expectation management. Investors will also have to come to terms with increased transparency as regulatory pressures mount against the tax arrangements of wealthy individuals and large corporations.

**Race to the Corporate Bottom** The general direction of tax rates will be downwards for corporations and upwards for individuals. We have already seen President Trump slash US corporation tax from 35% to 21% – the biggest corporate tax cut in US history[4] – and Prime Minister Theresa May has indicated a desire for the UK to have the lowest corporate tax rate in the G20.[5] But tax revenue has to come from somewhere, so high earners will be expected to make up the short-fall – through complex measures no doubt, as blatant tax hikes run the risk of encouraging wealth creators to pick up sticks and get the next EasyJet flight out to the country offering the best rates.

For asset managers themselves, tax is a pressing issue as governments begin to turn their attention to carried interest for untapped revenue. In both the US and UK, legislation has been proposed to re-designate sums received in the form of carry as chargeable to income tax rather than the far less burdensome capital gains tax.

**IT** Thankfully, the strain of tax-related bureaucracy can largely be handled by computers. Technology can decrease the time spent accumulating relevant data, running calculations, and filing reports. Therefore, the headache of tax should be limited to the decision-making process as after that, institutional investors and asset managers can implement IT systems to take care of the hard work.

## TECHNOLOGY

Technology will be one of the big themes for the future, but making predictions is a dangerous game. Technology has been both underrated in terms of predictions – 'The Internet? Bah!' (*Newsweek*, 27 February, 1995) – as well as, to put it mildly, vastly over-promoted – just look at some of the recent hype around blockchain and crypto replacing all software and all currencies. Blockchain has in my view many problems, not least cost, excessive power use (think ESG), and the ability to get lost – or mugged – in its blocks.

Here are some more predictions.

IT infrastructure, both hardware and software, will become increasingly outsourced and viewed as a service to be paid for according to the variable needs of managers and increasing pace of technological change.

With this modern approach to IT, managers will need to take data protection and cyberse-curity seriously – I predict many data-leak and hacking scandals to come. Cybersecurity threats will be exacerbated by the rise of flexible working practices (which is seeing computers and smartphones being used for professional purposes ever more commonly in public spaces and home environments) and increased reliance on the internet to store, support and access data and software.

We will also see a rise in outsourced research and analytics, as competition within the knowledge industry heats up (driving down costs) and smaller managers seek to take advantage of big data analytics that would otherwise be inaccessible to them (on account of the expense of doing it in-house). Providing outsourced services to smaller managers is also seen as a useful additional income stream for companies that are able to run their own heavy-duty analytics.

Efficiency gains are not limited to outsourcing technology – blockchain (although over-rated) promises to bring revolutionary levels of efficiency and security to transactions. Cost savings can be passed on to clients in the battle to remain competitive in a market that already has its eyes focused keenly on management fees and value for money.

I also expect to see a steep increase in the use of automation, with the rise of AI and so-called robo-advisers. As asset managers are squeezed on fees, the industry will, like others, find it difficult to resist the move toward technology-assisted solutions. In the short term, we can rest assured that there is still a place for humans in asset management, as the advice current AI systems can offer is limited and investors do not seem ready just yet to place full faith in computers. The trend, however, will undeniably be toward fewer staff and more computers.

**Interfaces** One of the chief areas of growth in this space will be a rise in digital interfaces for retail investors to make, monitor, and exit their investments. This may also pave the way for open-ended retail funds that can be instantly traded in and out of via an app or website, as younger generations expect liquidity from illiquid assets. We can also expect a similar increase in online investor 'portals' or 'dashboards' for institutional investors too. Digitisation having already taken its toll on the bricks and mortar of the high street, we can expect continued pressure on businesses of all kinds to cut wasted expenditure on real property (as well as real people).

### Social Media

*Social media has peaked. Always on is too stressful.*

– Marcus Hudson, 2019, aged 17

Social media will continue, however, to be an important means of communication for asset managers and must not be overlooked in its potential to influence and attract investors (and investment opportunities). In the complex universe of financial services, customer relationship management is essential. Trust and friendship can be as highly valued as cold hard cash returns.

In the words of Alice Bentinck MBE of Entrepreneur First, 'to be a good asset manager, you have to be good with the people as well as the numbers'.

However, as well as providing useful marketing and communications platforms for asset managers, tech giants (FAANG) pose a significant threat to incumbent managers as they eye-up the opportunities that the industry offers them. Look out for Google and Facebook's entry into the asset management space as it takes advantage of its advanced analytic capabilities, brand strength, and deep pockets. Not to mention its billions of fanatical users. Only GDPR and similar data protection rules stands in their way.

## SCALE

Join the USD 1 trillion AuM club or get merged.

Increased regulation, costs, and the need to be at the top of your game on technology and digitisation (as discussed above) all means that scale is going to be a big theme. Resources, expertise, and efficiency are not just key to succeeding, but necessary for survival. Managers are already merging. For example, Janus Capital Group and Henderson Group came together in 2017 to form Janus Henderson, and Standard Life and Aberdeen Asset Management formed Standard Life Aberdeen the same year – reportedly targeting GBP 200 million in cost savings (in part funded by an 8% cut in staff).[6] In 2018, the value of deals where an asset manager was the target was over USD 21 billion[7] – the highest it has been in a decade. The number of mergers between asset managers is only going to increase. Interestingly, we have seen some asset managers begin to acquire wealth managers as well, in a move to capture more HNWI investors.[8]

**Going Public** The demand for scale will also lead to more listings on stock markets for managers – as well as more listed funds. Unfortunately, listed managers get whacked thrice when stock markets fall. Once, because they are listed and the market has declined. Twice, because they have portfolios of listed stocks that will hit their fees. Thrice, because cash flows out fast. Just look at 2018.

Similarly, suppliers to managers will merge and list for matching scale.

Assisting this mass upscale of asset managers will be increased cooperation between jurisdictions in the realm of cross-border fund marketing. Schemes such as ARFP, ASEAN, and MRF are opening up the Asia-Pacific region and we can expect more arrangements like this in that region and elsewhere. As it becomes easier to market funds internationally, it becomes easier for asset managers to expand internationally.

**Due Diligence** Expect an increase in DD on managers and funds. This will involve enhanced legal, operational, as well as financial, and technology systems and cybersecurity due diligence.

Any more fund or manager scandals will only increase the DD – get used to it.

## INSOURCE OR OUTSOURCE

The need for scale leads increasingly to the debate around insourcing or outsourcing.

Part of the rationale behind MJ Hudson is to democratise the industry by providing managers with an outsourced solution for many parts of their front, mid, and back offices, as AuM increasingly flows towards the very largest management groups.

That said, even the largest groups will outsource parts of their back to mid office, either in less significant jurisdictions for them or where they feel that the expertise is better held by an outsourced expert – for example, legal services. Outsourcing allows managers to focus on generating returns and is often more cost-efficient than in-house operations, so we are likely to see outsourcing increase across the industry.

If the FAANGs do indeed make an entry into asset management, we can obviously expect them to have excellent IT and data analysis infrastructure and also strong front-office capabilities, but they will likely outsource many of the back-office functions – perhaps even the front desk or portfolio management in a joint venture with an asset management behemoth. This might help keep the passive bubble pumped up for a while longer.

## ESG AND IMPACT

Since we know that ESG policies do not necessarily result in lower returns and ESG considerations weigh increasingly heavier on the minds of investors, I anticipate that ESG policies will become standard for all investment schemes. In 2018, funds investing by reference to ESG criteria reached USD 1 trillion, which is an increase in 60% from 2012.[9] Man Group is one of the most notable hedge fund groups to have embraced ESG recently, excluding investments in coal and tobacco stocks amongst others.[10] They have reported plans to catalogue their funds into three categories according to their ESG compliance.

Expect increased focus on which companies do good and which companies do bad. Investors want to know. Interestingly, companies can move from good to bad. Silicon Valley is full of mini-Messiahs that convince you they are saving the world. Then a few days later they are blamed for a data breach and doing bad. So expect ESG fickleness too.

So-called 'impact funds' will grow. Cynics believe impact is throwing money away into corruption in poorer countries. Evangelical street charity sales folk believe they are making the world a better place. Somewhere in this impact noise lies truth and meaning, and I firmly believe in impact. We can expect so much more from impact, because the actual AuM right now is tiny. Nigel Kershaw OBE explains, it 'is possible to have a growth economy – combined with a social economy. Capital can be democratized, with no impact on economic return. It's not about bringing impact into the mainstream – it's actually about impacting the mainstream'.

With this increase in attention toward ESG considerations, passive fund managers will need to start getting at least a bit active given that the market indices they track have no ESG conscience. We should also see an increase in the quality of data measuring the performance of funds from a social perspective, as managers will be competing for business on the basis of both financial returns and social impact, and will need something to show for their efforts. This means a new expense for asset managers, as fee income gravitates into the pockets of a new generation of ESG compliance analysts.

## ASSET CLASSES

**Alternatives**   We can expect alternative asset classes to grow ever more popular as the performance of traditional asset classes continue to disappoint during the Long Sideways. The mounting piles of dry powder in the industry certainly suggest that investors are optimistic about alternatives. In their 2014 report, PwC predicted the global share of AuM in alternatives to grow from 10% to 13%.[11] In their 2017 update, they remained confident of this, noting that alternatives already accounted for 11% of global AuM in 2015.[12]

**Crowdfunding** In particular, investment into crowdfunding is set to grow, at least for now. Online peer-to-peer (P2P) lending sites have begun to enjoy mainstream success, driven by the lack of credit available to SMEs and the wonders of the internet. There has also been a growing market for invoice-exchange platforms and other online business models providing alternative finance solutions to SMEs. That said, I see some scandals emerging from these platforms on account of their lack of due diligence. Also regulators do not like these crowd-type platforms. Retail could lose money.

**Private Debt** Private debts funds are growing fast too. Certain PE managers see it as a faster way to scale, with hedge having taken a whacking for the last ten years. The challenge of ageing populations means pension funds are under much more pressure to deliver strong and predictable results. The institutional pursuit of income-generating (and particularly fixed-income) assets is a major driving force for growth in private debt investments.

Countries like Italy have just allowed private debt funds to be created by managers, as opposed to banks (Italy has all been about banks for 500 years, having invented them – although Arabic states might beg to differ). Also in the struggle to keep pace, private debt could offer governments a solution to a lack of otherwise readily available finance.

**Private Equity** PE and VC is set to grow as an asset class as investors look for so-called 'uncorrelated returns' or perhaps more simply – returns! Traditional asset classes have not offered particularly exciting returns in the era of the Long Sideways; meanwhile, hands-on investment in young tech start-ups or fast-growing established business ventures can produce a very healthy financial crop in a short time frame. Activist investing is much easier in a PE or VC context too, since a significant or controlling interest is often acquired – which is great for ESG-conscious investors.

**Infra and (also) New Energy** Additionally, governments around the world are faced with the challenges of a rapidly growing population, which, as we face crises in healthcare, housing, transport, and energy, demands new and ambitious infrastructure. Tony Dalwood, CEO of Gresham House, notes in particular the vast demand for renewable energy infrastructure.

## ACTIVE VS. PASSIVE

*The passives bubble will burst shortly.*

– Matthew Hudson, January 2018.

Yes, I said that then.

Passives have made a good name for themselves and grown significantly in the wake of the financial crisis as investors were given a sudden reminder of the benefits of long-term, though perhaps less exciting, capital growth. Richard Novack of Alpha Hawk notes that the 'post-financial crisis emphasis on risk management' has lowered Vol and returns and that 'QE has promoted passive investments via ETFs and systematic strategies, whereas the removal of volatility has diminished the discretionary element to investing.' This has kick-started a battle between actively and passively managed funds.

Passive investment involves the buying of an index fund that tracks the entirety of a major index – the FTSE 100 or S&P 500, for example. If a company's stock drops out of either of those indices, the fund that a passive investor drops them too, usually ensuring a mirroring of that index. These portfolio adjustments are positively Darwinian in their ruthless simplicity and science. This type of investing charges a lower fee than those funds that are actively managed. Fidelity recently launched an index fund with a 0% fee, signalling the price pressures that are present in the passives market (although it makes it back by lending stock out to hedge funds to be able to short). The growth of ETFs has meant that investors have plenty of choice, but their overriding concern is typically cost) and it is always clear to the investor what constitutes their portfolio. But the stocks purchased automatically by the index tracker may not always have merit which may in turn distort the price of each company's share – enter active managers. However, the simplicity of passive investing means that it is unlikely to go away anytime soon as many investors look for consistent returns with generally lower levels of risk due to the wide spread of capital.

Passive funds and their proponents articulate their perceived advantages regularly. Some of the typical arguments that are made are they are cheaper and have performed better than their active counterparts since the last financial crisis. Richard Novack comments that 'returns are broadly falling, resulting in investors being less willing to pay the discretionary fees traditionally paid for alpha generation'. Research has shown that 75–85% of active managers in the US underperform their benchmark. Investing in a passive fund also, they claim, prevents the risk of an investor inadvertently choosing an active fund that is actually, in secret, an index tracker in disguise. This is perhaps more common than realised and certainly a pitfall an investor would hope to avoid given the cost implications. There is also an argument put forward that investing in passive funds will limit harmful investor behaviour.

However, two issues stand to challenge passive in the coming years. First, the passive market has grown so large that it begins to beg the question of whether you can track a market and make it too. I would suggest that energy in the active management scene is the lifeblood of the index trackers. Over the past five years the proportion of passively managed assets has increased to 21.6%. Indeed, according to Moody's by 2024 passive investments will have a larger market share than active investments in the US. Yet the increasing popularity in passives has prompted warnings about momentum play. The reality of passive investing is different to many peoples interpretation of what they are doing with their money. For example, the S&P 500 is the most popular index in the world for investors to follow. A common misconception is that tracking this index is a neutral approach – it is not. The index is cap-weighted, which means that investors are actually putting an increasing amount of money into a smaller pool of options (typically tech stocks). As the largest stocks keep growing, more and more people are actually risking their money on a particular sector. This contributes to what is known as momentum investing, which promotes the perpetual success of popular stocks and resigns unpopular stocks to further underperformance. A side effect of this is the potential for abrupt market corrections. This is particularly concerning as a large number of investors may not appreciate their exposure to this potential downside risk. An obvious solution that does not undermine the autonomy of investors would be to educate them further about the potential risks they are taking.

Second, trends in ESG as well as smart beta and factor investing strategies have introduced a new level of activity to passive management. There are a growing number of passive funds that have begun to question the established wisdom of copying traditional market capitalisation-based indices, and have instead turned toward building their own, focused on alternative measures of value, which seek improved returns. Passives also cannot continue to simply copy indices that do not take into account ESG considerations. So perhaps passives will increasingly lean towards active investing.

On the active side, most significantly, the return of Vol marks the arrival of new opportunity. Hedge funds put in their worst display in seven years in 2018, but also outperformed the S&P 500 for the first time in ten years.[13] Volatile markets have always been to active managers as clay courts are to Rafael Nadal, and reports like this reminds us of that. Vol creates opportunities to take short positions, exploit arbitrage, and pick the winners and losers. So with the return of Vol, I can see the return of the active. Although we will have to see how they fare in competition with the new and improved passive, or perhaps 'hybrid', funds.

I strongly believe that low cost, Darwinian, passive funds have a large role to play in asset management and their investors. However actives are vital too. In fact, possibly many funds may be seen to sit in the future somewhere on a hybrid scale. As passive managers begin to look for a slice of the alpha, higher fee paying, pie, active managers can also seek some beta. The divide looks set to crumble.

## ANY CONCLUSIONS?

**All Trends Overshoot**   The trends that currently exist will carry on longer than they legitimately should. Passives will continue to grow, until investors look more to performance than cost. The cost at all costs trend will overshoot.

The Long Sideways is long.

**We Live in Certain Times**   All this talk about uncertain times – frankly, in 2019, we in the UK or the US have never had it so good. Our economies are strong, there is near full employment, interest rates are phenomenally low, we do not get falsely arrested or imprisoned, we are not at war, we are not dying of untreatable diseases, and drinkable water comes out of a tap. Most of us can find love and declare it. There is no crash. Boy, it could not get much better.

**Twenty Years' Time?**   Hmm – the big guess: well apart from the obvious such as asset management is set to grow – and alternative assets in particular.

Technology will be major. Social media  in its current form though will sink with time, as fines and a rising lack of social and industrial confidence take their toll.

Climate change will make parts of the world more habitable (I am sure the Chinese and Russians have worked that one out), and other parts of the world less so, or indeed uninhabitable. Weather might become less predictable, but we can expect it to continue on as a staple of British small talk.

The big one, though, is that some governments will work out that wealth and thus improved public services is the new war. As the population becomes older and more expensive, and overly-generous house price inflation and pensions wealth sits with people no longer working or contributing, taxing the heck out of the younger wealth creators will not help you. Beat your neighbours or lose the war. Thus, some countries will reduce both tax and regulation, despite global trends such as GDPR and data protection. Although counter-intuitive to the average politician, this will lead cutting edge countries to become global asset manager dominators in twenty years' time. Which countries? Well, it is up to them, although Singapore has a start on all of us. Hong Kong looks in trouble politically. London and New York will both depend on the Americans. The West Coast in my view has peaked and will suffer a collapse of confidence when it sinks in that they have not made the world a better place.

**Rest of the Century** The US will still be the dominant world empire. No world empire lasts fewer than 100 years and typically they last a multiple of that. UK, Portugal, France, Holland – it's debatable. Also, is the US Empire just a continuation of the Anglo-Saxon UK one? However, the US Empire ranks alongside Rome and Persia in terms of power, military strength, and economic muscle. The US dollar is *the* currency. Its language is *the* language. I can't see anyone catching the US this century. Investment will become very self-powered, very immediate, and very liquid. Gigantic houses will dominate. Trusted brands will win.

## ENDNOTES

1. www.abi.org.uk/globalassets/files/publications/public/data/abi_bro4467_state_of_market_v10.pdf
2. https://ec.europa.eu/info/sites/info/files/business_economy_euro/banking_and_finance/documents/190110-aifmd-operation-report_en.pdf
3. www.ft.com/content/40723bc4-bda7-3a4c-a6fc-3d9dd79b56eb
4. www.bbc.co.uk/news/world-43790895
5. www.theguardian.com/politics/2016/nov/21/theresa-may-cuts-to-corporation-tax-cbi-speech
6. www.bbc.co.uk/news/uk-scotland-scotland-business-40922985
7. FT, 10 December 2018.
8. www.pwc.com/gx/en/asset-management/asset-management-insights/assets/am-insights-june-2017.pdf
9. FT, 19 November 2018.
10. FT, 10 December 2018.
11. www.pwc.com/gx/en/asset-management/publications/pdfs/pwc-asset-management-2020-a-brave-new-world-final.pdf
12. www.pwc.com/gx/en/asset-management/asset-management-insights/assets/am-insights-june-2017.pdf
13. FT article, Hedge Fund Research index.

# Some Conclusions

*Be yourself; everyone else is already taken.*

– Oscar Wilde

So where has this merry dance led us?

## SCALE UP OR FOCUS

Asset management is growing. Alternative asset management is growing even faster. Regulation is labyrinthine. Operational costs travel in one direction. Outsourcing is vital, to operate at industrial scale and with institutional quality. Expect more manager consolidation. Scale or niche is vital.

## A WINNING STRATEGY

Diversification of investment strategies stretches categorisation to breaking point. General funds may diversify their investment strategies to provide a balanced portfolio. Not so niche strategies. Multi-boutique, multi-niche... a library of knowledge can prove a winning formula. Listed funds multiply. Private debt is growing fastest. Private debt continues to fill the RE leverage (and especially development) void. Banks are making a comeback – up to a point – providing corporate debt and buy-out leverage, but not in the way they used to (*Barbarians at the Gate*). Infra will continue to rise. Expect new energy to be huge. Private equity is very popular, but has too much dry powder. Is mass cash investing VC a bubble waiting to burst? Thirst for yield persists in a low interest desert. Alternatives are not as alternative as they used to be. Actives versus passives: the battle continues.

## MACRO GOES GLOBAL

As politics is not going away, and history has not ended, learn to adapt. Globalisation versus populism. Global growth seems to be slowing and interest rates stay low in developed countries. The US dollar is still king. The US is the only empire of the twenty-first century. Rumours of its demise were premature. The Western world is getting older, and China is maturing. The UK, US, EU, and Japanese Long Sideways is here to stay. Asia is rising. Think India, not just China. India has youth, growth, language, political, and legal advantages. Africa and South America will make faltering progress, with a few backward steps thrown in. Trade and foreign policy are increasingly becoming the same thing. Brexit will weaken the UK, especially its global reputation. Nor is Brexit good news for the EU project. And the UK's breakaway will not benefit global security. Remember the European project was formed in response to the Second World War. Populism continues to undermine the EU from within. There is a global race to zero for corporation tax, as countries realise they can reduce headline taxes to reap more from indirect taxes.

## SOCIAL IMPACT

ESG policies do not always lower returns make. ESG is here to stay. Managers will be required to incorporate these norms and investors will expect managers to select portfolio companies that employ them. ESG is like advertising in the 1950s. It is no longer new and the new pressure is the fear that your peer group are more advanced than you. Impact – and charitable – investing has the potential to grow and grow. Diversity and gender inequality are still problems. Do women make better managers? They are less driven by ego and gut. Discuss.

## THE THIRD WAVE

Technology disrupts, that much we do know. Competition can be ruthless. Witness the ravages of the provincial high street. However, new behemoth platforms continue to strut around like nineteenth-century monopolies. AI, big data, blockchaining, cybersecurity, robo-advisers, and biometrics sweep the land. And everything is on, all the time, blinking. Welcome HAL. While wealth accumulation, and taxing it sensibly, becomes ever more challenging. The IT in cybercrime exposes shortfalls and continues to proliferate: The Panama Papers, The Luxembourg Leaks, the ever-present WikiLeaks. And more nakedly commercial attacks, like WannaCry.

Competing drivers pivot off technology and data and their impact on asset managers. Transparency and AML versus data protection (GDPR). Social media versus personal privacy. Immediacy of communications versus bots and fake news.

How can I leverage data and charge subscriptions on my portal? When will social media and tech giants start to compete directly with asset managers? Where are the bubbles waiting to burst?

## GOVERNANCE, REGULATION, TAXATION

Changes brought by the Dodd–Frank Act and FATCA are having far-reaching effects on the alternative asset management industry. The Dodd–Frank Act significantly reduces the scope for small private fund managers to market in the US to private investors without SEC approval. This increases costs and time delays for fund managers outside the US who wish to source US investors. FATCA increases the burden on alternative asset managers who have accepted US investors into their funds.

CRS is following everywhere else. BEPs and global transparency are increasing, as are beneficial registries. The Volcker Rule is by far the most controversial plank of all the reforms that have emerged from the crisis. It has decimated banking profitability but has opened up a shadow sector in which private investors trade or borrow. Will Trump burn Volcker? MiFID II chokes the supply of information to all but privileged investors – the opposite of what it was supposed to do. AIFMD had had a widespread effect on asset managers that are based in, or wish to market in, Europe. Will AIFMD ever be finished and fully implemented? Are we all waiting for AIFMD II? Where will Brexit leave UK managers marketing in the EU? Where will Brexit leave EU managers marketing in the UK? Will the Brexit fallout have undesired consequences, such as the cutting of the delegation model for US managers operating in Europe? Will substance rules finally finish off any last vestiges of delegation not bumped off by the Brexit revenge or Brexit greed?

Technological advances, third-party intrusions and cyber risk intensify the need for the correct structures and right people to be in place. The growing utility of data for managers brings with it new challenges under GDPR and other regulation that both protects and requires information to be shared. The overarching impact of all these rules introduces higher costs to the operation of an investment fund. AML, conflicts, and anti-bribery, together with recent rules around transparency and beneficial ownership, add further to cost. Since the start of the financial crisis, reform has been considerable. Some new regulations will be diluted or be more narrowly defined over time. Indeed, much of it will be properly understood only sometime after its implementation. But never have the roles of compliance and risk been more important. Being prepared for regulatory change and having a proactive regulatory culture is vital to managing compliance and risk systems. By giving your firm time and putting the right people and processes in place, you are de-risking both yourself and your investors. Having the right technical systems – and keeping it up to date – is critical. This can be seen by the increase in awareness not just within the industry but also amongst the public.

Ensuring substance, from both a regulatory and a tax perspective, is one-way traffic. More knowledgeable boards – with more time – and with greater diversity on boards – are on the rise. How an asset management firm deals with tax risk will be viewed as a competitive advantage or disadvantage. Investors will expect robust and efficient tax infrastructure and will have minimal tolerance of tax uncertainty or tax adjustments. As a result, tax will be a key operational and business activity, requiring specialist resources, a new approach and integration into front-, back-, and middle-office activities.

## INCUBATION, PLATFORMS, SEEDING AND OUTSOURCING

Increased costs and the need for increased skills, in mid to back office, leads to the need to outsource. Incubators will emerge from the ashes left behind by the investment banks. These incubators and platforms can provide industrial strength – full suite – infrastructure. They can also help distribute.

Incubators and outsourcers will help democratise the industry, faced with unprecedented need for substance, skills, and scale. Without them, only the large will win. Also, expect increased seeding of managers, as well as funds taking stakes in managers. This helps smaller managers grow as well as deal with succession issues.

## YOUR INVESTORS

Raising money is becoming more sophisticated. Use excellent and simple materials. Add understandable messages. Short sentences! Transparency and informationally always-on. Slick, simple interfaces, but with very deep analytical content. Knowledge is king. In the new era of asset management, managers are splitting between the haves and the have-nots. It is not just about returns equating to increased funding. Many of the larger, more-scaled, or library brands, have huge internal placement and investor relations squadrons. Fund raising is a 365 days a year, every year, project; not once every four years, and then reluctantly.

The requirement to bridge a culture gap is important when working between investors and managers. SWFs, state-sponsored funding bodies, banks, pension funds, and charities represent different investment classes, but they are habitual sources of investment funding as well as being significant market players. Each of these organisations have their own cultures and requirements. Learn them. Pension funds are the single largest sector source of funding. Pension plans have entered the debate around managers' fees and charging. SWFs are also a substantial source of funds. Middle Eastern state-backed funds invest up to one third of their new investment into PE. SWFs focus more on the long-term wealth preservation model and tend to favour coinvestment models. SWFs are also building their own in-house teams to conduct their own deals – so partner with them. Pension plans and SWFs are only increasing their investment into alternatives.

Asset allocation is one of the key forms of diversification – it is the diversification of asset categories. This can potentially offer less erratic performance and act as an emotional buoy when certain asset classes take a hit. Asset allocation is not easy. The precise mix of assets requires considerable analysis of a variety of factors, namely, capital markets, past performance, expected market movements, etc., and therefore necessitates a huge amount of work and intellect. Moreover, these variables are in a constant state of flux further complicating the situation. Asset allocation as a 'free lunch' could be over, and could lead to other forms of investing such as more active management and alternative approaches to asset allocation to gain more appeal.

## AND FINALLY, FINALLY

I will probably have to produce a new edition of this book fairly soon.

Asset management has really entered a new era.

It is fast-moving.

We have great responsibility – asset management is vital to the wealth and health of people – as well as affecting the air that we breathe and the food on our table.

*So long, and thanks for all the fish.*

*– Douglas Adams, novelist.*

# Glossary of Terms

| Term | Definition |
|------|------------|
| Abu Dhabi Global Market | an international financial centre based in Abu Dhabi |
| Abu Dhabi Investment Authority | a UAE SWF |
| Abu Dhabi Investment Council | a UAE SWF |
| acquisition cost | the aggregate cost of all aspects of an acquisition, including legal, accounting and any necessary registration fees and tax liabilities |
| active | a fund management approach according to which the fund manager selects investments based on their own particular investment strategy in an attempt to beat the market and maximise returns |
| Administradoras de Fondo de Pensiones | a Chilean pension fund |
| advisory / investors committee | a committee or board made up of representatives of certain investors. The role of the advisory committee is limited to being consulted on matters such as conflicts of interest, approving exceptions to the investment restrictions and potentially certain other matters set out in the LPA and discussing the performance and operation of the fund. Their role in the management of a fund structured as a limited partnership is often restricted to avoid becoming a general partner |
| African Venture Capital Association | an industry body for PE and VC in Africa |
| alpha | a measure of investment performance which compares returns to a benchmark index. Actively managed funds tend to aim for high alpha (i.e. to outperform the market by as much as possible) |
| alternative assets | any asset class falling outside of traditional listed equities and bonds |
| alternative beta | an investment strategy focused on reducing the Vol of alternative investments, often using hedging techniques |
| Alternative für Deutschland | a right-wing political party in Germany |
| alternative investment fund | a fund focused on investment in alternative assets |
| alternative investment fund manager | the manager of an AIF |

| Term | Definition |
|------|-----------|
| Alternative Investment Market | a sub-market of the London Stock Exchange on which earlier-stage companies can float owing to looser regulation |
| annual venture capital operating company | an investment company with at least half of its assets invested in operating companies and exercising management rights in relation to at least one of those companies |
| anti-money laundering | the practice of investigating the source and movement of funds involved in a transaction or used to pay professional fees to avoid being embroiled in money laundering or financing terrorism |
| approved person | a person approved by the FCA to conduct Controlled Functions |
| approved persons regime | the FCA regime under which a person must be approved to conduct Controlled Functions |
| Arab Spring | the period from 18 December 2010 to the current date of violent and non-violent protests and civil wars in the Arab world |
| arbitrage | the contemporaneous sale and purchase of an asset in different markets to profit from price discrepancies caused by market inefficiencies |
| arrival price | the actual price at which a trade or deal is executed |
| articles of association | a UK company's most important constitutional document which sets out the rules of the company and which takes effect as a contract between the company and its shareholders |
| Asian Century | the predicted dominance of Asian political and cultural influence in the twenty-first century |
| Asian region funds passport | an initiative led by Australia, New Zealand, the Republic of Korea, and Singapore which aims to facilitate cross-border fund marketing between participating Asian and Pacific economies |
| asset manager | a firm or individual that manages a fund (or funds) on behalf of investors (and themselves) |
| asset-backed securities | securities (typically bonds) issued by an SPV that derive their value from the performance of a pool of typically illiquid income-generating assets (e.g. mortgage loans or royalties) |
| assets under management | the total market value of assets managed by an asset manager |
| Association for Private Capital Investment in Latin America | an industry body for PE and VC in Latin America |

| Term | Definition |
| --- | --- |
| Association of Southeast Asian Nations Collective Investment Scheme Framework | an international arrangement facilitating cross-border fund marketing between Singapore, Malaysia, and Thailand |
| austerity | a fiscal policy programme that aims to reduce a government's budget deficit and a country's national debt by increasing taxation and decreasing public expenditure |
| Australian Prudential Regulation Authority | an independent statutory authority that oversees and promotes stability of the financial system in Australia |
| Australian Securities and Investments Commission | an independent government body that regulates the corporate, financial services and consumer credit industries in Australia |
| authorised fund manager | a fund manager authorised by the FCA |
| authorised unit trust | an FCA-regulated collective investment vehicle established as a trust |
| Autorité des Marchés Financiers | the French financial markets regulator |
| B15 cities | the top 15 cities by GDP ranking below the T15 cities |
| Baby Boomers | the demographic cohort of those born during the period after the second world war up to 1964 |
| back office | includes support roles such as IT, human resources, and accounting |
| BAK Taxation Index | a list comparing the tax regimes of various international cities and Swiss cantons, published by BAK Basel Economics AG |
| Bank of England | the central bank of the UK |
| Basel Committee | Basel Committee on Banking Supervision, a forum of national banking supervisory authorities established in 1974 by the then G10 countries |
| Basel III | a collection of measures designed by the Basel Committee that have been internationally agreed as a response to the Financial Crisis and which are followed on a voluntary basis |
| bear market | a market in which prices are generally falling |
| beta | a measure of investment Vol – passively managed funds tend to aim for a beta of 1 (i.e. to replicate the performance of the market) |
| Big Bang | the period of drastic financial services deregulation in the UK during the 1980s under Prime Minister Margaret Thatcher |
| big data | any data set, the size and/or complexity of which requires powerful computer software to analyse |

| Term | Definition |
| --- | --- |
| Black Wednesday | 16 September 1992, the date on which Prime Minister John Major's Conservative government had to withdraw sterling from the ERM because it was not able to keep the currency above the agreed lower limit |
| blind-pool fund | a fund where the investors' capital is committed to be used in any investment. The investor cannot opt out of a specified investment and the fund is 'blind' as it has made no investments at the point of commitment |
| blockchain | a system of data storage based on a digital list of data 'blocks' which are connected by unique timestamps, the system offers greater efficiency and security than previous approaches to data storage and has given rise to the development of cryptocurrencies |
| bond | a debt security issued by companies and governments. The holder typically derives value from repayment of capital and interest |
| bottom line | a company's net profit (a reference to the bottom line of a company's profit and loss account) |
| Brazilian Central Bank | the central bank of Brazil |
| Brexit | a portmanteau of the words 'Britain' and 'exit', referring to the UK's proposed withdrawal from the EU |
| Bribery Act 2010 | UK legislation covering criminal offences related to bribery |
| BRICS | the emerging economies of Brazil, Russia, India, China and South Africa |
| British Business Bank | a state-owned development bank established by the UK government |
| British Overseas Territories | the 14 territories outside of the UK which fall under the sovereignty of the UK. They are former territories of the British Empire that have not voted for independence but they are largely independent in their internal governance and rely on the UK for international representation and defence |
| British Private Equity and Venture Capital Association | an industry body for PE and VC in the UK |
| bulge bracket | a term used to define a globally-minded, multi-service line and multi-product investment bank pre-financial crisis |
| bull market | a market in which prices are generally rising |
| business cycle | the fluctuation in an economy's real GDP through periods of growth and contraction, within the context of a long-term growth trend |
| Business Finance Taskforce | a group consisting of chief executives from Barclays, HSBC, Lloyds, Santander, Standard Chartered, RBS, and the British Bankers' Association, set up in 2010 to review and address public perceptions of the UK banking industry's contribution to the UK economy |

| Term | Definition |
|---|---|
| Business Growth Fund | a PE investment company founded by Barclays, HSBC, Lloyds, RBS, and Standard Chartered in 2011 to provide capital to SMEs |
| capital expenditure | company spending attributable to the purchase or maintenance of fixed assets such as property, plant or machinery |
| Capital Markets Union | an EC initiative for increased capital market integration across the EU |
| Capital Requirements Directive IV | an EU Directive providing prudential rules for financial institutions in the EU |
| carried interest | the PE equivalent of the performance fee in a hedge fund context. During the distribution (or 'waterfall'), following the return of capital to the investors and the payment of a preferred return to investors (usually 8% of capital, also known as the 'hurdle rate'), the manager and its executives receive a percentage (usually 20%) of all profits thereafter with catch-up of the hurdle |
| carry | shorthand term for carried interest |
| carry deed | the legal document under which the carry vehicle is established |
| carry holder | the manager and the senior members of its team that receive the carried interest |
| carry partner | the carry vehicle is a partner in the fund, and is assigned this label in the fund documentation and structure |
| carry vehicle | the legal entity which receives the carried interest from the fund and passes it on to the manager and those individuals who are entitled to receive it |
| catch-up | during the waterfall, the carry partner is paid a percentage of the preferred return to investors – which will, if the carried interest is 20%, be 25% of the amount paid as a preferred return |
| central bank | a financial institution which manages a national economy's currency, money supply and base interest rate, often referred to as the 'lender of last resort' |
| central counterparty | a third-party financial institution which takes on the credit risk in derivatives transactions and provides clearing services |
| Central Mediterranean Route | the most used migration route to the EU during the Migration Crisis which typically entails travel from sub-Saharan Africa through Libya, across the Mediterranean Sea, to Italy |
| Certification Regime | a part of the UK financial services regulatory framework, which requires annual certification of the fitness and propriety of staff |

| Term | Definition |
| --- | --- |
| Chancellor of the Exchequer | equivalent to the finance minister in other countries, the senior government minister in charge of the Treasury |
| China Mainland-Hong Kong Mutual Recognition of Funds | an international arrangement facilitating cross-border fund marketing between China and Hong Kong |
| China Securities Regulatory Commission | the Chinese securities market regulator |
| clawback | in the context of fund distributions, any amount which an LP is obliged to return to the fund after distributions have been made, pursuant to the terms of the LPA |
| close company | a company which is UK resident and controlled by five or fewer participants who either have control of the company or are entitled to receive a majority of its assets on winding up (s 439 CoTA 2010) |
| closed-ended fund | a fund which has a fixed number of investor interests (whether represented by units, shares, etc.). Following its final closing, investors cannot cancel (or redeem) interests until the fund is terminated and the fund has a predetermined lifespan |
| closing | the date on which the fund will admit a round of investors. A fund may have only one closing, but often there are multiple rounds |
| Code 03 | a code of practice published by The Pensions Regulator relating to funding defined benefits |
| collateralised debt obligation | a type of structured asset-backed security consisting of various tranches of pooled assets |
| collateralised loan obligation | a type of asset-backed security where the backing asset is a pool of debt |
| collective investment scheme | an arrangement for the pooling of capital contributed by more than one person or company for the purpose of investment |
| Commissao de Valores Mobiliarios (Brazilian Securities Commission) | Brazilian capital markets regulator |
| commitment | the amount that an investor is bound to provide when called upon by the fund manager |
| committed capital fund | a fund in which the investors are committed to provide funds when called upon to do so |
| commodities trading adviser | a US term for a person or company who provides advice to a fund in relation to commodity derivatives |
| Commodity Futures Trading Commission | an independent US government agency which regulates the US futures and options market |

| Term | Definition |
| --- | --- |
| Common Reporting Standards regime | an OECD arrangement according to which participating states exchange certain information on an annual basis concerning financial institutions based in their jurisdiction to support efforts to fight tax evasion |
| Companies House | the UK registrar of companies |
| Competition Commission | the predecessor of the Competition and Markets Authority in the UK |
| compound annual growth rate | the rate of return on an investment that would be necessary for it to reach a target value assuming annual profits were reinvested |
| Conduct Rules | a part of the UK financial services regulatory framework, which provides two sets of rules – one set for all individuals and an additional set for senior managers |
| controlled functions | functions which can only be performed by Approved Persons under FSMA, e.g. being a director of a regulated firm |
| controller | a person or body who determines how and why personal data is used |
| cornerstone investor | an investor that provides a significant early commitment to provide capital to a fund, usually on more favourable terms than later investors. They will also assist in the promotion of the fund |
| corporate social responsibility | a form of corporate self-regulation focused on sustaining ethical business practices |
| Corporation Tax Act 2010 | UK legislation concerning corporation tax and company distributions |
| Council of Appeals of the National Financial System | an appellate body, which reviews decisions of both the BCB and the CVM |
| credit | the ability to obtain capital, goods, or services, based on the promise of future payment |
| credit crisis (credit crunch) | a drastic reduction in the availability of credit or ease of access to credit in an economy (especially in reference to the period during 2008 which saw the bankruptcy of Lehman Brothers) |
| Credit Rating Agency Reform Act 2006 | US legislation regulating the US credit rating agency industry |
| CRISIL | formerly an initialisation of Credit Rating Information Services of India Limited, a global ratings company majority-owned by S&P |
| C-suite | a company's most senior executives, derived from the titles of senior executives which start with the letter 'C' (e.g. CEO, CIO, CFO) |

| Term | Definition |
| --- | --- |
| Cuban Missile Crisis | the 13-day non-violent confrontation between the US and Soviet Union which is considered the height of Cold War tensions, and which was caused by US missiles being stationed in Europe and consequently Soviet missiles being stationed in Cuba |
| custody rule | Rule 206 of the IAA requiring investment advisers to comply with detailed procedures that are designed to keep investors informed about the location and person that maintains the custody of their assets |
| Data Protection Act 2018 | UK legislation updating data protection laws |
| delegation model | under AIFMD, portfolio management decisions can be delegated in their entirety to a UK or US-based investment manager, and enjoy EU passporting rights |
| Democratic National Committee | the US Democratic Party governing body |
| derivative | a financial product (such as an option or future), the value of which is derived from the value of an underlying asset (e.g. gold or oil) |
| derivatives clearing organisations | an entity that facilitates derivative transactions through the provision of clearing services |
| development capital | an investment in a business which is beyond the start-up phase but is not considered a mature business, with the aim of funding further expansion |
| development finance institution | a financial institution which provides investment in development projects |
| directive | a legislative instrument of the EU, which requires member states to achieve a particular outcome, but leaves the member states with the freedom to implement their own domestic legislation in order to do so |
| Directive 2003/41/EC - Institutions for Occupational Retirement Provision Directive | EU legislation regulating pensions schemes |
| Directive 2011/61/EU Alternative Investment Fund Managers Directive | European legislation regulating the management of AIFs |
| Directive 2014/57/EU Market Abuse Directive | EU legislation to prevent market abuses such as market manipulation and insider dealing |
| disguised investment management fees | profit sharing arrangements deemed to exploit tax rules on carried interest in order that fee income can be charged to capital gains tax instead of income tax |
| disinflation | a period of reduced inflation |
| diversification | the practice of allocating investment capital across different markets and asset classes in order to reduce a portfolios overall exposure to any one particular risk |

| Term | Definition |
|---|---|
| diverted profits tax | a UK tax designed to capture certain profits which are connected to or generated within the UK but moved outside of the UK through careful tax planning and would therefore otherwise not be subject to UK tax |
| dividend yields | the value of a dividend as a percentage of the current share price of the stock to which the dividend relates |
| Division of Clearing and Risk | a division of the CFTC, providing oversight of derivatives clearing organisations in the US |
| Division of Investment Management | SEC division which aims to protect investors and promotes informed investment decision-making |
| Division of Market Oversight | a division of the CFTC, which promotes fair, competitive and secure derivative markets through oversight of trading platforms and repositories in the US |
| Dodd–Frank Wall Street Reform and Consumer Protection Act | landmark US legislation affecting financial services regulation, passed in response to the credit crisis and ensuing financial crisis |
| dry powder | money raised by PE managers that has not yet been allocated towards the purchase of assets |
| Dubai International Finance Centre | a financial hub based in Dubai |
| due diligence | the process of gathering information about an investment target and assessing the risks and opportunities associated with it |
| dynamic asset allocation | a portfolio management strategy that usually entails no target mix of asset allocation and frequent adjustments to the mix as the manager sees fit |
| Economic and Monetary Union | the integration and coordination of eurozone economic and monetary policy |
| efficient market hypothesis | the theory that asset prices are fully reflective of all available information (and therefore it is impossible to buy undervalued or overvalued stock) |
| Emerging Market Index in the MSCI | a market capitalisation-weighted index consisting of 24 countries which represent 10% of global market capitalisation |
| Employee Retirement Income Security Act of 1974 | US legislation regulating private pension plans, with the aim of protecting the interests of employee participants in such plans |
| environmental, social, governance | criteria for the measurement of an investment's ethical standards and impact beyond financial returns |
| equities | shares (ownership interests) in privately or publicly owned companies. The holder typically derives value from capital gains on resale and/or income in the form of dividends |
| escrow | a third-party account where monies may be held on trust until payment is due |

| Term | Definition |
| --- | --- |
| Eskom Pension and Provident Fund | a South African pension fund |
| establishment expenses | the costs of setting up a fund, including legal fees, administrative fees, and marketing costs |
| euro | the official currency of 19 of the EU Member States |
| European Central Bank | the eurozone's central bank |
| European Commission | an EU institution responsible for management of the EU and proposing EU legislation |
| European Economic Area | the single market for goods, services, capital and labour within the EU and EFTA states |
| European Exchange Rate Mechanism | a system intended to avoid large fluctuations in the exchange rates between the Euro and other EU currencies, participation is voluntary and currently only the Danish krone is included |
| European Financial Stability Facility | an SPV funded by eurozone members in order to tackle the European sovereign debt crisis |
| European Free Trade Association | a free trade area consisting of Norway, Iceland, Liechtenstein, and Switzerland |
| European Fund for Strategic Investments | a key component of the 'Juncker Plan', a EUR 33.5 billion initiative funded by the EIB and EC to encourage private investment in the EU |
| European Insurance and Occupational Pensions Authority | an EU body which supports the stability of the EU financial system by promoting transparency and protecting insurance policyholders and pension scheme beneficiaries |
| European Investment Bank | a lending institution jointly owned by member states which provides funding for EU projects |
| European Investment Fund | an EU vehicle for the purpose of providing finance to SMEs |
| European Market Infrastructure Regulation | EU legislation for the regulation of OTC derivatives |
| European Organization for Nuclear Research | the world's largest particle physics laboratory based in Geneva, Switzerland |
| European Securities and Markets Authority | the EU financial markets (particularly credit ratings agencies) regulator |
| European Stability Mechanism | a eurozone organisation established in 2012 to provide loans to eurozone member states in financial difficulty |
| European System of Central Banks | a co-operative network of central banks consisting of the ECB and the 28 central banks of the EU member states |
| European Union | the political and economic union of the 28 participating member states in Europe |
| Eurosystem | the ECB and national central banks of the 19 eurozone member states |
| eurozone | the monetary union of 19 member states which have adopted the euro as their currency |

| Term | Definition |
|---|---|
| EU–Turkey deal | an agreement reached in March 2016 between the EU and Turkey in relation to the Migration Crisis, pursuant to which migrants arriving 'irregularly' in Greece would be returned to Turkey and the member states would take one Syrian refugee for every migrant returned to Turkey |
| exchange-traded funds | an investment fund traded on a stock exchange (and which usually tracks an index) |
| family office | a private company that manages investments and trusts either for a single wealthy family or for several families |
| fatwa | a ruling on a point of Islamic law given by a recognised authority |
| FCA Code of Conduct | the set of rules governing the professional conduct of certain SM&CR employees |
| FCA individual conduct rules | the rules set out under COCON 2.1 governing individual conduct |
| FCA remuneration codes | a set of rules published by the FCA which set out the requirements certain firms must fulfil when setting pay and bonuses for their employees |
| Federal Reserve | the Federal Reserve System is the central banking system of the United States. Aside from the provision of finance to the government and key financial institutions, it also has regulatory and supervisory functions and plays an active role in monetary policy |
| Financial Action Task Force | an intergovernmental organisation of 37 countries which aims to combat money laundering and terrorist financing |
| Financial Conduct Authority | the UK financial services market regulator |
| financial crisis | the period of negative to low growth across many developed economies from 2007 to 2013 |
| financial due diligence | DD focused on financial issues |
| Financial Intelligence Analysis Units | member state national bodies with the objective of reducing money laundering and the financing of terrorism |
| Financial Services and Markets Act 2000 | UK legislation which sets out the regulatory framework for financial services in the UK and established the Financial Ombudsman Service and the FSA |
| Financial Services and Markets Act 2000 (Regulated Activities) Order 2001 | UK legislation specifying activities which are regulated under FSMA |
| Financial Services Authority | the predecessor to the FCA |
| Financial Stability Board | an international body based in Switzerland and established by the G20 in 2009 to monitor the global financial system and make recommendations |
| Financial Stability Oversight Council | a US government organisation established by the Dodd–Frank Act to monitor the US financial system and make recommendations |

| Term | Definition |
|---|---|
| Financial Times Stock Exchange | a share-index of the top 100 companies by market capitalisation listed on the LSE |
| FINMA | the Swiss financial services market regulator |
| first closing | where a fund has multiple closings, the first is usually the most significant |
| FIS Law | the Law of the People's Republic of China on Funds for Investment in Securities |
| fiscal policy | the use of fiscal mechanisms (i.e. taxation and public expenditure) to influence an economy |
| Foreign Account Tax Compliance Act | US legislation requiring all non-US financial institutions to report certain information about US taxpayers, and entities in which US taxpayers hold a significant interest, to the IRS |
| Fourth EU Money Laundering Directive | EU legislation relating to AML |
| Frontex | the European Border and Coast Guard Agency, responsible for control of the Schengen Area (area of passport-free travel within the EU) border |
| front office | includes client-facing roles such as managers, analysts, and sales people |
| FTSE All-Share Index | a market capitalisation-weighted index consisting of over a quarter of the companies traded on the LSE |
| G20 | an international forum for the governments of 20 of the most influential countries to discuss global economic issues |
| Gates Foundation | the Bill & Melinda Gates Foundation, a privately owned charitable organisation controlled by Bill Gates, Melinda Gates, and Warren Buffett |
| General Data Protection Regulation | EU data protection legislation |
| general partner | a partner to a Limited Partnership with unlimited liability and responsibility for the management of the day-to-day business of the partnership |
| general partner's share | the share of a fund's profits paid to the GP which is used to pay the management fee |
| Generally Accepted Principles and Practices | see 'Santiago Principles' |
| Generation X | the demographic cohort of those born after the Baby Boomers and before the Millennials |
| gharar | Arabic for 'uncertainty', which encompasses financial risk |
| gilt | a UK government-issued bond |
| GIs | originally an abbreviation of 'galvanised iron', these initials have come to be used in reference to US soldiers |
| Global Financial Centres Index | a ranking of the world's top financial cities |
| Global Impact Investing Network | a private New York based organisation that promotes the development of impact investing internationally |

| Term | Definition |
|---|---|
| Global Impact Investing Ratings System | an ESG analysis and ratings tool which uses IRIS metrics |
| globalisation | the phenomenon of increasing worldwide interaction between individuals, businesses, and nations |
| Government Pension Investment Fund | a Japanese state pension fund |
| Great Depression | the worldwide economic depression beginning with the crash of the New York Stock Exchange in 1929 and lasting until the late 1930s |
| gross domestic product | the total monetary value of all the goods and services produced by a national economy |
| growth capital | a typically minor investment in a mature company for the purpose of funding growth or other expansion |
| Harmonised Index of Consumer Prices | used as the indicator of inflation by the ECB, a consumer price index which is compiled using a harmonised approach across all member states |
| hedge fund | an actively managed and generally open-ended investment fund trading in a variety of asset classes, though chiefly equities, derivatives and bonds, and which often employs sophisticated investment strategies in an effort to outperform the market |
| Her Majesty's Revenue and Customs | the UK government department responsible for tax collection |
| High-net-worth individual | a person whose investable assets are of an exceptionally high value, enabling them to access investment opportunities not available to retail investors (a HNWI holds millions of USD in investable assets) |
| high water mark | a mechanism often included in hedge fund (and other open-ended fund) LPAs which ensures that if the NAV of a fund falls in one period, the performance fee can only later be charged on any outperformance above the highest value the fund reached in a previous period |
| Hong Kong Monetary Authority | the de facto central bank of Hong Kong |
| hurdle | a rate of return that must be paid to investors before the manager can claim its entitlement to (catch-up and) carried interest |
| IBM Institute for Business Value | a business research organisation run by IBM |
| impact fund | a fund which places particular emphasis on social returns in addition to financial returns |
| income-based carried interest | carried interest which does not meet the investment holding period required under UK tax law to qualify for capital gains tax treatment instead of income tax treatment |

| Term | Definition |
|---|---|
| independent financial adviser | a professional financial adviser not representing an insurer or bank |
| individual retirement agreement | a form of tax-advantageous private pension plan in the US |
| inflation | the rate at which the average price of goods and services increases in an economy |
| Information Commissioners Office | the UK's data protection authority |
| information memorandum | also referred to as an offering memorandum or private placement memorandum (PPM), a document provided by managers to potential investors containing important information about a fund they are marketing |
| infrastructure | an alternative investment class encompassing major building projects such as hospitals, power supplies, and transport links |
| initial coin offering | a type of funding using cryptocurrency which has recently been used by start-ups |
| initial public offering | the first sale of shares in a company to investors as a company goes public, underwritten by an investment bank |
| Institutional Limited Partners Association | a trade association for PE investors |
| intellectual property | intangible property which is the product of human intellect, including trademarks, patents, and copyrights |
| interest rate | the rate a lender charges a borrower for credit |
| Internal Revenue Code | the consolidated and codified US tax laws enforced by the IRS |
| Internal Revenue Service | the US federal tax authority |
| International Consortium of Investigative Journalists | an international network of investigative journalists collaborating on large-scale investigations and responsible for the release of the Panama Papers and Paradise Papers |
| International Finance Corporation | an independent arm of the World Bank that provides asset management and financial advisory services to the private sector in developing economies |
| International Forum of Sovereign Wealth Funds | a non-profit group of SWF managers established in 2009 and based in London with the objective of promoting the Santiago Principles |
| International Monetary Fund | an international organisation based in Washington, DC for the promotion of economic growth, international trade and monetary co-operation |
| International Working Group of Sovereign Wealth Funds | the predecessor of the IFSWF |

| Term | Definition |
|------|------------|
| investment adviser | some fund structures require the engagement of an investment adviser separate from the manager. This is often an entity associated with the manager. It is often necessary in hedge funds, where the jurisdiction of the fund requires a manager within that territory |
| Investment Advisors Act of 1940 | US legislation regulating investment advisers |
| investment advisery model | under AIFMD, portfolio management decisions can be made at the fund level, under advice from a UK or US based investment adviser and enjoy EU passporting rights |
| Investment Company Act of 1940 | US legislation regulating investment fund vehicles |
| Investment Company Institute | a worldwide association of regulated funds which promotes ethical investment and management practices |
| investment management / manager | an individual or corporation that makes investment decisions on behalf a fund |
| investment objective | the aim of a fund, the strategy of a fund is geared towards the overall investment objective |
| investment period | the period of time in which a fund with a fixed lifespan makes investments. This is usually from first closing to the midway stage of the fund's life |
| investment vehicle | any legal entity or arrangement, such as a limited company or partnership, used for the purpose of making and/or holding investments |
| investor | in a funds context, any provider of capital to a fund (in a broader context, any person who allocates capital with the expectation of financial gain) |
| IRIS | a company which produces a set of defined metrics for measuring ESG performance |
| Irish Collective Asset-Management Vehicle | an Irish investment vehicle |
| iShares | a group of ETFs managed by BlackRock |
| Islamic bank | a banking institution which adheres to the requirements of Sharia law and Islamic principles |
| Jersey property unit trust | a property-holding vehicle under Jersey law |
| jumbo director | a person holding board positions with a large number of companies |
| Jumpstart Our Business Startups Act of 2012 | US legislation intended to promote private investment in small businesses in the US |
| key person | the management team is as much about individuals as the collective. Investors are often attracted to a fund by the persons involved in running it and will want to ensure that they remain so, and have control over any succession to other persons |

| Term | Definition |
|---|---|
| KKR & Co. Inc. | one of the world's largest asset managers, headquartered in New York |
| know your customer | the practice of verifying the identity of a business' customers and identifying any potential risks of being embroiled in illegal activity |
| Kuwait Investment Authority | Kuwait's SWF |
| legal due diligence | DD focused on legal issues |
| legal entity identifier | a unique 20-character code designed to enable international identification of legal entities engaging in financial transactions |
| leverage | the use of debt to increase the potential return of an investment |
| leveraged buyout | the purchase of a company using debt (in addition to equity) |
| liability-driven investing | an investment strategy focused on delivering sufficient returns to meet future liabilities, the prime example of a fund which might use LDI is a pension fund |
| LIBOR | the London Inter-Bank Offered Rate. Various LIBOR rates exist for different financial institutions, but it also is a headline figure of the rate at which banks will lend to each other. It is used as a reference point in calculating other payments of interest (e.g. 4% above LIBOR) |
| limited liability company | a US corporate entity that protects members of the company from personal liability |
| limited liability partnership | a UK tax-transparent corporate entity that protects members of the partnership from personal liability |
| limited partner | in a limited partnership, the limited partner provides equity capital to the fund and has an interest in the profits and capital distributions made by the partnership. A limited partner will not have unlimited exposure to the liabilities of the fund, in contrast with a general partner. A limited partner may become a general partner by taking a role in the management of the fund |
| limited partner advisory committee | a committee, formed of LP representatives, which normally advises the GP on particular issues relating to a fund such as conflicts of interests and LP consent matters, but may also be consulted on investment decisions |
| limited partnership | a limited partnership is established under the Limited Partnership Act 1907. Unlike a partnership, where all partners are jointly and severally liable for the liabilities of the fund, a limited partnership allows for certain partners to have liability limited to their capital contributions |

| Term | Definition |
|------|-----------|
| limited partnership agreement | the key constitutional document of a Limited Partnership, which sets out the terms of participation in a fund |
| listed | traded on a public stock exchange |
| Local Government Pension Scheme | a pension scheme for employees working in local government in the UK |
| London Stock Exchange | one of the world's largest and oldest stock exchanges, based in London |
| Long Sideways | the period beginning just after the dot-com bust to the present day of relatively low growth and low Vol |
| Long-Term Capital Management L.P. | a US-based hedge fund management firm |
| LPX indices | market capitalisation indices following the performance of publicly traded PE companies |
| Luxembourg Leaks | documents leaked in 2016 revealing controversial tax rulings issued by Luxembourg tax authorities in relation to hundreds of companies, helping to reduce their tax liabilities |
| managed accounts | a managed account is an alternative to a fund structure whereby the assets are held by a custodian on behalf of the investor, rather than pooled by a manager into a fund |
| management fee | an annualised fee payable to the manager of the fund to cover the operating costs it encounters. It is not intended to act as a source of profit, and some investors will require audited accounts to show that the fee covers no more than costs |
| manager | the entity representing the investment team which promotes and manages the fund and makes investments on behalf of the fund |
| Mandatory Provident Funds Authority | the regulator of privately managed compulsory pension funds in Hong Kong |
| Market Abuse Regulation | EU legislation aimed at increasing market integrity and boosting investor protection in EU securities markets |
| Markets in Financial Instruments Directive 2004/39/EC | EU legislation regulating EU financial markets |
| Markets in Financial Instruments Directive II-Directive 2014/65/EU | EU legislation regulating EU financial markets, in particular by increasing transparency through additional reporting requirements |
| Meet ASEAN's Talents and Champions | a roadshow aimed at promoting investment in ASEAN and engagement with ASEAN businesses and investors |
| member state | a country party to the treaties of the EU |
| mezzanine debt | subordinated debt or preferred equity, i.e. debt or debt-like capital which is senior to ordinary equity but is junior to senior debt |

| Term | Definition |
|---|---|
| mid office | includes strategic management roles such as risk, compliance, and legal |
| migration crisis | the European migrant crisis, a term given to the period since 2015 during which an increasingly large number of migrants began arriving in the EU from North Africa and the Middle East across the Mediterranean Sea or through South-East Europe |
| Millennials | the demographic cohort of those born during the decades of 1980 and 1990 |
| minimum capital requirement | a minimum amount of capital required by regulators to be held by a financial services provider such as a bank or insurer in the interests of financial stability and consumer protection |
| modern portfolio theory | in broad terms, the theory that the combination of assets chosen as well as the class of assets themselves impacts the results of a portfolio. Before this, portfolio construction theory was focussed on the individual risks or rewards of each security |
| Monetary Authority of Singapore | the central bank of Singapore |
| monetary policy | the use of monetary mechanisms (for example, money supply and interest rates) to influence an economy |
| money laundering | the process of disguising of the origins of illegally obtained money, such that it appears to have been obtained legally, usually by transferring the money to and from reputable financial institutions and legitimate corporate entities |
| Money Laundering, Terrorist Financing and Transfer of Funds (Information on the Payer) Regulations 2017 | UK legislation relating to AML |
| mortgage-backed security | a typed of asset-backed security, where the assets are mortgages |
| MS15/2.3 | a FCA market study concerning asset management |
| Mubadala Investment Company | a UAE SWF |
| mutual fund | essentially, a synonym of 'fund' |
| national competent authority | the authority responsible, in each EU member state, for the domestic authorisation of medicines |
| National Council for Social Security Fund | a Chinese state-run fund used for social security |
| National Futures Association | a self-regulatory organisation concerning the US derivatives market |
| national insurance contribution | a tax paid by UK workers to fund state benefits |

| Term | Definition |
|---|---|
| National Stock Exchange of India | the principal stock exchange in India |
| net asset value | the value of a business of funds' assets minus liabilities |
| net investable assets | the total value of assets an investor has available to invest, calculated by deducting debts and, in the case of individuals, personal property (cars and houses etc.) from the total assets they own |
| Netherlands Development Finance Company | a Dutch DFI |
| New York Stock Exchange | the world's largest stock exchange, based in New York City |
| Non-Cooperative Country and Territory | the FATF 'blacklist' of countries which are considered to be uncooperative in international endeavours to curb money laundering and terrorist financing |
| non-executive director | a board member who is not involved in the day-to-day management of a company and offers an external and independent view on board matters |
| OECD Anti-Bribery Convention | a convention of the OECD which aims to tackle political corruption and corporate crime |
| OECD G20 Base Erosion and Profit Sharing Project | an international initiative to combat tax avoidance by multinational corporations |
| Office of the Commissioner of Insurance | in the US, the office of an elected representative at state level, responsible for regulation of the insurance industry |
| Official List | the UK Official List is maintained by the UKLA. It is a list of all securities which are traded on a regulated market within the UK |
| open-ended fund | an investment vehicle which can freely issue and redeem shares or other interests as investors subscribe to and leave the fund |
| open-ended investment company | a UK-incorporated investment vehicle, in which shares can be bought and sold by investor-shareholders as in an open-ended fund |
| operating company | a company which derives its profits from the sale of goods or services (as opposed to a holding company, which derives profits from the ownership of other companies) |
| Operation Sophia | an EU military operation to tackle refugee smuggling routes in the Mediterranean |
| operational due diligence | DD focused on operational issues |
| operational efficiency | a measure of business productivity, based on the ratio of input to output |
| operational expenditure | company spending attributable to the ongoing costs of running a business such as electricity and salaries |
| order management system | a computer software system used for processing high volumes of trades in financial securities |

| Term | Definition |
|------|-----------|
| Organisation for Economic Co-operation and Development | an international organisation promoting co-operation between the 36 member countries on questions of economic policy |
| outsourced chief investment officer | the engagement of external resources (either human, IT, or both) in the management of an investment portfolio, particularly in respect of decisions relating to asset allocation |
| over-the-counter derivatives | a derivative contract privately agreed between counterparties, as opposed to the standardised contracts traded on public exchanges |
| Ovum | a data and research company |
| P&L method | a method of complying with MiFID II requirements, by paying for research fees out of an asset manager's own profit and loss account |
| P22 countries | countries whose pension funds manage the most assets |
| P7 countries | the seven countries with the largest holdings of pension assets |
| Panama Papers | over 11 million electronic documents leaked in 2016 from Panama-based law firm Mossack Fonseca exposing sensitive information about investors, including 12 national leaders, and their tax-efficient investment structures |
| Paradise Papers | over 13 million electronic documents leaked in 2016 from various sources (over half from international law firm Appleby) exposing sensitive information about investors, including Queen Elizabeth II, and their tax-efficient investment structures |
| Paris Agreement | an international agreement between 195 countries designed to tackle climate change |
| partnership agreement | a partnership agreement is the constitutional document at the heart of a partnership. It is not necessary for the legal establishment of a partnership, but any well advised person will formally set out the rights and responsibilities of partners together with the procedures necessary for running of the partnership |
| passive | a fund management approach based on following a particular index by trying to own all the stocks in that index in the proportion they are held in that index |
| payment in kind | use of good or services as payment as oppose to cash |
| performance fee | an additional fee usually paid to (open-ended) fund managers if they are successful, usually around 20% |
| plan asset regulations | see 'ERISA' |
| plan assets | assets held for the use of a defined benefit pension plan |

| Term | Definition |
|------|------------|
| politically exposed person | an individual holding an important public position and generally presenting a higher risk of bribery and corruption due to their power and influence |
| Ponzi scheme | a fraudulent investment structure made famous by Charles Ponzi in the 1920s which involves paying returns to early investors with the contributions of later investors – the scheme can generally work for as long as new investors join. Investors are unaware of the scheme and believe they are invested in a legitimate fund structure |
| post-modern portfolio theory | an extension and amendment to MPT with a revised view of risk |
| President's Working Group on Financial Markets | a US working group consisting of the Secretary of the Treasury, the Chairperson of the Board of Governors of the Federal Reserve, the Chairperson of the SEC, and the Chairperson of the CFTC |
| PricewaterhouseCoopers | an international professional services business and one of the 'Big Four' auditors |
| Principles Operating System | a technological platform designed to assist in investment decision-making, developed by Bridgewater Associates |
| private equity | generally, a term for investments made into companies which are either unlisted private entities or listed entities with the intention of delisting the target company |
| private equity principles | a set of principles published by ILPA in January 2011 to promote alignment of interests between GPs and LPs, good governance, and transparency in fund partnerships |
| private finance initiative | a form of public-private partnership pursuant to which a private investor completes and manages a public project using their own capital and then leases use of it to public authorities |
| processor | a person or body which processes personal data on behalf of a controller |
| Prudential Regulation Authority | a regulatory body, forming part of the Bank of England, which prudentially regulates and supervises various financial services firms (chiefly, banks and insurers) |
| PSC register | a public register of people with significant control of privately owned UK companies |
| Public Company Accounting Oversight Board | a US statutory non-profit corporation responsible for overseeing public company audits |
| public pension fund | a retirement savings fund for public sector employees |
| publicly traded partnership | a partnership which is listed and traded on a public exchange |
| public–private partnership | an arrangement between a public body and a private company, typically long-term, to finance, build and operate public projects |

| Term | Definition |
|------|-----------|
| PULSE | a portfolio management tool using IRIS metrics |
| quantitative easing | expansionary monetary policy aimed at increasing market liquidity through the purchase of government bonds and other financial assets by a central bank |
| quantitative tightening | contractionary monetary policy aimed at reducing market liquidity through the holding or selling of bonds and increasing interest rates by a central bank |
| real estate | broadly, the asset class encompassing land and buildings |
| Real Estate Investment Trust | a property investment company that owns, and usually operates, revenue-generating RE |
| Real Estate Operating Company | similar to a REIT, except a REOC generates revenue through the sale of new or refurbished RE |
| real GDP | an inflation-adjusted measure of GDP |
| recession | a period of economic contraction within the business cycle, generally defined within Europe as two consecutive quarters of negative growth in real GDP |
| redemption fee | a fee charged to investors for withdrawing money from a fund |
| regulated activity | an activity which is regulated under RAO |
| Remainers | those in favour of the UK remaining within the EU |
| Renminbi Qualified Foreign Institutional Investor Scheme | a Chinese policy initiative allowing international institutional investors, who meet certain requirements, to invest directly into the Chinese mainland capital markets |
| Report of Foreign Bank and Financial Accounts | a statutory filing that must be made by certain US citizens with substantial holdings in foreign bank accounts |
| research payment account | a separate account for payment of research fees, used by asset managers to comply with MiFID when using investor money to pay for research fees |
| Retail Distribution Review 2012 | a review of the UK market for retail investment products conducted by the FSA |
| return on investment | a performance measure used to evaluate investment efficiency |
| riba | Arabic for 'usury', which is generally understood to include interest |
| risk | the possibility of losing economic value, a consequence of any financial decision made in a context of uncertainty |
| risk-weighted assets | assets forming part of a regulator's assessment of the minimum capital requirement for a financial institution, these assets are given a weighing according to their perceived risk and this value is used in the final computation |
| robotic process automation | the use of robots (with or without learning capabilities) to perform often tedious and repetitive tasks normally requiring human involvement, thereby removing humans from a process |

| Term | Definition |
|------|------------|
| Santiago Principles | a set of principles endorsed by the IFSWF to promote good governance and transparency |
| Saudi Stock Exchange | the largest stock exchange in the Middle East, based in Riyadh, Saudi Arabia |
| Scheme Advisory Board | the advisory board to the UK Local Government Pension Scheme |
| secondary | secondary investments in PE (or RE or hedge) are effectively buyouts by a second PE fund of PE assets from a first PE fund |
| Securities Act of 1933 | US legislation enacted in response to the stock market crash in 1929 and ensuing Great Depression which regulates certain securities transactions |
| Securities and Exchange Board of India | the securities market regulator in India |
| Securities and Exchange Commission | an independent US federal government agency overseeing preservation of fair and orderly functioning of the securities market, protection of investor's rights and steady capital formation in the market |
| Securities and Futures Commission of Hong Kong | the securities and futures market regulator in Hong Kong |
| Securities Exchange Act of 1934 | US legislation which regulates the secondary trading of securities |
| senior debt | debt which enjoys first right of payment ahead of any other debts |
| Senior Insurance Managers Regime | the UK regulatory regime which preceded SM&CR for senior managers at insurance firms |
| senior management functions | functions that involve responsibility for management of certain aspects (defined by statute) of a firm's affairs which includes the functions of the C-Suite |
| Senior Managers and Certification Regime | the UK regulatory regime for senior managers in FCA-regulated firms |
| Senior Managers Regime | a part of the UK financial services regulatory framework, which increases the personal accountability of senior staff |
| shareholders agreement | a contract, separate from a company's Articles of Association, between the shareholders of a company which sets out their rights and obligations in relation to each other |
| Sharia advisory board | an advisory panel which certifies Sharia compliance |
| Sharia-compliant fund / financial product | an investment fund or financial product which adheres to the requirements of Sharia law and Islamic principles |
| Shenzen–Hong Kong Stock Connect | a scheme connecting the Shenzhen Stock Exchange and Hong Kong Stock Exchange |
| small and medium-sized enterprises | representing the majority of businesses, a non-subsidiary business employing fewer than 250 people with annual turnover of under EUR 50 million |

| Term | Definition |
|------|------------|
| Small Business Administration | a US government agency which supports small US businesses and entrepreneurs |
| Small Business Jobs Act of 2010 | US legislation which authorised the creation of the Small Business Lending Fund Program which is a government-backed investment program to support small US businesses |
| smart beta | an investment strategy which aims to achieve alpha (i.e. outperform the market) whilst minimising risk and cost, by using alternative index constructions to traditional beta-seeking tracker funds |
| Social Impact Accelerator | an EIF VC fund |
| Solvency Capital Requirement | the minimum capital which EU insurance companies must hold under Solvency II |
| Solvency II | Solvency II Directive (2009/138/EC), which imposes certain rules on insurance groups to protect consumers, including a minimum capital requirement |
| South African Government Employees Pension Fund | a South African civil servant pension |
| sovereign wealth fund | a state-owned investment fund |
| special purpose vehicle | a company established for a narrow and specific function (for example, a 'bidco' or 'midco' used in a corporate acquisition to structure investment from various debt and equity sources) |
| sponsor | a sponsor in a PE context is the PE firm establishing a fund, and in a listed fund context, is usually a separate investment bank |
| Standard & Poor's | a US-based credit rating agency, also well known for its S&P 500 index |
| State Earnings-Related Pension Scheme | a UK government pension arrangement that existed between 1978 and 2002, when it was replaced by the State Second Pension, which in turn was partially replaced by the State Pension. They are all forms of state-funded additional pension provision on top of the basic state pension |
| Stewardship Principles | GPIF-published principles for responsible investment |
| Stichting Pensioenfonds ABP | the Dutch national pension fund |
| Stichting Pensioenfonds Zorg en Welzijn | the second largest Dutch pension fund |
| substance | the substantive activities of a business, which, in a funds context, means activities such as portfolio management, risk management, investment analysis, trading, fundraising, valuation, and compliance |
| sukuk | Arabic for 'legal instrument', the Shariah-compliant equivalent to a bond |
| sunnah | the traditional customs of the Islamic community, based on the teachings of the prophet Muhammad |

| Term | Definition |
| --- | --- |
| superannuation | an alternative term for a pension, commonly used in Australia |
| Swap Dealer and Intermediary Oversight Division | the division of CFTC responsible with the supervision of derivatives market intermediaries |
| T15 cities | the top 15 cities by GDP |
| Tax Cuts and Jobs Act of 2017 | US legislation most notable for introducing personal and corporate tax reductions |
| tax evasion | the illegal avoidance of tax payments due under the relevant tax regime(s) |
| tax haven | a jurisdiction in which rates of taxation are very low (and levels of financial secrecy may be higher) |
| technological due diligence | DD focused on technological issues |
| Telkom Pension Fund | a South African pension fund |
| tier 1 capital | essentially cash in the bank, used to describe the most liquid assets of a bank in the context of capital adequacy |
| toshin | an abbreviation of 'toshin-shintaku' which means 'investment trust', 'toshin' has become a synonym in Japan for 'fund' |
| Treasury | Her Majesty's Treasury, the government agency responsible for the UK's economic policy |
| Treaty on the Functioning of the European Union | one of the two primary EU treaties |
| troika | the EC, the ECB, and the IMF |
| UK Debt Management Office | the government agency responsible for managing the UK government's debt |
| UK Innovation Investment Fund | a UK government-backed VC fund which invests in high growth technology businesses |
| UK Listing Authority | the official listing maintained by the FCA to regulate the companies for trading on UK Stock Exchange |
| ultra high-net-worth individual | a person whose investable assets are of such an exceptionally high value as to distinguish them from HNWIs (an UHNWI holds tens of millions of USD in investable assets) |
| unauthorised unit trust | a unit trust which does not obtain authorisation from the FCA which is treated differently for tax purposes |
| Undertakings For Collective Investment In Transferable Securities Directive | EU legislation providing for a type of regulated open-ended fund established in the EU which can be freely marketed within the EU. The first directive was introduced in 1985, but several updated versions have been introduced since, with UCITS V being the most recent |
| unicorn | a private company valued at over USD 1 billion |
| United Nations Principles for Responsible Investment | UN-supported principles that encourage responsible investment practices |

| Term | Definition |
| --- | --- |
| value added tax | a consumption tax applied to EU goods and services, charged at 20% in the UK |
| venture capital | a form of PE investing which targets early stage and start-up operations with funding requirements and cash flow profiles distinct from other PE targets, often (but not always) investing in technology-driven businesses |
| Verohallinto | the Finnish tax authorities |
| volatility | a measurement of the fluctuation in a market or security's value |
| Volcker Rule | a reference to section 619 of the US Dodd-Frank Wall Street Reform and Consumer Protection Act, implemented after the Financial Crisis to restrict the kinds of speculative investments banks can make and restricts their dealings with hedge and PE funds |
| Western world | (generally speaking) the US, Canada, Europe, Australia, and New Zealand |
| WikiLeaks | a non-profit organisation that publishes confidential information which it deems to be in the public interest |
| Willis Towers Watson | an international risk management company |
| withdrawal agreement | the agreement to be made between the UK and EU regarding the terms of the UK's withdrawal from the EU |
| World Bank | an international financial institution that provides finance to government bodies for development projects |
| World Trade Organization | an intergovernmental organisation which regulates international trade |
| Yale University Endowment | the second largest university endowment in the world, known also for being one of the best-performing |
| zakat | Arabic for 'charity', or alms-giving, one of the five pillars of Islam |
| zero-hour contract | a contract of employment under which the employee is not guaranteed any minimum working hours |

# Abbreviations

| Initials | Term |
|----------|------|
| ABP | Stichting Pensioenfonds ABP |
| ABS | asset-backed securities |
| ADGM | Abu Dhabi Global Market |
| ADIA | Abu Dhabi Investment Authority |
| ADIC | Abu Dhabi Investment Council |
| AfD | Alternative für Deutschland |
| AFP | Administradoras de Fondo de Pensiones (Chilean pension fund) |
| AIF | alternative investment fund |
| AIFM | alternative investment fund manager |
| AIFMD | Directive 2011/61/EU Alternative Investment Fund Managers Directive |
| AIM | Alternative Investment Market |
| AMF | Autorité des Marchés Financiers |
| AML | anti-money laundering |
| APRA | Australian Prudential Regulation Authority |
| ARFP | Asian region funds passport |
| ASEAN | Association of Southeast Asian Nations Collective Investment Scheme Framework |
| ASIC | Australian Securities and Investments Commission |
| AUD | Australian dollar |
| AuM | assets under management |
| AUT | authorised unit trust |
| AVCA | African Venture Capital Association |
| BBB | British Business Bank |
| BCB | Brazilian Central Bank |
| BEPS | OECD G20 Base Erosion and Profit Sharing Project |
| BFT | Business Finance Taskforce |
| BGF | Business Growth Fund |
| BoE | Bank of England |
| BVCA | British Private Equity and Venture Capital Association |
| CAGR | compound annual growth rate |
| CAPEX | capital expenditure |
| CCP | central counterparty |
| CDO | collateralised debt obligation |
| CERN | European Organization for Nuclear Research |
| CFA | Chartered Financial Analyst |
| CFTC | Commodity Futures Trading Commission |

| Initials | Term |
| --- | --- |
| CHF | Swiss Franc |
| CIS | collective investment scheme |
| CLO | collateralised loan obligation |
| CMU | Capital Markets Union |
| COCON | FCA Code of Conduct |
| CoTA | Corporation Tax Act 2010 |
| CRS | Common Reporting Standards |
| CSR | corporate social responsibility |
| CSRC | China Securities Regulatory Commission |
| CTA | commodities trading adviser |
| CVM | Commissao de Valores Mobiliarios (Brazilian Securities Commission) |
| DCO | derivatives clearing organisations |
| DCR | Division of Clearing and Risk |
| DD | due diligence |
| DFI | development finance institution |
| DIFC | Dubai International Finance Centre |
| DIMF | disguised investment management fees |
| DMO | Division of Market Oversight |
| DNC | Democratic National Committee |
| DPT | diverted profits tax |
| DSIO | Division of Swap Dealer and Intermediary Oversight |
| EC | European Commission |
| ECB | European Central Bank |
| EEA | European Economic Area |
| EFSF | European Financial Stability Facility |
| EFSI | European Fund for Strategic Investments |
| EFTA | European Free Trade Association |
| EIB | European Investment Bank |
| EIF | European Investment Fund |
| EIOPA | European Insurance and Occupational Pensions Authority |
| EMIR | European Market Infrastructure Regulation |
| EMU | Economic and Monetary Union |
| ERISA | Employee Retirement Income Security Act of 1974 |
| ERM | European Exchange Rate Mechanism |
| ESCB | European System of Central Banks |
| ESG | environmental, social, governance |
| ESM | European Stability Mechanism |
| ESMA | European Securities and Markets Authority |
| ETF | exchange-traded funds |
| EU | European Union |
| EUR | Euro |
| FAANG | Facebook, Amazon, Apple, Netflix, Google |
| FATCA | Foreign Account Tax Compliance Act |
| FATF | Financial Action Task Force |

| Initials | Term |
| --- | --- |
| FBAR | Report of Foreign Bank and Financial Accounts |
| FCA | Financial Conduct Authority |
| FDD | financial due diligence |
| FINMA | Swiss Financial Market Supervisory Authority |
| FMO | Nederlandse Financierings-Maatschappij voor Ontwikkelingslanden (Netherlands Development Finance Company) |
| FSA | Financial Services Authority |
| FSB | Financial Stability Board |
| FSMA | Financial Services and Markets Act 2000 |
| FSOC | Financial Stability Oversight Council |
| FTSE | Financial Times Stock Exchange |
| GAPP | Generally Accepted Principles and Practices |
| GBP | pound sterling |
| GDP | gross domestic product |
| GDPR | General Data Protection Regulation |
| GFCI | Global Financial Centres Index |
| GIIN | Global Impact Investing Network |
| GIIRS | Global Impact Investment Ratings System |
| GP | general partner |
| GPIF | Government Pension Investment Fund |
| GPS | general partner's share |
| HKMA | Hong Kong Monetary Authority |
| HMRC | Her Majesty's Revenue and Customs |
| HNWI | high-net-worth individual |
| IAA | Investment Advisers Act of 1940 |
| IBCI | income-based carried interest |
| IC | advisory / investors committee |
| ICA | Investment Company Act of 1940 |
| ICAV | Irish Collective Asset-Management Vehicle |
| ICIJ | International Consortium of Investigative Journalists |
| ICO | Information Commissioners Office |
| ICO | initial coin offering |
| IFC | International Finance Corporation |
| IFSWF | International Forum of Sovereign Wealth Funds |
| ILPA | Institutional Limited Partners Association |
| IM | information memorandum |
| IMF | International Monetary Fund |
| IORP | Directive 2003/41/EC – Institutions for Occupational Retirement Provision Directive |
| IP | intellectual property |
| IPO | initial public offering |
| IRA | individual retirement agreement |
| IRC | Internal Revenue Code |
| IRS | Internal Revenue Service |

| Initials | Term |
|----------|------|
| IWG | International Working Group of Sovereign Wealth Funds |
| JOBS Act | Jumpstart Our Business Startups Act of 2012 |
| JPUT | Jersey property unit trust |
| KIA | Kuwait Investment Authority |
| KKR | KKR & Co. Inc. |
| KYC | know-your-customer |
| LAVCA | Association for Private Capital Investment in Latin America |
| LBO | leveraged buy-out |
| LDD | legal due diligence |
| LDI | liability-driven investing |
| LEI | legal entity identifier |
| LGPS | Local Government Pension Scheme |
| LIBOR | London Inter-Bank Offered Rate |
| LLC | limited liability company |
| LLP | limited liability partnership |
| LP | limited partner / limited partnership |
| LPA | limited partnership agreement |
| LPAC | limited partner advisory committee |
| LSE | London Stock Exchange |
| LTCM | Long-Term Capital Management LP |
| MAD II | Directive 2014/57/EU Market Abuse Directive |
| MAR | Market Abuse Regulation |
| MAS | Monetary Authority of Singapore |
| MATCH | Meet ASEAN's Talents and Champions |
| MBS | mortgage-backed security |
| MCR | minimum capital requirement |
| MENA | Middle East and North Africa |
| MiFID | Markets in Financial Instruments Directive 2004/39/EC |
| MiFID II | Markets in Financial Instruments Directive II – Directive 2014/65/EU |
| MLD4 | Fourth EU Money Laundering Directive |
| MPFA | Mandatory Provident Funds Authority |
| MPT | modern portfolio theory |
| MRF | China Mainland-Hong Kong Mutual Recognition of Funds |
| NAV | net asset value |
| NCA | national competent authority |
| NCSSF | National Council for Social Security Fund |
| NED | non-executive director |
| NFA | National Futures Association |
| NIA | net investable assets |
| NIC | national insurance contribution |
| NSE | National Stock Exchange of India |
| NYSE | New York Stock Exchange |
| OCI | Office of the Commissioner of Insurance |
| oCIO | outsourced chief investment officer |

| Initials | Term |
|----------|------|
| ODD | operational due diligence |
| OECD | Organisation for Economic Co-operation and Development |
| OEIC | open-ended investment company |
| OPEF | operational efficiency |
| OPEX | operational expenditure |
| OTC | over-the-counter |
| PCAOB | Public Company Accounting Oversight Board |
| PE | private equity |
| PEP | politically exposed person |
| PFI | private finance initiative |
| PFZW | Stichting Pensioenfonds Zorg en Welzijn |
| PIK | payment in kind |
| PMPT | post-modern portfolio theory |
| PPP | public–private partnership |
| PRA | Prudential Regulation Authority |
| PriOs | Principles Operating System |
| PSC | people with significant control |
| PTP | publicly traded partnerships |
| PwC | PricewaterhouseCoopers |
| QE | quantitative easing |
| QT | quantitative tightening |
| RAO | Financial Services and Markets Act 2000 (Regulated Activities) Order 2001 |
| RDR | Retail Distribution Review 2012 |
| RE | real estate |
| REIT | Real Estate Investment Trust |
| REOC | Real Estate Operating Company |
| ROI | return on investment |
| RPA | research payment account |
| RPA | robotic process automation |
| RQFII | Renminbi Qualified Foreign Institutional Investor Scheme |
| RWA | risk-weighted assets |
| S&P | Standard & Poor's |
| SBA | Small Business Administration |
| SBJ Act | Small Business Jobs Act of 2010 |
| SCR | Solvency Capital Requirement |
| SEA | Southeast Asia |
| SEBI | Securities and Exchange Board of India |
| SEC | Securities and Exchange Commission |
| SERPS | State Earnings-Related Pension Scheme |
| SFC | Securities and Futures Commission of Hong Kong |
| SIA | Social Impact Accelerator |
| SIMR | Senior Insurance Managers Regime |
| SM&CR | Senior Managers and Certification Regime |
| SME | small and medium-sized enterprises |

| Initials | Term |
| --- | --- |
| SPV | special purpose vehicle |
| SWF | sovereign wealth fund |
| TDD | technological due diligence |
| TFEU | Treaty on the Functioning of the European Union |
| UAE | United Arab Emirates |
| UCITS | Undertakings For Collective Investment In Transferable Securities Directive |
| UHNW | ultra high-net-worth individual |
| UK | United Kingdom |
| UKIIF | UK Innovation Investment Fund |
| UKLA | UK Listing Authority |
| UNPRI | United Nations Principles for Responsible Investment |
| US | United States of America |
| USD | US dollar |
| VAT | value added tax |
| VC | venture capital |
| VCOC | annual venture capital operating company |
| Vol | volatility |
| WTO | World Trade Organization |

# Acknowledgments

I would like to thank members of the MJ Hudson team, especially John Cormie, Jake Fleming, Jacob Freeman, Jack Fishburn, and Sam Burford.

Also thanks as always to the Hudson family for their immeasurable support and humour – see some of their quotes dotted throughout the book. Also to my father Norman Geoffrey Hudson, for his inspiration (he was a prolific technical author in insurance); my mother Anne Yvonne Hudson, for her line that I always have another mountain to climb; and my wife Katherine, for covering many other bases to allow me the time to write this book and have a career in asset management, as well as providing thoughtful industry ideas from her marketing and public relations career (and many grammatical corrections!).

Finally, thanks to the five asset management founder-CEOs that I interviewed for their insight. Below is a short biography on each.

## WOL KOLADE

Wol is the CEO of Livingbridge, a private equity firm investing across business services, consumer markets, healthcare, education, technology, media, and communications. In 2017, Livingbridge won UK House of the Year at the Private Equity Awards.

Wol is a Kings College London engineering graduate and has an MBA from Exeter Business School. He started his career with Barclays in 1990 and after a short period in various head office roles, joined the predecessor firm of Livingbridge in 1993.

A few years ago, Wol was appointed to chair the Private Equity Industry Association at a difficult time for the industry. During this time, he has worked with governments and media outlets to explain how the work that private equity houses do with entrepreneurial companies is hugely beneficial to the wider economy.

Wol has a deep interest in healthcare and education, and sits on the boards of a number of schools and universities. He is chairman of the Guys and St Thomas' Charity, a 500-year-old charitable foundation with total assets of GBP 600 million. Wol also sit on the board of NHS Improvement as a non-executive director, working to help the NHS to meet its short-term challenges and secure its future.

## RICHARD NOVACK

Richard is the founder of Alpha Hawk, a new multi-boutique hedge manager investing platform based in London, which he created because of his conviction that niche hedge fund managers can generate alpha. Alpha Hawk reviews dozens of hedge fund managers and backs a very select few specialist players. It is a venture demonstrative of the niche, rather than scale, approach to asset management.

Richard studied at Temple University, graduating in Molecular Biology before beginning his career in proprietary trading. Richard created and managed a wholly independent proprietary trading desk at Amikon Investments before founding a specialist proprietary trading boutique hedge fund of his own and then a niche hedge fund incubator called Matrix Investments, which he directed for more than a decade.

## ALICE BENTINCK, MBE

Alice is the co-founder of Entrepreneur First, a start-up accelerator with offices in London, Singapore, Paris, Berlin, Bangalore, and Hong Kong. They now have a portfolio of 200 start-ups with a total value of more than USD 1.5 billion.

Alice studied at Nottingham University Business School, graduating with first class honours in management studies. Prior to founding Entrepreneur First, Alice interned in the office of Tony Blair, where she assisted with the Africa Governance Initiative. From 2009 to 2011 she was a management consultant with McKinsey & Company.

In 2012, Alice also co-founded Code First: Girls, a non-profit initiative providing free web programming courses for female university students from arts backgrounds, giving them the skills to switch to the tech sector. In 2014, Alice was appointed as one of the Prime Minister's advisers for the Northern Future Forum in Helsinki. She has been a member of the advisory board of Founders4Schools since April 2014, and a member of the Computer Science Department Industrial Liaison Board at Imperial College London since April 2015.

Alice was appointed Member of the Order of the British Empire (MBE) in the 2016 Birthday Honours for services to business.

## TONY DALWOOD

Tony is an experienced investor, with over 20 years in the industry, and has advised numerous public and private equity businesses. In December 2014, Tony became CEO of Gresham House and brought in a new management team that has transformed the company from an investment trust into an AIM-listed specialist asset management group.

Tony studied at the University of Bristol, graduating in Economics & Accounting, and continued his postgraduate studies in management at the University of Cambridge. Tony started his career at Phillips & Drew Fund Management (later UBS Global Asset Management), one of the UK's most prominent value investment firms with GBP 60 billion in assets at its peak. He was a member of the UK Equity Investment Committee with responsibility for managing over GBP 1.5 billion of UK equities.

In 2002 Tony founded and became CIO of SVG Investment Managers and CEO of SVG Advisers (formerly Schroder Ventures (London) Limited), the global private equity funds business and specialist alternatives manager. He established and led the growth of SVG Investment Managers, before launching Strategic Equity Capital plc, a London listed Investment Trust in 2005.

Tony currently chairs the London Pension Fund Authority's Investment Panel, which oversees GBP 4.6 billion in AuM. He is also an Independent non-executive director of JPEL plc (formerly JP Morgan Private Equity Limited plc), and advises the endowment fund of St Edmund's College, University of Cambridge.

## NIGEL KERSHAW, OBE

Nigel serves as Executive Chairman of The Big Issue Group, known for *The Big Issue* magazine. It is also responsible for Big Issue Invest, which manages or advises on over GBP 150 million worth of social funds.

Nigel trained as a four colour lithographic printer and gained his Diploma at the London College of Communication, (now the University of the Arts). Previous to joining The Big Issue in 1994, he founded three employee-owned printing and publishing companies and has worked as a Systems Analyst, Project Manager, Litho Printer, and trade union official.

Nigel is a member of both the Big Society Capital and the British Venture Capital Association's Responsible Investment Advisory Boards. Nigel is also a Social Enterprise UK Ambassador. He has extensive experience of building and restructuring operational businesses and launching successful, innovative new ventures as well as attracting financial investment and delivering both a financial and social return on investment.

In 2010, Nigel was awarded an OBE for services to Social Enterprise and in 2013 was named Social Enterprise UK's 'Champion of Champions'.

### Further Acknowledgments

Alternative Investment Management Association

Association of the Luxembourg Fund Industry

Australian Government Website

Australian Securities and Investments commission

Australian Stock Exchange

Autorité des Marches Financiers

Bank of England

Central Bank of Ireland

Channel Islands Stock Exchange

CIA World Factbook

Citibank

Cyprus Stock Exchange

Deutsche Börse

European Union

Financial Conduct Authority

Financial Times

Gates Foundation

Global Economics

Government of Brazil Website

Government of Singapore Website

Government of The Netherlands Website

Her Majesty's Revenue and Customs

Internal Revenue Service
Jersey Financial Services Commission
London Stock Exchange
Luxembourg Stock Exchange
National Portal of India
New York Stock Exchange
Partners Group
Principles for Responsible Investment
Private Equity Growth Capital Council
Securities and Exchange Board of India
Securities and Exchange Commission
Shanghai Stock Exchange
Shenzhen Stock Exchange
Singapore Stock Exchange
Sovereign Wealth Fund Institute
States of Alderney Website
The Charity Commission
The Daily Telegraph
The Economist
The Wall Street Journal
Tom Wolfe
UK Legislation Website
United Nations Statistics Division
US Treasury Department

# About the Author

**M**atthew Hudson is CEO and Founder of MJ Hudson, a specialised law firm and international asset management and investment consultancy that offers infrastructure and multiple services to asset managers and asset owners.

Matthew is a builder of businesses within asset management and private equity, having started and built a number of financial and professional services firms.

Matthew is a well-known industry figure and regularly speaks on new developments concerning the Alternative Assets industries. He is the author of the leading text, *Funds: Private Equity, Hedge and All Core Structures*, also published by Wiley Finance.

Instrumental in helping to build and manage four of the major Alternative Asset law firms, his achievements include:

- Founding MJ Hudson
- Co-founding the Private Equity Group of SJ Berwin, the European law firm
- Re-establishing the London office for O'Melveny & Myers, the large US West Coast law firm
- Creating the London office for the large US East Coast law firm, Proskauer.

Matthew has also worked in four Private Equity houses, being involved with:

- Leveraged buyouts for a group built within CSFB
- Founding Far Blue Ventures, the Venture Capital house, backing IP spin-outs from universities

- Co-founding Tower Gate Capital, making small cap investments
- Coller Capital, the global Secondaries firm.

In his involvement with investment groups, Matthew has helped to build a number of software, financial, and other services businesses – many of which have subsequently exited.

In connection with his law firm consultancies, Matthew has represented many of the larger private equity, venture capital, SWF, and family office groups.

# Index